DIVORCE AND DISSOLUTION OF CIVIL PARTNERSHIP IN THE SHERIFF COURT

DIVORCE AND DISSOLUTION OF CIVIL PARTNERSHIP IN THE SHERIFF COURT

An exposition of the law and practice
relating to divorce and dissolution of
civil partnership in the sheriff court

Ninth Edition

by

S. A. Bennett, LL.B. (Hons)
Advocate

Barnstoneworth Press
2012

First published, 1984
Second edition, 1987
Third edition, 1991
Fourth edition, 1994
Fifth edition, 1997
Sixth edition, 2000
Seventh edition, 2005
Eighth edition, 2007
Ninth edition, 2012

© S. A. Bennett

ISBN 978-0-9562478-2-7

Published by S. A. Bennett, Advocate, Advocates' Library,
Parliament House, Edinburgh EH1 1RF
under the name 'Barnstoneworth Press'.

Website: www.barnstoneworthpress.co.uk

Typeset by Initial Typesetting Services, Edinburgh
Printed by Multiprint (Scotland) Limited, Kirkcaldy

CONTENTS

v

FOREWORD

by

The Hon. Lord Pentland,
Senator of the College of Justice

Twenty-eight years after its first appearance, Mr Bennett's renowned *Divorce and Dissolution of Civil Partnership in the Sheriff Court* now reaches its ninth edition.

Just as divorce law during this period has undergone a radical transformation through a plethora of new statutes, rules and cases, so too has this work evolved to reflect the many changes. But the author's succinct writing style remains, an essential ingredient in the text's continuing success; and the book's structure, mirroring a divorce writ, has stood the test of time. The book continues to be both comprehensive and easy to read; no small achievement.

This excellent book should enable any lawyer, or judge, to find his or her way around an increasingly complex area of the law with far greater facility than might otherwise be possible. I have no hesitation in commending it to practitioners and judicial colleagues alike.

Edinburgh   Paul B. Cullen
1 May 2012

TABLE OF CASES

A page number in **bold type** indicates that a digest of the case is printed on that page.

TABLE OF STATUTES

xvii

TABLE OF STATUTORY INSTRUMENTS

TABLE OF ORDINARY CAUSE RULES

CHAPTER 1

SPECIAL RULES OF PROCEDURE

The Ordinary Cause Rules include special procedural requirements applicable to actions of divorce or dissolution of civil partnership. Some of these are drawn to the attention of practitioners under the relevant subject heading (*e.g.* mental disorder). Others are mentioned in this chapter.

CITATION AND INTIMATION

There is a wide range of procedural requirements relating to citation and intimation in actions of divorce or dissolution of civil partnership.

Citation

No warrant for citation of a defender in an action of divorce or dissolution of civil partnership may be granted without there being produced with the initial writ an extract of the relevant entry in the register of marriages or equivalent document, or an extract of the relevant entry in the civil partnership registry or an equivalent document, unless the sheriff otherwise directs.[1]

Citation in such an action requires to be in Form F15 or Form CP15, which must be attached to a copy of the initial writ and warrant of citation in Form F14 or Form CP14 and must have appended to it a notice of intention to defend in Form F26 or Form CP16.[2] The certificate of citation requires to be in Form F16 or Form CP17 and must be appended to the initial writ.[3]

---

[1] r. 33.9(a) or r. 33A.9(1) and (2)(a). See also r. 33.9(b) or r. 33A.9(3) (birth certificate also requiring to be produced with initial writ where section 11 order craved).

[2] rr 33.10 and 33.11(1) or rr. 33A.10 and 33A.11(1). As to service in cases of mental disorder, see Chap. 2.

[3] r. 33.11(2) or r. 33A.11(2).

Where the address of the defender is not known to the pursuer and cannot reasonably be ascertained, citation must be effected in accordance with Rule 5.6, which provides:

"(1) Where the address of a person to be cited or served with a document is not known and cannot reasonably be ascertained, the sheriff shall grant warrant for citation and service upon that person—

    (a) by the publication of an advertisement in Form G3 in a specified newspaper circulating in the area of the last known address of that person; or

    (b) by displaying on the walls of court a copy of the instance and crave of the initial writ, the warrant of citation and a notice in Form G4;

and the period of notice fixed by the sheriff shall run from the date of publication of the advertisement or display on the walls of court, as the case may be.

(2) Where service requires to be executed under paragraph (1), the pursuer shall lodge a service copy of the initial writ and a copy of any warrant of citation with the sheriff clerk from whom they may be uplifted by the person for whom they are intended.

(3) Where a person has been cited or served in accordance with paragraph (1) and, after the cause has commenced, his address becomes known, the sheriff may allow the initial writ to be amended subject to such conditions as to re-service, intimation, expenses or transfer of the cause as he thinks fit.

(4) Where advertisement in a newspaper is required for the purposes of citation or service under this rule, a copy of the newspaper containing the advertisement shall be lodged with the sheriff clerk by the pursuer.

(5) Where display on the walls of court is required under paragraph (1)(b), the pursuer shall supply to the sheriff clerk for that purpose a certified copy of the instance and crave of the initial writ and any warrant of citation."

The pursuer must aver in the condescendence what steps have been taken to ascertain the defender's whereabouts[4], and intimation falls also to be made in accordance with Rule 33.7(1)(a) or Rule 33A.7(1) (a), considered next.

---

[4] r. 3.1(6).

Intimation

There are various warrants and orders for intimation or dispensing with intimation that may be required in actions of divorce or dissolution of civil partnership.

The pursuer requires to include in the initial writ a crave for a warrant for intimation—

    (a) in an action for divorce or dissolution of civil partnership where the address of the defender is not known to the pursuer and cannot reasonably be ascertained, to—

        (i) every child of the marriage between the parties who has reached the age of 16 years or every person who was a child of the family (within the meaning of section 101(7) of the Civil Partnership Act 2004) who has reached the age of 16 years,[5] as the case may be, and

        (ii) one of the next-of-kin of the defender who has reached that age,

    unless the address of such a person is not known to the pursuer and cannot reasonably be ascertained; and a notice of intimation in Form F1 or Form CP1 must be attached to the copy of the initial writ intimated to any such person;[6]

    (b) in an action for divorce where the pursuer alleges that the defender has committed adultery with another person, to that person, unless—

        (i) that person is not named in the initial writ and, if the adultery is relied on for the purposes of section 1(2)(a) of the Divorce (Scotland) Act 1976 (irretrievable breakdown of marriage by reason of adultery), the initial writ contains an averment that his or her identity is not known to the pursuer and cannot reasonably be ascertained; or

        (ii) the pursuer alleges that the defender has been guilty of rape upon or incest with, that named person,

    and a notice of intimation in Form F2 must be attached to the copy of the initial writ intimated to any such person; and where the address of any such named person is not known and cannot reasonably be ascertained, there must be included a crave to dispense with intimation;[7]

---

[5] See Chap. 5, n. 9.
[6] r. 33.7(1)(a) or r. 33A.7(1)(a).
[7] r. 33.7(1)(b) and (5).

(c) in an action for divorce or dissolution of civil partnership, where the defender is a person suffering from a mental disorder,[8] to—
  (i) those persons mentioned in subparagraph (a)(i) and (ii) *supra*, unless the address of such person is not known to the pursuer and cannot reasonably ascertained; and
  (ii) any person holding the office of guardian or continuing or welfare attorney to the defender under or by virtue of the Adults with Incapacity (Scotland) Act 2000 (or, in the case of divorce only, the *curator bonis* to the defender, if one has been appointed),
and a notice of intimation in Form F3 or Form CP2 must be attached to the copy of the initial writ intimated to any such person;[9]

(d) in an action for divorce relating to a marriage which was entered into under a law which permits polygamy where—
  (i) one of the decrees specified in section 2(2) of the Matrimonial Proceedings (Polygamous Marriages) Act 1972 is sought; and
  (ii) either party to the marriage in question has any spouse additional to the other party,
to any such additional spouse, and a notice of intimation in Form F4 must be attached to the initial writ intimated to any such person; and where the address of any such additional spouse is not known and cannot reasonably be ascertained, there must be included a crave to dispense with intimation;[10]

(e) in an action for divorce or dissolution of civil partnership where the sheriff may make an order under section 11 of the Children (Scotland) Act 1995 in respect of a child—
  (i) who is in the care of a local authority, to that authority and a notice of intimation in Form F5 or Form CP3 must be attached to the notice intimated to that authority;
  (ii) who, being a child of one party to the marriage or one party to the civil partnership, as the case may be, has been accepted as a child of the family by the other party to the marriage or the other party to the civil partnership, as the case may be, and who is liable to be maintained by a third party, to that third party; and a notice of

---

[8] "Mental disorder" has the meaning assigned in s. 328 of the Mental Health (Care and Treatment) (Scotland) Act 2003—r. 33.1(2) or r. 33A.1(2). See further Chap.2.
[9] r. 33.7(1)(c) or r. 33A.7(1)(b).
[10] r. 33.7(1)(d) and (5).

          intimation in Form F5 or Form CP3 must be attached to the initial writ intimated to that third party; or

   (iii) in respect of whom a third party in fact exercises care and control, to that third party, and a notice of intimation in Form F6 or Form CP4 must be attached to the initial writ intimated to that third party;

and where the address of any such third party as is mentioned in paragraph (ii) or (iii) *supra* is not known and cannot reasonably be ascertained, there must be included a crave to dispense with intimation;[11]

(f) in an action for divorce or dissolution of civil partnership where the pursuer craves an order under section 11 of the Children (Scotland) Act 1995, to any parent or guardian of the child who is not a party to the action, and a notice of intimation in Form F7 or Form CP5 must be attached to the initial writ intimated to any such parent or guardian; and where the address of any such parent or guardian is not known and cannot reasonably be ascertained, there must be included a crave to dispense with intimation;[12]

(g) in an action for divorce or dissolution of civil partnership which includes a crave for an order under section 11 of the Children (Scotland) Act 1995, to the child to whom such an order would relate if not a party to the action, and a notice of intimation in Form F9 or Form CP7 must be intimated to that child; and where the address of any such child is not known and cannot reasonably be ascertained, there must be included a crave to dispense with intimation; but where the pursuer considers that to order intimation to the child is inappropriate, he must

   (i) include a crave in the initial writ to dispense with intimation to that child; and

   (ii) include in the initial writ averments setting out the reasons why such intimation is inappropriate;[13]

(h) in an action for divorce or dissolution of civil partnership where the pursuer makes an application for an order under section 8(1)(aa) of the Family Law (Scotland) Act 1985 (transfer of property) and—

---

[11] r. 33.7(1)(e) and (5) or r. 33A.7(1)(c) and (5).

[12] r. 33.7(1)(f) and (5) or r. 33A.7(1)(d) and (5).

[13] r. 33.7(1)(h), (5) and (7) or r. 33A.7(1)(f), (5) and (7). *C.f. Gallacher v. Gallacher,* 1997 S.L.T. (Sh. Ct.) 42 (sheriff expected to see crave to dispense with intimation to six-year-old child in initial writ). See further Chap 6. Note that the initial writ itself does not fall to be intimated to the child in terms of the Rules.

(i) the consent of a third party to such a transfer is necessary by virtue of an obligation, enactment or rule of law, or

(ii) the property is subject to a security,

to the third party or creditor, as the case may be, and a notice of intimation in Form F10 or Form CP8 must be attached to the initial writ intimated to any such person; and where the address of any such third party or creditor is not known and cannot reasonably be ascertained, there must be included a crave to dispense with intimation;[14]

(i) in an action for divorce or dissolution of civil partnership where the pursuer makes an application for an order under section 18 of the Family Law (Scotland) Act 1985 (which relates to avoidance transactions), to—

(i) any third party in whose favour the transfer of, or transaction involving, the property is to be or was made, and

(ii) any other person having an interest in the transfer of, or transaction involving, the property,

and a notice of intimation in Form F11 or Form CP9 must be attached to the initial writ intimated to any such person; and where the address of any such third party or other person is not known and cannot reasonably be ascertained, there must be included a crave to dispense with intimation;[15]

(j) in an action for divorce or dissolution of civil partnership where the pursuer makes an application for an order under the Matrimonial Homes (Family Protection) (Scotland) Act 1981, where the application is under section 3(1), 3(2), 4, 7 or 13 of that Act, and the entitled spouse is a tenant or occupies the matrimonial home by permission of a third party or the pursuer makes an application for an order under Chapter 3 of Part 3 of the Civil Partnership Act 2004, where the application is under section 103(1), 103(2), 104, 107 or 112 of that Act, and the entitled civil partner is a tenant or occupies the family home by permission of a third party, as the case may be, to the landlord or the third party, as the case may be, and a notice of intimation in Form F12 or Form CP10 must be attached to the initial writ intimated to any such person; and

---

[14] r. 33.7(1)(i) and (5) or r. 33A.7(1)(g) and (5).
[15] r. 33.7(1)(j) and (5) or r. 33A.7(1)(h) and (5).

where the address of any such landlord or third party is not known and cannot reasonably be ascertained, there must be included a crave to dispense with intimation;[16]

(k) in an action for divorce or dissolution of civil partnership where the pursuer makes an application for an order under section 8(1)(ba) of the Family Law (Scotland) Act 1985 (orders under section 12A of the 1985 Act for pension lump sum), to the person responsible for the pension arrangement, and a notice of intimation in Form F12A or Form CP11 must be attached to the initial writ intimated to any such person; and where the address of any such person is not known and cannot reasonably be ascertained, there must be included a crave to dispense with intimation;[17]

(l) in an action for divorce or dissolution of civil partnership where the pursuer makes an application for an order under section 8(1)(baa) of the Family Law (Scotland) Act 1985 (pension sharing orders), to the person responsible for the pension arrangement, and a notice in Form F12B or Form CP12 must be attached to the initial writ intimated to any such person; and where the address of any such person is not known and cannot reasonably be ascertained, there must be included a crave to dispense with intimation;[18]

(m) in an action for divorce or dissolution of civil partnership where a pursuer makes an application for an order under section 8(1)(bab) of the Family Law (Scotland) Act 1985 (pension compensation sharing order), to the Board of the Pension Protection Fund, and a notice of intimation in Form F12C or Form CP12A must be attached to the initial writ intimated to that Board;[19] and

(n) in an action for divorce or dissolution of civil partnership where a pursuer makes an application for an order under section 8(1)(bb) of the Family Law (Scotland) Act 1985 (an order under section 12B(2) of the 1985 Act for pension compensation), to the Board of the Pension Protection Fund, and a notice of intimation in Form F12D or Form CP12B must be attached to the initial writ intimated to that Board.[20]

---

[16] r. 33.7(1)(k) and (5) or r. 33A.7(1)(i) and (5).
[17] r. 33.7(1)(l) and (5) or r. 33A.7(1)(j) and (5).
[18] r. 33.7(1)(m) and (5) or r. 33A.7(1)(k) and (5).
[19] r. 33.7(1)(n) or r. 33A.7(1)(l).
[20] r. 33.7(1)(o) or r. 33A.7(1)(m).

Each notice of intimation must be on a period of notice of 21 days unless the sheriff otherwise orders, but the sheriff cannot order a period of notice of less than two days.[21]

Where any party makes a crave or averment which, had it been made in an initial writ, would have required any of the foregoing warrants for intimation, he must include a crave in his writ for a warrant for intimation or to dispense with such intimation.[22]

Where the identity or address of any person in respect of whom a warrant for intimation requires to be applied for is not known and cannot reasonably be ascertained, the party required to apply for the warrant must include in his pleadings an averment of that fact and averments setting out what steps have been taken to ascertain the identity or address, as the case may be, of that person;[23] and where that identity or address becomes known during the course of the action, the party who would have been required to insert the crave for warrant for intimation to that person must lodge a motion for a warrant for intimation to that person or to dispense with intimation.[24]

The sheriff may grant any of the foregoing craves to dispense with intimation or make such other order as he thinks fit.[25]

Where the pursuer founds upon an association[26] between the defender and another named person, the pursuer must, immediately after the expiry of the period of notice, lodge a motion for an order for intimation to that person or to dispense with such intimation.[27] In determining such a motion, the sheriff may —

(a) make such order for intimation as he thinks fit; or
(b) dispense with intimation; and
(c) where he dispenses with intimation, order that the name of that person be deleted from the condescendence of the initial writ.[28]

---

[21] r. 33.7(3) or r. 33A.7(3).

[22] r. 33.15(3) or r. 33A.15(3), also providing that r. 33.7 or r. 33A.7 shall, with the necessary modifications, apply to a crave for a warrant under r. 33.15(3) or r. 33A.15(3) as it applies to a crave for a warrant under r. 33.7 or r. 33A.7.

[23] r. 33.4 or r. 33A.4.

[24] r. 33.7(6) or r. 33A.7(6).

[25] rr. 33.7(5) and (7) and 33.15(3) or rr. 33A.7(5) and (7) and 33A.15(3).

[26] "Association", in the case of divorce, means "sodomy, incest or any homosexual relationship" and, in the case of dissolution of civil partnership, means "sodomy, incest or any homosexual or heterosexual relationship"—r. 33.8(4) or r. 33A.8(4).

[27] r. 33.8(1) or r. 33A.8(1).

[28] r. 33.8(2) or r. 33A.8(2).

Where intimation is so ordered, a copy of the initial writ and an intimation in Form F13 or Form CP13 must be intimated to the named person.[29]

Where the pursuer craves a residence order in respect of a child, the sheriff may, if he thinks fit, order intimation to the local authority in which area the pursuer resides; and such intimation shall be in Form F8 or Form CP6.[30] Where such an order for intimation is made, intimation to that local authority must be given within 7 days after the date on which an order for intimation has been made.[31]

More generally, in relation to intimation of an action for divorce or dissolution of civil partnership, the sheriff may, at any time—

(a) order intimation to be made on such person as he thinks fit;

(b) postpone intimation where he considers that such postponement is appropriate and, in that case, make such order in respect of postponement as thinks fit; or

(c) dispense with intimation, where he considers that such dispensation is appropriate.[32]

Where the sheriff is considering whether to make an order under section 11 of the Children (Scotland) Act 1995 by virtue of section 12 of that Act (restrictions on decrees for divorce affecting children), he must, subject to paragraph (c) *supra*, order intimation in Form F9 or Form CP7 to the child to whom the section 11 order would relate unless—

(a) intimation has been given to the child under Rule 33.7(1)(h) or Rule 33A.7(1)(f); or

(b) the sheriff considers that the child is not of sufficient age and maturity to express his views.[33]

UNDEFENDED ACTIONS

Any action of divorce or dissolution of civil partnership that is undefended is subject to certain evidential requirements.

---

[29] r. 33.8(3) or r. 33A.8(3).

[30] r. 33.12(1) or r. 33A.12(1).

[31] r. 33.12(2) or r. 33A.12(2).

[32] r. 33.15(1) or r. 33A.15(1).

[33] r. 33.15(2) or r. 33A.15(2). Note that the initial writ itself does not fall to be intimated to the child in terms of the rules.

The requirement of proof

In an action of divorce or dissolution of civil partnership, whether or not appearance has been entered for the defender, no decree or judgment in favour of the pursuer may be pronounced until the grounds of action have been established by evidence.[34]

As a consequence of this requirement of proof, default by the defender in an action of divorce or dissolution of civil partnership entitles the sheriff only to allow the case to proceed as undefended.[35]

Affidavits

In actions for divorce or dissolution of civil partnership to which Rule 33.28 or Rule 33A.29 applies, evidence requires to be given by affidavit, unless the sheriff otherwise directs.[36] The foregoing Rules apply to—

(a) actions in which no notice of intention to defend has been lodged;

(b) an action in which a curator *ad litem* has been appointed under Rule 33.16 or Rule 33A.16 where the curator *ad litem* to the defender has lodged a minute intimating that he does not intend to lodge defences;

(c) any action which proceeds at any stage as undefended where the sheriff so directs; and

(d) the merits of an action which is undefended on the merits where the sheriff so directs, notwithstanding that the action is defended on an ancillary matter.[37]

In any such case, the Practice Note relative to affidavits in family actions, reproduced in Appendix IV *infra*, requires to be complied with.[38]

Unless the sheriff otherwise directs, evidence relating to the welfare of a child must be given by affidavit, at least one affidavit being emitted by a person other than a parent or party to the action.[39] Where the child is in the care of a local authority, it is sufficient to tender evidence

---

[34] Civil Evidence (Scotland) Act 1988, s. 8(1) and (2), as amended by the Civil Partnership Act 2004, Sched. 28, para. 55.

[35] r. 33.37(2)(a) or r. 33A.37(2)(a).

[36] r. 33.28(2) or r. 33A.29(2).

[37] r. 33.28(1) or r. 33A.29(1).

[38] As to the court's requirements in relation to financial and other ancillary craves, set forth in paras. 17–19 of the Practice Note, see further *Ali v. Ali*, 2001 S.C. 618; *Ali v. Ali (No. 3)*, 2003 Fam. L.R. 13; *Sullivan v. Sullivan*, 2003 Fam. L.R. 53; *Thirde v. Thirde*, 1987 S.C.L.R. 335.

[39] r. 33.28(3) or r. 33A.29(3).

of that fact by affidavit from a person qualified to speak to that fact, and it is not necessary that the person emitting the affidavit should personally have knowledge of and speak to the arrangements made by the local authority for the welfare of such child.[40]

Evidence in the form of a written statement bearing to be the professional opinion of a duly qualified medical practitioner, which has been signed by him and lodged in process, is admissible in place of parole evidence by him.[41]

At any time after the expiry of the period for lodging a notice of intention to defend, the pursuer requires to

(a) lodge in process the affidavit evidence; and
(b) endorse a minute in Form F27 or Form CP27 on the initial writ as follows:

"(*Insert name of solicitor for the pursuer*) having considered the evidence contained in the affidavits and the other documents[42] all as specified in the Schedule hereto and being satisfied that upon the evidence a motion for decree (in terms of the crave(s) of the initial writ) [*or in such restricted terms as may be appropriate*] may properly be made, moves the court accordingly.

In respect whereof

Signed

Solicitor for the pursuer (add designation and business address)

SCHEDULE

(number and specify documents considered)"[43]

---

[40] *Hunter v. Hunter*, 1979 S.L.T. (Notes) 2.

[41] r. 33.28(4) or r. 33A.29(4).

[42] Such other documents include any marriage or civil partnership certificate and birth certificate requiring to be lodged along with the initial writ in terms of r. 33.9 or r. 33A.9 as well as any notice of consent, joint minute, extract decree, extract conviction, photograph, medical report or other production relevant to the case.

[43] r. 33.29(1) or r. 33A.30(1), subject to the rule of law that an action falls if no procedure has followed within a year and a day of the expiry of the period of notice—*McCulloch v. McCulloch*, 1990 S.L.T. (Sh. Ct.) 63; *Dunnett v. Dunnett*, 1990 S.C.L.R. 135 (*c.f. Donnelly v. Donnelly*, 1991 S.L.T. (Sh. Ct.) 9; *The Royal Bank of Scotland plc v. Mason*, 1995 S.L.T (Sh. Ct.) 32).

The sheriff may at any time after the pursuer has complied with the foregoing, without requiring the appearance of parties—

   (a) grant decree in terms of the motion for decree;[44] or

   (b) remit the cause for such further procedure, if any, including proof by parole evidence, as the sheriff thinks fit.[45]

The sheriff may accept evidence by affidavit at any hearing for an order or interim order.[46]

DEFENDED ACTIONS

Part III of Chapter 33 and Part III of Chapter 33A of the Rules comprise rules applicable to actions for divorce and dissolution of civil partnership that are defended.

Rule 33.34 or Rule 33A.34 makes provision regarding notices of intention to defend and defences, applying where the defender seeks—

   (a) to oppose any crave in the initial writ;

   (b) to make a claim for—

       (i) aliment;[47]

      (ii) an order for financial provision within the meaning of section 8(3) of the Family Law (Scotland) Act 1985;[48] or

     (iii) a section 11 order;[49]

   (c) an order—

       (i) under section 16(1)(b) or (3) of the 1985 Act (setting aside or varying agreement as to financial provision);[50]

---

[44] Where any parties have reached agreement in relation to a section 11 order, aliment for a child or an order for financial provision, a joint minute may be entered into expressing that agreement and, subject to r. 33.19(3) or r. 33A.19(3) (no order before views of child expressed), the sheriff may grant decree in respect of those parts of the joint minute in relation to which he could otherwise make an order, whether or not a decree would include matter for which there was no crave—r. 33.26 or r. 33A.27. Note, further, that the requirement to intimate motions does not apply in an action of divorce or dissolution of civil partnership where no notice of intention to defend has been lodged or insofar as it proceeds as undefended—r. 33.33 and r. 33A.33.

[45] r. 33.29(2) or r. 33A.30(2). It is not necessary to record the evidence at any proof in an action of divorce or dissolution of civil partnership which is not defended—r. 33.32 or r. 33A.32.

[46] r. 33.27 or r. 33A.28.

[47] Also provided for by r. 33.39(1)(a) and (2)(b) or r. 33A.39(1)(a) and (2)(b).

[48] Also provided for by r. 33.48(1)(a) and (2)(a) or r. 33A.45(1)(a) and (2)(a).

[49] Also provided for by r. 33.39(1)(a) and (2)(a) or r. 33A.39(1)(a) and (2)(a). See, however, r. 9.6(3) (neither crave nor averments need be made in the defences which relate to any section 11 order).

[50] Also provided for by r. 33.48(1)(a) and (2)(b) or r. 33A.45(1)(a) and (2)(b).

(ii) under section 18 of the 1985 Act (which relates to avoidance provisions);[51] or

(iii) under the Matrimonial Homes (Family Protection) (Scotland) Act 1981 or under Chapter 3 or Chapter 4 of Part 3 or section 127 of the Civil Partnership Act 2004; or

(d) to challenge the jurisdiction of the court.

In such an action, the defender must —

(a) lodge a notice of intention to defend in Form F26 or Form CP16 before the expiry of the period of notice;[52] and

(b) make any claim or seek any order, as above referred to, in those defences by setting out in his defences —

(i) craves;

(ii) averments in the answers to the condescendence in support of those craves; and

(iii) appropriate pleas-in-law.[53]

Notwithstanding abandonment by a pursuer, the court may allow a defender to pursue an order or claim sought in his defences; and the proceedings in relation to that order or claim shall continue in dependence as if a separate cause.[54]

All parties to a defended action of divorce or dissolution of civil partnership must, except on cause shown, attend the Options Hearing in the case.[55] Failure by a party to attend, however, attracts no sanction provided that he or she is represented at the diet.[56]

Provision is made by Rule 33.37 or Rule 33A.37 for the granting of decree by default, the rule applying in an action in which the defender has lodged a notice of intention to defend where a party fails —

---

[51] Also provided for by r. 33.48(1)(a) and (2)(c) or r. 33A.45(1)(a) and (2)(c).

[52] Note that where a defender intends to make an application for a section 11 order which, had it been made in an initial writ, would have required a warrant for intimation under r. 33.7 or r. 33A.7, the defender must include a crave in his notice of intention to defend for a warrant for intimation or to dispense with such intimation, and r. 33.7 or r. 33A.7 applies with the necessary modifications to such a crave as it applies to a crave for a warrant under those rules — r. 33.34(3) or r. 33A.34(3).

[53] r. 33.34(2) or r. 33A.34(2). *C.f. Bell v. MacPherson*, 1997 S.L.T. (Sh. Ct.) 62 at p. 63 (where defender making a claim which it is not possible to deal with in an answer to an article of condescendence [because pursuer not making a similar claim or at least has made no averments in relation to that matter], defender should insert additional answers to condescendence in support of his claim). See also n. 49, *supra*.

[54] r. 33.35 or r. 33A.35.

[55] r. 33.36 or r. 33A.36. The parties are similarly obliged to attend any Child Welfare Hearing fixed in the case, along with any child who has indicated his or her wish to attend — r. 33.22A(5) or r. 33A.23(5).

[56] *Grimes v. Grimes*, 1995 S.C.L.R. 268.

(a) to lodge, or intimate the lodging of, any production or part of process;[57]
(b) to implement an order of the sheriff within a specified period;[58]
(c) to appear or be represented at any diet;[59] or
(d) otherwise to comply with any requirement imposed upon that party by the rules.[60]

Where a party has so failed, and is thereby in default, the sheriff may—

(a) allow the action to proceed as undefended under Part II of Chapter 33 or Chapter 33A of the Rules; or
(b) grant decree of absolvitor; or
(c) dismiss the action or any claim made or order sought; or
(d) make such other order as he thinks fit to secure the expeditious progress of the cause; and
(e) award expenses.[61]

Provision is also made in the Rules for late appearance by the defender in an action of divorce or dissolution of civil partnership. The sheriff is thereby empowered, at any stage of the action before the granting of final decree, to make an order with such conditions, if any, as he thinks fit—

(a) directing that a defender who has not lodged a notice of intention to defend be treated as if he had lodged such a notice and the period of notice had expired on the date on which the order was made; or
(b) allowing a defender who has not lodged a notice of intention to defend to appear and be heard at a diet of proof although he has not lodged defences, but he shall not, in that event, be allowed to lead evidence without the pursuer's consent.[62]

An application under the foregoing provision must be made by note setting out the proposed defence and explaining the defender's failure to appear.[63] Such a note must be served on the pursuer and any other

---

[57] The sheriff may, on cause shown, prorogate the time for lodging any production or part of process—r. 33.37(4) or r. 33A.37(4).
[58] The sheriff may, on cause shown, prorogate the time for intimating or implementing any order—r. 33.37(4) or r. 33A.37(4).
[59] Where no party appears at a diet, the sheriff may dismiss the action—r. 33.37(3) or r. 33A.37(3).
[60] r. 33.37(1) or r. 33A.37(1).
[61] r. 33.37(2) or r. 33A.37(2).
[62] r. 33.33A(1) or r. 33A.33A(1).
[63] r. 33.33A(5) or r. 33A.33A(5).

party.[64] Any such application shall not affect any right of appeal the defender may otherwise have.[65]

Where the sheriff makes such an order, the pursuer may recall a witness already examined or lead other evidence whether or not he closed his proof before that order was made.[66] Where no such order has been sought by a defender who has not lodged a notice of intention to defend and decree is granted against him, the sheriff may, on an application made within 14 days of the date of the decree, and with such conditions, if any, as he thinks fit, make an order recalling the decree.[67] Where the sheriff does this, the cause shall thereafter proceed as if the defender had lodged a notice of intention to defend and the period of notice had expired on the date on which the decree was recalled.[68]

SIMPLIFIED PROCEDURE

Simplified divorce applications and simplified dissolution of civil partnership applications may be made in certain circumstances.

Such applications are competent if, but only if—

(a) the applicant relies upon the facts set out in section 1(2(d) of the Divorce (Scotland) Act 1976 or section 117(3)(c) of the Civil Partnership Act 2004 (no cohabitation for one year with consent of defender to decree), or section 1(2)(e) of the 1976 Act or section 117(3)(d) of the 2004 Act (no cohabitation for two years), or section 1(1)(b) of the 1976 Act or section 117(2)(b) of the 2004 Act (issue of interim gender recognition certificate);

(b) in an application under section 1(2)(d) of the 1976 Act or section 117(3)(c) of the 2004 Act, the other party consents to decree of divorce or dissolution of civil partnership being granted;

(c) no other proceedings are pending in any court which could have the effect of bringing the marriage or civil partnership to an end;

(d) there are no children of the marriage or child of the family (as defined in section 101(7) of the 2004 Act) under the age of 16 years;

(e) neither party to the marriage or civil partnership applies for

---

[64] r. 33.33A(7) or r. 33A.33A(7).
[65] r. 33.33A(6) or r. 33A.33A(6).
[66] r. 33.33A(2) or r. 33A.33A(2).
[67] r. 33.33A(3) or r. 33A.33A(3).
[68] r. 33.33A(4) or r. 33A.33A(4).

an order for financial provision on divorce or dissolution of civil partnership;

(f) neither party to the marriage or civil partnership suffers from mental disorder;[69] and

(g) in the case of divorce, neither party to the marriage applies for the postponement of decree under section 3A of the Divorce (Scotland) Act 1976 (postponement of decree where religious impediment to remarriage exists).[70]

If an application ceases to be one to which the foregoing applies at any time before the final decree, it is deemed to be abandoned and must be dismissed.[71]

A simplified application must be made in Form F31 or Form CP29 (no cohabitation for one year with consent of defender to decree) or Form F33 or Form CP30 (no cohabitation for two years) or Form F33A or Form CP31 (issue of interim gender recognition certificate) and must be signed by the applicant.[72] The applicant requires to send the application to the sheriff clerk with—

(a) an extract or certified copy of the marriage or civil partnership certificate;

(b) the appropriate fee; and

(c) in an application under section 1(1)(b) of the Divorce (Scotland) Act 1976 or section 117(2)(b) of the Civil Partnership Act 2004, the interim gender recognition certificate or a certified copy within the meaning of Rule 33.9A(3) or Rule 33A.9(4).[73]

It is the duty of the sheriff clerk to cite any person and intimate any document in connection with a simplified application.[74]

A simplified application in which the facts set out in section 1(2)(d) of the Divorce (Scotland) Act 1976 or section 117(3)(c) of the Civil Partnership Act 2004 (no cohabitation for one year with consent of defender to decree) are relied on shall only be of effect if the form of consent in Part 2 of Form F31 or Form CP29 is signed by the party to the marriage or civil partnership giving consent.[75] Parole evidence cannot be given in a simplified application.[76]

---

[69] As to "mental disorder", see *B v. B*, 2009 S.L.T. (Sh. Ct.) 43 at p. 46.
[70] r. 33.73(1) and (3) or r. 33A.66(1) and (3).
[71] r. 33.73(2) or r. 33A.66(2).
[72] r. 33.74 or r. 33A.67.
[73] r. 33.75 or r. 33A.68.
[74] r. 33.76(2) or r.33A.69(2).
[75] r. 33.74(1)(b) or r. 33A.67(1)(b).
[76] r. 33.79 or r. 33A.72.

Any person on whom service or intimation of a simplified application has been made may give notice by letter sent to the sheriff clerk that he challenges the jurisdiction of the court or opposes the grant of decree of divorce or dissolution of civil partnership and giving reasons for his opposition to the application.[77] The sending of such a letter does not imply acceptance of the jurisdiction of the court.[78] Where such opposition is made, the sheriff must dismiss the application unless he is satisfied that the reasons given for the opposition are frivolous.[79] Any reason that cannot in law justify not granting decree of divorce, such as an objection to divorce on religious grounds, falls to be regarded as frivolous.[80] The sheriff clerk must intimate the sheriff's decision to the applicant and the respondent.[81]

The sheriff may grant decree in terms of the simplified divorce application on the expiry of the period of notice if such application has been properly served provided that, when the application has been served in a country to which the Hague Convention on the Service Abroad of Judicial and Extra-Judicial Documents in Civil and Commercial Matters dated 15 November 1965 applies, decree shall not be granted until it is established to the satisfaction of the sheriff that the requirements of Article 15 of that Convention have been complied with.[82]

Any appeal against an interlocutor granting decree in terms of the simplified application may be made, within 14 days after the date of decree, by sending a letter to the court giving reasons for the appeal.[83]

Any application to the court after decree has been granted in a simplified application which could have been made if it had been made in an action of divorce or dissolution of civil partnership, requires to be made by minute.[84]

---

[77] r. 33.78(1) or r. 33A.71(1).
[78] r. 33.78(4) or r. 33A.71(4).
[79] r. 33.78(2) or r. 33A.71(2).
[80] *Waugh v. Waugh*, 1992 S.L.T. (Sh. Ct.) 17.
[81] r. 33.78(3) or r. 33A.71(3).
[82] r. 33.80(1) or r. 33A.73(1).
[83] r. 33.81 or r. 33A.74. As to "reasons for the appeal", see *Colville v. Colville*, 1988 S.L.T. (Sh. Ct.) 23; *Norris v. Norris*, 1992 S.L.T. (Sh. Ct.) 51.
[84] r. 33.82 or r. 33A.75.

CHAPTER 2

MISCELLANEOUS TOPICS

Miscellaneous topics of significance in the law and practice relating to divorce and dissolution of civil partnership are considered in this chapter.

JURISDICTION

A sheriff court has jurisdiction to entertain actions of divorce and dissolution of civil partnership by virtue of section 8 of the Domicile and Matrimonial Proceedings Act 1973 and section 225(2) of the Civil Partnership Act 2004, respectively.

Actions for divorce

A sheriff court may have jurisdiction to entertain actions of divorce by virtue of section 8(1)(a) and (2) or section 8(1)(a) and (3) of the Domicile and Matrimonial Proceedings Act 1973.

A sheriff court has jurisdiction by virtue of section 8(1)(a) and (2) of the Domicile and Matrimonial Proceedings Act 1973[1] to entertain an action of divorce if (and only if)[2] each of the following applies:

    (a)   either—
          (i)   the Scottish courts have jurisdiction under the Council Regulation; or
         (ii) the action is an excluded one and either party to the marriage in question is domiciled in Scotland at the date when the action is begun;[3]
    and
    (b)   either party to the marriage—

---

[1] As amended by the Divorce Jurisdiction, Court Fees and Legal Aid (Scotland) Act 1983, Sched. 1, para. 18, the European Communities (Matrimonial Jurisdiction and Judgments) (Scotland) Regulations 2001 (S.S.I. 2001 No. 36), reg. 2(3)(a) and the European Communities (Matrimonial and Parental Responsibility Jurisdiction and Judgments) (Scotland) Regulations 2005 (S.S.I. 2005 No. 42), reg. 2(3)(a).

[2] Prorogation, for example, is not a ground of jurisdiction in actions of divorce or dissolution of civil partnership—*Singh v. Singh*, 1988 S.C.L.R. 541.

[3] *C.f. City of Edinburgh Council v. Davis*, 1987 S.L.T. (Sh. Ct.) 33 (action "raised" when citation of defender effected).

(i)   was resident in the sheriffdom for a period of 40 days ending with that date; or

(ii) was resident in the sheriffdom for a period of not less than 40 days ending not more than 40 days before the said date and has no known residence in Scotland at that date.

With respect to section 8(2)(a)(i), "the Council Regulation" is Council Regulation (EC) No. 2201/2003 of 27 November 2003 concerning jurisdiction and the recognition and enforcement of judgments in matrimonial matters and matters of parental responsibility.[4] The Scottish courts have jurisdiction in accordance with article 3 thereof, which provides:

"1. In matters relating to divorce, legal separation or marriage annulment, jurisdiction shall be with the courts of the Member State:

(a)   in whose territory:
— the spouses are habitually resident, or
— the spouses were last habitually resident, in so far as one of them still resides there, or the respondent is habitually resident, or
— in the event of a joint application, either of the spouses is habitually resident, or
— the applicant is habitually resident if he or she resided there for at least a year immediately before the application was made, or
— the applicant is habitually resident if he or she resided there for at least six months immediately before the application was made, and is either a national of the Member State in question or, in the case of the United Kingdom and Ireland, has his 'domicile' there;

(b)   of the nationality of both spouses or, in the case of the United Kingdom, and Ireland, of the 'domicile' of both spouses.

2. For the purpose of this regulation, 'domicile' shall have the same meaning as it has under the legal systems of the United Kingdom and Ireland."

---

[4] 1973 Act, s. 12(5)(c), as amended by the European Communities (Matrimonial and Parental Responsibility Jurisdiction and Judgments) (Scotland) Regulations 2005 (S.S.I. 2005 No. 42), reg. 2(6)(b).

Whether a party is "habitually resident" is a question of fact that encompasses the idea of where the person normally lives.[5] It has been suggested that a habitual residence is one that is being enjoyed voluntarily for the time being and with the settled intention that it should continue for some time, and that a person can have only one habitual residence at any one time.[6]

"Domicile" is an idea of law, namely the relation that the law creates between an individual and a particular locality or country; to every adult person the law ascribes a domicile, and that domicile remains his fixed attribute until a new and different attribute takes its place.[7] A person becomes capable of having a domicile when he attains the age of 16 years.[8] This is a "domicile of choice", which is a conclusion or inference that the law derives from the fact of a man fixing voluntarily his sole or chief residence in a particular place, with the unlimited intention of continuing to reside there.[9]

With regard to section 8(2)(a)(ii), an action is "an excluded one" if it is an action in respect of which no court of a Contracting State[10] has jurisdiction under the Council Regulation and the defender is not a person who is—

(i) a national of a Contracting State (other than the United Kingdom or Ireland); or
(ii) domiciled in Ireland.[11]

In relation to section 8(2)(b), the term "resident" points to a requirement for something more than mere presence at or occupation of a particular place and it is only when such presence or occupation is vested with a particular character that one can properly refer to it as

---

[5] *Morris v. Morris*, 1993 S.C.L.R. 144 at p. 145.

[6] *Dickson v. Dickson*, 1990 S.C.L.R. 692 at p. 703.

[7] *Bell v. Kennedy* (1869) 6 M. (H.L.) 69 at p. 78.

[8] Age of Legal Capacity (Scotland) Act 1991, s. 7.

[9] *Udny v. Udny* (1869) 7 M. (H.L.) 89 at p. 99; *Spence v. Spence*, 1995 S.L.T. 335; *Marsh v. Marsh*, 2002 S.L.T. (Sh. Ct.) 87.

[10] "Contracting State" means Belgium, Cyprus, Czech Republic, Germany, Greece, Spain, Estonia, France, Hungary, Ireland, Italy, Latvia, Lithuania, Luxemburg, Malta, Netherlands, Austria, Poland, Portugal, Slovak Republic, Slovenia, Finland, Sweden and the United Kingdom—1973 Act, s. 12(5)(b), as inserted by the European Communities (Matrimonial Jurisdiction and Judgments) (Scotland) Regulations 2001 (S.S.I. 2001 No. 36), reg. 2(5)(b) and amended by the European Communities (Matrimonial and Parental Responsibility Jurisdiction and Judgments) (Scotland) Regulations 2005 (S.S.I. 2005 No. 42), reg. 2(6)(a).

[11] 1973 Act, s. 12(5)(d), as inserted by the European Communities (Matrimonial Jurisdiction and Judgments) (Scotland) Regulations 2001 (S.S.I. 2001 No. 36), reg. 2(5)(b) and amended by the European Communities (Matrimonial and Parental Responsibility Jurisdiction and Judgments) (Scotland) Regulations 2005 (S.S.I. 2005 No. 42), reg. 2(6)(a).

"residence".[12] A person may be resident in more than one place and it must follow that continuous and uninterrupted occupation is not a necessary requirement for a finding of "residence".[13] However, some degree of actual physical occupation of a particular place is necessary before one can be said to reside at that place.[14] Whether or not a defender in an action of divorce is "resident" in any particular sheriffdom is therefore a question of fact and degree.[15]

Residence within the sheriffdom after the action is begun cannot be taken into account in determining whether or not there is jurisdiction.[16] Special cause must be shown to obtain warrant for citation from any court within a sheriffdom other than that in which the cause would normally fall to be dealt, namely the court within the district of which the defender was resident.[17]

A sheriff court has jurisdiction to entertain an action of divorce by virtue of section 8(1)(a) and (3) of the Domicile and Matrimonial Proceedings Act 1973 (notwithstanding that jurisdiction would not be exercisable under section 8(2)) if it is begun at a time when an original action is pending in respect of the marriage; and for this purpose "original action" means an action in respect of which the court has jurisdiction by virtue of section 8(2) or (3). This does not however give the court jurisdiction to entertain an action in contravention of Article 6 of the Council Regulation (exclusive nature of jurisdiction under Article 3 [general jurisdiction], Article 4 [counterclaim] and Article 5 [conversion of legal separation to divorce]).[18] The foregoing provisions are without prejudice to any sheriff court's jurisdiction to entertain an action of divorce remitted to it in pursuance of any enactment or rule of court,[19] provided that entertaining the action would not contravene Article 6 of the Council Regulation.[20]

---

[12] *Williamson v. Williamson*, 2010 S.L.T. (Sh. Ct.) 41 at p. 44.

[13] *Ibid.*

[14] *Ibid.*

[15] *Ibid.*

[16] *McNeill v. McNeill*, 1960 S.C. 30.

[17] *Simpson v. Bruce*, 1984 S.L.T. (Sh. Ct.) 38.

[18] 1973 Act, s. 8(3A), as inserted by the European Communities (Matrimonial Jurisdiction and Judgments) (Scotland) Regulations 2001 (S.S.I. 2001 No. 36), reg. 2(3)(b) and amended by the European Communities (Matrimonial and Parental Responsibility Jurisdiction and Judgments) (Scotland) Regulations 2005 (S.S.I. 2005 No. 42), reg. 2(3) (b). As to Art. 6, see further *Lopez v. Lopez Lizazo*, 2008 Fam. L.R. 2.

[19] See, *e.g.*, *Gribb v. Gribb*, 1992 S.C.L.R. 776 (action of divorce remitted from Court of Session to sheriff court under the Law Reform (Miscellaneous Provisions) (Scotland) Act 1985, s. 14).

[20] 1973 Act, s. 8(4), as amended by the European Communities (Matrimonial Jurisdiction and Judgments) (Scotland) Regulations 2001 (S.S.I. 2001 No. 36), reg. 2(3)(c) and the European Communities (Matrimonial and Parental Responsibility Jurisdiction and Judgments) (Scotland) Regulations 2005 (S.S.I. 2005 No. 42), reg. 2(3)(c).

Actions for dissolution of civil partnership

A sheriff court has jurisdiction by virtue of section 225(2) of the Civil Partnership Act 2004 to entertain an action for the dissolution of a civil partnership if (and only if)—

    (a) the court has jurisdiction under section 219 regulations (*viz.* regulations issued under section 219 of the Civil Partnership Act 2004); or

    (b) no court has, or is recognised as having, jurisdiction under section 219 regulations and either civil partner is domiciled in Scotland[21] on the date when the proceedings are begun

and either partner

    (a) was resident in the sheriffdom[22] for a period of 40 days ending with the date when the action is begun; or

    (b) had been resident in the sheriffdom for a period of not less than 40 days ending not more than 40 days before that date and has no known residence in Scotland at that date.[23]

The regulations issued under section 219 of the Civil Partnership Act 2004 are The Civil Partnership (Jurisdiction and Recognition of Judgments) (Scotland) Regulations 2005.[24] Regulation 5 thereof provides:

> "The courts in Scotland shall have jurisdiction in relation to proceedings for the dissolution . . . of a civil partnership . . . where—
>
>   (a) both civil partners are habitually resident in Scotland;
>
>   (b) both civil partners were last habitually resident in Scotland and one of the partners continues to reside there; .
>
>   (c) the defender is habitually resident in Scotland;
>
>   (d) the pursuer is habitually in Scotland and has resided there for at least one year immediately preceding the date on which the action is begun; or
>
>   (e) the pursuer is domiciled and habitually resident in Scotland and has resided there for at least six months immediately preceding the date on which the action is begun."[25]

---

[21] As to "domiciled in Scotland", see text accompanying nn. 7–9, *supra.*

[22] As to "resident in the sheriffdom", see text accompanying nn. 12–17, *supra.*

[23] 2004 Act, s. 225(1)(a) and (b) and (2)(a) and (b).

[24] S.S.I. 2005 No. 629.

[25] As to "habitually resident in Scotland", see text accompanying nn. 5 and 6, *supra.*

At any time when proceedings for the dissolution of a civil partnership or for separation of civil partners are pending in respect of which the sheriff court has jurisdiction, it also has jurisdiction to entertain other proceedings, in respect of the same civil partnership, for dissolution, even though that jurisdiction would not be exercisable under section 225(2) of the 2004 Act.[26]

CONCURRENT PROCEEDINGS

Where more than one legal system has jurisdiction in relation to divorce or dissolution of civil partnership, complex rules are required to avoid conflicts of jurisdiction. These are principally to be found in Schedule 3 to the Domicile and Matrimonial Proceedings Act 1973[27] (for actions of divorce) and in rules of court corresponding thereto made by virtue of section 226 of the Civil Partnership Act 2004 (for actions of dissolution of civil partnership).

These rules require parties to actions of divorce or dissolution of civil partnership to inform the court about any proceedings continuing outside Scotland which are in respect of the marriage or civil partnership, or capable of affecting its validity, and they make provision regarding mandatory and discretionary sists of such actions by the Scottish court where there are such concurrent proceedings elsewhere.

Duty to furnish particulars

The duty incumbent upon the pursuer and any other person who has entered appearance in the action to furnish particulars of any proceedings which he knows to be continuing in another jurisdiction,[28]

---

[26] 2004 Act, s. 225(4).

[27] Sched. 3 is subject to Art. 19 of the Council Regulation (lis pendens and dependent actions) — 1973 Act, s. 11(2), as inserted by the European Communities (Matrimonial and Parental Responsibility Jurisdiction and Judgments) (Scotland) Regulations 2005 (S.S.I. 2005 No. 42), reg. 2(5)(b). Art. 19 *inter alia* states that where proceedings relating to divorce between the same parties are brought before courts of different Member States, the court second seised must of its own motion stay its proceedings until such times as the jurisdiction of the court first seised is established; that where the jurisdiction of the court first seised is established the court second seised must decline jurisdiction in favour of that court; and that in that case, the party who brought the relevant action before the court second seised may bring that action before the court first seised.

[28] Any reference in Sched. 3 to the 1973 Act to proceedings in another jurisdiction is a reference to proceedings in a court of that jurisdiction and to any other proceedings in that jurisdiction which are of a prescribed description — 1973 Act, Sched. 3, para. 5. Any reference in Part XIII of the Ordinary Cause Rules (sisting of civil partnership actions) to proceedings in another jurisdiction is to proceedings in a court or before an administrative authority of that jurisdiction — r. 33A.79(4).

and which are in respect of the marriage or civil partnership with which the action is concerned or capable of affecting its validity, subsists while the action is pending and until proof in the action has begun.[29]

Rule 33.2 or Rule 33A.2 provides the machinery whereby each party may discharge this duty, requiring the pursuer to state in the condescendence of the initial writ whether to her knowledge any proceedings are continuing[30] in Scotland or in any other country which are in respect of the marriage or civil partnership to which the initial writ relates or are capable of affecting its validity or subsistence.[31] Where such proceedings are continuing, the pursuer must also state —

(a) the court, tribunal or authority before which they have been commenced;
(b) the date of commencement;
(c) the names of the parties;
(d) the date or expected date of any proof (or its equivalent) in the proceedings; and
(e) such other facts as may be relevant to the question of whether or not the action before the sheriff should be sisted under Schedule 3 to the 1973 Act or Council Regulation (EC) No. 2201/2003 of 27 November 2003 concerning jurisdiction and the recognition and enforcement of judgments in matrimonial matters and matters of parental responsibility, or under Part XIII of Chapter 33A of the Rules (sisting of civil partnership actions).[32]

The foregoing rules also provide that where —

(a) such proceedings are continuing;
(b) the action before the sheriff is defended; and
(c) either the initial writ does not contain the statement anent those proceedings above referred to or the particulars mentioned in (a) to (e) above are incomplete or incorrect,

---

[29] 1973 Act, Sched. 3, para. 7 or r. 33A.80. Neither the taking of evidence on commission nor a separate proof relating to any preliminary plea is to be regarded as part of the proof in the action — 1973 Act, Sched. 3, para. 4(a) or r. 33A.79(3)(a). See also n. 45 and accompanying text, *infra*.

[30] Proceedings are "continuing" at any time after they have been commenced and before they have been finally disposed of — r. 33.1(3) or r. 33A.1(3). An action is continuing if it is pending and not sisted — 1973 Act, Sched. 3, para. 4(b) or r. 33A.79(3)(b).

[31] r. 33.2(2)(a) or r. 33A.2(2)(a).

[32] r. 33.2(2)(b) or r. 33A.2(2)(b).

any defences or minute, as the case may be, lodged by any person to the action must include that statement and, where appropriate, the further or correct particulars.[33]

Mandatory sists

Where before the beginning of the proof in a continuing action of divorce or dissolution of civil partnership it appears to the sheriff, on the application[34] of a party to the marriage or civil partnership—

(a) that in respect of the same marriage or civil partnership proceedings for divorce or nullity of marriage or dissolution or nullity of civil partnership are continuing in a related jurisdiction (*i.e.* another country within the United Kingdom);[35] and

(b) that the parties to the marriage or civil partnership have resided together after the marriage was contracted or the civil partnership was formed or treated as having been formed within the meaning of section 1(1) of the Civil Partnership Act 2004; and

(c) that the place where they resided together when the action was begun or, if they did not then reside together, where they last resided together before the date on which that action was begun is in that jurisdiction; and

(d) that either of the said parties was habitually resident in that jurisdiction throughout the year ending with the said date on which they last resided together before the date on which that action was begun;

it is the duty of the sheriff to sist the action before him.[36]

Where an action is sisted by reference to proceedings in a related jurisdiction for the aforementioned remedies, then, without prejudice to the effect of the sist otherwise—

(a) the court shall not have power to make a relevant order (*i.e.* an interim order made relating to aliment or children)[37] in connection with the sisted action except in pursuance of paragraph (c) below; and

---

[33] r. 33.2(3) or r. 33A.2(3).

[34] Application for a sist must be made by written motion—r. 33.17 or r. 33A.17.

[35] Any of the following countries fall within the meaning of "related jurisdiction": England and Wales, Northern Ireland, Jersey, Guernsey (including Alderney and Sark) and the Isle of Man—1973 Act, Sched. 3, para. 3(2) or r. 33A.79(2).

[36] 1973 Act, Sched. 3, para. 8 or r. 33A.81.

[37] 1973 Act, Sched. 3, para. 11(1) or r. 33A.84(1).

(b) subject to the said paragraph (c), any relevant order made in connection with the sisted action shall (unless the sist or the relevant order has been previously recalled) cease to have effect on the expiration of the period of three months beginning with the date on which the sist comes into operation; but

(c) if the court considers that as a matter of necessity and urgency it is necessary during or after that period to make a relevant order in connection with the sisted action or to extend or further extend the duration of a relevant order made in connection with the sisted action, the court may do so, and the order shall not cease to have effect by virtue of paragraph (b) above.[38]

Where any action of divorce or dissolution of civil partnership is sisted and at the time the sist comes into operation, an order is in force, or at a subsequent time an order comes into force, being an order made in connection with the other proceedings and providing for any of the following four matters, namely periodical payments for a spouse of the marriage in question or for a party to the civil partnership in question, periodical payments for a child, arrangements to be made concerning with whom a child is to live, contact with a child, and any other matter relating to parental responsibilities within the meaning of section 1(3) of the Children (Scotland) Act 1995 or parental rights within the meaning of section 2(4) of that Act, then, as from the time when the sist comes into operation (in a case where the order is in force at that time) or (in any other case) on the coming into force of the order—

(a) any relevant order made in connection with the sisted action shall cease to have effect in so far as it makes for a spouse or civil partner, or child, any provision for any of the said matters as respects which the same or different provision for that spouse or civil partner, or child, is made by the other order; and

(b) the court shall not have power in connection with the sisted action to make a relevant order containing for a spouse or civil partner, or child, provision for any of the matters aforesaid as respects which any provision for that spouse or civil partner, or child, is made by the other order.[39]

These provisions have no effect on any power of a court—

(a) to vary or recall a relevant order in so far as the order is for the time being in force; or

---

[38] 1973 Act, Sched. 3, para. 11(2) or r. 33A.84(2).
[39] 1973 Act, Sched. 3, para. 11(3) or r. 33A.84(3).

(b) to enforce a relevant order as respects any period when it is or was in force; or

(c) to make a relevant order in connection with an action which was, but is no longer, sisted.[40]

The court may, on the application of a party to the action, recall a mandatory sist if it appears to the court that the other proceedings by reference to which the action was sisted are sisted or concluded or that a party to those other proceedings has delayed unreasonably in prosecuting those other proceedings.[41] Application for the recall of a sist must be made by written motion.[42]

Discretionary sists

Where before the beginning of a proof in a continuing action of divorce or dissolution of civil partnership it appears to the sheriff —

(a) that any other proceedings in respect of the marriage or civil partnership in question or capable of affecting its validity are continuing in another jurisdiction (*i.e.* any country outside Scotland);[43] and

(b) that the balance of fairness (including convenience) as between the parties to the civil partnership is such that it is appropriate for those proceedings to be disposed of before further steps are taken in the action;

the sheriff may then if he thinks fit sist that action.[44]

This discretionary power may be exercised after the beginning of a proof in a continuing action of divorce or dissolution of civil partnership in the event that the court is satisfied that a person has failed to perform the aforementioned duty imposed on him to furnish particulars of concurrent proceedings in another jurisdiction.[45]

In considering the foregoing issue of the balance of fairness and convenience, the court requires to have regard to all factors appearing to be relevant, including the convenience of witnesses and any delay or expense which may result from the proceedings being sisted, or not being sisted.[46] The proper initial approach to the question is to consider the overall connection of the marriage or civil partnership with the

---

[40] 1973 Act, Sched. 3, para. 11(4) or r. 33A.84(4).
[41] 1973 Act, Sched. 3, para. 10(1) or r. 33A.83(1).
[42] r. 33.17 or r. 33A.17.
[43] 1973 Act, Sched. 3, para. 3(1) or r. 33A.79(2).
[44] 1973 Act, Sched. 3, para. 9(1) or r. 33A.82(1).
[45] 1973 Act, Sched. 3, para. 9(4) or r. 33A.82(4). No action in respect of the failure of a person to perform such a duty is competent — *ibid.*
[46] 1973 Act, Sched. 3, para. 9(2) or r. 33A.82(2).

jurisdictions in question; and if that overall connection is *prima facie* with Scotland, the court would only be entitled to grant the sist if it were to take the view that there were, nevertheless, other circumstances by reason of which justice required that a sist should be granted.[47]

The court may, on the application of a party to the action, recall a discretionary sist if it appears to the court that the other proceedings by reference to which the action was sisted are sisted or concluded or that a party to those other proceedings has delayed unreasonably in prosecuting those other proceedings.[48] Application for the recall of a sist must be made by written motion.[49]

MENTAL DISORDER

Where a party to a marriage or a civil partnership suffers from mental disorder, special rules apply in the context of actions for divorce or dissolution of civil partnership.[50]

Mentally disordered pursuer

An insane person cannot competently prosecute an action of divorce or dissolution of civil partnership.[51] Mental disorder falling short of insanity does not of itself preclude the raising of such an action, but the pursuer must have the capacity to give instructions for the prosecution of the action.[52] A preliminary proof as to the pursuer's mental condition is competent; however, the onus on the defender to establish incapacity is a heavy one.[53]

Mentally disordered defender

The defender in an action of divorce or dissolution of civil partnership may be a person who is suffering from a mental disorder, which means any—

    (a)   mental illness;
    (b)   personality disorder; or
    (c)   learning disability,

---

[47] *Mitchell v. Mitchell*, 1992 S.C. 372. See also *De Dampierre v. De Dampierre* [1988] A.C. 92.
[48] 1973 Act, Sched. 3, para. 10(1) or r. 33A.83(1).
[49] r. 33.17 or r. 33A.17.
[50] As to the effect of mental disorder on the use of the simplified procedure, see Chap. 1.
[51] *Thomson v. Thomson* (1887) 14 R. 634.
[52] *Gibson v. Gibson*, 1970 S.L.T. (Notes) 60.
[53] *AB v. CB*, 1937 S.C. 408.

however caused or manifested (and cognate expressions are to be construed accordingly), but a person is not mentally disordered by reason only of any of the following:

(a) sexual orientation;
(b) sexual deviancy;
(c) transsexualism;
(d) transvestism;
(e) dependence on, or use of, alcohol or drugs;
(f) behaviour that causes, or is likely to cause, harassment, alarm or distress to any other person;
(g) acting as no prudent person would act.[54]

In the case of a defender who is suffering from a mental disorder, intimation of the action falls to be made in accordance with Rule 33.7(1)(c) or Rule 33A.7(1)(b).[55]

Where the defender suffers or appears to suffer from mental disorder and is resident in a hospital or other similar institution, citation must be made in compliance with Rule 33.13 or Rule 33A.13. This requires citation to be executed by registered post or the first class recorded delivery service addressed to the medical officer in charge of that hospital or institution; and there requires to be included with the copy of the initial writ—

(a) a citation in Form F15 or Form CP15;
(b) any notice required by Rule 33.14(1) or Rule 33A.14(1);[56]
(c) a request in Form F17 or Form CP18;
(d) a form of certificate in Form F18 or Form CP19 requesting the medical officer to—
    (i) deliver and explain the initial writ, citation and any notice or form of notice of consent required under Rule 33.14(1) or Rule 33A.14(1) personally to the defender; or
    (ii) certify that such delivery or explanation would be dangerous to the health or mental condition of the defender; and
(e) a stamped envelope addressed for return of that certificate to the pursuer or his solicitor, if he has one.[57]

The medical officer must send the certificate in Form F18 or Form CP19 duly completed to the pursuer or his solicitor, as the case may

---

[54] Mental Health (Care and Treatment) (Scotland) Act 2003, s. 328, applied by r. 33.1(2) or r. 33A.1(2).
[55] As to which, see Chap. 1, text accompanying nn. 8–9.
[56] As to which, see Chap. 3, nn. 35 and 47.
[57] r. 33.13(1) or r. 33A.13(1).

be, and that certificate must be attached to the certificate of citation.[58] Where such a certificate bears that the initial writ has not been delivered to the defender, the sheriff may, at any time before decree—

(a) order such further medical inquiry; and
(b) make such order for further service or intimation, as he thinks fit.[59]

Rule 33.16 or Rule 33A.16 applies where it appears to the court that the defender is suffering from a mental disorder. In that event, the sheriff must—

(a) appoint a curator *ad litem* to the defender;
(b) where the facts set out in section 1(2)(d) of the Divorce (Scotland) Act 1976 or section 117(3)(c) of the Civil Partnership Act 2004 (no cohabitation for one year with consent of defender to decree) are relied on—
    (i) make an order for intimation of the ground of the action to the Mental Welfare Commission for Scotland; and
    (ii) include in such an order a requirement that the Commission sends to the sheriff clerk a report indicating whether in its opinion the defender is capable of deciding whether or not to give consent to the granting of decree.[60]

Within seven days after the appointment of a curator *ad litem*, the pursuer must send to him—

(a) a copy of the initial writ and any defences (including any adjustments and amendments) lodged; and
(b) a copy of any notice in Form G5 sent to him by the sheriff clerk.[61]

On receipt of any report from the Mental Welfare Commission for Scotland required as aforesaid, the sheriff clerk must—

(a) lodge the report in process; and
(b) intimate that this has been done to—
    (i) the pursuer;
    (ii) the solicitor for the defender, if known; and
    (iii) the curator *ad litem*.[62]

The curator *ad litem* requires to lodge in process within 14 days after the report of the Mental Welfare Commission for Scotland has

---

[58] r. 33.13(2) and (3) or r. 33A.13(2) and (3).
[59] r. 33.13(4) or r. 33A.13(4).
[60] r. 33.16(1) and (2) or r. 33A.16(1) and (2).
[61] r. 33.16(3) or r. 33A.16(3).
[62] r. 33.16(4) or r. 33A.16(4).

been lodged in process or, where no such report is required, within 21 days after the date of his appointment, one of the following:

(a) a notice of intention to defend;
(b) defences to the action;
(c) a minute adopting defences already lodged; or
(d) a minute stating that the curator *ad litem* does not intend to lodge defences.[63]

Notwithstanding that he has lodged a minute stating that he does not intend to lodge defences, a curator *ad litem* may appear at any stage of the action to protect the interests of the defender.[64] If, at any time, it appears to the curator *ad litem* that the defender is not suffering from mental disorder, he may report that fact to the court and seek his own discharge.[65] The pursuer is responsible, in the first instance, for payment of the fees and outlays of the curator *ad litem* incurred during the period from his appointment until—

(a) he lodges a minute stating that he does not intend to lodge defences;
(b) he decides to instruct the lodging of defences or a minute adopting defences already lodged; or
(c) being satisfied after investigation that the defender is not suffering from mental disorder, he is discharged.[66]

PUBLICITY OF PROCEEDINGS

Statutory restrictions concerning what may lawfully be printed or published in connection with an action of divorce or dissolution of civil partnership are set forth in the Judicial Proceedings (Regulation of Reports) Act 1926.

Section 1(1) of the Act[67] provides:

"It shall not be lawful to print or publish, or cause or procure to be printed or published—
(a) in relation to any judicial proceedings any indecent matter or indecent medical, surgical or physiological details being matters or details the publication of which would be calculated to injure public morals;
(b) in relation to any judicial proceedings for dissolution

---

[63] r. 33.16(5) and (6) or r. 33A.16(5) and (6).
[64] r. 33.16(7) or r. 33A.16(7).
[65] r. 33.16(8) or r. 33A.16(8).
[66] r. 33.16(9) or r. 33A.16(9).
[67] As amended by the Civil Partnership Act 2004, Sched. 27, para. 8(2).

of marriage . . . or for the dissolution . . . of a civil partnership . . ., any particulars other than the following, that is to say—

    (i)   the names, addresses and occupations of the parties and witnesses;

    (ii)   a concise statement of the charges, defences and counter-charges in support of which evidence has been given;

    (iii)   submissions on any point of law arising in the course of the proceedings, and the decision of the court thereon;

    (iv)   the summing-up of the judge and the finding of the jury (if any) and the judgment of the court and observations made by the judge in giving judgment:

Provided that nothing in this part of this subsection shall be held to permit the publication of anything contrary to the provisions of paragraph (a) of this subsection."

The Act does not apply to:

(a)   the printing of any pleading, transcript of evidence or other document for use in connection with any judicial proceeding or the communication thereof to persons concerned in the proceedings; or

(b)   the printing or publishing of any notice or report in pursuance of the directions of the court; or

(c)   the publishing of any matter in any separate volume or part of any bona fide series of law reports which does not form part of any other publication and consists solely of reports of proceedings in courts of law, or in any publication of a technical character bona fide intended for circulation among members of the legal or medical professions.[68]

No person other than a proprietor, editor, master printer or publisher is liable to be convicted under the Act.[69] The Act does not give a divorce litigant any civil law right to recover damages for its breach.[70]

---

[68] 1926 Act, s. 1(4).

[69] 1926 Act, s. 1(2).

[70] *Nicol v. Caledonian Newspapers Ltd*, 2003 S.L.T. 109.

CHAPTER 3

THE MERITS

The grounds upon which the court may grant decree for divorce or the dissolution of a civil partnership, namely (i) the irretrievable breakdown of the marriage or civil partnership; or (ii) the issue of an interim gender recognition certificate, are recognised in this chapter. The court's powers in certain cases of irretrievable breakdown to postpone the grant of decree are considered first.

POSTPONEMENT OF DECREE

Reconciliation

One of the aims of the Divorce (Scotland) Act 1976, according to its long title, is to "facilitate reconciliation between the parties in consistorial causes".

To that end the court is empowered in appropriate cases to continue any pending action of divorce for such period as it thinks proper to enable attempts to be made to effect reconciliation (and any cohabitation during this period is disregarded for the purposes of that action).[1] A similar provision exists in the Civil Partnership Act 2004 with respect to actions for dissolution of civil partnership.[2]

Religious impediment to remarriage

Notwithstanding that irretrievable breakdown of a marriage has been established in an action of divorce, the court may—

(a) on the application of a party; and
(b) if satisfied—
   (i) that the applicant is prevented from entering into a religious marriage (*i.e.* a marriage solemnised by a marriage celebrant of a prescribed religious body)[3] by

---

[1] Divorce (Scotland) Act 1976, s. 2(1).
[2] Civil Partnership Act 2004, s. 118.
[3] 1976 Act, s. 3A(7), as inserted by the Family Law (Scotland) Act 2006, s. 15. Any Hebrew Congregation is a religious body for the purposes of s. 3A(7) by virtue of the Divorce (Religious Bodies) (Scotland) Regulations 2006 (S.S.I. 2006 No. 253), reg. 2. A marriage celebrant of a prescribed religious body is a reference to—(a) a minister, clergyman,

virtue of a requirement of the religion of that marriage; and the other party can act so as to remove, or enable or contribute to the removal of, that impediment which prevents that marriage; and

(ii)   that it is just and reasonable to do so,

postpone the grant of decree until it is satisfied that the other party has so acted.[4] Any application for such postponement must be made by minute in the process to which the application relates.[5]

The court may, whether or not on the application of a party, recall such a postponement and may, before doing so, order the other party to produce a certificate from a relevant religious body confirming that the other party has acted as above described.[6] A religious body is "relevant" for these purposes if the applicant considers the body competent to provide the aforesaid confirmation.[7] Any application for such recall of postponement must be made by minute in the process to which the application relates.[8]

IRRETRIEVABLE BREAKDOWN

In an action for divorce, on the application of the pursuer,[9] the court may grant decree if it is established that the marriage has broken down irretrievably.[10] Likewise, in an action for dissolution of civil partnership, on the application of the pursuer, the court may grant decree if it is established that the civil partnership has broken down irretrievably.[11]

In either case, the onus of proving irretrievable breakdown is on the pursuer.[12] The evidence establishing the grounds must consist of

---

pastor or priest of such a body; (b) a person who has, on the nomination of such a body, been registered under s. 9 of the Marriage (Scotland) Act 1977 as empowered to solemnise marriages; or (c) any person who is recognised by such a body as entitled to solemnise marriages on its behalf—1976 Act, s. 3A(8), as inserted by the Family Law (Scotland) Act 2006, s. 15.

[4] 1976 Act, s. 3A(1), (2) and (3), as inserted by the Family Law (Scotland) Act 2006, s. 15.

[5] r. 33.27A.

[6] 1976 Act, s. 3A(4) and (5), as inserted by the Family Law (Scotland) Act 2006, s. 15.

[7] 1976 Act, s. 3A(6), as inserted by the Family Law (Scotland) Act 2006, s. 15.

[8] r. 33.27A.

[9] A counter claim by the defender for divorce is incompetent—*Farley v. Farley*, 1990 S.C. 279.

[10] 1976 Act, s. 1(1)(a).

[11] 2004 Act, s. 117(1) and (2)(a).

[12] *Paterson v. Paterson*, 1938 S.C. 251 at p. 256; *Ross v. Ross*, 1997 S.L.T. (Sh. Ct.) 51 at p. 53.

or include evidence other than that of a party to the marriage or civil partnership.[13] In the event of failure to lead evidence from a witness other than the parties, the court has power to allow further proof.[14] The standard of proof required to establish the ground of action is on the balance of probability.[15]

In terms of section 1(2) of the Divorce (Scotland) Act 1976, the irretrievable breakdown of a marriage is taken to be established in an action of divorce if—

(a) since the date of the marriage the defender has committed adultery; or

(b) since the date of the marriage the defender has at any time behaved (whether or not as a result of mental abnormality and whether such behaviour has been active or passive) in such a way that the pursuer cannot reasonably be expected to cohabit with the defender; or

(c) there has been no cohabitation between the parties at any time during a continuous period of one year after the date of the marriage and immediately preceding the bringing of the action and the defender consents to the granting of decree of divorce; or

(d) there has been no cohabitation between the parties at any time during a continuous period of two years after the date of the marriage and immediately preceding the bringing of the action.

In terms of section 117(3) of the Civil Partnership Act 2004, the irretrievable breakdown of a civil partnership is taken to be established in an action of dissolution of civil partnership if—

(a) since the date of registration of the civil partnership the defender has at any time behaved (whether or not as a result of mental abnormality and whether such behaviour has been

---

[13] Civil Evidence (Scotland) Act 1988, s. 8(3) and (3A), as amended and inserted, respectively, by the 2004 Act, Sched. 28, para. 55. The Lord Advocate may by order made by statutory instrument provide that this requirement should not apply, or should apply subject to such modifications as may be specified in the order, in respect of such class or classes of action as may be so specified—1988 Act, s. 8(4), as so amended. Relevant orders so made are the Evidence in Divorce Actions (Scotland) Order 1989 (S.I. 1989 No. 582) and the Evidence in Civil Partnership and Divorce Actions (Scotland) Order 2012 (S.S.I. 2012 No. 111), which relate to cases which may proceed under the simplified procedure. See also *Taylor v. Taylor*, 2000 S.L.T. 1419 (s. 8(3) of the 1988 Act provided safeguard against collusion but did not require corroboration or that all witnesses should be led who might provide corroboration).

[14] *Symanski v. Symanski*, 2005 Fam. L.R. 6.

[15] 1976 Act, s. 1(6); 2004 Act, s. 117(8).

active or passive) in such a way that the pursuer cannot reasonably be expected to cohabit with the defender; or

(b) there has been no cohabitation between the parties at any time during a continuous period of one year after the date of registration of the civil partnership and immediately preceding the bringing of the action and the defender consents to the granting of decree of dissolution of the civil partnership; or

(c) there has been no cohabitation between the parties at any time during a continuous period of two years after the date of registration of the civil partnership and immediately preceding the bringing of the action.

Each of the foregoing grounds is now considered in turn.

Adultery

Adultery is ". . . sexual intercourse or carnal connection between a consenting spouse and a member of the opposite sex who is not the other spouse . . .".[16]

One act of adultery is sufficient to constitute irretrievable breakdown. How the offended spouse responds to it or perceives it is immaterial.[17] Whether or not the marriage partners were cohabiting at the time is irrelevant. Good faith (*e.g.* committing adultery in the genuine belief that the marriage partner is dead) is not a defence.[18] Adminicles of evidence relevant to proof of adultery include admissions of adultery,[19] opportunity plus,[20] diaries and letters,[21] fathering or mothering a child by a third party[22] and other sexual behaviour on the part of the offending spouse.[23]

Irretrievable breakdown is however not to be taken to be established if—

---

[16] *MacLennan v. MacLennan*, 1958 S.C. 105 at p. 109.

[17] *Stewart v. Stewart*, 1987 S.L.T. (Sh. Ct.) 48 at p. 50.

[18] *Hunter v. Hunter* (1900) 2 F. 774.

[19] *Sinclair v. Sinclair*, 1986 S.L.T. (Sh. Ct.) 54 at p. 56. *C.f. Cooper v. Cooper*, 1987 S.L.T. (Sh. Ct.) 37 (admission of adultery by affidavit inadmissible where not disclosed *in gremio* that witness warned that he or she need not give evidence tending to indicate guilt of adultery).

[20] *Hannah v. Hannah*, 1931 S.C. 275 (shared hotel bedroom); *Hall v. Hall*, 1958 S.C. 206 (late night home visits).

[21] *Creasey v. Creasey*, 1931 S.C. 9; *Argyll v. Argyll*, 1963 S.L.T. (Notes) 42 (diary); *Rattray v. Rattray* (1897) 25 R. 315 (letter).

[22] *MacKay v. MacKay*, 1946 S.C. 78 (wife having child by another man); *Campbell v. Campbell* (1860) 23 D. 99 (husband fathering child by another woman).

[23] *Collins v. Collins* (1884) 11 R. (H.L.) 19 at pp. 29, 33 (condoned adultery); *Whyte v. Whyte* (1884) 11 R. 710 (husband behaving indecently towards another woman); *Wilson v. Wilson*, 1955 S.L.T. (Notes) 81 (wife embracing another man).

(a) the adultery has been connived at in such a way as to raise the defence of *lenocinium*, which is that the defender has actively promoted the adultery in question;[24] or

(b) the adultery has been condoned by the pursuer's cohabitation with the defender in the knowledge and belief that the defender has committed the adultery; but adultery will not be held to have been so condoned by reason only of the fact that after the commission of the adultery the pursuer has continued or resumed cohabitation with the defender, provided that the pursuer has not cohabited with the defender at any time after the end of the period of three months from the date on which cohabitation was continued or resumed with the aforesaid knowledge or belief.[25]

Intimation where adultery between a pursuer or defender and a named third party is alleged falls to be made in accordance with Rule 33.7(1)(b) and Rule 33.15(3).[26]

Behaviour

Whereas adultery is based on objective fact and affords a ground for divorce however the offended spouse responds to it or perceives it, in relation to behaviour as establishing irretrievable breakdown in actions of divorce or dissolution of civil partnership, the effective question is how the offended spouse or civil partner could reasonably be expected to react to specific behaviour on the part of the other spouse or civil partner.[27]

The question as to whether the pursuer can reasonably be expected to cohabit with the defender is one as to the position at the date of proof and the court is entitled to take into account the pursuer's circumstances at that date and the changes that will have occurred in the parties' lives since they separated.[28] Irretrievable breakdown is however only to be taken to be established where the fact that the pursuer cannot reasonably be expected to cohabit with the defender flows, in a causal sense, from the nature of the relevant behaviour of the defender.[29]

---

[24] 1976 Act, s. 1(3); Scottish Law Commission, *Report on Family Law* (Scot. Law Com. No. 135, 1992), para. 13.2. An example is where the husband has encouraged the wife to prostitute herself (*Marshall v. Marshall* (1881) 8 R. 702).

[25] 1976 Act, ss. 1(3) and 2(2).

[26] See Chap. 1, text accompanying nn. 7 and 22.

[27] *Stewart v. Stewart*, 1987 S.L.T. (Sh. Ct.) 48 at p. 50 (admission of extra-marital "association" after persistent late homecoming justified divorce).

[28] *Findlay v. Findlay*, 1991 S.L.T. 457.

[29] *Ibid*. See also *Knox v. Knox*, 1993 S.C.L.R. 381; *Smith v. Smith*, 1994 S.C.L.R. 244.

The more obvious examples of behaviour establishing irretrievable breakdown include habitual abuse of alcohol or drugs, violence directed at the pursuer (including attempted or threatened violence) and extra-marital sexual activity.[30] Relevant conduct may be persistent, or cumulative, or may be of such a nature that even if there is no risk of a repetition it is so destructive of a marriage or civil partnership relationship as to make it unreasonable to expect the pursuer to cohabit with the defender.[31]

Where the defender has been convicted of a criminal offence upon which the pursuer wishes to found (*e.g.* assault upon her) she may rely upon section 10 of the Law Reform (Miscellaneous Provisions) (Scotland) Act 1968 to establish the commission of the offence.

Non-cohabitation

In cases of one year's non-cohabitation with the defender's consent to the granting of decree of divorce or dissolution of civil partnership, and in cases of two years' non-cohabitation, it must be averred and proved that the parties have not cohabited for the requisite period of time. Any action raised before the expiry of that period is therefore manifestly groundless.[32]

The question of when the parties ceased to cohabit is one of fact to be determined, at least in divorce actions, under reference to section 13(2) of the Divorce (Scotland) Act 1976, which provides:

> "For the purposes of this Act, the parties to a marriage shall be held to cohabit with one another only when they are in fact living together as man and wife; and 'cohabitation' shall be construed accordingly."[33]

In considering whether or not a period of non-cohabitation has been continuous no account is to be taken of any period (or periods) not exceeding six months in all during which the parties cohabited with one another, any such period (or periods) however not counting as part of the period of non-cohabitation.[34]

---

[30] *C.f.* Chap. 1, nn. 26–29 (procedure when "association" with third party alleged).
[31] *Hastie v. Hastie*, 1985 S.L.T. 146 at p. 148 (false accusations of infidelity and of an incestuous association).
[32] *Matthews v. Matthews*, 1985 S.L.T. (Sh. Ct.) 68. Conversion of an action of divorce or dissolution of civil partnership based on other grounds to a one-year with consent or two-years action by amendment after the expiry of the requisite period of non-cohabitation is competent—*Duncan v. Duncan*, 1986 S.L.T. 17.
[33] *C.f. Buczynska v. Buczynski*, 1989 S.L.T. 558; *Brown v. Brown*, 1998 Fam. L.R 81; *Banks v. Banks*, 2005 Fam. L.R. 116; *Bain v. Bain*, 2008 Fam. L.R. 81.
[34] 1976 Act, s. 2(4) and 2004 Act, s. 119(3).

With respect to one-year cases, Rule 33.14 or Rule 33A.14 and Rule 33.18 or Rule 33A.18 provide the machinery for the giving and the withdrawal of consent to the granting of decree of divorce or dissolution of civil partnership.

The pursuer requires to attach to the copy initial writ served upon the defender a notice in Form F19 or Form CP20 and a notice of consent in Form F20 or Form CP21.[35] The certificate of citation must state which notice or form has been attached to the initial writ.[36]

The defender thereafter indicates to the court his consent by giving notice in writing in Form F20 or Form CP21 to the sheriff clerk.[37] It is incompetent to give consent in any other way, such as by oral evidence.[38] The defender is free to deliver the notice personally or have an intermediary (*e.g.* the pursuer's solicitor) deliver it.[39] The evidence of one witness is sufficient for the purpose of establishing that the signature on the notice of consent is that of the defender.[40] Where a lengthy period of time has elapsed since the date of the defender's signature, the sheriff has a discretion as to whether or not to treat the consent form as valid.[41]

The defender is entitled to withdraw his consent at any time and for any reason. Where the initial writ contains an averment that the defender consents to the grant of decree, he may give notice in writing that he has not consented to decree being granted or that he withdraws any consent which he has already given.[42] Where he does so, the sheriff clerk must intimate the terms of the letter to the pursuer who is required within 14 days after the date of the intimation, if none of the other facts mentioned in section 1(2) of the Divorce (Scotland) Act 1976 (or section 117(3) of the Civil Partnership Act 2004, as the case may be) is averred in the initial writ, to lodge a motion for the action to be sisted.[43] If no such motion is lodged, the pursuer shall be deemed to have abandoned the action and the action must be dismissed.[44] If the motion is granted and the sist is not recalled or renewed within a period of six months from the date of the interlocutor granting the sist, the pursuer is deemed to have abandoned the action and the action must

---

[35] r. 33.14(1)(a)(i) or r. 33A.14(1)(a)(i).
[36] r. 33.14(2) or r. 33A.14(2).
[37] r. 33.18(1) or r. 33A.18(1).
[38] *Rodgers v. Rodgers*, 1994 S.C.L.R. 750.
[39] *Taylor v. Taylor*, 1988 S.C.L.R. 60.
[40] r. 33.18(2) or r. 33A.18(2).
[41] *Donnelly v. Donnelly*, 1991 S.L.T. (Sh. Ct.) 9.
[42] r. 33.18(3) or r. 33A.18(3).
[43] r. 33.18(4) and (5) or r. 33A.18(4) and (5).
[44] r. 33.18(6) or r. 33A.18(6).

be dismissed.[45] In any case where the defender has not given or has withdrawn his consent, it is incompetent or at least inappropriate for the court to pronounce any interlocutor in the process, save as already mentioned.[46]

In relation to two-year cases, the pursuer requires to send with the copy initial writ served upon the defender a notice as nearly as may be in terms of Form F23 or Form CP24.[47] The certificate of citation must state which notice or form has been attached to the initial writ.[48]

INTERIM GENDER RECOGNITION CERTIFICATE

In an action for divorce the court may grant decree if an interim gender recognition certificate under the Gender Recognition Act 2004 has, after the date of the marriage, been issued to either party of the marriage.[49] Similarly, in an action for dissolution of civil partnership the court may grant decree if an interim gender recognition certificate under the Gender Recognition Act 2004 has, after the date of the registration of the civil partnership, been issued to either of the civil partners.[50]

Gender Recognition Panels issue gender recognition certificates upon applications under section 1 of the Gender Recognition Act 2004. Such an application may be made by a person of either gender who is aged at least 18 on the basis of

(a)   living in the other gender; or
(b)   having changed gender under the law of a country or territory outside the United Kingdom.[51]

Unless the applicant is married or a civil partner, any certificate so issued is to be a full gender recognition certificate.[52] If the applicant is married or a civil partner, the certificate is to be an interim gender recognition certificate.[53]

---

[45] r. 33.18(7) or r. 33A.18(7).
[46] *Boyle v. Boyle*, 1977 S.L.T. (Notes) 69.
[47] r. 33.14(1)(b)(i) or r. 33A.14(1)(b)(i).
[48] r. 33.14(2) or r. 33A.14(2).
[49] Divorce (Scotland) Act 1976, s. 1(1)(b).
[50] Civil Partnership Act 2004, s. 117(2)(b).
[51] Gender Recognition Act 2004, s. 1(1).
[52] Gender Recognition Act 2004, s. 4(1) and (2), as amended by the Civil Partnership Act 2004, s. 250(2)(b).
[53] Gender Recognition Act 2004, s. 4(1) and (3), as amended by the Civil Partnership Act 2004, s. 250(2)(b).

Unless the sheriff otherwise directs, a warrant of citation shall not be granted in an action of divorce or dissolution of civil partnership without there being produced with the initial writ—

    (a) where the pursuer is the subject of the interim gender recognition certificate, the interim gender recognition certificate or, failing that, a certified copy of the interim gender recognition certificate; or

    (b) where the pursuer is the spouse or civil partner of the person who is the subject of an interim gender recognition certificate, a certified copy of the interim gender recognition certificate.[54]

For the purposes of the foregoing, a certified copy of an interim gender recognition certificate shall be a copy of that certificate sealed with the seal of the Gender Recognition Panels and certified to be a true copy by an officer authorised by the President of Gender Recognition Panels.[55]

A court which grants decree of divorce or a decree of dissolution of civil partnership on the ground that an interim gender recognition certificate has been issued to a party to the marriage or the civil partnership must, on doing so, issue a full gender recognition certificate to that party and send a copy to the Secretary of State.[56]

---

[54] r. 33.9A(1) and (2) or r. 33A.9(1) and (2)(b).

[55] r. 33.9A(3) or r. 33A.9(4).

[56] Gender Recognition Act 2004, ss. 5(1)(b) and 5A(1)(b), as amended by the Civil Partnership Act 2004, s. 250(4).

CHAPTER 4

PROTECTIVE MEASURES

In this chapter various measures for the protection of a party's position in an action of divorce or dissolution of civil partnership are discussed. These range in importance and effect from the accommodation address to interim exclusion orders.

ACCOMMODATION ADDRESS

Where the pursuer does not wish to disclose his or her whereabouts to the defender, he or she may be designed as care of his or her solicitors in the instance of the initial writ.

Use of an accommodation address is a privilege for when a party's address is not given, that party is not properly designed and, accordingly, the initial writ is not properly framed.[1]

There are circumstances in which the court will allow the use of an accommodation address (*e.g.* where there would otherwise be a risk of abuse); facts to justify the privilege must however be fully stated in the pleadings.[2]

All parties to an action of divorce or dissolution of civil partnership are under a continuing duty to disclose their true address to the court.[3] Application may be made to the court by motion to ordain a party to comply with this requirement.[4]

INTERDICTS

The court may grant interdicts and interim interdicts in the context of actions for divorce ("matrimonial interdicts") or dissolution of civil partnership ("relevant interdicts"). It may also make a determination that any such interdict or interim interdict obtained by an applicant is a domestic abuse interdict for the purposes of the Domestic Abuse (Scotland) Act 2011.

---

[1] *Doughton v. Doughton*, 1958 S.L.T. (Notes) 34; *B v. P*, 2010 Fam. L.R. 118.
[2] *Ibid.*
[3] *B v. P*, 2010 Fam. L.R. 118.
[4] *Stein v. Stein*, 1936 S.L.T. 103; *B v. P*, 2010 Fam. L.R. 118.

Matrimonial interdicts and relevant interdicts

An interdict is a matrimonial interdict if it is:

"an interdict, including an interim interdict, which—
  (a) restrains or prohibits any conduct of one spouse towards the other spouse or a child of the family;[5] or
  (b) prohibits a spouse from entering or remaining in—
      (i) a matrimonial home;[6]
      (ii) any other residence occupied by the applicant spouse;
      (iii) any place of work of the applicant spouse;
      (iv) any school attended by a child in the permanent or temporary care of the applicant spouse."[7]

An interdict is a relevant interdict if it is:

"an interdict, including an interim interdict, which—
  (a) restrains or prohibits any conduct of one civil partner towards the other civil partner or a child of the family;[8] or
  (b) prohibits a civil partner from entering or remaining in—
      (i) a family home;[9]
      (ii) any other residence occupied by the applicant civil partner;
      (iii) any place of work of the applicant civil partner;
      (iv) any school attended by a child in the permanent or temporary care of the applicant civil partner."[10]

It is not incompetent for the court to entertain an application for a matrimonial interdict or relevant interdict, including an interim interdict, by reason only that the spouses or civil partners are living together as man and wife or in civil partnership, as the case may be.[11] If the non-applicant spouse is an entitled spouse or has occupancy

---

[5] As to the meaning of "child of the family", see Chap.5, n. 6.

[6] For the meaning of "matrimonial home", see Chap. 5, n. 3.

[7] Matrimonial Homes (Family Protection) (Scotland) Act 1981, s. 14(2), as amended by the Family Law (Scotland) Act 2006, s. 10. "Applicant spouse" means the spouse who has applied for the interdict and "non-applicant spouse" is to be construed accordingly—1981 Act, s. 14(6), as inserted by the Family Law (Scotland) Act 2006, s. 10(3).

[8] As to the meaning of "child of the family", see Chap. 5, n. 6.

[9] For the meaning of "family home", see Chap. 5, n. 4.

[10] Civil Partnership Act 2004, s. 113(2), as amended by the Family Law (Scotland) Act 2006, Sched. 1, para. 8. "Applicant civil partner" means the civil partner who has applied for the interdict; and "non-applicant civil partner" is to be construed accordingly—2004 Act, s. 113(6), as inserted by the 2006 Act, Sched. 1, para. 8.

[11] 1981 Act, s. 14(1) and (2) and 2004 Act, s. 113(1) and (2).

rights, the court may only grant a matrimonial interdict prohibiting him or her from entering or remaining in the matrimonial home if the interdict is ancillary to an exclusion order or by virtue of section 1(3) of the Matrimonial Homes (Family Protection) (Scotland) Act 1981 the court refuses leave to exercise occupancy rights.[12] If the non-applicant civil partner is an entitled partner or has occupancy rights, the court may only grant a relevant interdict prohibiting him or her from entering or remaining in the family home if the interdict is ancillary to an exclusion order or by virtue of section 101(4) of the Civil Partnership Act 2004 the court refuses leave to exercise occupancy rights.[13]

The terms of any matrimonial interdict or relevant interdict must be no wider than are necessary to curb the illegal actings complained of, and so precise and clear that the person interdicted is left in no doubt what he is forbidden to do, and must be justified by the applicant's pleadings.[14] Where there is no information of a wrong actually being committed by the defender against the pursuer, there must be reasonable apprehension that the defender may in the future do the illegal acts which the pursuer seeks to have him restrained from doing.[15]

When an interim interdict is claimed to have been breached, a minute may be lodged containing detailed averments in support of a crave for the court to ordain the defender to appear at the bar of the court to explain his actings.[16] A breach of interdict constitutes a contempt of court that may lead to punishment, and it is necessary in the interests of fairness that the alleged contempt should be clearly and distinctly averred.[17] Such a minute can only be presented with the concurrence of the procurator fiscal concerned with any criminal proceedings that may be taken as a result of the actings in question,[18] and the minute is incompetent where the defender has already been convicted of an offence under section 2 of the Domestic Abuse (Scotland) Act 2011 in respect of the conduct in question.[19] If the minute can proceed, and the alleged breach is denied, answers may be ordered and a proof held. The evidence led should be confined to the parties' averments and

---

[12] 1981 Act, s. 14(3), (4) and (5), as inserted by the Family Law (Scotland) Act 2006, s. 10(3). As to the meaning of "non-applicant spouse", see n. 7, *supra*.

[13] 2004 Act, s. 113(3), (4) and (5), as inserted by the Family Law (Scotland) Act 2006, Sched. 1, para. 8. As to the meaning of "non-applicant civil partner", see n.10, *supra*.

[14] *Murdoch v. Murdoch*, 1973 S.L.T. (Notes) 13; *McKenna v. McKenna*, 1984 S.L.T. (Sh. Ct.) 92.

[15] *Bailey v. Bailey*, 1987 S.C.L.R. 1. *C.f. Inverurie Magistrates v. Sorrie*, 1956 S.C. 175 at p. 179.

[16] *Gribben v. Gribben*, 1976 S.L.T. 266.

[17] *Byrne v. Ross*, 1992 S.C. 498.

[18] *Gribben v. Gribben*, 1976 S.L.T. 266.

[19] Domestic Abuse (Scotland) Act 2011, s. 2(5).

corroboration is not required.[20] The standard of proof is proof beyond reasonable doubt.[21] If the breach is admitted or proved, the defender is liable to punishment by fine or imprisonment.[22]

An interim interdict ceases to be operative when the action in which it was granted ceases to be pending.[23] In any application for perpetual interdict, whether or not the action is defended, it is the duty of the court to exercise a sound judicial discretion in deciding whether interdict should be granted, and such grant can only be made on strong or at least reasonable grounds.[24]

When a perpetual interdict is claimed to have been breached, procedure is by way of initial writ to which the foregoing considerations apply.[25] Proceedings taken by way of initial writ for breach of interdict are civil proceedings to which the appeal provisions of the Sheriff Courts (Scotland) Act 1907 apply.[26]

Domestic abuse interdicts

A person who is applying for, or who has obtained, a matrimonial interdict or a relevant interdict, including an interim interdict, may apply to the court for a determination that the interdict applied for or obtained is a domestic abuse interdict.[27]

Application for such a determination made before the interdict in question is obtained must be made by crave in the initial writ, defences or counterclaim in which the interdict is sought.[28] Application for such a determination after the interdict in question is obtained must be made by minute.[29] The court may make the determination if satisfied that the interdict is, or is to be, granted for the protection of the applicant against a person who is (or was) the applicant's spouse or civil partner.[30] However, before making such a determination, the court must give the

---

[20] *Byrne v. Ross*, 1992 S.C. 498.

[21] *Gribben v. Gribben*, 1976 S.L.T. 266.

[22] *Byrne v. Ross*, 1992 S.C. 498. In *Forbes v. Forbes*, 1993 S.C. 271 the Inner House observed that it is proper not to call on the minuter in hearing submissions as to penalty, except with respect to matters of competency.

[23] *Stewart v. Stallard*, 1995 S.C.L.R. 167.

[24] *Bailey v. Bailey*, 1987 S.C.L.R. 1; *Cunningham v. Cunningham*, 2001 Fam. L.R. 12; *S v. Q*, 2005 S.L.T. 53. See also *Gunn v. Gunn*, 1955 S.L.T. (Notes) 69.

[25] *Forbes v. Forbes*, 1993 S.C. 271.

[26] *Maciver v. Maciver*, 1996 S.L.T. 733.

[27] Domestic Abuse (Scotland) Act 2011, ss. 2(7) and 3(1).

[28] r. 41A.1 and 41A.2(1).

[29] r. 41A.1 and 41A.2(2).

[30] 2011 Act, s. 3(2).

person against whom the interdict is, or is to be, granted an opportunity to make representations.[31]

Where such a determination is made, the interlocutor must be in Form DA1.[32] The determination however is of no effect until a copy of the interlocutor containing it has been served.[33] In this connection, Rule 41A.2(4) requires the applicant to serve a copy of the interlocutor in Form DA1 on the person against whom the interdict has been granted and lodge in process a certificate of service in Form DA2.

In a case where, in respect of the same interdict, a power of arrest is in effect and such a determination is made, the sheriff must appoint a person to send forthwith to such chief constable as the sheriff thinks fit a copy of the interlocutor in Form DA1 and the certificate of service in Form DA2.[34] Such person must, after such compliance, lodge in process a certificate of sending in Form DA4.[35]

Where such a determination has been made and is in effect, and a power of arrest is attached to the interdict under section 1(1A) or (2) of the Protection from Abuse (Scotland) Act 2001 and is in effect, a person who breaches the interdict is guilty of an offence under section 2(2) of the Domestic Abuse (Scotland) Act 2011.[36] This does not apply, however, in respect of any conduct which has already been punished as a contempt of court.[37]

A person guilty of an offence under section 2(2) of the 2011 Act is liable (only) —

(a) on summary conviction to imprisonment for a term not exceeding 12 months or to a fine not exceeding the statutory maximum or to both;

(b) on conviction on indictment, to imprisonment for a term not exceeding 5 years or to a fine or to both.[38]

Where a person has been convicted of such an offence in respect of any conduct, that conduct is not punishable as a contempt of court.[39]

Where a court varies an interdict in relation to which such a determination is in effect, the court must—

(a) review whether the interdict as varied continues to be a domestic abuse interdict; and

---

[31] 2011 Act, s. 3(3).
[32] r. 41A.2(3).
[33] 2011 Act, s. 3(4).
[34] r. 41A.2(6) and (7)(a).
[35] r. 41A.2(8).
[36] 2011 Act, s. 2(1) and (2).
[37] 2011 Act, s. 2(6).
[38] 2011 Act, s. 2(3) and (4).
[39] 2011 Act, s. 2(5).

(b) if not, recall the determination (in which event, it ceases to have effect for the purposes noted *supra*).[40]

Where a determination is so recalled, the interlocutor must be in Form DA3.[41] In a case where, in respect of the same interdict, a power of arrest is in effect and such a determination is recalled, the sheriff must appoint a person to send forthwith to such chief constable as the sheriff thinks fit, a copy of the interlocutor in Form DA3.[42] Such person must, after such compliance, lodge in process a certificate of sending in Form DA4.[43]

POWERS OF ARREST

The Protection from Abuse (Scotland) Act 2001 empowers the court to attach powers of arrest to interdicts and interim interdicts granted to protect individuals from abuse. Where a power of arrest attached to an interdict or interim interdict has effect, a constable may arrest the interdicted person without warrant if the constable—

(a) has reasonable cause for suspecting that person of being in breach of interdict; and
(b) considers that there would, if that person were not arrested, be a risk of abuse or further abuse by that person in breach of the interdict.[44]

In the case of an interdict or interim interdict which is—

(a) a matrimonial interdict which is ancillary to—
    (i) an exclusion order within the meaning of section 4(1) of the Matrimonial Homes (Family Protection) (Scotland) Act 1981; or
    (ii) an interim order within the meaning of section 4(6) of that Act,
(b) a relevant interdict which is ancillary to—
    (i) an exclusion order within the meaning of section 104(1) of the Civil Partnership Act 2004; or
    (ii) an interim order within the meaning of section 104(6) of that Act,

---

[40] 2011 Act, s. 3(5) and (6).
[41] r. 41A.2(5).
[42] r. 41A.2(6) and (7)(b).
[43] r. 41A.2(8).
[44] 2001 Act, s. 4(1). Police powers and procedure thereafter are set forth in ss. 4(2)–(6) and 5.

the court must, on an application under section 1 of the Protection from Abuse (Scotland) Act 2001, attach a power of arrest to the interdict.[45]

In the case of any other interdict or interim interdict sought or obtained for the purpose of protection against abuse, the court must, on such application, attach a power of arrest to the interdict if satisfied that—

(a)   the interdicted person has been given the opportunity to be heard by, or represented before, the court; and

(b)   attaching the power of arrest is necessary to protect the applicant from a risk of abuse in breach of the interdict.[46]

Application for attachment of a power of arrest to an interdict requires to be made by way of a crave in the initial writ or defences in which the interdict to which it relates is applied for, or, if made after the application for interdict, by motion in the process of the action in which interdict was sought, or by minute, with answers if appropriate, should the sheriff so order.[47] The application requires to be intimated to the person against whom the interdict is sought or was obtained.[48] The court, on attaching a power of arrest, must specify a date of expiry for the power, being a date not later than three years after the date when the power is attached.[49]

A power of arrest comes into effect only when it has been served on the interdicted person along with such documents as may be prescribed.[50] In terms of Rule 41.2(2), where the sheriff attaches a power of arrest to an interdict as aforesaid, the documents to be served on the interdicted person are the following:

(a)   a copy of the application for interdict;

(b)   a copy of the interlocutor granting interdict; and

(c)   where the application to attach a power of arrest was made after the interdict was granted, a copy of the certificate of service of the interdict.

As soon as possible after a power of arrest has been served, the person who obtained it, or such other person as may be prescribed, must deliver such documents as may be prescribed to the chief constable of any police area in which the relevant interdict (*viz.* the interdict to

---

[45]   Protection from Abuse (Scotland) Act 2001, s. 1(1) and (1A), as amended by the Family Law (Scotland) Act 2006, s. 32(1) and (2).

[46]   2001 Act, s. 1(1) and (2), as amended by the Family Law (Scotland) Act 2006, s. 32(1) and (3).

[47]   r. 41.2(1)(a).

[48]   r. 41.2(1)(b).

[49]   2001 Act, s. 1(3).

[50]   2001 Act, s. 2(1).

which the power of arrest is attached)[51] has effect.[52] By virtue of Rule 41.2(3), the documents to be delivered by the person who obtained the power of arrest to the chief constable are the following:

(a) a copy of the application for interdict;

(b) a copy of the interlocutor granting interdict;

(c) a copy of the certificate of service of the interdict;

(d) where the application to attach the power of arrest was made after the interdict was granted—

    (i) a copy of the application for the power of arrest;

    (ii) a copy of the interlocutor granting it; and

    (iii) a copy of the certificate of service of the power of arrest and the documents that required to be served along with it; and

(e) where a determination has previously been made in respect of such interdict under section 3(1) of the Domestic Abuse (Scotland) Act 2011, a copy of the interlocutor in Form DA1.

Such person must, after such compliance, lodge in process a certificate of delivery in Form PA1.[53]

A power of arrest ceases to have effect—

(a) on the date of expiry specified by the court;

(b) when it is recalled by the court; or

(c) when the interdict to which the power is attached is varied or recalled whichever is the earliest.[54]

The duration of a power of arrest must, on the application of the person who obtained it, be extended by the court, if satisfied that—

(a) the interdicted person has been given an opportunity to be heard by, or represented before, the court; and

(b) the extension is necessary to protect the applicant from a risk of abuse in breach of interdict.[55]

Such application requires to be made by minute in the process of the action in which the power of arrest was attached.[56] The court, on extending or further extending, the duration of a power of arrest, must

---

[51] 2001 Act, s. 3(2).
[52] 2001 Act, s. 3(1).
[53] r. 41.5.
[54] 2001 Act, s. 2(2).
[55] 2001 Act, s. 2(3).
[56] r. 41.3(1)(a).

specify a new date of expiry for the power, being a date not later than three years after the date when the extension is granted.[57]

Where the duration of a power of arrest has been extended, or further extended, the extension or further extension comes into effect only when it has been served on the interdicted person along with such documents as may be prescribed.[58] In terms of Rule 41.3(2), when the sheriff extends the duration of a power of arrest, the person who obtained the extension must deliver a copy of the interlocutor granting the extension to the chief constable of any police area in which the interdict has effect. Such person must, after such compliance, lodge in process a certificate of delivery in Form PA1.[59]

A power of arrest must be recalled by the court if—

(a)   the person who obtained it applies for recall; or

(b)   the interdicted person applies for recall and the court is satisfied that—

   (i)   the person who obtained the power has been given an opportunity to be heard by, or represented before, the court; and

   (ii)   the power is no longer necessary to protect that person from a risk of abuse in breach of the interdict.[60]

Such application requires to be made by minute in the process of the action in which the power of arrest was attached.[61]

By virtue of Rule 41.3(2), where the sheriff recalls a power of arrest, the person who obtained the recall must deliver a copy of the interlocutor granting the recall to the chief constable of any police area in which the relevant interdict (*viz.* the interdict to which the power of arrest was attached)[62] has effect. Such person must, after such compliance, lodge in process a certificate of delivery in Form PA1.[63]

Where an interdict to which a power of arrest has been attached is varied or recalled, the person who obtained the variation or recall must deliver a copy of the interlocutor varying or recalling the interdict to the chief constable of any police area in which the interdict has effect.[64] Such person must, after such compliance, lodge in process a certificate of delivery in Form PA1.[65]

---

[57]   2001 Act, s. 2(4) and (6).
[58]   2001 Act, s. 2(5) and (6).
[59]   r. 41.5.
[60]   2001 Act, s. 2(7).
[61]   r. 41.3(1)(b).
[62]   2001 Act, s. 3(2).
[63]   r. 41.5.
[64]   r. 41.4.
[65]   r. 41.5.

INTERIM EXCLUSION ORDERS

The Matrimonial Homes (Family Protection) (Scotland) Act 1981 and the Civil Partnership Act 2004 empower the court to suspend the occupancy rights of a spouse or a civil partner in a matrimonial home or a family home, respectively.

Where there is an entitled spouse and a non-entitled spouse,[66] or where both spouses are entitled, or permitted by a third party, to occupy a matrimonial home,[67] either spouse, whether or not in occupation at the time of the application, may apply to the court for an order (an "exclusion order") under the 1981 Act suspending the occupancy rights of the other spouse in the matrimonial home.[68] Where there is an entitled partner and a non-entitled partner,[69] or where both partners are entitled, or permitted by a third party, to occupy a family home,[70] either partner, whether or not in occupation at the time of the application, may apply to the court for an order (an "exclusion order") under the 2004 Act suspending the occupancy rights of the other partner in the family home.[71]

Any exclusion order, unless previously varied or recalled, ceases to have effect on the termination of the marriage or on the dissolution of the civil partnership.[72] This would seem to limit its relevance in actions of divorce or dissolution of civil partnership. However, the court has power, pending the making of such an order, to make an interim order suspending the occupancy rights of the non-applicant spouse or partner in the matrimonial home or family home to which the application for the exclusion order relates in terms of section 4(6) of the 1981 Act or section 104(7) of the 2004 Act.

Application for an exclusion order is by crave in the initial writ or defences, as the case may be, intimated to any landlord or third party by whose permission the matrimonial home or family home is occupied by the entitled spouse or partner.[73]Application for an interim order (hereinafter "interim exclusion order") is made by motion intimated —

    (a)   to the other spouse or partner;

    (b)   where the entitled spouse or partner is a tenant or occupies

---

[66] As to "entitled spouse" and "non-entitled spouse", see Chap. 5.

[67] For the meaning of "matrimonial home", see Chap. 5, n. 3 and accompanying text.

[68] 1981 Act, s. 4(1), as amended by the Law Reform (Miscellaneous Provisions) (Scotland) Act 1985, s. 13(5).

[69] As to "entitled partner" and "non-entitled partner," see Chap. 5.

[70] For the meaning of "family home", see Chap. 5, n. 4 and accompanying text.

[71] Civil Partnership Act 2004, s. 104(1).

[72] 1981 Act, s. 5(1)(a) and 2004 Act, s. 105(2)(a).

[73] rr. 33.7(1)(k), 33.15(3), 33.34(1)(c) (iii) and (2)(b)(i) and 33.67(1)(b) or rr. 33A.7(1)(i), 33A.15(3), 33A.34(1)(c)(iii) and (2)(b)(i) and 33A.60(1)(b).

the matrimonial home or family home by the permission of a third party, to the landlord or third party, as the case may be; and

(c) to any other person to whom intimation was or is to be made by virtue of Rule 33.7(1)(k) or Rule 33A.7(1)(i) (warrant for intimation to certain persons in actions for orders under the 1981 Act or the 2004 Act) or Rule 33.15 or Rule 33A.15 (order for intimation by sheriff).[74]

An interim exclusion order may only be made if the non-applicant spouse or non-applicant partner has been afforded an opportunity of being heard by or represented before the court, and accordingly failure to intimate the motion to the non-applicant spouse or non-applicant partner precludes the sheriff from granting it.[75] The court should ordinarily give the non-applicant spouse or non-applicant partner an opportunity to lodge affidavit evidence.[76]

The court requires to make the order if it appears to the court that the making of the order is necessary for the protection of the applicant or any child of the family[77] from any conduct[78] or threatened or reasonably apprehended conduct of the non-applicant spouse or partner which is or would be injurious to the physical or mental health of the applicant or child.[79] The court does not however require, before granting an interim exclusion order, to be satisfied that the applicant would otherwise be in immediate danger of suffering irreparable harm.[80] The court cannot be satisfied that the making of the interim exclusion order is necessary on the basis of *ex parte* statements alone.[81] There must be sufficient material before the court to enable it to be satisfied on a *prima facie* basis that the applicant requires the protection of such an order.[82] Such material might take the form of documents (*e.g.* affidavits,[83] extract convictions, medical reports) or any report ordered by the court as to the welfare of any children of the family.[84] The fact that the parties are not

---

[74] r. 33.69(1)(b) and (2) or r. 33A.62(1)(b) and (2). As to r. 33.15 or r. 33A.15, see Chap. 1, text accompanying n. 32.

[75] 1981 Act, s 4(6) and 2004 Act, s. 104(7); *Nelson v. Nelson*, 1988 S.L.T. (Sh. Ct.) 26.

[76] *Armitage v. Armitage*, 1993 S.C.L.R. 173.

[77] As to the meaning of "child of the family", see Chap. 5, n. 6.

[78] As to "conduct", see *Matheson v. Matheson*, 1986 S.L.T. (Sh. Ct.) 2 (threat to safety or health must originate from personal behaviour).

[79] 1981 Act, s. 4(2) and 2004 Act, s. 104(2).

[80] *McCafferty v. McCafferty*, 1986 S.C. 178 at p. 182.

[81] *Ward v. Ward*, 1983 S.L.T. 472.

[82] *Ibid.*; *Colagiacomo v. Colagiacomo*, 1983 S.L.T. 559; *Boyle v. Boyle*, 1986 S.L.T. 656; *Coster v. Coster*, 1992 S.C.L.R. 210.

[83] r. 33.27 or r. 33A.28.

[84] *Ward v. Ward*, 1983 S.L.T. 472. *C.f. Assar v. Assar*, 1994 G.W.D. 2–102 (preliminary proof ordered on minute and answers).

at the time of the motion living together is not a bar to the obtaining of an order, even where they have been separated for a lengthy period.[85]

The court must not however make the order if it appears to the court that the making of the order would be unjustified or unreasonable—

(a) having regard to all the circumstances of the case, including the following matters—

    (i) the conduct of the spouses or partners in relation to each other and otherwise;

    (ii) the respective needs and financial resources of the spouses or partners;

    (iii) the needs of any child of the family;

    (iv) the extent (if any) to which the matrimonial home or family home is used in connection with a trade, business or profession of either spouse or partner; and

    (v) whether the entitled spouse or the entitled partner offers or has offered to make available to the non-entitled spouse or the non-entitled partner any suitable alternative accommodation; and

(b) where the matrimonial home or family home—

    (i) is or is part of an agricultural holding within the meaning of section 1 of the Agricultural Holdings (Scotland) Act 1949; or

    (ii) is let, or is a home in respect of which possession is given, to the non-applicant spouse or non-applicant partner or to both spouses or partners by an employer as an incident of employment,

subject to a requirement that the non-applicant spouse or non-applicant partner, or as the case may be, both spouses or partners must reside in the matrimonial home or family home, having regard to that requirement and the likely consequences of the exclusion of the non-applicant spouse or partner from the matrimonial home or family home.[86]

If it appears to the court that an interim interdict (with or without the attachment of a power of arrest, as the case may be) is providing or would provide adequate protection to the applicant spouse or applicant partner, an interim exclusion order will not be granted.[87]

---

[85] *Brown v. Brown*, 1985 S.L.T. 376; *Millar v. Millar*, 1991 S.C.L.R. 649.

[86] 1981 Act, s. 4(3) and 2004 Act, s. 104(3).

[87] *Bell v. Bell*, 1983 S.C. 182 (*c.f. Brown v. Brown*, 1985 S.L.T. 376; *Colagiacomo v. Colagiacomo*, 1983 S.L.T. 559). For illustrations of circumstances where means other than an interim exclusion order would be unlikely to secure the desired degree of protection, see *Ward v. Ward*, 1983 S.L.T. 472 (drink-related course of conduct over a long period) and *Robertson v. Robertson*, 1999 S.L.T. 38 (unreasonably intrusive and jealous behaviour).

The court has a discretion as to whether or not to make an interim exclusion order and an appellate court could only interfere with any decision taken in exercise of this discretion if it were to be satisfied that the sheriff had misdirected himself and had erred in law, or, if he had applied the correct test, that he had reached an unwarranted conclusion.[88] An appeal can competently be taken without leave of the sheriff against the award of an interim exclusion order where an ancillary interim interdict has also been granted.[89] Failure by the defender to lodge a notice of intention to defend does not mean that he has no locus to appeal.[90] An interim exclusion order is an exception to the general rule that the effect of an appeal is to sist execution on a decree.[91]

In making an interim exclusion order the court *must*, on the application of the applicant spouse or applicant partner—

(i)   grant a warrant for the summary ejection of the non-applicant spouse or the non-applicant partner from the matrimonial home or family home, unless the non-applicant spouse or the non-applicant partner satisfies the court that it is unnecessary to grant such a warrant;[92]

(ii) grant an interdict prohibiting the non-applicant spouse or the non-applicant partner from entering the matrimonial home or family home without the express permission of the applicant spouse or the applicant partner;[93] and

(iii) grant an interdict prohibiting the removal by the non-applicant spouse or the non-applicant partner, except with the written consent of the applicant spouse or applicant or by a further order of the court, of any furniture and plenishings in the matrimonial home or family home, unless the non-applicant spouse or non-applicant partner satisfies the court that it is unnecessary to grant such an interdict.[94]

---

[88] *McCafferty v. McCafferty*, 1986 S.C. 178.

[89] *Oliver v. Oliver*, 1989 S.L.T. (Sh. Ct.) 1.

[90] *Nelson v. Nelson*, 1988 S.L.T. (Sh. Ct.) 26.

[91] *Orr v. Orr*, 1989 G.W.D. 12–506.

[92] 1981 Act, s. 4(4)(a) and 2004 Act, s. 104(4)(a). *C.f. Mather v. Mather*, 1987 S.L.T. 565 (interim exclusion order granted but suspended for three months to allow husband to find alternative accommodation).

[93] 1981 Act, s. 4(4)(b) and 2004 Act, s. 104(4)(b).

[94] 1981 Act, s. 4(4)(c) and 2004 Act, s. 104(4)(c). "Furniture and plenishings" means any article situated in a matrimonial home or family home which (a) is owned by either spouse or partner or is being acquired by either under a hire-purchase agreement or conditional sale agreement; and (b) is reasonably necessary to enable the home to be used as a family residence, but does not include any vehicle, caravan, houseboat or other structure as is mentioned in the definitions of "matrimonial home" or "family home"—1981 Act, s. 22(1) and 2004 Act, s. 135(1).

In making an interim exclusion order the court *may*—

(a) grant an interdict prohibiting the non-applicant spouse or non-applicant partner from entering or remaining in a specified area in the vicinity of the matrimonial home or family home;[95]

(b) where the warrant for the summary ejection of the non-applicant spouse or non-applicant partner has been granted in his or her absence, give directions as to the preservation of the non-applicant's goods and effects which remain in the matrimonial home or family home;[96]

(c) on the application of either spouse or partner, make an interim exclusion order, or the warrant or interdict mentioned in (i), (ii) or (iii) *supra*, subject to such terms and conditions as the court may prescribe;[97] and

(d) on the application of either spouse or partner, make such other order as it may consider necessary for the proper enforcement of any of the foregoing orders.[98]

The court may, on the application of either spouse or partner, vary or recall an interim exclusion order in relation to a matrimonial home or family home.[99] Applications for such variation or recall require to be made by minute intimated—

(a) to the other spouse or partner;

(b) where the entitled spouse or entitled partner is a tenant or occupies the matrimonial home or family home by the permission of a third party, to the landlord or third party, as the case may be; and

(c) to any other person to whom intimation is ordered by the sheriff to be made by virtue of Rule 33.7(1)(k) or Rule 33A.7(1)(i) (warrant for intimation to certain persons in actions for orders under the 1981 Act or the 2004 Act) or Rule 33.15 or Rule 33A.15 (order for intimation by sheriff).[100]

ORDERS RELATING TO AVOIDANCE TRANSACTIONS

The court has power under section 18(2) of the Family Law (Scotland) Act 1985 to make certain orders relating to avoidance transactions.

---

[95] 1981 Act, s. 4(5)(a) and 2004 Act, s. 104(5)(a).
[96] 1981 Act, s. 4(5)(b) and 2004 Act, s. 104(5)(b).
[97] 1981 Act, s. 4(5)(c) and 2004 Act, s. 104(5)(c).
[98] 1981 Act, s. 4(5)(d) and 2004 Act, s. 104(5)(d).
[99] 1981 Act, s. 5(1) and 2004 Act, s. 105(1).
[100] r. 33.70(1)(a) and (2) or r. 33A.63.

Where a claim has been made in an action of divorce or dissolution of civil partnership under section 8(1) of the Family Law (Scotland) Act 1985 for an order for financial provision, or for variation or recall of such an order, the person making the claim may, not later than one year from the date of disposal of the claim, apply to the court under section 18(1) of the Act for an order—

(i)   setting aside or varying any transfer of, or transaction involving, property effected by the other party not more than five years before the date of the making of the claim; or

(ii) interdicting the other party from effecting any such transfer or transaction.[101]

The power to set aside a transaction implies a power to reduce a writing or deed by which the transaction is effected.[102] An act of giving notice to dissolve a partnership is not a transaction involving property within the meaning of section 18(1), nor is the enforcement of a court decree.[103]

Application to the court under section 18(1) before final decree must be made by crave in the initial writ or defences, as the case may be, intimated to any third party in whose favour the transfer of, or transaction involving, the property is to be or was made and any other person having an interest in the transfer of, or transaction involving, the property.[104] Application to the court under section 18(1) after final decree must be made by minute in the process of the action to which the application relates.[105]

If the court is satisfied that the transfer or transaction had the effect of, or is likely to have the effect of, defeating in whole or in part the applicant's claim, it may make the order applied for or such other order as it thinks fit.[106] It is not necessary to demonstrate that

---

[101] As amended by the Civil Partnership Act 2004, Sched. 28, para. 24. See, for example, *M v. M and Wards Estate Trustees Ltd*, 2009 S.L.T. 750 (pursuer sought decree for the setting aside and reduction of a deed of trust executed by the defender and court granted interim interdict against the trustees from distributing or otherwise transferring the trust property). In *Wilson v. Wilson*, 1999 S.L.T. 249, an order was refused after proof in the absence of any real grounds in equity or otherwise to grant it.

[102] *Hernandez-Cimorra v. Hernandez-Cimorra*, 1992 S.C.L.R. 611. A letter purporting to acknowledge a loan was set aside in *Tahir v. Tahir (No. 2)*, 1995 S.L.T 451. See also *Harris v. Harris*, 1988 S.L.T. 101; *M v. M and Wards Estate Trustees Ltd*, 2009 S.L.T. 750.

[103] *Robertson v. Robertson*, 2009 Fam. L.R. 13; *Steel v. Steel*, 2010 Fam. L.R. 108.

[104] rr. 33.7(1)(j) and (5), 33.15(3) and 33.48(1)(a) and (2)(c) or rr. 33A.7(1)(h) and (5), 33A.15(3) and 33A.45(1)(a) and (2)(c).

[105] r. 33.52(b) or r. 33A.49(b).

[106] 1985 Act, s. 18(2). In *Tahir v. Tahir (No. 2)*, 1995 S.L.T. 451 the Lord Ordinary reduced a sheriff court decree in order to give effect to the setting aside of a fictitious borrowing transaction.

the transfer or transaction in question was intended to defeat a claim for financial provision, but it would be a rare case in which the court would intervene if it has concluded that the transfer or transaction in question was not so intended.[107] The court may include in the order such terms and conditions as it thinks fit and make any ancillary order which it considers expedient to ensure that the order is effective.[108]

The order must not prejudice any rights of a third party in or to the property where that third party—

(a) has in good faith acquired the property or any of it or any rights in relation to it for value; or

(b) derives title to such property or rights from any person who has done so.[109]

DILIGENCE ON THE DEPENDENCE

Circumstances may arise in actions of divorce or dissolution of civil partnership where a financial claim is being made by one spouse or civil partner against the other in which some security for the claim would be desirable. Inhibition or arrestment on the dependence of the action executed upon a warrant granted under the Debtors (Scotland) Act 1987[110] by the sheriff[111] may be very effective remedies for this purpose.

The Scottish Law Commission has described these diligences in the following terms:

"Inhibition is a procedure whereby the defender in an action can be prevented, pending the disposal of the action, from disposing of his heritable property. Arrestment on the dependence is a procedure whereby a third party holding moveable property for the defender or owing money to the defender can be prevented from parting with the property or money pending the disposal of the action."[112]

A spouse or civil partner claiming aliment or an order for financial provision ("the creditor") may make an application under section 15D(1) of the Debtors (Scotland) Act 1987 for warrant for diligence

---

[107] *M v. M, W Estate Trustees Ltd and Another*, 2011 Fam. L.R. 24.

[108] 1985 Act, s. 18(4).

[109] 1985 Act, s. 18(3). *C.f. Leslie v. Leslie,*1987 S.L.T. 232.

[110] As amended by the Bankruptcy and Diligence etc. (Scotland) Act 2007, s. 169.

[111] Debtors (Scotland) Act 1987, s. 15A(1).

[112] *Report on Aliment and Financial Provision* (Scot. Law Com. No. 67, 1981), para. 3-152.

by arrestment or inhibition on the dependence of the action.[113] The application requires to be made by motion[114] and must be accompanied by a statement in Form G4A.[115] The application must be intimated to the opposing party ("the debtor") and any other person having an interest,[116] except where the application states that the creditor is seeking the grant, under section 15E(1) of the Act, of warrant for diligence on the dependence in advance of a hearing on the application under section 15F of the Act.[117]

The court, on receiving an application for warrant for diligence on the dependence, must fix a date for a hearing on the application under section 15F of the Act, and order the creditor to intimate that date to the debtor and any other person appearing to the court to have an interest.[118] However, the court may, if satisfied as to certain matters, make an order granting warrant for diligence on the dependence *without* a hearing under section 15F of the Act.[119] The matters as to which the court must be satisfied are —

(a)   that the creditor has a *prima facie* case on the merits of the action;

(b)   that there is a real and substantive risk enforcement of any decree in the action in favour of the creditor would be defeated or prejudiced by reason of —
   (i)   the debtor being insolvent or verging on insolvency; or
   (ii) the likelihood of the debtor removing, disposing of, burdening, concealing or otherwise dealing with all or some of the debtor's assets,
   were warrant for diligence on the dependence not granted in advance of such a hearing; and

(c)   that it is reasonable in all the circumstances, including the effect granting warrant may have on any person having an interest, to do so.[120]

The onus is on the creditor to satisfy the court that the order granting warrant should be made.[121] Where the court is so satisfied and grants the warrant without a section 15F hearing, it must then fix a date for a

---

[113] s. 15C(1) of the 1987 Act renders it competent for the court to grant warrant for diligence on the dependence where the sum concluded for is a future or contingent debt.
[114] r. 6.A2(1).
[115] r. 6.A2(2).
[116] 1987 Act, s. 15D(2)(b).
[117] 1987 Act, s. 15D(2)(c) and (3).
[118] 1987 Act, s. 15D(4).
[119] 1987 Act, s. 15E(1).
[120] 1987 Act, s. 15E(2).
[121] 1987 Act, s. 15E(3).

hearing under section 15K of the Act (recall or restriction of diligence on dependence) and order the creditor to intimate that date to the debtor and any other person appearing to the court to have an interest.[122] Where such a hearing is fixed, section 15K of the Act applies as if an application had been made to the court for an order under that section.[123] Where the court refuses to make an order granting a warrant without a hearing under section 15F of the Act and the creditor insists in the application, the court must fix a date for a section 15F hearing on the application and order the creditor to intimate that date to the debtor and any other person appearing to the court to have an interest.[124]

At any hearing on an application for warrant for diligence on the dependence under section 15F of the Act, the court must not make any order without first giving any person to whom intimation of the date of the hearing was made, and any other person the court is satisfied has an interest, an opportunity to be heard.[125] At the section 15F hearing the court may, if satisfied as to certain matters, make an order granting warrant for diligence on the dependence.[126] The matters as to which the court must be satisfied are—

(a) that the creditor has a *prima facie* case on the merits of the action;

(b) that there is a real and substantive risk enforcement of any decree in the action in favour of the creditor would be defeated or prejudiced by reason of—

    (i) the debtor being insolvent or verging on insolvency; or

    (ii) the likelihood of the debtor removing, disposing of, burdening, concealing or otherwise dealing with all or some of the debtor's assets,

were warrant for diligence on the dependence not granted; and

(c) that it is reasonable in all the circumstances, including the effect granting warrant may have on any person having an interest, to do so.[127]

The onus is on the creditor to satisfy the court that the order granting warrant should be made.[128] Where the court makes an order granting, or as the case may be, refusing warrant for diligence on the dependence,

---

[122] 1987 Act, s. 15E(4).
[123] 1987 Act, s. 15E(5).
[124] 1987 Act, s. 15E(6).
[125] 1987 Act, s. 15F(1).
[126] 1987 Act, s. 15F(2).
[127] 1987 Act, s. 15F(3).
[128] 1987 Act, s. 15F(4).

the court must order the creditor to intimate that order to the debtor and any other person appearing to the court to have an interest.[129] Where the court makes an order refusing warrant for diligence on the dependence, it may impose such conditions (if any) as it thinks fit.[130] Without prejudice to that generality, those conditions may require the debtor to consign into court such sum, or to find caution to give such other security, as the court thinks fit.[131]

Where granting warrant for diligence on the dependence, the court may impose restrictions on the property attached. In the case of warrant for arrestment on the dependence, the court may limit the sum that may be attached to funds not exceeding such amount as the court may specify.[132] The maximum amount that the court may so specify is the aggregate of the following—

    (a) the principal sum craved;

    (b) a sum equal to 20 per cent of that sum or such other percentage as the Scottish Ministers may, by regulation, prescribe;

    (c) a sum equal to 1 year's interest on the principal sum at the judicial rate; and

    (d) any sum prescribed by the Scottish Ministers, by regulations, as appearing to them to be reasonable having regard to the expenses likely to be incurred by a creditor and chargeable against a debtor in executing an arrestment on the dependence.[133]

In the case of warrant for diligence by inhibition on the dependence, the court may limit the property inhibited to such property as may be specified.[134]

A certified copy of an interlocutor granting a motion for warrant for diligence by arrestment or inhibition on the dependence of the action is sufficient authority for the execution of the diligence concerned.[135] In the case of inhibition on the dependence of the action, the certified copy interlocutor may be registered with a certificate of execution in the Register of Inhibitions and Adjudications; and a notice of a certified copy of an interlocutor granting authority for inhibition on the dependence may be registered in the Register of Inhibitions and Adjudications and such registration has the same effect as registration

---

[129] 1987 Act, s. 15F(5).
[130] 1987 Act, s. 15F(6).
[131] 1987 Act, s. 15F(7).
[132] 1987 Act, s. 15H(1)
[133] 1987 Act, s. 15H(2) and (3).
[134] 1987 Act, s. 15J(b).
[135] r. 6.A2(3).

of a notice of inhibition under section 155(2) of the Titles to Land Consolidation (Scotland) Act 1868.[136] Where the debtor's address is not known to the creditor, an inhibition is deemed to have been served on the debtor if the schedule of inhibition is left with or deposited at the office of the sheriff clerk of the sheriff court district where the debtor's last known address is located.[137] An arrestment on the dependence must be served by serving the schedule of arrestment on the arrestee in Form G4B.[138] A certificate of execution must be lodged with the sheriff clerk in Form G4C.[139] If a schedule of arrestment has not been personally served on an arrestee, the arrestment has effect only if a copy of the schedule is also sent by registered post or the first class recorded delivery service to the last known place of residence of the arrestee, or if such place of residence is not known, or if the arrestee is a firm or corporation, to the arrestee's principal place of business, if known, or, if not known, to any known place of business of the arrestee; and the sheriff officer must, on the certificate of execution, certify that this has been done and specify the address to which the copy of the schedule was sent.[140]

Where diligence by arrestment or inhibition on the dependence of an action is executed before service of the initial writ on the debtor, the diligence ceases to have effect if the initial writ is not served on the debtor before the end of the period of 21 days beginning with the day on which the diligence is executed.[141] The court may however make an order extending that period, and in determining whether to make such an order the court must have regard to the efforts of the creditor to serve the initial writ within the period of 21 days, and any special circumstances preventing or obstructing service within that period.[142]

Where warrant is granted for diligence on the dependence, the debtor and any person having an interest may apply to the court for an order—

(a) recalling the warrant;
(b) restricting the warrant;
(c) if an arrestment or inhibition has been executed in pursuance of the warrant—
  (i) recalling; or
  (ii) restricting, that arrestment or inhibition;

---

[136] r. 6.A3.
[137] r. 6.A7.
[138] r. 6.A8(1).
[139] r. 6.A8(2).
[140] r. 6.1.
[141] 1987 Act, s. 15G(1) and (2).
[142] 1987 Act, s. 15G(3) and (4).

(d) determining any question relating to the validity, effect or operation of the warrant; or

(e) ancillary to any of the foregoing orders.[143]

The application requires to be made by motion.[144] The application must be intimated to the creditor and any other person having an interest.[145]

A hearing on such an application falls to be held under section 15K of the 1987 Act. At any such hearing, the court must not make any order without first giving any person to whom intimation of the application was made, and any other person the court is satisfied has an interest, an opportunity to be heard.[146] Where the court is satisfied that the warrant is invalid it must make an order recalling the warrant and, if an arrestment or inhibition has been executed in pursuance of the warrant, recalling that arrestment or inhibition; and may make an order ancillary thereto.[147] Where the court is satisfied that an arrestment or inhibition executed in pursuance of the warrant is incompetent, it must make an order recalling that arrestment or inhibition, and may make an order ancillary thereto.[148] Where the court is satisfied that the warrant is valid but that an arrestment or inhibition executed in pursuance to it is irregular or ineffective, or it is reasonable in all the circumstances, including the effect granting warrant may have had on any person having an interest, to do so, the court may make any of the orders listed *supra*.[149] The court must also make an order recalling the warrant and, if an arrestment or inhibition has been executed in pursuance of the warrant, recalling that arrestment or inhibition; and may make an order ancillary thereto, if no longer satisfied as to certain matters.[150] These matters are the following—

(a) that the creditor has a *prima facie* case on the merits of the action;

(b) that there is a real and substantive risk enforcement of any decree in the action in favour of the creditor would be defeated or prejudiced by reason of—

    (i) the debtor being insolvent or verging on insolvency; or

---

[143] 1987 Act, s. 15K(1) and (2). Warrant to arrest on the dependence was recalled in *Matheson v. Matheson*, 1995 S.L.T. 765. An inhibition was recalled in *Thom v. Thom*, 1990 S.C.L.R. 800.

[144] r. 6.A4.

[145] 1987 Act, s. 15K(3).

[146] 1987 Act, s. 15K(4).

[147] 1987 Act, s. 15K(5).

[148] 1987 Act, s. 15K(6).

[149] 1987 Act, s. 15K(7).

[150] 1987 Act, s. 15K(8).

(ii) the likelihood of the debtor removing, disposing of, burdening, concealing or otherwise dealing with all or some of the debtor's assets; and

(c) that it is reasonable in all the circumstances, including the effect granting warrant may have on any person having an interest, for the warrant or, as the case may be, any arrestment or inhibition executed in pursuance of it to continue to have effect.[151]

The onus is on the creditor to satisfy the court that no order recalling or restricting diligence should be made.[152] In granting an application for an order recalling or restricting diligence on the dependence, the court may impose such conditions (if any) as it thinks fit.[153] Without prejudice to that generality, the court may impose conditions that require the debtor to consign into court such sum, or to find such caution or to give such other security, as the court thinks fit.[154] Where the court makes an order recalling or restricting diligence on the dependence, the court must order the debtor to intimate that order to the creditor and any other person appearing to the court to have an interest.[155]

Where an order restricting warrant for diligence on the dependence is made under section 15K(7), or a condition is imposed by virtue of section 15F(6) or section 15K(11), the debtor may apply to the court for variation of the order or, as the case may be, variation or removal of the condition.[156] The application requires to be made by motion.[157] The application must be intimated to the creditor and any other person having an interest.[158]

A hearing on such an application falls to be held under section 15L of the 1987 Act. At any such hearing, the court must not make any order without first giving any person to whom intimation of the application was made, and any other person the court is satisfied has an interest, an opportunity to be heard.[159] On such an application, the court may if it thinks fit vary the order, or vary or remove the condition.[160] Where the court makes an order varying the order or, as the case may be, varying or removing the condition, the court must order the debtor to

---

[151] 1987 Act, s. 15K(9).
[152] 1987 Act, s. 15K(10).
[153] 1987 Act, s. 15K(11).
[154] 1987 Act, s. 15K(12).
[155] 1987 Act, s. 15K(13).
[156] 1987 Act, s. 15L(1). As to ss. 15F(6) and 15K(7) and (11), see text accompanying nn. 130, 140 and 153, *supra.*
[157] r. 6.A5.
[158] 1987 Act, s. 15L(2).
[159] 1987 Act, s. 15L(3).
[160] 1987 Act, s. 15L(4).

intimate that order to the creditor and any other person appearing to the court to have an interest.[161]

A creditor is entitled to such expenses as the creditor incurs in obtaining warrant for diligence on the dependence and, where an arrestment or inhibition is executed in pursuance of the warrant, in so executing the arrestment or inhibition, but the court may modify or refuse such expenses if it is satisfied that the creditor was acting unreasonably in applying for the warrant or that such modification or refusal is reasonable in all the circumstances and having regard to the outcome of the action.[162]

A debtor is entitled, where warrant for diligence on the dependence is granted, and the court is satisfied that the creditor was acting unreasonably in applying for it, to the expenses incurred in opposing that warrant, but the court may modify or refuse those expenses if it is satisfied that such modification or refusal is reasonable in all the circumstances and having regard to the outcome of the action.[163]

Subject to the foregoing provisions, the court may make such finding as it thinks fit in relation to such expenses.[164] Expenses incurred as mentioned *supra* in obtaining or, as the case may be, opposing an application for warrant shall be expenses of process.[165] The foregoing is without prejudice to any enactment or rule of law as to the recovery of expenses chargeable against the debtor as are incurred in executing an arrestment or inhibition on the dependence of an action.[166]

---

[161] 1987 Act, s. 15L(5).
[162] 1987 Act, s. 15M(1) and (3).
[163] 1987 Act, s. 15M(2) and (3).
[164] 1987 Act, s. 15M(4).
[165] 1987 Act, s. 15M(5).
[166] 1987 Act, s. 15M(6).

CHAPTER 5

PROPERTY ORDERS

The sheriff is empowered by statute[1] to make various orders, described herein as "property orders", relative to a matrimonial home or family home. These orders, excepting exclusion orders and related measures, are discussed in this chapter.[2]

ORDERS CONCERNING OCCUPANCY RIGHTS

The Matrimonial Homes (Family Protection) (Scotland) Act 1981 provides for the granting of certain orders concerning occupancy rights in relation to any matrimonial home, namely any house, caravan, houseboat or other structure which has been provided or has been made available by one or both spouses as, or has become, a family residence and includes any garden or other ground or building usually occupied with, or otherwise required for the amenity or convenience of, the house, caravan, houseboat or other structure but does not include a residence provided or made available by a person for one spouse to reside in, whether with any child of the family or not, separately from the other spouse.[3] The Civil Partnership Act 2004 provides for the granting of similar orders concerning occupancy rights in relation to any family home of the civil partnership, similarly defined.[4]

Occupancy rights

A spouse may be entitled, or permitted by a third party, to occupy a matrimonial home (an "entitled spouse") and a civil partner may be entitled, or permitted by a third party, to occupy a family home (an

---

[1] The statutes are the Matrimonial Homes (Family Protection) (Scotland) Act 1981 and the Civil Partnership Act 2004. The court's powers under the Family Law (Scotland) Act 1985 to make incidental orders *inter alia* regulating the occupation of the matrimonial home or family home after divorce or dissolution of civil partnership are mentioned in Chap. 7.

[2] Exclusion orders and related measures are considered in Chap. 4.

[3] Matrimonial Homes (Family Protection) (Scotland) Act 1981, s. 22(1), as amended by the Law Reform (Miscellaneous Provisions) (Scotland) Act 1985, s. 13(10) and the Family Law (Scotland) Act 2006, s. 9 and Sched. 3. See also text accompanying n. 9, *infra*.

[4] Civil Partnership Act 2004, s. 135(1), as amended by the Family Law (Scotland) Act 2006, Sched. 1, para. 12. See also text accompanying n. 9, *infra*.

"entitled partner").[5] If a spouse is not so entitled or permitted (a "non-entitled spouse") or a civil partner is not so entitled or permitted (a "non-entitled partner"), he or she nevertheless has occupancy rights *ex lege* as follows:

(a) if in occupation, to continue to occupy the matrimonial home or family home, together with any child of the family;[6] and

(b) if not in occupation, to enter and occupy the matrimonial home or family home, together with any child of the family,[7]

except that if there has been no cohabitation between an entitled spouse or partner and a non-entitled spouse or partner during a continuous period of two years and during that period the non-entitled spouse or partner has not occupied the matrimonial home or family home, the non-entitled spouse or partner shall, on the expiry of that period, cease to have occupancy rights in the matrimonial home or family home.[8] The non-entitled spouse or partner will also cease to have occupancy rights in a matrimonial home or family home if it ceases to be a matrimonial home or family home, as is the case once the tenancy of a matrimonial home or family home is transferred from one spouse or civil partner to the other by agreement or under any enactment, and following the transfer the spouse or civil partner to whom the tenancy was transferred occupies the home but the other spouse or civil partner does not.[9]

---

[5] "Entitled spouse" includes a spouse who is entitled, or permitted by a third party, to occupy a matrimonial home along with an individual who is not the other spouse only if that individual has waived his or her right of occupation in favour of the spouse so entitled or permitted – 1981 Act, s. 1(2). "Entitled partner" includes a civil partner who is entitled, or permitted by a third party, to occupy a family home along with an individual who is not the other civil partner only if that individual has waived his or her right of occupation in favour of the civil partner so entitled or permitted – 2004 Act, s. 101(3).

[6] "Child of the family" includes any child or grandchild of either spouse or civil partner, and any person who has been brought up or treated by either spouse or civil partner as if he were a child of that spouse or civil partner, whatever the age of such a child, grandchild or person may be – 1981 Act, s. 22(1), as amended by the Children (Scotland) Act 1995, s. 105(4) and Sched. 4, para. 30, and 2004 Act, s. 101(7), as substituted by the Family Law (Scotland) Act 2006, s. 33 and Sched. 1, para. 3.

[7] 1981 Act, s. 1(1), (1A) and (4), as amended by the Law Reform (Miscellaneous Provisions) (Scotland) Act 1985, s. 13, and 2004 Act, s. 101(1) and (2). If the entitled spouse or partner refuses to allow the non-entitled spouse or partner to exercise the right if not in occupation to enter and occupy the matrimonial home or family home, the non-entitled spouse or partner may exercise that right only with the leave of the court under s. 3(3) or (4) of the 1981 Act or s. 103(3) or (4) of the 2004 Act – 1981 Act, s. 1(3) and 2004 Act, s. 101(4), considered *infra*.

[8] 1981 Act, s. 1(7), as inserted by the Family Law (Scotland) Act 2006, s. 5, and 2004 Act, s. 101(6A), as inserted by the 2006 Act, s. 33 and Sched. 1, para. 3.

[9] 1981 Act, s. 22(2), as amended by the Family Law (Scotland) Act 2006, s. 9 and 2004 Act, 135(2), as inserted by the 2006 Act, Sched. 1, para. 12. Note that where (a) the entitled spouse or partner is a tenant of a matrimonial home or family home; and (b) possession thereof

The 1981 Act and the 2004 Act provide for the protection of the occupancy rights of one spouse against the other by way of orders for which either spouse or civil partner who has occupancy rights[10] may apply –

    (i)   declaring the occupancy rights of the applicant spouse or partner;

    (ii) enforcing the occupancy rights of the applicant spouse or partner;

    (iii) restricting the occupancy rights of the non-applicant spouse or partner;

    (iv) regulating the exercise by either spouse or partner of his or her occupancy rights;

    (v) protecting the occupancy rights of the applicant spouse or partner in relation to the other spouse or partner; and

    (vi) granting to the applicant spouse or partner with occupancy rights in a matrimonial home or family home the possession or use in the matrimonial home or family home of furniture and plenishings owned or hired or being acquired under a hire-purchase or conditional sale agreement by the other spouse or partner.[11]

An order in category (i) must be granted if it appears to the court that the application relates to a matrimonial home or family home, as the case may be.[12] As regards the remaining categories, the court may make such order as appears to it to be just and reasonable having regard to all the circumstances of the case, including the matters specified in paragraphs (a) to (e) of section 3(3) of the 1981 Act or section 103(3) of the 2004 Act, detailed below, except that no such order may be made if it appears that the effect of the order would be to exclude the non-applicant from the matrimonial home or family home, as the case may be.[13]

Any order in categories (i) to (vi) above, unless previously varied or recalled, ceases to have effect on the termination of the marriage or

---

is necessary in order to continue the tenancy; and (c) the entitled spouse or partner abandons such possession, the tenancy shall be continued by such possession by the non-entitled spouse or partner – 1981 Act, s. 2(8) and 2004 Act, s. 102(8).

[10] A non-entitled spouse or partner who has ceased to have occupancy rights in a matrimonial home or family home by virtue of s. 1(7) of the 1981 Act or s. 101(6A) of the 2004 Act (as to which, see text accompanying n. 8 *supra*), may not apply to the court for an order under s. 3(1) of the 1981 Act or s. 103(1) of the 2004 Act – 1981 Act, s. 1(8) or 2004 Act, s. 101(6B).

[11] 1981 Act, s. 3(1) and (2) and 2004 Act, s. 103(1) and (2).

[12] 1981 Act, s. 3(3) and 2004 Act, s. 103(3).

[13] 1981 Act, s. 3(5) and 2004 Act, s. 103(5).

on the dissolution of the civil partnership.[14] This would seem to limit their relevance in actions of divorce or dissolution of civil partnership. However, the court has power, pending the making of any such order, to make an interim order relating to occupancy rights in terms of section 3(4) of the 1981 Act or section 103(4) of the 2004 Act.

Application for an order concerning occupancy rights is by crave in the initial writ or defences, as the case may be, intimated to any landlord or third party by whose permission the matrimonial home or family home is occupied by the entitled spouse or partner.[15] Application for an interim order is made by motion intimated—

(a) to the other spouse or partner;
(b) where the entitled spouse or entitled partner is a tenant or occupies the matrimonial home or family home by the permission of a third party, to the landlord or third party, as the case may be; and
(c) to any other person to whom intimation was or is to be made by virtue of Rule 33.7(1)(k) or Rule 33A.7(1)(i) (warrant for intimation to certain persons in actions for orders under the 1981 Act or the 2004 Act) or Rule 33.15 or Rule 33A.15 (order for intimation by sheriff).[16]

The interim order may be made only if the non-applicant spouse or partner has been afforded an opportunity of being heard by or represented before the court.[17] An interim order is not an interim version of a final order relating to occupancy rights, to which a different test applies.[18] The court, on the application of either spouse or partner, may make such interim order as it considers necessary or expedient in relation to—

(a) the residence of either spouse or partner in the home to which the application relates;
(b) the personal effects of either spouse or partner or of any child of the family;

---

[14] 1981 Act, s. 5(1)(a) and 2004 Act, s. 105(2)(a). The orders in categories (i) to (v) also cease to have effect where any entitled spouse or partner ceases to be so entitled in relation to the matrimonial home or family home in question—1981 Act, s. 5(1)(b) and (c) and 2004 Act, s. 105(2)(b) and (c). As to orders in category (vi), see 1981 Act, s. 5(2) and 2004 Act, s. 105(3).

[15] rr. 33.7(1)(k), 33.15(3), 33.34(1)(c) (iii) and (2)(b)(i) and 33.67(1)(b) or rr. 33A.7(1)(i), 33A.15(3), 33A.34(1)(c)(iii) and (2)(b)(i) and 33A.60(1)(b).

[16] r. 33.69(1)(a) and (2) or r. 33A.62(1)(a) and (2). As to r. 33.15 or r. 33A.15, see Chap. 1, text accompanying n. 32.

[17] 1981 Act, s. 3(4) and 2004 Act, s. 103(4).

[18] *Black v. Black*, 2011 S.L.T. (Sh. Ct.) 157.

(c) the furniture and plenishings.[19]

However, no such order may be made if it appears that the effect of the order would be to exclude the non-applicant from the matrimonial home or family home.[20]

The court may, on the application of either spouse or partner, vary or recall any interim order concerning occupancy rights in relation to a matrimonial home or family home.[21] Applications for such variation or recall require to be made by minute intimated —

(a) to the other spouse or partner;
(b) where the entitled spouse or entitled partner is a tenant or occupies the matrimonial home or family home by the permission of a third party, to the landlord or third party, as the case may be; and
(c) to any other person to whom intimation is ordered by the sheriff to be made by virtue of Rule 33.7(1)(k) or Rule 33A.7(1)(i) (warrant for intimation to certain persons in actions for orders under the 1981 Act or the 2004 Act) or Rule 33.15 or Rule 33A.15 (order for intimation by sheriff).[22]

Occupancy: subsidiary and consequential rights

For the purpose of securing the occupancy rights of a non-entitled spouse or partner, that spouse or partner shall, in relation to a matrimonial home or family home, be entitled without the consent of the entitled spouse or partner –

(a) to make any payment due by the entitled spouse or partner in respect of rent, rates, secured loan instalments, interest or other outgoings (not being outgoings on repairs or improvements);
(b) to perform any other obligation incumbent on the entitled spouse or partner (not being an obligation in respect of non-essential repairs or improvements);
(c) to enforce performance of an obligation by a third party which that third party has undertaken to the entitled spouse or partner to the extent that the entitled spouse or partner may enforce such performance;
(d) to carry out such essential repairs as the entitled spouse or partner may carry out;

---

[19] 1981 Act, s. 3(4) and 2004 Act, s. 103(4).
[20] 1981 Act, s. 3(5) and 2004 Act, s. 103(5).
[21] 1981 Act, s. 5(1) and 2004 Act, s. 105(1).
[22] r. 33.70(1)(a) and (2) or r. 33A.63.

(e) to carry out such non-essential repairs or improvements as may be authorised by an order of the court, being such repairs or improvements as the entitled spouse or partner may carry out and which the court considers to be appropriate for the reasonable enjoyment of the occupancy rights;

(f) to take such other steps, for the purpose of protecting the occupancy rights of the non-entitled spouse or partner as the entitled spouse or partner may take to protect the occupancy rights of the entitled spouse or partner.[23]

Where there is an entitled spouse or partner and a non-entitled spouse or partner, the court, on the application of either of them, may, having regard in particular to the respective financial circumstances of the spouses or partners, make an order apportioning expenditure incurred or to be incurred by either spouse or partner –

(a) without the consent of the other spouse or partner, on any of the items mentioned in paragraphs (a) and (d), *supra*;

(b) with the consent of the other spouse or partner, on anything relating to a matrimonial home or family home.[24]

Where both spouses or partners are entitled, or permitted by a third party, to occupy a matrimonial home or family home –

(a) either spouse or partner shall be entitled, without the consent of the other spouse or partner, to carry out such non-essential repairs or improvements as may be authorised by an order of the court, being such repairs or improvements as the court considers to be appropriate for the reasonable enjoyment of the occupancy rights;

(b) the court, on the application of either spouse or partner, may, having regard in particular to the respective financial circumstances of the spouses or partners, make an order apportioning expenditure incurred or to be incurred by either spouse or partner, with or without the consent of the other spouse or partner, on anything relating to the matrimonial home or family home.[25]

Where one spouse or partner owns or hires, or is acquiring under a hire-purchase or conditional sale agreement, furniture and plenishings in a matrimonial home or family home –

---

[23] 1981 Act, s. 2(1) and 2004 Act, s. 102(1). "Improvements" includes alterations and enlargement – 1981 Act, s. 2(9) and 2004 Act, s. 102(9).

[24] 1981 Act, s. 2(3) and 2004 Act, s. 102(3).

[25] 1981 Act, s. 2(4) and 2004 Act, s. 102(4).

(a) the other spouse or partner may, without the consent of the first mentioned spouse or partner –

    (i) make any payment due by the first mentioned spouse or partner which is necessary, or take any other step which the first mentioned spouse or partner is entitled to take, to secure the possession or use of any such furniture and plenishings (and any such payment shall have effect in relation to the rights of a third party as if it were made by the first mentioned spouse or partner); or

    (ii) carry out such essential repairs to the furniture and plenishings as the first mentioned spouse or partner is entitled to carry out;

(b) the court, on the application of either spouse or partner, may, having regard in particular to the respective financial circumstances of the spouses or partners, make an order apportioning expenditure incurred or to be incurred by either spouse or partner –

    (i) without the consent of the other spouse or partner, in making payments under a hire, hire-purchase or conditional sale agreement, or in paying interest charges in respect of the furniture and plenishings, or in carrying out essential repairs to the furniture and plenishings; or

    (ii) with the consent of the other spouse, on anything relating to the furniture and plenishings.[26]

Any application for any order apportioning expenditure as above must be made within five years of the date on which any payment in respect of such incurred expenditure was made.[27] Any such order may require one spouse or partner to make a payment to the other spouse or partner in implementation of the apportionment.[28] It is competent to make such an order before final decree, *i.e.* as an interim order.[29] An appeal without leave of the sheriff against any interim order apportioning expenditure is incompetent.[30]

---

[26] 1981 Act, s. 2(5) and 2004 Act, s. 102(5).

[27] 1981 Act, s. 2(7) and 2004 Act, s. 102(7).

[28] 1981 Act, s. 2(6) and 2004 Act, s. 102(6).

[29] *Porter v. Porter*, 1990 S.C.L.R. 752 (interim order ordaining defender to service mortgage and clear arrears).

[30] *Wilson v. Wilson*, 2001 S.L.T. (Sh. Ct.) 55.

ORDERS DISPENSING WITH CONSENT TO DEALING

The Matrimonial Homes (Family Protection) (Scotland) Act 1981 and the Civil Partnership Act 2004 make provision for the granting of orders dispensing with the consent of a non-entitled spouse or a non-entitled partner to a dealing that has taken place, or a proposed dealing, relating to a matrimonial home or family home.

In terms of section 6(1) of the 1981 Act or section 106(1) of the 2004 Act, the continued exercise of occupancy rights conferred on a non-entitled spouse or non-entitled partner in respect of a matrimonial home or family home, as the case may be, cannot be prejudiced by reason only of any dealing of the entitled spouse or entitled partner relating to that home; and a third party is not by reason only of any such dealing entitled to occupy that matrimonial home or family home or any part of it.[31]

However, these sections do not apply where—

(a) The non-entitled spouse or the non-entitled partner in writing either—
   (i) consents or has consented to the dealing in the pre-scribed form; or
   (ii) renounces or has renounced his or her occupancy rights in relation to the matrimonial home, or family home, or property to which the dealing relates;
(b) The court has made an order under section 7 of the 1981 Act or section 104 of the 2004 Act dispensing with the consent of the non-entitled spouse or the non-entitled partner, as the case may be, to the dealing;
(c) The dealing occurred, or implements a binding obligation entered into by the entitled spouse or the entitled partner, before his or her marriage to the non-entitled spouse or the registration of the civil partnership, as the case may be;
(d) The dealing occurred or implements a binding obligation entered into before the commencement of the 1981 Act or the 2004 Act, as the case may be;
(e) The dealing comprises a transfer for value to a third party

---

[31] "Dealing" includes the grant of a heritable security and the creation of a trust but does not include a conveyance under s. 80 of the Lands Clauses Consolidation (Scotland) Act 1845 – 1981 Act, s. 6(2) and 2004 Act, s. 106(2). "Entitled spouse" or "entitled partner" does not include a spouse or partner who, apart from the provisions of the 1981 or 2004 Acts, is permitted by a third party to occupy a matrimonial home or family home; or is entitled to occupy a matrimonial home or family home along with an individual who is not the other spouse or partner, whether or not that individual has waived his or her right of occupation in favour of the spouse or partner so entitled—*ibid.*

who has acted in good faith, if there is produced to the third party by the transferor—

    (i) a written declaration signed by the transferor, or a person acting on behalf of the transferor under a power of attorney or as a guardian (within the meaning of the Adults with Incapacity (Scotland) Act 2000), that the subjects of the transfer are not, or were not at the time of the dealing, a matrimonial home in relation to which a spouse of the transferor has or had occupancy rights or a family home in relation to which a civil partner of the transferor has or had occupancy rights; or

    (ii) a renunciation of occupancy rights or consent to the dealing which bears to have been properly made or given by the non-entitled spouse or the non-entitled partner or a person acting on behalf of the non-entitled spouse or the non-entitled partner under a power of attorney or as a guardian (within the meaning of the Adults with Incapacity (Scotland) Act 2000);

(f) The entitled spouse or the entitled partner has permanently ceased to be entitled to occupy the matrimonial home or the family home, as the case may be, and at any time thereafter a continuous period of 2 years has elapsed during which the non-entitled spouse or the non-entitled partner has not occupied the home; or

(g) A person acquires a matrimonial home or a family home, or an interest in it, in good faith and for value from a person other than the person who is or, as the case may be, was the entitled spouse or the entitled partner; or a person derives title to the home from a person who so acquired title.[32]

With respect to category (b), section 7 of the 1981 Act or section 107 of the 2004 Act entitles the court, on the application of an entitled spouse or an entitled partner (as the case may be) or any other person having an interest, to make an order dispensing with the consent of the non-entitled spouse or the non-entitled partner to a dealing which has taken place or a proposed dealing, if—

(a) such consent is being unreasonably withheld;

(b) such consent cannot be given by reason of physical or mental disability;

(c) the non-entitled spouse or the non-entitled partner cannot be

---

[32] 1981 Act. s. 6(1A) and (3), as amended by the Law Reform (Miscellaneous Provisions) (Scotland) Act 1985, s. 13(6) and as amended and inserted by the Family Law (Scotland) Act 2006, s. 6, and 2004 Act, s. 106(1A) and (3).

found after reasonable steps have been taken to trace him or her; or

(d) the non-entitled spouse or the non-entitled partner is under legal disability by reason of nonage.[33]

Application for such an order must be made by motion intimated to the other spouse or civil partner and any other person to whom intimation is ordered to be made.[34] If relevant and material facts are in dispute, the court may order that the matter proceed by way of minute and answers.[35]

As regards paragraph (a) above, the onus is on the applicant to show that consent is being unreasonably withheld.[36] Such onus may be discharged where the purpose of withholding is shown not to have been to protect occupancy rights but to attempt to force the other spouse or partner into certain actings in exchange.[37] Furthermore, consent is taken to be unreasonably withheld where it appears to the court that—

(a) the non-entitled spouse or the non-entitled partner has led the entitled spouse or entitled partner to believe that such consent would be given and that the non-entitled spouse or the non-entitled partner would not be prejudiced by any change in the circumstances of the case since such apparent consent was given; or

(b) that the entitled spouse or the entitled partner has, having taken all reasonable steps to do so, been unable to obtain an answer to a request for consent.[38]

In considering whether or not to make the order, the court must have regard to all the circumstances of the case, including the matters specified in paragraphs (a) to (e) of section 3(3) of the 1981 Act or section 103(3) of the 2004 Act, namely—

(a) the conduct of the spouses or partners in relation to each other and otherwise;

(b) the respective needs and financial resources of the spouses or partners;

(c) the needs of any child of the family;

(d) the extent (if any) to which the matrimonial home or family

---

[33] 1981 Act, s. 7(1) and 2004 Act, s. 107(1).

[34] r. 33.69(1)(c) and (2)(a) and (c) or r. 33A.62(1)(c) and (2)(a) and (c).

[35] *Longmuir v. Longmuir*, 1985 S.L.T. (Sh. Ct.) 33 at p. 36.

[36] *Hall v. Hall*, 1987 S.L.T. (Sh. Ct.) 15.

[37] *O'Neill v. O'Neill*, 1987 S.L.T. (Sh. Ct.) 26.

[38] 1981 Act, s. 7(2) or 2004 Act, s. 107(2).

home is used in connection with a trade, business or profession of either spouse or partner; and

(e) whether the entitled spouse or the entitled partner offers or has offered to make available to the non-entitled spouse or the non-entitled partner any suitable alternative accommodation.[39]

If in relation to a proposed sale —

(a) negotiations with a third party have not begun; or
(b) negotiations have begun but a price has not been agreed,

an order dispensing with consent may be made only if —

(i) the price agreed for the sale is no less than such amount as the court specifies in the order dispensing with the consent of the non-entitled spouse or the non-entitled partner to the proposed dealing; and
(ii) the contract for the sale is concluded before the expiry of such period as may be so specified.[40]

If the proposed dealing is the grant of a heritable security, the order may be made only if —

(a) the heritable security is granted for a loan of no more than such amount as the court specifies in the order; and
(b) the security is executed before the expiry of such period as may be so specified.[41]

Where an application is made for an order dispensing with consent to a dealing or a proposed dealing and an action is or has been raised by a non-entitled spouse or non-entitled partner to enforce occupancy rights, such part of the action as relates to the enforcement of the occupancy rights is to be sisted until the conclusion of the proceedings on the application.[42] An application will be refused where the non-applicant spouse or partner craves a transfer of property order relative to the matrimonial home or family home.[43]

If the court refuses an application for an order dispensing with consent to a dealing or proposed dealing, it may make an order requiring a non-entitled spouse or non-entitled partner who is or becomes the occupier of the matrimonial home or family home —

---

[39] 1981 Act, s. 7(3) or 2004 Act, s. 107(3).
[40] 1981 Act, s. 7(1A) and (1B) and 2004 Act, s. 107(1A) and (1B), as inserted by the Family Law (Scotland) Act 2006, s. 7 and Sched. 1, para. 6.
[41] 1981 Act, s. 7(1C) and (1D) and 2004 Act, s. 107(1C) and (1D), as inserted by the Family Law (Scotland) Act 2006, s. 7 and Sched. 1, para. 6.
[42] 1981 Act, s. 7(4) and r. 33.71 and 2004 Act, s. 107(4) and r. 33A.64.
[43] *Rae v. Rae*, 1991 S.L.T. 454.

(a) to make such payments to the owner of the home in respect of its occupation as may be specified in the order;

(b) to comply with such other conditions relating to the occupation of the matrimonial home or family home as may be so specified.[44]

ORDERS TRANSFERRING TENANCY

The Matrimonial Homes (Family Protection) (Scotland) Act 1981 and the Civil Partnership Act 2004 enable the sheriff in an action of divorce or dissolution of civil partnership, on granting decree or within such period as he may specify on granting decree, to make an order transferring tenancy.[45]

Such may be an order —

(a) transferring the tenancy of a matrimonial home or family home to a non-entitled spouse or non-entitled partner; or

(b) where the spouses or partners are joint or common tenants of a matrimonial home or family home, vesting the tenancy in one spouse or partner only.[46]

In either case, the court may provide for payment by the applicant to the non-applicant of such compensation as seems just and reasonable in all the circumstances of the case, but in assessing the amount of any such compensation no account is to be taken of any right to purchase under Part III of the Housing (Scotland) Act 1987.[47] The effect of the order is to vest the tenancy (or sole tenancy, as the case may be) in the applicant, subject to all the liabilities under the lease other than any arrears of rent for the period before the making of the order.[48]

It is not competent for a non-entitled spouse or partner to apply for an order transferring tenancy where the matrimonial home or family home —

(a) is let to the entitled spouse or partner as an incident of employment, and the lease is subject to a requirement that the entitled spouse or partner must reside therein;

---

[44] 1981 Act, s. 7(3A) and 2004 Act, s. 107(3A), as inserted by the Family Law (Scotland) Act 2006, s. 7 and Sched. 1, para. 6.

[45] "Tenancy" includes sub-tenancy, statutory tenancy (as defined in s. 3 of the Rent (Scotland) Act 1971) and statutory secured tenancy (as defined in s.16(1) of the Housing (Scotland) Act 1988) – 1981 Act, s. 22(1) and 2004 Act, s. 135(1).

[46] 1981 Act, s. 13(1), (2), (9) and (10), as amended by the Family Law (Scotland) Act 1985, Sched. 1, para. 11, and 2004 Act, s. 112 (1), (2), (10) and (11).

[47] 1981 Act, s. 13(1), (9) and (11) and 2004 Act, s. 112(1), (10) and (12).

[48] 1981 Act, s. 13(5) and 2004 Act, s. 112(5) and (6).

(b) is on or pertains to land comprised in an agricultural lease or agricultural holding;[49]

(c) is on or pertains to a croft[50] or the subject of a cottar[51] or the holding of a landholder or a small statutory tenant;[52]

(d) is let on a long lease;[53]

(e) is part of the tenancy land of a tenant-at-will.[54]

Application for an order transferring tenancy must be made by a crave[55] in the initial writ or defences, as the case may be, intimated to the landlord, who must have an opportunity of being heard by the court before the order may be granted.[56] The court is required in determining whether or not to grant the order to have regard to all the circumstances of the case, including the matters specified in paragraphs (a) to (e) of section 3(3) of the Matrimonial Homes (Family Protection) (Scotland) Act 1981 or section 103(3) of the Civil Partnership Act 2004, namely —

(a) the conduct of the spouses or partners in relation to each other and otherwise;

(b) the respective needs and financial resources of the spouses or partners;

(c) the needs of any child of the family;

(d) the extent (if any) to which the matrimonial home or family home is used in connection with a trade, business or profession of either spouse or partner; and

(e) whether the entitled spouse or the entitled partner offers or

---

[49] "Agricultural lease" means a lease constituting a 1991 Act tenancy within the meaning of the Agricultural Holdings (Scotland) Act 2003 or a lease constituting a limited duration tenancy or a short limited duration tenancy (within the meaning of that Act) — 1981 Act, s. 13(8). "Agricultural holding" has the same meaning as in s. 1 of the Agricultural Holdings (Scotland) Act 1991 – 2004 Act, s. 112(9).

[50] "Croft" has the same meaning as in the Crofters (Scotland) Act 1955 or the Crofters (Scotland) Act 1993 – 1981 Act, s. 13(8) and 2004 Act, s. 112(9).

[51] "Cottar" has the same meaning as in s. 28(4) of the Crofters (Scotland) Act 1955 or s. 12(5) of the Crofters (Scotland) Act 1993 – 1981 Act, s. 13(8) and 2004 Act, s. 112(9).

[52] "Holding" in relation to a landholder and a statutory small tenant, "landholder" and "statutory small tenant" have the same meanings respectively as in ss. 2(1), 2(2) and 32(1) of the Small Landholders (Scotland) Act 1911 – 1981 Act, s. 13(8) and 2004 Act, s. 112(9).

[53] "Long lease" has the same meaning as in s. 28(1) of the Land Registration (Scotland) Act 1979 – 1981 Act, s. 13(8) and 2004 Act, s. 112(9).

[54] 1981 Act, s. 13(7) and 2004 Act, s. 112(8). "Tenant-at-will" has the same meaning as in s. 20(8) of the Land Registration (Scotland) Act 1979 – 1981 Act, s. 13(8) and 2004 Act, s. 112(9).

[55] rr. 33.48(1)(a) and (2)(d) and 33.34(1)(c)(iii) and (2)(b)(i) or r. 33A.45(1)(a) and (2)(d) and 33A.34(1)(c)(iii) and (2)(b)(i).

[56] 1981 Act, s. 13(4) and 2004 Act, s. 112(4). As to intimation, see further Chap. 1, text accompanying nn. 16 and 22.

has offered to make available to the non-entitled spouse or the non-entitled partner any suitable alternative accommodation,

and the suitability of the applicant to become the tenant (or sole tenant, as the case may be) and his or her capacity to perform the obligations under the lease.[57]

The clerk of court must notify the landlord of the making of an order transferring tenancy.[58]

---

[57] 1981 Act, s. 13(3) and 2004 Act, s. 112(3). For an illustration of circumstances justifying the granting of an order transferring tenancy, see *McGowan v. McGowan*, 1986 S.L.T. 112; *Guyan v. Guyan*, 2001 Fam. L.R. 99.

[58] 1981 Act, s. 13(6) or 2004 Act, s. 112(7).

CHAPTER 6

CHILDREN

The subject of children in the context of the law and practice relating to divorce and dissolution of civil partnership is discussed in this chapter; and the jurisdiction, duties and powers of the court in this connection are considered in turn.

JURISDICTION OF THE COURT

A sheriff court has jurisdiction by virtue of section 10(1) and (1A) of the Domicile and Matrimonial Proceedings Act 1973[1] to entertain an application competently made to it for the making, variation or recall of an order relating to children which is ancillary or collateral to an action for divorce (whether the application is made before or after the pronouncement of a final decree in the action) if the court has, or as the case may be, had jurisdiction to entertain the action for divorce. Similar provisions exist in section 227 of the Civil Partnership Act 2004 with respect to actions for dissolution of civil partnership.[2]

The court does not however have such jurisdiction where—

(a) in the case of divorce, the court is exercising jurisdiction in the proceedings by virtue of Article 3 of the Council Regulation (*i.e.* Council Regulation (EC) No. 2201/2003 of 27 November 2003 concerning jurisdiction and the recognition and enforcement of judgments in matrimonial matters and matters of parental responsibility) and the making or variation of an order in consequence of the application would contravene Article 6 of the Council Regulation;[3] or

---

[1] As amended and inserted, respectively, by para. 20(2)(a) and 20(2)(b) of Sched. 4 to the Children (Scotland) Act 1995.

[2] Civil Partnership Act 2004, s. 227(1), (2), (3) and (5).

[3] Domicile and Matrimonial Proceedings Act 1973 s. 10(1B), as inserted by the European Communities (Matrimonial Jurisdiction and Judgments) (Scotland) Regulations 2001 (S.S.I. 2001 No. 36), reg. 2(4) and amended by the European Communities (Matrimonial and Parental Responsibility Jurisdiction and Judgments) (Scotland) Regulations 2005 (S.S.I. 2005 No. 42), reg. 2(4). Art. 3 of the Council Regulation is reproduced in Chap. 2. As to Art. 6 of the Council Regulation, see Chap. 2, n. 18 and accompanying text.

(b) in the case of dissolution of civil partnership, jurisdiction to entertain the action was under section 219 regulations and to make, vary or recall the order to which the application relates would contravene the regulations.[4]

The court does not have jurisdiction to entertain an application for an order with respect to the residence, care or control of a child or contact with a child or the education or upbringing of a child after the dismissal of an action of divorce or after decree of absolvitor is granted therein, or after the dismissal of an action of dissolution of civil partnership, unless the application for the order was made on or before such dismissal or the granting of the decree of absolvitor.[5]

The court does not have jurisdiction to entertain an application for the variation of any such order made in an action of divorce or dissolution of civil partnership where it has refused to grant the principal remedy sought in the proceedings if, on the date of the application, matrimonial proceedings in respect of the marriage concerned are continuing in another court in the United Kingdom.[6]

In terms of section 13(6) of the Family Law Act 1986[7] a court which has jurisdiction in actions of divorce or dissolution of civil partnership to entertain an application for an order with respect to the residence, care or control of a child or contact with a child or the education or upbringing of a child may make an order declining such jurisdiction if—

(a) it appears to the court with respect to that child that—

(i) but for section 11(1) of the Act (exclusion of jurisdiction of Scottish court), another court in Scotland would have jurisdiction to entertain an application for such an order; or

(ii) but for section 3(2), 5(3), 20(2) or 23(3) of the Act (exclusion of jurisdiction of English and Northern Irish courts), a court in another part of the United Kingdom

---

[4] Civil Partnership Act 2004, s. 227(3A). As to section 219 regulations, see Chap. 2, nn. 24–26 and accompanying text.

[5] Family Law Act 1986, s. 13(2), as substituted by the Civil Partnership Act 2004 (Consequential Amendments) (Scotland) Order 2005 (S.S.I. 2005 No. 623), art. 15(3).

[6] 1986 Act, s. 13(4), as amended by the Children (Scotland) Act 1995, Sched. 4, para. 41(3) and the Civil Partnership Act 2004 (Consequential Amendments) (Scotland) Order 2005 (S.S.I. 2005 No. 623), art. 15(5). This is subject to s. 13(5), as amended (subs. (4) not to apply if the court in which the other proceedings are continuing has made any of certain specified orders and that order is in force).

[7] As amended by the Civil Partnership Act 2004 (Consequential Amendments) (Scotland) Order 2005 (S.S.I. 2005 No. 623), art. 15(6).

would have jurisdiction to make such an order or an order varying such an order; and

  (b) the court considers that it would be more appropriate for such matters relating to that child to be determined in that other court or part.

The court may recall an order made under section 13(6) of the 1986 Act.[8]

A court which has such jurisdiction to entertain an application for order with respect to the residence, care or control of a child or contact with a child or the education or upbringing of a child may refuse the application in any case where the matter in question has been determined in other proceedings.[9]

Where, at any stage of the proceedings on an application made to a court in Scotland for such an order, it appears to the court—

  (a) that proceedings with respect to the matters to which the application relates are continuing outside Scotland or in another court in Scotland;

  (b) that it would be more appropriate for those matters to be determined in proceedings outside Scotland or in another court in Scotland and that such proceedings are likely to be taken there; or

  (c) that it should exercise its powers under Article 15 of the Council Regulation (transfer to a court better placed to hear the case),

the court may sist the proceedings on that application or (as the case may be) exercise its powers under Article 15 of the Council Regulation.[10]

DUTIES OF THE COURT

The Children (Scotland) Act 1995 imposes certain duties upon the court in any action of divorce or dissolution of civil partnership with respect to section 11 orders (*viz.* orders under section 11(1) of the Act relating to parental responsibilities and parental rights).

---

[8] 1986 Act, s. 13(7).

[9] 1986 Act, s. 14(1).

[10] 1986 Act, s. 14(2), as amended by the European Communities (Matrimonial and Parental Responsibility Jurisdiction and Judgments) (Scotland) Regulations 2005 (S.S.I. 2005 No. 42), reg. 4(2). See *Hill v. Hill*, 1991 S.L.T. 189; *B v. B*, 1998 S.L.T. 1245; *M v. M*, 2002 S.C. 103.

These duties are that—

(a) in considering whether or not to make a section 11 order and what order to make, the court must regard the welfare of the child concerned as its paramount consideration and must not make any such order unless it considers that it would be better for the child that the order be made than that none should be made at all, and in so doing must have regard to certain matters;[11]

(b) in considering whether or not to make a section 11 order and what order to make, taking account of the child's age and maturity, the court must so far as practicable give him an opportunity to indicate whether he wishes to express his views, give him an opportunity to express them if he does so wish and have regard to such views as he may express;[12]

(c) where it is considering making a section 11 order and in pursuance of that order two or more relevant persons would have to co-operate with one another as respects matters affecting the child, the court must consider whether it would be appropriate to make the order;[13]

(d) the court must endeavour to ensure that any section 11 order which it makes, or any determination by it not to make an order, does not adversely affect the position of a person who has, in good faith and for value, acquired any property of the child concerned, or any right or interest in such property;[14]

(e) where any child of the family[15] has not reached the age of

---

[11] Children (Scotland) Act 1995, s. 11(7)(a), (7A) and (7B), as inserted by the Family Law (Scotland) Act 2006, s. 24. The matters to which it must have regard are detailed *infra* (text accompanying nn. 21 and 22).

[12] 1995 Act, s. 11(7)(b).

[13] 1995 Act, s. 11(7D), as inserted by the Family Law (Scotland) Act 2006, s. 24. "Relevant person", in relation to a child, means—(a) a person having parental responsibilities or parental rights in respect of the child; or (b) where a parent of the child does not have parental responsibilities or parental rights in respect of the child, a parent of the child—1995 Act, s. 11(7E), as so inserted.

[14] 1995 Act, s. 11(8).

[15] "Child of the family", in relation to the parties to a marriage, means—(i) a child of both of them; or (ii) any other child, not being a child who is placed with them as foster parents by a local authority or voluntary organisation, who has been treated by both of them as a child of the family—Children (Scotland) Act 1995, s. 12(4)(a), as amended by the Family Law (Scotland) Act 2006, Sched. 2, para. 8. "Child of the family", in relation to the partners in a civil partnership, means a child—(i) who has been treated by both partners as a child of the family which their partnership constitutes; or (ii) whose parents are the partners (being parents by virtue of ss. 33 and 42 of the Human Fertilisation and Embryology Act 2008)— Children (Scotland) Act 1995, s. 12(4)(b), as amended by the Family Law (Scotland) Act 2006, Sched. 2, para. 8 and 2008 Act, Sched. 6, para. 53.

16 years, the court must consider (in the light of such information as is before the court as to the arrangements which have been, or are proposed to be, made for the upbringing of each child) whether to exercise with respect to him the powers conferred by section 11 or 54 of the Act;[16] and

(f) where the court is of the opinion that the circumstances of the case require, or are likely to require, it to exercise any power under section 11 or 54 of the Act with respect to a child and it is not in a position to do so without giving further consideration to the case and there are exceptional circumstances which make it desirable in the interests of that child that it should not grant decree in the action until it is in a position to exercise such a power, it must postpone its decision on the granting of decree in the action until it is in such a position.[17]

The duties set forth in paragraphs (a) and (b) *supra* are now considered in more detail.

The welfare principle

In considering whether or not to make a section 11 order and what order to make, the court must regard the welfare of the child[18] as its paramount consideration and must not make any such order unless it considers that it would be better for the child that the order be made than that none should be made at all.[19] There is no presumptive rule or guideline tending to favour the wishes or interests of either parent.[20]

In carrying out the duties imposed by the foregoing provision, the court must have regard in particular to the following matters:

---

[16] 1995 Act, s. 12(1), as amended by the Civil Partnership Act 2004, s. 261(2) and Sched. 28, para. 60. The section applies where a child of the family has not reached the age of 16 years at the date when the question first arises as to whether the court should give such consideration as is mentioned in s. 12(1)—1995 Act, s. 12(3). Powers conferred by s. 11 or s. 54 of the 1995 Act are considered, *infra*. As to the sheriff's duty to order intimation to the child when so considering, see r. 33.15(2) or r. 33A.15(2), mentioned in Chap. 1, text accompanying n. 33.

[17] 1995 Act, s. 12(2).

[18] *C.f. Birmingham City Council v. H (A Minor)* [1994] 2 A.C. 212 (regard not to be had to welfare of 15-year-old mother in application for contact with baby) and *Re T and E (Proceedings: Conflicting Interests)* [1995] 1 F.L.R. 581 at p. 587 (competing interests of sibling children required to be balanced and situation of least detriment to all of them achieved).

[19] 1995 Act, s. 11(7)(a).

[20] *Sanderson v. McManus*, 1997 S.C. (H.L.) 55; *M v. M*, 2012 S.L.T. 428.

(a) the need to protect the child from—
  (i) any abuse;[21] or
  (ii) the risk of any abuse,
  which affects, or might affect, the child;
(b) the effect such abuse, or the risk of such abuse, might have on the child;
(c) the ability of a person—
  (i) who has carried out abuse which affects or might affect the child; or
  (ii) who might carry out such abuse,
  to care for, or otherwise meet the needs of, the child; and
(d) the effect any abuse, or the risk of any abuse, might have on the carrying out of responsibilities in connection with the welfare of the child by a person who has (or, by virtue of a section 11 order would have) those responsibilities.[22]

"Welfare" is not statutorily defined but has been judicially explained as follows:

"'Welfare' is an all encompassing word. It includes material welfare, both in the sense of adequacy of resources to provide a pleasant home and a comfortable standard of living and in the sense of adequacy of care to ensure that good health and due personal pride are maintained. However, while material considerations have their place they are secondary matters. More important are the stability and the security, the loving and understanding, care and guidance, the warm and compassionate relationships, that are essential for the full development of the child's own character, personality and talents."[23]

What is in the best interests of any particular child is essentially a question of fact; and since cases can vary infinitely on their facts, case law assumes a lesser significance in this area. Worthy of particular note, however, are the judicial expressions of (1) a general preference that the mother should have custody of the very young child;[24] (2) the need

---

[21] "Abuse" includes (a) violence, harassment, threatening conduct and any other conduct giving rise, or likely to give rise, to physical or mental injury, fear, alarm or distress; (b) abuse of a person other than the child; and (c) domestic abuse—1995 Act, s. 11(7C), as inserted by the Family Law (Scotland) Act 2006, s. 24. "Conduct" includes (a) speech; and (b) presence in a specified place or area—*ibid*. This provision was considered in *R v. R*, 2010 Fam. L.R. 123.

[22] 1995 Act, s. 11(7A) and (7B), as inserted by the Family Law (Scotland) Act 2006, s. 24.

[23] Per Hardie Boys J. in *Walker v. Walker and Harrison*, noted in [1981] NZ Recent Law 257.

[24] *Brixey v. Lynas*, 1997 S.C. (H.L.) 1. *C.f. MacMillan v. Brady*, 1997 Fam. L.R. 29.

for close and anxious attention to the possible effects on the child of any change to existing arrangements;[25] (3) the desirability of placing very great and usually decisive weight on the wishes of the teenage child;[26] and (4) a preference that all children of a marriage (or civil partnership) should be brought up together.[27]

The paramountcy formulation connotes—

". . . a process whereby, when all the facts, relationships, claims and wishes of parents, risks, choices, and other circumstances are taken into account and weighed, the course to be followed will be that which is most in the interests of the child's welfare as that term has now to be understood. That is the . . . paramount consideration because it rules on or determines the course to be followed."[28]

The court must consider all the relevant circumstances and decide what in its judgment the welfare of the child requires.[29] There may not be a strict legal onus of proof in this regard, but in the absence of relevant material on which the court could properly take the view that it would be in the interests of a child for a given order to be granted, then an application must fail.[30] That being so, a party who seeks to alter the status quo must have some liability to furnish the court with material potentially capable of justifying the making of a relevant order.[31]

---

[25] *J v. C* [1970] A.C 668 at p. 715.

[26] *Gover v. Gover*, 1969 S.L.T. (Notes) 78; *Blance v. Blance*, 1978 S.L.T. 74.

[27] *Early v. Early*, 1990 S.L.T. 221 at p. 224. But see *H v. H*, 2010 S.L.T. 395 (although preservation of sibling relationship a central consideration, the relationship between child and parent was primary and an important counterweight).

[28] Per Lord MacDermott in *J v. C* [1970] A.C. 668 at p. 710, under reference to the formulation "its first and paramount consideration", thought to amount to the same thing in *C v. C (A Minor: Custody Appeal)* [1991] 1 F.L.R. 223 at p. 230.

[29] *Osborne v. Matthan (No. 2)*, 1998 S.C. 682 at p. 688; *Pearson v. Pearson*, 1999 S.L.T. 1364 at p. 1367. *C.f. O v. O*, 1994 S.C. 569 (not normally appropriate, where welfare of children is involved, to dispose of an application solely on the pleadings, and the court will not do so, except on a point of law only, without conducting some kind of inquiry into the facts). Note that professional advisers have a duty to take steps to identify and concentrate on, and only on, the issue, which is the welfare of the subject child or children—*NJDB v. JEG*, 2011 S.C. 191.

[30] *White v. White*, 2001 S.C. 689 at p. 698.

[31] *S v. S*, 2012 Fam. L.R. 32.

Views of the child

In considering whether or not to make a section 11 order and what order to make, the court, taking account for the child's age and maturity[32], must so far as practicable —

    (i)   give him an opportunity to indicate whether he wishes to express his views;

    (ii) if he does so wish, give him an opportunity to express them; and

    (iii) have regard to such views as he may express.[33]

The duty on the court to comply with the foregoing requirements is one which continues until the relevant order is made and the fact that formal intimation may have been dispensed with as inappropriate in no way relieves the court of complying with that continuing duty, if necessary *ex proprio motu.*[34]

Rule 33.19 or Rule 33A.19 provides the machinery whereby the aforesaid requirements may be complied with. These provide that in an action of divorce or dissolution of civil partnership, in relation to any matter affecting a child, where that child has —

    (a) returned to the sheriff clerk Form F9 or Form CP7; or

    (b) otherwise indicated to the court a wish to express views on a matter affecting him,

the court must not grant any order unless an opportunity has been given for the views of that child to be obtained or heard.[35] Where a child has indicated a wish to express his views, the sheriff must order such

---

[32] A child who is 12 years or more is presumed to be of sufficient age and maturity to form a view — 1995 Act, s. 11(10). *C.f. G v. G,* 2003 Fam. L.R. 118 (6-year-old child's views not sought).

[33] 1995 Act, s. 11(7)(b). This provision gives effect to Art. 12 of the United Nations Convention on the Rights of the Child, reproduced in App. V. See, *e.g., Henderson v. Henderson,* 1997 Fam. L.R. 120 (child's views of importance in conjunction with other factors); *Perendes v. Sim,* 1998 S.L.T. 1382 (children's wishes accorded limited weight); *H v. H,* 2000 Fam. L.R. 73 (child's wishes determinative); *M v. M,* 2000 Fam. L.R. 84 (child's wishes of importance in conjunction with other factors); *S v. S,* 2002 S.C. 246 (child's wishes determinative); *Ellis v. Ellis,* 2003 Fam. L.R. 77 (children's wishes not given decisive weight); *J v. J,* 2004 Fam. L.R. 20 (children's wishes not given decisive weight) and *C v. McM,* 2005 Fam. L.R. 36 (children's views ambivalent).

[34] *S v. S,* 2002 S.C. 246 at p. 250. In a case where the parties' children had been interviewed by a social worker at an earlier stage of the proceedings and had shown divided loyalty, the sheriff was held to have correctly exercised his discretion not to give them a further opportunity to express views (*C v. McM,* 2005 Fam. L.R. 36). See also *X v. Y,* 2007 Fam. L.R. 153 (sheriff declining to interview children to ascertain whether they had been untruthful in expressing their views to a consultant psychologist).

[35] r. 33.19(1) or r. 33A.19(1).

steps to be taken as he considers appropriate to ascertain the views of that child.[36] The sheriff cannot grant an order in an action of divorce or dissolution of civil partnership, in relation to any matter affecting a child who has indicated a wish to express his views, unless due weight has been given by the sheriff to the views expressed by that child, having due regard to his age and maturity.[37]

So far as affording the child the opportunity to make known his or her views is concerned, the only proper and relevant test is one of practicability, and how the child should be given such an opportunity will depend on the circumstances of each case and, in particular, on his or her age:

"At one extreme, intimation in terms of Form F9 [or Form CP7] may be appropriate whereas, at the other extreme, a much less formal method will be appropriate. Seeing a child in chambers is, of course, always open to the court but, in the case of a very young child, we do not discount the possibility that his or her views, or the lack of them, could properly be made known to the court through the agency of, for example, a private individual who is well known to the child or perhaps by a child psychologist. But, if, by one method or another it is practicable to give a child the opportunity of expressing his views, then, in our view, the only safe course is to employ that method. What weight is thereafter given to such views as may be expressed is, of course, an entirely different matter. It follows that we do not agree . . . that the formal process of intimation in terms of Form F9 [or Form CP7] should necessarily be seen as the principal mode of compliance with s. 11(7)(b). In particular, where younger children are involved or where there is a risk of upsetting the child, other methods may well be preferable."[38]

The child may express his or her views personally to the sheriff orally or in writing.[39] Alternatively, somebody else, who need not be an advocate or a solicitor, may do so on the child's behalf.[40] The sheriff, or the person appointed by the sheriff, must record the views of the child in writing.[41] Careful consideration will always have to be given to the question of whether to embark on the process of interviewing

---

[36] r. 33.19(2) or r. 33A.19(2).
[37] r. 33.19(3) or r. 33A.19(3).
[38] *S v. S*, 2002 S.C. 246 at p. 250.
[39] r. 33.20(1) or r. 33A.20(1). Note that an interview cannot be substituted for a proof—
      Macdonald v. Macdonald, 1985 S.L.T. 244.
[40] Sheriff Courts (Scotland) Act 1971, s. 32(1)(j) and Form F9 or Form CP7.
[41] r. 33.20(2) or r. 33A.20(2).

a child and, if it is to be undertaken, the most appropriate method of approaching this most sensitive task.[42]

The sheriff may direct that such views, and any written views, given by a child be —

(a) sealed in an envelope marked "Views of the child—confidential";

(b) be kept in the court process without being recorded in the inventory of process;

(c) be available to a sheriff only;

(d) not be opened by any person other than a sheriff; and

(e) not form a borrowable part of the process.[43]

The practicalities involved in reconciling the parties' right to a fair hearing and a child's right to express his views are of immense difficulty, best resolved by taking the fundamental principle that a party is entitled to disclosure of all materials as the starting point and next considering whether disclosure would involve a real possibility of significant harm to the child.[44]

The court's aforesaid duties in relation to the child's views do not require a child to be legally represented if he does not wish to be.[45] In the event that he wants to be a party to the proceedings, the child may apply by minute for leave to enter the process and to lodge defences.[46] His right is not only one to have his views conveyed to the court but also to have his position advocated in accordance with his instructions.[47] The court may nevertheless decline to exercise its discretion so as to allow the child to enter the process.[48]

POWERS OF THE COURT

The court's powers in connection with children in actions of divorce or dissolution of civil partnership are wide and include the power—

---

[42] *W v. W*, 2003 S.L.T. 1253 at p. 1259. *C.f. X v. Y*, 2007 Fam.L.R. 153 (children interviewed by consultant psychologist); *McG v. McG*, 2007 Fam. L.R. 62 (children aged 7 and 5 considered too young to be interviewed).

[43] r. 33.20(2) or r. 33A.20(2).

[44] *McGrath v. McGrath*, 1999 S.L.T. (Sh. Ct.) 90. *C.f. Dosoo v. Dosoo*, 1999 S.L.T. (Sh. Ct.) 86.

[45] 1995 Act, s. 11(9).

[46] r. 13(1). *C.f. Fourman v. Fourman*, 1998 Fam. L.R. 98 (14-year-old girl given leave to enter process); *H v. H*, 2000 Fam. L.R. 73 (11-year-old boy, with learning disabilities but competent, sisted as a party); *B v. B*, 2011 S.L.T. (Sh. Ct.) 225 (12-year-old boy, probably confused, refused leave to enter process at late stage of action).

[47] *B v. B*, 2011 S.L.T. (Sh. Ct.) 225 at p. 228.

[48] *Ibid.*

(a) to make orders in relation to parental responsibilities and parental rights under section 11(1) of the Children (Scotland) Act 1995;

(b) to prevent the removal of children under section 35(3) and (5) of the Family Law Act 1986;

(c) to make provision for the maintenance of children under section 8 of the Child Support Act 1991;

(d) to make a reference to the Principal Reporter under section 54(1) of that Act; and

(e) to restrict publicity concerning a person under the age of 17 years under section 46(1) of the Children and Young Persons (Scotland) Act 1937.

The powers set forth in paragraphs (a) to (e) *supra* are now considered in more detail.

Section 11 orders

In terms of section 11(1) of the Children (Scotland) Act 1995, an order[49] (known as a "section 11 order")[50] may be made in an action of divorce or dissolution of civil partnership in relation to parental responsibilities or parental rights.[51]

"Parental responsibilities" are the responsibilities that a parent has in relation to his child—

(a) to safeguard and promote the child's health, development and welfare;

(b) to provide, in a manner appropriate to the stage of development of the child—
   (i) direction;
   (ii) guidance,
   to the child;

(c) if the child is not living with the parent, to maintain personal relations and direct contact with the child on a regular basis; and

(d) to act as the child's legal representative,

---

[49] "Order" includes an interim order or an order varying or discharging an order—1995 Act, s. 11(13).

[50] r. 33.1(2) or r. 33A.1(2).

[51] Orders under s. 11(1) and (2)(g) and (h) in relation to guardianship and the administration of a child's property are not discussed herein.

but only in so far as compliance with the foregoing is practicable and in the interests of the child.[52]

"Parental rights" are the rights that a parent, in order to enable him to fulfil his parental responsibilities in relation to his child, has—

(a) to have the child living with him or otherwise to regulate the child's residence;

(b) to control, direct or guide, in a manner appropriate to the stage of development of the child, the child's upbringing;

(c) if the child is not living with him, to maintain personal relations and direct contact with the child on a regular basis; and

(d) to act as the child's legal representative,

and, where two or more persons have a parental right as respects a child, each of them may exercise that right without the consent of the other or, as the case may be, of any of the others, unless any decree or deed conferring the right, or regulating its exercise, otherwise provides.[53]

A person who has parental responsibilities or parental rights in relation to a child shall not abdicate those responsibilities or rights to anyone else but may arrange for some or all of them to be fulfilled or exercised on his behalf; and without prejudice to that generality any such arrangement may be made with a person who already has parental responsibilities or parental rights in relation to the child concerned.[54] The fact that a person has parental responsibilities or parental rights in relation to a child does not entitle that person to act in any way which would be incompatible with any court order relating to the child or the child's property, or with any supervision requirement made under section 70 of the 1995 Act.[55]

The court may make such order under section 11(1) as it thinks fit, and without prejudice to the generality of that subsection, may make any of the following orders—

(a) an order depriving a person of some or all of his parental responsibilities or parental rights in relation to a child;

(b) an order—

---

[52] 1995 Act, s. 1(1) and (3). "Child" means, for the purposes of paras. (a), (b)(i), (c) and (d), a person under the age of 16 years, and, for the purposes of para. (b)(ii), a person under the age of 18 years—*ibid.*, s. 1(2).

[53] 1995 Act, s. 2(1), (2) and (4). "Child" means a person under the age of 16 years—*ibid.*, s. 2(7).

[54] 1995 Act, s. 3(5), as amended by the Human Fertilisation and Embryology Act 2008, Sched. 6, para. 50(4). The provision is subject to ss. 4 and 4A of the Act (acquisition of parental rights and responsibilities by natural father and by second female parent by agreement with mother).

[55] 1995 Act, s. 3(4).

       (i)   imposing upon a person (provided he is at least sixteen years of age or is a parent of the child) such responsibilities; and

      (ii)   giving that person such rights;

   (c)   an order regulating the arrangements as to—

       (i)   with whom; or

      (ii)   if with different persons alternately or periodically, with whom during what periods,

a child under the age of sixteen years is to live (any such order being known as a "residence order");

   (d)   an order regulating the arrangements for maintaining personal relations and direct contact between a child under that age and a person with whom the child is not, or will not be, living (any such order being known as a "contact order");

   (e)   an order regulating any specific question which has arisen, or may arise, in connection *inter alia* with parental responsibilities or parental rights (any such order being known as a "specific issue order"); and

   (f)   an interdict prohibiting the taking of any step of a kind specified in the interdict *inter alia* in the fulfilment of parental responsibilities or the exercise of parental rights relating to a child.[56]

The existence of a supervision requirement does not serve to make a section 11 order incompetent.[57] On the other hand, where a permanence order (as defined in section 80(2) of the Adoption and Children (Scotland) Act 2007) is in force in respect of a child, the court may not make a section 11 order such as is mentioned in paragraphs (a) to (e) *supra*.[58]

A section 11 order has the effect of depriving a person of parental responsibility or parental right only in so far as the order expressly so provides and only to the extent necessary to give effect to the order, but in making any such order as is mentioned in paragraph (a) and (b) *supra*, the court may revoke any agreement which, in relation to the child concerned, has effect by virtue of section 4(2) or 4A(2) of the 1995 Act (acquisition of parental rights and responsibilities by natural father, and by second female parent, by agreement with mother).[59]

---

[56] 1995 Act, s. 11(2).

[57] *P v. P*, 2000 S.L.T. 781.

[58] 1995 Act, s. 11A, as inserted by the Adoption and Children (Scotland) Act 2007, s. 103.

[59] 1995 Act, s. 11(11), as amended by the Human Fertilisation and Embryology Act 2008, Sched. 6, para. 52(3).

Where the court makes a residence order which requires that a child live with a person who, immediately before the order is made does not have in relation to the child all the parental responsibilities listed in paragraphs (a), (b) and (d), *supra*, and the parental rights listed in paragraphs (b) and (d), *supra*, that person shall, subject to the provisions of the order or of any other section 11 order, have the missing responsibilities and rights while the residence order remains in force.[60]

A joint residence order may competently be made.[61] A residence order is intended to regulate where a child is to make his home, and so a contact order is the appropriate order to regulate overnight or longer stays.[62] The person with whom the child lives has a responsibility to help make contact orders work.[63] An award of postal or letterbox contact may be made.[64]

Where the court at its own instance or on the motion of a party is considering making a contact order or interim contact order subject to supervision by the social work department of a local authority, it must ordain the party moving for such an order to intimate to the chief executive of that local authority (where not already a party to the action and represented at the hearing at which the issue arises) the following—

  (a)   the terms of any relevant motion;
  (b)   the intention of the sheriff to order that the contact be supervised by the social work department of that local authority; and
  (c)   that the local authority shall, within such period as the sheriff has determined
       (i)   notify the sheriff clerk whether it intends to make representations to the sheriff; and
       (ii) where it intends to make representations in writing, to do so within that period.[65]

There does not have to be a dispute between the parties in order for the court to have the power to make a specific issue order; it is sufficient that there is a question to be answered.[66] Specific issue orders have been sought in relation to whether—

---

[60]   1995 Act, s. 11(12).
[61]   *Fourman v. Fourman*, 1998 Fam. L.R. 98.
[62]   *McBain v. McIntyre*, 1997 S.C.L.R. 181; *R v. R*, 2010 Fam. L.R. 123.
[63]   *Cosh v. Cosh*, 1979 S.L.T. (Notes) 72 at p. 73.
[64]   *A v. M*, 1999 Fam. L.R. 42; *R v. R*, 2010 Fam. L.R. 123.
[65]   r. 33.25 or r. 33A.26.
[66]   *C.f. Re H G (Specific Issue Order: Sterilisation)* [1993] 1 F.L.R. 587.

(a) a child should attend a particular school against the wishes of the non-applicant parent;[67]

(b) a child should be required to attend classes in religious instruction without the non-applicant's consent;[68]

(c) the applicant parent should be allowed to relocate to another country with a child;[69] and

(d) the non-applicant parent should be prevented from unilaterally changing a child's surname.[70]

A section 11 order may be made—

(1) on an application by—

(a) a person who—

(i) not having, and never having had, parental responsibilities or parental rights in relation to the child, claims an interest;

(ii) has parental responsibilities or parental rights in relation to the child;[71]

(b) in the case of a contact order, with the leave of the court by a person whose parental responsibilities or parental rights in relation to the child were extinguished on the making of an adoption order;[72]

(c) in the case of any section 11 order other than a contact order, by a person who has had, but no longer has, parental responsibilities or parental rights in relation to the child for a reason other than that they have been extinguished on the making of an adoption order or by virtue of section 55(1) of the Human Fertilisation and Embryology Act 2008;[73] or

---

[67] *G v. G*, 2002 Fam. L.R. 120.

[68] *M v. C*, 2002 S.L.T. (Sh. Ct.) 82.

[69] *M v. M*, 2000 Fam. L.R. 84; *S v. S*, 2002 S.C. 246; *McShane v. Duryea*, 2006 Fam. L.R. 15; *X v. Y*, 2007 Fam. L.R. 153; *M v. M*, 2008 Fam. L.R. 90; *M v. M*, 2012 S.L.T. 428; *S v. S*, 2012 Fam. L.R. 32. See also *S v. FD*, 2010 S.L.T. (Sh. Ct.) 107 (specific issue order sought allowing applicant parent to take the children to Spain for six weeks every year).

[70] *M v. C*, 2002 S.L.T. (Sh. Ct.) 82. An application by a child for a specific issue order that she be known by a different surname in future was refused as incompetent in *S v. D*, 2007 S.L.T. (Sh. Ct.) 37.

[71] 1995 Act, s. 11(3)(a), as amended by the Adoption and Children (Scotland) Act 2007, s. 107(a). "Person" includes (without prejudice to the generality of s. 11(3)(a)) the child concerned; but it does not include a local authority—s. 11(5). A local authority may nevertheless competently make representations to the court to the effect that the court should make no order in favour of a party applying for a s. 11 order, and may do so by way of a minute—*McLean v. Dornan*, 2001 Fam. L.R. 58.

[72] 1995 Act, s. 11(3)(aa), as inserted by the Adoption and Children (Scotland) Act 2007, s. 107(b).

[73] 1995 Act, s. 11(3)(ab) and (4), as inserted, substituted and amended by the Adoption and Children (Scotland) Act 2007, s. 107(b) and Sched. 2, para. 9(2)(a)(i) and (ii) and Sched.

(2) where no application has been made, and the court (even if it declines to make any other order) considers that it should make such an order.[74]

Application for a section 11 order is made by the pursuer by a crave in the initial writ,[75] accompanied by any appropriate crave for warrant for intimation or to dispense with intimation.[76] Application for a section 11 order is made by the defender by lodging a notice of intention to defend in Form F26 or Form CP16 and setting out in his defences:

(i)   craves;
(ii) averments in the answers to the condescendence in support of those craves;
(iii) appropriate pleas-in-law.[77]

In terms of Rule 9.6(3), though, neither a crave nor averments need be made in the defences which relate to any section 11 order. The defender must however include in his notice of intention to defend a crave for a warrant for intimation or to dispense with intimation in respect of any application for a section 11 order which, had it been made in an initial writ, would have required a warrant for intimation under Rule 33.7 or Rule 33A.7.[78] Application for a section 11 order by a person other than the pursuer or defender is made by minute in the cause.[79]

Unless the sheriff on cause shown otherwise directs, a warrant for citation cannot be granted in an action of divorce or dissolution of civil partnership which includes a crave for a section 11 order without there being produced with the initial writ an extract of the relevant entry in the register of births or equivalent document.[80]

3, para. 1 and substituted by the Human Fertilisation and Embryology Act 2008, Sched. 6, para. 52(2)(a) and (b). "Person" includes (without prejudice to the generality of s. 11(3) (ab)) the child concerned; but it does not include a local authority—s. 11(5). "Adoption order" has the meaning given by s. 119 of the Adoption and Children (Scotland) Act 2007—s. 11(6).

[74] 1995 Act, s. 11(3)(b), as substituted by the Adoption and Children (Scotland) Act 2007, s. 107(c).

[75] r. 33.39(1)(a) and (2)(a) or r. 33A.39(1)(a) and (2)(a).

[76] r. 33.7(1)(e) or r. 33A.7(1)(c) (intimation where child in care of local authority or third party, or liable to be maintained by third party); r. 33.7(1)(f) or r. 33A.7(1)(d) (intimation where section 11 order craved and parent or guardian not party to the action); r. 33.7(1) (h) or r. 33A.7(1)(f) (intimation to child to whom section 11 order craved would relate); r. 33.7(5) or r. 33A.7(5) (intimation dispensed with where address unknown); and r. 33.7(7) or r. 33A.7(7) (intimation dispensed with where inappropriate for child).

[77] r. 33.34(1)(b)(iii) and (2)(b)(i) or r. 33A.34(1)(b)(iii) and (2)(b)(i) and r. 33.39(1)(a) and (2)(a) or r. 33A.39(1)(a) and (2)(a).

[78] r. 33.34(3) or r. 33A.34(3).

[79] r. 33.39(1)(b) and (2)(a) or r. 33A.39(1)(b) and (2)(a).

[80] r. 33.9(b) or r. 33A.9(3).

A party to an action of divorce or dissolution of civil partnership, who makes an application for a section 11 order in respect of a child shall include in his pleadings—

(i) averments giving particulars of any other proceedings known to him, whether in Scotland or elsewhere and whether concluded or not, which relate to the child in respect of whom the section 11 order is sought;[81] and

(ii) where the party seeks an order such as is mentioned in section 11(2)(a) to (e), *supra*, an averment that no permanence order (as defined in section 80(2) of the Adoption and Children (Scotland) Act 2007) is in force in respect of the child.[82]

Where such other proceedings are continuing[83] or have taken place, and the averments of the applicant do not contain particulars of the other proceedings, or contain particulars which are incomplete or incorrect, any defences or minute, as the case may be, lodged by any party to the action must include such particulars or such further or correct particulars as are known to him or her.[84]

Where—

(a) on the lodging of a notice of intention to defend in an action of divorce or dissolution of civil partnership in which the initial writ seeks or includes a crave for a section 11 order, a defender wishes to oppose any such crave or order, or seeks the same order as that craved by the pursuer;

(b) on the lodging of a notice of intention to defend in such an action, the defender seeks a section 11 order which is not craved by the pursuer; or

(c) in any other circumstances in such an action, the sheriff considers that a Child Welfare Hearing under Rule 33.22A or Rule 33A.23 should be fixed and makes an order (whether at his own instance or on the motion of a party) that such a hearing shall be fixed,[85]

the sheriff clerk requires to fix a date and time for a Child Welfare Hearing on the first suitable court date occurring not sooner than 21 days after the lodging of such notice of intention to defend, unless the

---

[81] r. 33.3(1)(a) or r. 33A.3(1)(a), implementing s. 39 of the Family Law Act 1986.

[82] r. 33.3(1)(c) or r. 33A.3(1)(c).

[83] Proceedings are "continuing" at any time after they have been commenced and before they have been finally disposed of—r. 33.1(3) or r. 33A.1(3).

[84] r. 33.3(2) or r. 33A.3(2).

[85] Thus the sheriff may fix a Child Welfare Hearing after hearing evidence at a proof (*M v. M*, 2012 Fam. L.R. 14) and even after issuing his judgment (*G v. B*, 2011 S.L.T. 1253).

sheriff directs the hearing to be held on an earlier date.[86] On fixing the date for the Child Welfare Hearing, the sheriff clerk must intimate that date in Form F41 or Form CP26 to the parties, whose right to make any other application to the court whether by motion or otherwise is unaffected thereby.[87]

At the Child Welfare Hearing (which may be held in private), the sheriff must seek to secure the expeditious resolution of disputes in relation to the child by ascertaining from the parties the matters in dispute and any information relevant to that dispute, and may—

(a) order such steps to be taken, make such order, if any, or order further procedure, as he thinks fit; and

(b) ascertain whether there is or is likely to be a vulnerable witness within the meaning of section 11(1) of the Vulnerable Witnesses (Scotland) Act 2004 who is to give evidence at any proof or hearing and whether any order under section 12(1) of that Act requires to be made.[88]

All parties (including a child who has indicated his or her wish to attend) must, except on cause shown, attend the Child Welfare Hearing personally.[89] It is the duty of the parties to provide the sheriff with sufficient information to enable him to conduct the Child Welfare Hearing.[90] The sheriff is entitled under the rule to make a final order at the Child Welfare Hearing without hearing evidence, provided that he has material before him, of whatever description, which is sufficient to enable him to reach a view on the material questions.[91] The sheriff must not, however, conduct the Child Welfare Hearing in a manner that contravenes a party's right to a fair hearing such as by granting an order on the basis of a report not seen by the parties[92] or by dismissing

---

[86] r. 33.22A(1) or r. 33A.23(1). Except where r. 9.2(1A) applies, the fixing of a Child Welfare Hearing does not obviate the need to fix an Options Hearing under r. 9.2 (*Henderson v. Adamson*, 1998 S.C.L.R. 365). In terms of r. 9.2(1A), where the only matters in dispute in an action of divorce or dissolution of civil partnership are a section 11 order or the matters in dispute include a section 11 order, there is no requirement to fix an Options Hearing insofar as the matters in dispute relate to a section 11 order.

[87] r. 33.22A(2) and (3) or r. 33A.23(2) and (3).

[88] r. 33.22A(4) or r. 33A.23(4).

[89] r. 33.22A(5) or r. 33A.23(5). Failure by a party to attend, however, attracts no sanction provided that he or she is represented at the diet—*McLaren v. Henderson*, 2006 S.L.T. (Sh. Ct.) 68.

[90] r. 33.22A(6) or r. 33A.23(6).

[91] *Hartnett v. Harnett*, 1997 S.C.L.R. 525; *Morgan v. Morgan*, 1998 S.C.L.R. 681; *McCulloch v. Riach*, 1999 S.C.L.R. 159; *O'Malley v. O'Malley*, 2004 Fam. L.R. 44.

[92] *A v. B*, 2011 S.L.T. (Sh. Ct.) 131.

an action without having given the pursuer any prior indication of an intention to dismiss at that stage.[93]

Application by any party in an action of divorce or dissolution of civil partnership pending before the court for, or for variation of, a residence order or contact order must be made by motion.[94]

In any action of divorce or dissolution of civil partnership in which an order relating to parental responsibilities or parental rights is in issue, the sheriff may, at any stage of the action, where he considers it appropriate to do so, refer that issue to a mediator accredited to a specified family mediation organisation.[95] Reference to a mediator may therefore be made after proof.[96] Such a reference however is not a competent disposal as a final order.[97] In general, no information as to what occurred during family mediation is admissible as evidence in any civil proceedings.[98]

Where the court is considering any question relating to the care and upbringing of a child, it may, without prejudice to its power to appoint any other person (*e.g.* an advocate or a solicitor),[99] not being an officer of the local authority for the purpose, appoint an appropriate local authority[100] under section 11(1) of the Matrimonial Proceedings (Children) Act 1958[101] to investigate and report to the court on all the circumstances of the child and on the proposed arrangements for the care and upbringing of the child. Where, at any stage of the action, the sheriff appoints—

(a) a local authority under section 11(1) of the 1958 Act or otherwise; or

(b) another person (a "reporter"), whether under that statutory provision or otherwise,

to investigate and report on the circumstances of a child and on proposed arrangements for the care and upbringing of the child, Rule

---

[93] *Ross v. Ross*, 1999 S.C.L.R. 1112.

[94] r. 33.43(b) or r. 33A.40(b).

[95] r. 33.22 or r. 33A.22.

[96] *Harris v. Martin*, 1995 S.C.L.R. 580.

[97] *Patterson v. Patterson*, 1994 S.C.L.R. 166.

[98] Civil Evidence (Family Mediation) (Scotland) Act 1995, s. 1, subject to s. 2 (exceptions *inter alia* as to contracts and where every participant agrees on admissibility).

[99] Such appointments may most appropriately be made in cases of particular urgency, cases involving parties living in different local authority areas and cases where the local authority has already been extensively involved (*c.f. O v. O*, 1994 S.C. 569 at p. 572).

[100] "Local authority" has the same meaning as in the Social Work (Scotland) Act 1968— Matrimonial Proceedings (Children) Act 1958, s. 11(1A), as inserted by the Social Work (Scotland) Act 1968, Sched. 8, para. 43(1).

[101] As amended by the Social Work (Scotland) Act 1968, Sched. 8, para. 43(1) and the Children (Scotland) Act 1995, Sched. 4, para. 9.

33.21 or Rule 33A.21 applies. In terms thereof, the sheriff must, on making the appointment, direct that the party who sought the appointment or, where the court makes the appointment of its own motion, the pursuer or minuter, as the case may be, shall—

(a) instruct the local authority or reporter; and
(b) be responsible, in the first instance, for the fees and outlays of the local authority or reporter appointed.[102]

The party who sought the appointment or, where the court makes the appointment of its own motion, the pursuer or minuter, as the case may be, must also, within 7 days after the date of the appointment, intimate the name and address of the local authority or reporter to any local authority to which intimation of the action has been made.[103]

Where a local authority or reporter has been appointed, an application for a section 11 order in respect of the child concerned cannot be determined until the report has been lodged.[104] On completion of the report, the local authority or reporter, as the case may be, must send the report, with a copy of it for each party, to the sheriff clerk who must on receipt send a copy to each party.[105] Such a report may be a more satisfactory source of information than *ex parte* statements or affidavits in considering whether an interim order is or is not desirable.[106] The report is not evidence in the case.[107] If, however, on consideration of the report the court, either *ex proprio motu* or on the application of any person concerned, considers it expedient to do so, it may require the person who furnished the report to appear and to be examined on oath regarding any matter dealt with in the report, and any such person may be examined and cross-examined accordingly.[108] Even without such evidence from its author, the report may be of assistance to the sheriff in considering any oral evidence that he might hear before disposing of the application in the best interests of the child on a consideration of all the evidence.[109] Any expenses incurred in connection with the preparation of such a report by a local authority or other person appointed under section 11 of the

---

[102] r. 33.21(2) or r. 33A.21(2).
[103] r. 33.21(3) or r. 33A.21(3).
[104] r. 33.21(6) or r. 33A.21(6).
[105] r. 33.21(4) and (5) or r. 33A.21(4) and (5).
[106] *Hardie v. Hardie,* 1993 S.C.L.R. 60; *O v. O,* 1994 S.C. 569 at p. 572.
[107] *Whitecross v. Whitecross,* 1977 S.L.T. 225 at p. 227; *Kristiansen v. Kristiansen,* 1987 S.C.L.R. 462; *Oliver v. Oliver,* 1988 S.C.L.R. 285.
[108] Matrimonial Proceedings (Children) Act 1958, s. 11(4).
[109] *O v. O,* 1994 S.C. 569 at p. 572. See also *Bailey v. Bailey,* 2001 Fam. L.R. 133 at p. 137 (report prepared in order to assist the court at the time of the proof should have been considered by the sheriff on its merits before he reached his decision).

Matrimonial Proceedings (Children) Act 1958 shall form part of the expenses of the action and be defrayed by such party to the action as the court may direct, and the court may certify the amount of the expenses so incurred.[110]

Where in proceedings for or relating to a section 11 order in respect of a child there is not available to the court adequate information as to where the child is, the court may order any person who it has reason to believe may have relevant information to disclose it to the court.[111] Application for the order requires to be made by motion, and the sheriff may ordain the person against whom the order has been made to appear before him or to lodge an affidavit.[112] A person cannot be excused from complying with such an order by reason that to do so may incriminate him or his spouse or civil partner of an offence, but a statement or admission made in compliance with the order is not admissible in evidence against either of them in proceedings for any offence other than perjury.[113]

The courts of review will only interfere with the judgment of the court of first instance in exceptional circumstances.[114] There requires to be a disclosed inclusion of irrelevant or exclusion of relevant matters or a wrongness in the result of so striking a character as to make it a legitimate conclusion that there must have been an error of method.[115] Even so, the best interests of a child might well be better served by an application for variation, based on a change of circumstances, presented to the court of first instance rather than the pursuit of a sterile process of appeals.[116] An appeal without leave of the sheriff against the grant or refusal of an interim order relating to a child, such as a contact order, is incompetent.[117] The position is otherwise where an order for delivery is also granted.[118]

Where any parties have reached agreement in relation to a section 11 order, a joint minute may be entered into expressing that agreement, and, subject to Rule 33.19(3) or Rule 33A.19(3) (no order before views of child expressed), the sheriff may grant decree in respect of

---

[110] 1958 Act, s. 11(5), as amended by the Social Work (Scotland) Act 1968, Sched. 8, para. 43(2).

[111] Family Law Act 1986, s. 33(1). *C.f. Abusaif v. Abusaif*, 1984 S.L.T. 90.

[112] r. 33.23 or r. 33A.24.

[113] 1986 Act, s. 33(2).

[114] *Senna-Cheribbo v. Wood*, 1999 S.C. 328 at p. 331.

[115] *G v. G (Minors: Custody Appeal)* [1985] 1 W.L.R. 647 at p. 650; *M v. M*, 2012 S.L.T. 428; *S. v S.*, 2012 Fam. L.R. 32.

[116] *Sanderson v. McManus*, 1997 S.C. (H.L.) 55 at p. 58; *Stewart v. Stewart*, 2007 S.C. 451 at p. 454.

[117] *Fergus v. Eadie*, 2005 S.C.L.R. 176.

[118] *B v. B*, 2009 Fam. L.R. 129.

those parts of the joint minute in relation to which he could otherwise make an order, whether or not such a decree would include a matter for which there was no crave.[119] No agreement can however bind the court.[120]

To enforce section 11 orders the court may grant such orders as an order for delivery[121] or for sheriff officers to search for and take possession of a child.[122] Wilful failure to make a child available for the purposes of a contact order is punishable as a contempt of court, as is wilful failure to return a child after contact.[123] A party alleged to be in breach of an interim order may be ordained to appear at the bar to answer the charge and, in the event of denial, minute and answers may be ordered.[124] Where a final order is claimed to have been breached, procedure is by way of initial writ.[125] If the court is satisfied that the order or interim order has been breached, it may impose a penalty of imprisonment or a fine, or may admonish the party in breach.[126] The consideration that a sentence of imprisonment would separate a child from the primary carer is relevant but not paramount; the court must uphold the rule of law and protect the interests of the innocent party.[127]

A section 11 order relating to parental responsibilities or parental rights ceases to have effect where a relevant order made outwith Scotland comes into force, so far as it makes provision for any matter for which the same or different provision is made by that order,[128] or

---

[119] r. 33.26(a) or r. 33A.27(a).

[120] *Robson v. Robson*, 1973 S.L.T. (Notes) 4; *Anderson v. Anderson*, 1989 S.C.L.R. 475; *McKechnie v. McKechnie*, 1990 S.L.T. (Sh. Ct.) 75.

[121] *McEwen v. McEwen*, 2000 Fam. L.R. 116. *C.f. Brown v. Brown*, 1948 S.C. 5; *Thomson v. Thomson*, 1979 S.L.T. (Sh. Ct.) 11. As to the power of the court to make an order for the delivery of a child by one parent to the other parent other than in implement of a section 11 order, see the Family Law Act 1986, s. 17(1).

[122] *C.f. Caldwell v. Caldwell*, 1983 S.C. 137.

[123] *M v. S*, 2009 Fam. L.R. 149; *B v. R*, 2009 Fam. L.R. 146.

[124] *Johnston v. Johnston*, 1996 S.L.T. 499.

[125] *Celso v. Celso*, 1992 S.C.L.R. 175.

[126] Note that the standard of proof is proof beyond reasonable doubt (*Johnston v. Johnston*, 1996 S.L.T. 499).

[127] *M v. S*, 2009 Fam. L.R. 149 at p. 153.

[128] 1986 Act, s. 15(1), as amended by the Children (Scotland) Act 1995, Sched. 4, para. 41(4) and the European Communities (Matrimonial Jurisdiction and Judgments) (Scotland) Regulations 2001 (S.S.I. 2001 No. 36), reg. 4(2), the relevant orders being an order under Pt. 1 of the 1986 Act, or an order varying such an order, competently made by another court in any part of the United Kingdom with respect to the child in question; or an order relating to the parental responsibilities or parental rights in relation to that child which is made outside the United Kingdom and recognised in Scotland by virtue of s. 26 of the 1986 Act, or by virtue of the Council Regulation. Where, by virtue of s. 15(1), a child is to live with a different person, then, if there is in force an order made by a court in Scotland providing for the supervision of that child by a local authority, that order shall

in any event once the child reaches the age of 16 years.[129] Where a section 11 order made by a court in Scotland ceases by virtue of the coming into force of a relevant order to have effect so far as it makes provision for any matter, that court has no power to vary it so as to make provision for that matter.[130] Subject to that, the court may vary[131] or recall any section 11 order made by it notwithstanding that it would no longer have jurisdiction to make the original order.[132]

Application after final decree for, or for the variation or recall of, a section 11 order or in relation to the enforcement of such an order requires to be made by minute in the process of the action to which the application relates.[133] It is incompetent to proceed by way of a separate action.[134] Where a minute has been lodged, any party may apply by motion for any interim order which may be made pending the determination of the application.[135]

Where the court is asked to consider a variation of a section 11 order originally granted upon the parties' joint motion, it is of little value to look for a change of circumstances since the agreement was made.[136] The court is required to decide whether it is in the best interests of the child that the original order be varied or recalled.[137]

Prevention of removal of children

The sheriff may at any time after the commencement of proceedings, on an application by any of the following—

  (a) any party to the proceedings;
  (b) the guardian of the child concerned;
  (c) any other person who has or wishes to obtain the care of a child,

grant interdict or interim interdict prohibiting the removal of the child from the United Kingdom or any part thereof, or out of the control of

---

cease to have effect—1986 Act, s. 15(4), as amended by the Children (Scotland) Act 1995, Sched. 4, para. 41(4)(b) and Sched. 5.

[129] In the unlikely event of an order in relation to parental responsibility to provide guidance to the child (Children (Scotland) Act 1995, s. 1(1)(b)(ii)), the order would cease to have effect on the child's 18th birthday—1995 Act, s. 1(2)(b).

[130] 1986 Act, s. 15(2).

[131] An order varying an original order means any order made with respect to the same child as the original order was made—1986 Act, s. 15(3).

[132] 1986 Act, s. 15(2), subject to ss. 11(1) and 13(4).

[133] r. 33.44(1) or r. 33A.41(1).

[134] *McEwen v. McEwen*, 2000 Fam. L.R. 116.

[135] r. 33.44(2) or r. 33A.41(2).

[136] *McGhee v. McGhee*, 1998 Fam. L.R. 122.

[137] *Thomson v. Thomson*, 2000 G.W.D. 23–874.

the person in whose care the child is.[138] Proceedings shall be held to commence when the warrant of citation is signed.[139]

An application by a party to the proceedings requires to be made by motion,[140] and by any other party by minute.[141] The application need not be served or intimated.[142]

Any such interdict or interim interdict automatically has effect in the rest of the United Kingdom.[143] The court granting the interdict or interim interdict may order the surrender of any United Kingdom passport issued to or containing particulars of the child.[144]

Maintenance of children

The Child Support Act 1991 allocates responsibility to the Child Maintenance and Enforcement Commission for the calculation of periodical maintenance payable by certain parents with respect to children of theirs who are not in their care.

The residual role of the court with respect to maintenance of children is prescribed by section 8 of the 1991 Act, in terms of which the court's powers are restricted to—

(a)   varying maintenance orders, where no maintenance calculation has been made, if the maintenance order has been made after a prescribed date or, where the order was made before the prescribed date, an exclusion in respect of existing maintenance orders applies;[145]

(b)   revoking maintenance orders;[146]

(c)   making maintenance orders in line with written agreements;[147]

---

[138] Family Law Act, 1986, s. 35(3) and (4), as amended by the Children (Scotland) Act 1995, Sched. 4, para. 41(8) and Sched. 5 and the Age of Legal Capacity (Scotland) Act 1991, Sched. 1, para. 47. *C.f.* Children (Scotland) Act 1995, s. 2(3), (6) and (7) (nobody entitled to remove child from, or retain child outwith, United Kingdom without consent of persons with parental rights). Interdict was refused in *S v. Q*, 2005 S.L.T. 53.

[139] 1986 Act, s. 35(5)(b).

[140] r. 33.24(1)(a) or r. 33A.25(1)(a).

[141] r. 33.24(1)(b) or r. 33A.25(1)(b).

[142] r. 33.24(2) or r. 33A.25(2).

[143] 1986 Act, s. 36.

[144] 1986 Act, s. 37(1). "United Kingdom passport" means a current passport issued by the Government of the United Kingdom—s. 37(2).

[145] 1991 Act, s. 8(1), (2), (3) and (3A), as amended by the Child Support, Pensions and Social Security Act 2000, Sched. 3, para. 11(2) and the Child Maintenance and Other Payments Act 2008, Sched. 3(1), para. 6 and Sched. 8, para. 1. The prescribed date is 3 March 2003 — the Child Support (Applications: Prescribed Date) Regulations 2003 (S.I. 2003 No. 194).

[146] 1991 Act, s. 8(4).

[147] 1991 Act, s. 8(5), as amended by the Child Support, Pensions and Social Security Act 2000, Sched. 3, para. 11(2) and given effect by the Child Support (Written Agreements) (Scotland) Order 1997 (S.I. 1997 No. 2943), para. 2.

(d) making maintenance orders where a maintenance calculation is in force, the non-resident parent's net weekly income exceeds a prescribed amount, and the court is satisfied that the circumstances of the case make it appropriate for the non-resident parent to make periodical payments in addition to the child support maintenance payable by him in accordance with the maintenance calculation;[148]

(e) making maintenance orders for some or all of the expenses incurred in connection with the provision of instruction at an educational establishment or training for a trade, profession or vocation;[149]

(f) making maintenance orders for some or all of the expenses attributable to a child's disability;[150] and

(g) making maintenance orders against a person with care of the child.[151]

A maintenance order, in the context of actions of divorce or dissolution of civil partnership, is any order for aliment or interim aliment under the Family Law (Scotland) Act 1985.[152]

The court which refuses a decree of divorce or dissolution of a civil partnership shall not, by virtue of such refusal, be prevented from making an order for aliment.[153]

An application for an order for aliment in an action of divorce or dissolution of civil partnership requires to be made by a crave in the initial writ or defences, as the case may be.[154] Where made by a person

---

[148] 1991 Act, s. 8(6). The prescribed amount is the figure referred to in paragraph 10(3) of Sched. 1 to the Child Support Act 1991, as substituted by the Child Support, Pensions and Social Security Act 2000, Sched. 1. This figure is £2,000 (calculated in accordance with regulations issued under para. 10(1) of that Schedule, *videlicet* the Child Support (Maintenance Calculations and Special Cases) Regulations 2000 (S.I. 2001 No. 155). The figure is subject to alteration by regulations issued under para. 10A(1)(b) of that Schedule.

[149] 1991 Act, s. 8(7). An adult training centre attended by a handicapped child was held to be an educational establishment for the purposes of s. 8(7) in *McBride v. McBride*, 1995 S.C.L.R. 1021.

[150] 1991 Act, s. 8(8). For the purposes of subs. (8), a child is disabled if he is blind, deaf or dumb or is substantially and permanently handicapped by illness, injury, mental disorder or congenital deformity or such other disability as may be prescribed—1991 Act, s. 8(9).

[151] 1991 Act, s. 8(10).

[152] 1991 Act, s. 8(11)(d) and Family Law (Scotland) Act 1985, ss. 1(1)(c) and (d), 2(2)(a) and (aa) and 6(1)(b) and (c).

[153] Family Law (Scotland) Act 1985, s. 21, as amended by the Children (Scotland) Act 1995, Sched. 5 and the Civil Partnership Act 2004, Sched. 28, para. 25.

[154] r. 33.39(1)(a) and (2)(b) or r. 33A.39(1)(a) and (2)(b).

other than the pursuer or defender, the application must be by minute in the action.[155] A person—

(a) to whom an obligation of aliment is owed under section 1 of the Family Law (Scotland) Act 1985;

(b) in whose favour an order for aliment while under the age of 18 years was made in the action of divorce or dissolution of civil partnership; and

(c) who seeks, after attaining that age, an order for aliment against the person in that action against whom the order for aliment in his favour was made,

must apply by minute in the process of that action.[156]

In any action in which an order for aliment is sought, or is sought to be varied or recalled, the pleadings of the applicant must include an averment stating whether and, if so, when and by whom, a maintenance order (within the meaning of section 106 of the Debtors (Scotland) Act 1987) has been granted in favour of or against that party or of any other person in respect of whom the order is sought.[157]

An action containing a crave relating to aliment to which section 8(6), (7), (8) or (10) of the Child Support Act 1991 applies must—

(a) include averments stating, where appropriate—

(i) that a maintenance calculation under section 11 of the 1991 Act (maintenance calculations) is in force;

(ii) the date of the maintenance calculation;

(iii) the amount and frequency of periodical payments of child support maintenance fixed by the maintenance calculation; and

(iv) the grounds on which the sheriff retains jurisdiction under section 8(6), (7), (8) or (10) of the Act; and

(b) unless the sheriff on cause shown otherwise directs, be accompanied by any document issued by the Secretary of State to the party intimating the making of the foregoing maintenance calculation.[158]

An action containing a crave relating to aliment to which section 8(6), (7), (8) or (10) of the Child Support Act 1991 does not apply must include averments stating—

---

[155] r. 33.39(1)(b) and (2)(b) or r. 33A.39(1)(b) and (2)(b).
[156] r. 33.46(1) or r. 33A.43(1).
[157] r. 33.5 or r. 33A.5.
[158] r. 33.6(2) or r. 33A.6(2). As to s. 8(6), (7), (8) and (10) of the 1991 Act, see nn. 148–151 and accompanying text, *supra*.

(a) that the habitual residence of the absent parent, person with care or qualifying child within the meaning of section 3 of the 1991 Act is furth of the United Kingdom; or

(b) that the child is not a child within the meaning of section 55 of that Act.[159]

An action involving parties in respect of whom a decision has been made in any application, review or appeal under the Child Support Act 1991 relating to any child of those parties must—

(a) include averments stating that such a decision has been made and giving details of that decision; and

(b) unless the sheriff on cause shown otherwise directs, be accompanied by any document issued by the Secretary of State to the parties intimating that decision.[160]

Any application by a party in an action depending before the court for, or for variation of, an order for interim aliment for a child under the age of 18 years must be made by motion.[161] Any application for interim aliment by a person over 18 years for aliment pending the determination of an application for aliment must also be made by motion.[162]

Where any parties have reached agreement in relation to aliment for a child, a joint minute may be entered into expressing that agreement, and the sheriff may grant decree in respect of those parts of the joint minute in relation to which he could otherwise make an order, whether or not such a decree would include a matter for which there was no crave.[163]

Where an application is made after final decree for, or for the variation or recall of, an order for aliment for a child, it must be made by minute in the process of the action to which the application

---

[159] r. 33.6(3) or r. 33A.6(3). A child is a "qualifying child" within the meaning of s. 3 of the 1991 Act if – (a) one of his parents is, in relation to him, an absent parent; or (b) both of his parents are, in relation to him, absent parents— 1991 Act, s. 3(1). A person is a child within the meaning of s. 55 of the 1991 Act if – (a) he is under the age of 16; (b) he is under the age of 19 and receiving full-time education (which is not advanced education) – (i) by attendance at a recognised educational establishment; or (ii) elsewhere, if the education is recognised by the Secretary of State; or (c) he does not fall within para. (a) or (b) but – (i) he is under the age of 18, and (ii) prescribed conditions are satisfied with respect to him; but a person is not a child for the purposes of the Act if he is or has been married or a civil partner— 1991 Act, s. 55(1) and (2), as amended by the Civil Partnership Act 2004, Sched. 24, para. 3.

[160] r. 33.6(5) or r. 33A.6(5).

[161] r. 33.43(a) or r. 33A.40(a).

[162] r. 33.46(2) or r. 33A.43(2).

[163] r. 33.26(b) or r. 33A.27(b).

relates.[164] Any application for variation or recall of a decree for aliment requires that there has since the date of decree been a material change of circumstances.[165] Without prejudice to this generality, the making of a maintenance calculation with respect to a child for whom the decree of aliment was granted is a material change of circumstances for these purposes.[166]

The court has power to backdate any variation or recall of a decree for aliment to the date of the application for variation or recall or, on special cause shown, to a date prior to the making of the application, and in the event of backdating may require any sums paid under the decree to be repaid.[167] On an application for variation or recall of a decree, the court may, pending determination of the application, make such order as it thinks fit.[168]

Reference to the Principal Reporter

In terms of section 54(1) of the Children (Scotland) Act 1995, where it appears to the court that any of certain statutory conditions is satisfied with respect to a child, it may refer the matter to the Principal Reporter, specifying the condition.[169] This however can only be done where the relevant facts have been admitted or proved.[170] The statutory conditions are included in section 52(2) of the 1995 Act,[171] namely that the child—

    (a) is beyond the control of any relevant person;
    (b) is falling into bad associations or is exposed to moral danger;
    (c) is likely (i) to suffer unnecessarily; or (ii) be impaired in his health or development, due to a lack of parental care;

---

[164] rr. 33.45(1) and 33.46(3) or rr. 33A.42(1) and 33A.43(3). Note that any application for variation or recall of an order for aliment for a child must be made while the obligation to aliment still exists—*Paterson v. Paterson*, 2002 S.L.T. (Sh. Ct.) 65.

[165] Family Law (Scotland) Act 1985, s. 5(1).

[166] 1985 Act, s. 5(1A), as inserted by the Child Support (Amendments to Primary Legislation) (Scotland) Order 1993 (1993 S.I. No. 660 (S. 98)) and amended by the Child Support, Pensions and Social Security Act 2000, Sched. 3, para. 5(2).

[167] 1985 Act, ss. 3(1)(c) and 5(2) and (4). See *e.g. Hannah v. Hannah*, 1988 S.L.T. 82; *Dalgleish v. Robinson*, 1991 S.C.L.R. 892; *Mitchell v. Mitchell*, 1992 S.C.L.R. 553.

[168] 1985 Act, s. 5(3). Any party may lodge a motion for any interim order which may be made pending the determination of the application — r. 33.45(2) or r. 33A.42(2).

[169] The interlocutor making the reference must be intimated by the sheriff clerk forthwith to the Principal Reporter, the intimation specifying which of the conditions it appears to the sheriff has been satisfied—r. 33.93 or r. 33A.77. As to procedure thereafter, see r. 33.94 or r. 33A.78 (intimation of decision by Principal Reporter).

[170] *A v. B*, 2011 S.L.T. (Sh. Ct.) 131.

[171] As amended by the Criminal Procedure (Consequential Provisions) (Scotland) Act 1995, Sched. 4, para. 97 and the Adoption and Children (Scotland) Act 2007 (Modification of Enactments) Order 2010 (S.S.I. 2010 No. 21), Sched. 1, para. 5.

(d) is a child in respect of whom any of the offences mentioned in Schedule 1 to the Criminal Procedure (Scotland) Act 1995 (offences against children to which special provisions apply) has been committed;

(e) is, or is likely to become, a member of the same household as a child in respect of whom any of the offences referred to in paragraph (d) above has been committed;

(f) is, or is likely to become, a member of the same household as a person who has committed any of the offences referred to in paragraph (d) above;

(g) or is likely to become, a member of the same household as a person in respect of whom an offence under sections 1 to 3 of the Criminal Law (Consolidation) (Scotland) Act 1995 (incest and intercourse with a child by step-parent or person in position of trust) has been committed by a member of that household;

(h) has failed to attend school regularly without reasonable excuse . . .

(j) has misused alcohol or any drug, whether or not a controlled drug within the meaning of the Misuse of Drugs Act 1971;

(k) has misused a volatile substance by deliberately inhaling its vapour, other than for medicinal purposes;

(l) is being provided with accommodation by a local authority under section 25 of the 1995 Act, or is the subject of a permanence order made under section 80 of the Adoption and Children (Scotland) Act 2007 and, in either case, his behaviour is such that special measures are necessary for his adequate supervision in his interest or in the interest of others.

Where the court has referred a matter to the Principal Reporter under section 54(1) he must—

(a) make such investigations as he thinks appropriate; and

(b) if he considers that compulsory measures of supervision[172] are necessary, arrange a children's hearing to consider the case of the child under section 69 of the 1995 Act, and section 54(1) applies as if the condition specified by the court thereunder were a ground of referral established in accordance with section 68 of that Act.[173]

---

[172] "Supervision" in relation to compulsory measures of supervision may include measures taken for the protection, treatment or control of the child—1995 Act, s. 52(3).

[173] 1995 Act, s. 54(3).

Restriction of publicity concerning children

Section 46(1) of the Children and Young Persons (Scotland) Act 1937[174] provides:

> "In relation to any proceedings, the court may direct that—
>
> (a) no newspaper report of the proceedings shall reveal the name, address, or school, or include any particulars calculated to lead to the identification, of a person under the age of seventeen years concerned in the proceedings, either as being the person by or against or in respect of whom the proceedings are taken,[175] or as being a witness therein;
>
> (b) no picture shall be published in any newspaper as being or including a picture of any child or young person so concerned in the proceedings as aforesaid;
>
> except in so far (if at all) as may be permitted by the direction of the court."

Any person who publishes any matter in contravention of any such direction is liable to be convicted under the Act.[176] The foregoing applies, with the necessary modifications, in relation to sound and television broadcasts as it applies in relation to newspapers.[177]

---

[174] As amended by the Children and Young Persons Act 1963, s. 57(1) and the Social Work (Scotland) Act 1968, Sched. 2, para. 7.

[175] An order directing the media not to publish details which might identify a young child who was the subject of custody and access proceedings was granted in *C v. S*, 1989 S.C. 1.

[176] Children and Young Persons (Scotland) Act 1937, s. 46(2).

[177] Children and Young Persons (Scotland) Act 1963, s. 57(4).

CHAPTER 7

MONEY

The subject of money in the context of the law and practice relating to divorce and dissolution of civil partnership (excepting maintenance for children) is discussed in this chapter; and the court's power to make orders relative to the subject before, upon and after the granting of decree are examined in turn.

ORDERS MADE BEFORE THE GRANTING OF DECREE

Pending final disposal of an action of divorce or dissolution of civil partnership the court may make interim orders under the Family Law (Scotland) Act 1985, including interim aliment orders, incidental orders *pendente lite* and orders for the provision to the court by a party of details of his or her resources.

Interim aliment orders

A claim for interim aliment is competent in an action of divorce or dissolution of civil partnership by either party against the other in terms of section 6 of the Family Law (Scotland) Act 1985.[1]

Whether or not the claim is disputed, the court may award the sum claimed or any lesser sum or may refuse to make an award.[2] An award of interim aliment must consist of an award of periodical payments payable only until the date of the disposal of the action or such earlier date as the court may specify.[3] In the event of any appeal, the date of disposal of the action is the date upon which the appeal is determined.[4] It is incompetent to backdate an award of interim aliment.[5]

Application for interim aliment must be made by motion.[6] In deciding what award of interim aliment (if any) to make, the court may have regard to the criteria set out in section 4 of the Act, which

---

[1] Family Law (Scotland) Act 1985, s. 6(1)(b) and (c), as amended by the Civil Partnership Act 2004, Sched. 28, para. 13.
[2] 1985 Act, s. 6(2).
[3] 1985 Act, s. 6(3).
[4] *Lessani v. Lessani*, 2007 Fam. L.R. 81.
[5] *Kirk v. Kirk*, 2003 Fam. L.R. 50; *Adamson v. Adamson*, 1996 S.L.T. 427.
[6] r. 33.50 or r. 33A.47.

relates to claims for aliment.[7] Accordingly, the needs and resources of the parties, their respective earning capacities, and generally all the circumstances of the case are proper elements to consider in relation to a claim for interim aliment.[8]

With respect to earning capacity, the court can reasonably expect the parties to produce documentary evidence of their respective net incomes.[9] Both the benefits of a company car and payment by the company of pension contributions constitute resources that ought to be taken into account, at least to the extent that the recipient's cash income is thereby not subject to such outlays.[10] Likewise, a cohabitant's earnings are relevant where the defender claims deductions from his salary to be taken into account that include provisions for a home that he shares with another person with an income.[11] Child tax credit, which is unaffected by interim aliment payments, falls to be regarded as a resource in the hands of the recipient.[12] Any spouse or civil partner who cohabits with a third party cannot expect to obtain an award of interim aliment.[13]

Awards of interim aliment are within the discretion of the judge of first instance and an appellate court could only interfere if it were to be satisfied that the sheriff had erred in law, or that he had failed to notice a relevant factor, or that he had taken into account an irrelevant consideration, or that he had arrived at a wholly unreasonable decision or one that was plainly wrong.[14] An appeal without leave of the sheriff against an award of interim aliment or the refusal of an application for interim aliment is incompetent.[15] The position is otherwise if the sheriff's interlocutor is itself incompetent.[16]

An award of interim aliment may be varied or recalled by an order of the court.[17] Application for such variation or recall in a depending action must be made by motion.[18] A motion for variation or recall

---

[7] *McGeachie v. McGeachie*, 1989 S.C.L.R. 99 at p. 100.
[8] *Ibid. C.f. McGeoch v. McGeoch*, 1998 Fam. L.R. 130 (wealthy parties).
[9] *C.f. Wiseman v. Wiseman*, 1989 S.C.L.R. 757 and *Pryde v. Pryde*, 1991 S.L.T. (Sh. Ct.) 26.
[10] *Semple v. Semple*, 1995 S.C.L.R. 569.
[11] *Munro v. Munro*, 1986 S.L.T. 72.
[12] *Dupuy v. Dupuy*, 2010 Fam. L.R. 19.
[13] *Brunton v. Brunton*, 1986 S.L.T. 49.
[14] *Begg v. Begg*, 1987 S.C.L.R. 704 at p. 705; *Adams v. Adams*, 2002 S.C.L.R. 379 at p. 380.
[15] *Rixson v. Rixson*, 1990 S.L.T. (Sh. Ct.) 5; *Hulme v. Hulme*, 1990 S.L.T. (Sh. Ct.) 25; *Dickson v. Dickson*, 1990 S.L.T. (Sh. Ct.) 80; *Richardson v. Richardson*, 1991 S.L.T. (Sh. Ct.) 7.
[16] *Kirk v. Kirk*, 2003 Fam. L.R. 50.
[17] 1985 Act, s. 6(4).
[18] r. 33.50 or r. 33A.47.

may be granted without a change of circumstances having been established.[19] There must however be a sufficient reason to justify a variation or recall.[20] The making of a maintenance calculation in respect of any child of the parties could be such a reason.[21] The court's powers in relation to an application for variation or recall of interim aliment are the same as in the case of an application for interim aliment.[22] It is incompetent to backdate the variation or recall of an order for interim aliment.[23]

Incidental orders *pendente lite*

In terms of section 14(1) of the Family Law (Scotland) Act 1985[24] certain incidental orders may be made under section 8(2) of the Act before the granting or refusal of decree of divorce or dissolution of civil partnership.

The incidental orders in question are listed in section 14(2)(a) to (c) and (f) to (k) of the Act, detailed below. Incidental orders exist to facilitate the making of the main orders of capital payment, transfer of property, periodical allowance and pension sharing.[25] An incidental order *pendente lite* for the sale of a jointly owned matrimonial home or family home by a party not craving any financial provision is therefore incompetent.[26] The power to make orders before the granting or refusal of decree has content in a situation of regulation or reorganisation prior to examination of the parties' whole affairs by the court.[27] However, while the court may make an incidental order for the sale of the matrimonial home or family home *pendente lite*, it has no power to order vacant possession at that stage.[28] An incidental order for the valuation of a property is incompetent where the property in question does not belong to the parties or either of them.[29]

---

[19] *Bisset v. Bisset*, 1993 S.C.L.R. 284 at p. 287.

[20] *Ibid.* at p. 288.

[21] *Stokes v. Stokes*, 1999 S.C.L.R. 327. *C.f.* 1985 Act, s. 13(4A), as inserted by the Child Support (Amendments to Primary Legislation) (Scotland) Order 1993 (S.I. 1993 No. 660), art. 2(4) and amended by the Child Support, Pensions and Social Security Act 2000, Sched. 3, para. 5(4).

[22] 1985 Act, s. 6(4).

[23] *McColl v. McColl*, 1993 S.C. 276.

[24] As amended by the Civil Partnership Act 2004, Sched. 28, para. 21(2).

[25] *Amin v. Amin*, 2000 S.L.T. (Sh. Ct.) 115.

[26] *MacClue v. MacClue*, 1994 S.C.L.R. 933.

[27] *Amin v. Amin*, 2000 S.L.T. (Sh. Ct.) 115.

[28] *Adams v. Adams*, 2010 S.L.T. (Sh. Ct.) 2.

[29] *Demarco v. Demarco*, 1990 S.C.L.R. 635 (order for valuation of property owned by company of which husband a shareholder refused).

Section 14 of the 1985 Act gives the court a discretionary power to be exercised in the circumstances of each case.[30] An incidental order *pendente lite* may be regarded by the court as premature and refused on that basis.[31] Application for an incidental order *pendente lite* may be made by motion, but the sheriff is not bound to determine such a motion if he considers that the application should properly be by a crave in the initial writ or defences, as the case may be.[32]

An incidental order *pendente lite* may be varied or recalled by subsequent order on cause shown.[33] Application for such variation or recall in a depending action must be made by minute in the process of the action to which the application relates.[34]

Orders for provision of details of resources

By virtue of section 20 of the Family Law (Scotland) Act 1985, the court may order either party to provide details of his resources.[35]

The power may be exercised even where there is no suggestion that the party called upon to provide details is in some way concealing some resource.[36] If the party so called upon fails to provide details of his present and foreseeable resources he will be in contempt of an order of court.[37] Section 20 does not however give the court power to conduct an inquiry as to the extent of the disclosure.[38]

In order to fulfil his obligation, the party ordered must provide a figure for the value of each item of property but does not require to produce documentation vouching the figure.[39] The sheriff is entitled to seek clarification of matters in any list of resources and may appoint the solicitor for the party concerned to appear personally before him.[40] It remains for the party claiming a specific financial provision to formulate and prove the entitlement.[41]

---

[30]   *McKeown v. McKeown*, 1988 S.C.L.R. 355.
[31]   *Ibid.*
[32]   r. 33.49(1) or r. 33A.46(1).
[33]   1985 Act, s. 14(4).
[34]   r. 33.49(2) or r. 33A.46(2).
[35]   "Resources" means present and foreseeable resources — 1985 Act, s. 27(1).
[36]   *Lawrence v. Lawrence*, 1992 S.C.L.R. 199.
[37]   *Nelson v. Nelson*, 1993 S.C.L.R. 149.
[38]   *Ibid.*
[39]   *Ibid.*
[40]   *Ibid.*
[41]   *Williamson v. Williamson*, 1989 S.L.T. 866 at p. 867.

ORDERS MADE UPON THE GRANTING OF DECREE

When granting decree of divorce or dissolution of civil partnership the court may make one or more orders under section 8 of the Family Law (Scotland) Act 1985, such an order being referred to in the Act as "an order for financial provision".[42] The court also has power under section 16 of the 1985 Act to make an order setting aside or varying an agreement on financial provision.

As regards orders for financial provision, section 8(1) of the Act[43] provides that in an action for divorce, either party to the marriage and in an action for dissolution of a civil partnership, either partner may apply to the court for one or more of the following orders —

   (a)   an order for the payment of a capital sum to him by the other party to the action [capital sum order];

   (b)   an order for the payment of a pension lump sum towards discharge of liability under a capital sum order;

   (c)   an order for the payment of pension compensation towards discharge of liability under a capital sum order;

   (d)   an order for the transfer of property to him by the other party to the action [transfer of property order];

   (e)   a pension sharing order;

   (f)   a pension compensation sharing order;

   (g)   an order for the payment of a periodical allowance to him by the other party to the action [periodical allowance order]; and

   (h)   an incidental order.

These orders are now discussed, bearing in mind that no one method by which financial provision may be made has a preference over any other.[44] Thereafter, orders under section 16 of the 1985 Act relating to agreements on financial provision are considered.

Whether the order sought is under section 8 or section 16 of the Act, Rule 33.51A or Rule 33A.48A (Pension Protection Fund notification) applies.[45]

---

[42] 1985 Act, s. 8(3).

[43] As variously amended and inserted by the Law Reform (Miscellaneous Provisions) (Scotland) Act 1990, Sched. 8, para. 34 and Sched. 9, the Pensions Act 1995, s. 167(1), the Welfare Reform and Pensions Act 1999, Sched. 12, para. 6, the Civil Partnership Act 2004, Sched. 28, para. 14(2) and the Pensions Act 2008, Sched. 7, para. 2.

[44] *Christie v. Christie*, 2004 S.L.T. (Sh. Ct.) 95; *McKinnon v. McKinnon*, 2008 Fam. L.R. 25.

[45] Where a party at any stage in the proceedings applies for an order under s. 8 or s. 16, and the party against whom the order is sought has received notification in compliance with the Pension Protection Fund (Provision of Information) Regulations 2005 or does so after the order is sought that there is an assessment period in relation to his pension

Capital sum orders

The court may make an order for payment of a capital sum to one party to a marriage, or one civil partner, by the other under section 8(2) of the 1985 Act —

(a) on granting decree of divorce or of dissolution of a civil partnership; or

(b) within such period as the court on granting decree may specify.[46]

The court has power to stipulate that a capital sum order will come into effect at a specified future date.[47] Such might, for example, be wholly or partly after the expected date of sale of the matrimonial home or family home,[48] the date of vesting of the liable person's pension entitlement,[49] the likely date of conclusion of the liable person's sequestration,[50] or the date of death of the liable person.[51] Payment of a capital sum may also be deferred in whole or in part to give the liable party time to put together the necessary funding.[52]

The court may, on making a capital sum order, order that the capital sum will be payable by instalments.[53] Instalment payments may well be appropriate when the capital asset concerned is an income-generating

---

arrangement or that the Board of the Pension Protection Fund has assumed responsibility for all or part of his pension arrangement, he must lodge the notification and obtain and lodge as soon as reasonably practicable thereafter (i) a valuation summary; and (ii) a forecast of his compensation entitlement—r. 33.51A(1) – (4) or r. 33A.48A(1) – (4). Where the notification is received before the order is sought, it requires to be lodged within 7 days of the order being sought; where the notification is received after the order is sought, it must be lodged within 7 days of the notification being received— r. 33.51A(5) or r. 33A.48A(5). Where an order is sought against the defender before the defences are lodged, and the notification is received before that step occurs, the notification must be lodged with the defences—r. 33.51A(6) or r. 33A.48A(6). At the same time as lodging the valuation summary and forecast, copies must be sent to the other party to the proceedings—r. 33.51A(7) or r. 33A.48A(7).

[46] 1985 Act, s. 12(1), as amended by the 2004 Act, Sched. 28, para. 18(2). As to s. 12(1) (b), see text accompanying nn. 297–300, *infra*.

[47] 1985 Act, ss. 8(1) and (2) and 12(2), as amended by the 2004 Act, Sched. 28, para. 14(2).

[48] *Little v. Little*, 1990 S.L.T. 785.

[49] *Dorrian v. Dorrian*, 1991 S.C.L.R. 661; *Gulline v. Gulline*, 1992 S.L.T. (Sh. Ct.) 71; *Bannon v. Bannon*, 1993 S.L.T. 999; *Gracie v. Gracie*, 1997 S.L.T. (Sh. Ct.) 15.

[50] *Shand v. Shand*, 1994 S.L.T. 387.

[51] *Collins v. Collins*, 1997 Fam. L.R. 50.

[52] *Watt v. Watt*, 2009 S.L.T. 931.

[53] 1985 Act, s. 12(3). Payment by instalments was ordered in, *e.g., Bell v. Bell*, 1988 S.C.L.R. 457; *Buckle v. Buckle*, 1995 S.C.L.R. 590; *Gracie v. Gracie*, 1997 S.L.T. (Sh. Ct.) 15; *McEwan v. McEwan*, 1997 S.L.T. 118; *McHugh v. McHugh*, 2001 Fam. L.R. 30; *Carrol v. Carrol*, 2003 Fam. L.R. 108; *Sweeney v. Sweeney (No. 2)*, 2006 S.C. 82.

asset.[54] Where there is no such capital asset, for the court to require capital to be created by payment of instalments arising out of income would be quite wrong and contrary to the intention of the Family Law (Scotland) Act 1985 as this would merely establish a requirement to pay a periodical allowance for a very extended period but under another name.[55]

Application for a capital sum order must be made by a crave in the initial writ or defences, as the case may be.[56] Where any such application has been made, the court must make such order, if any, as is:

(a) justified by the principles set out in section 9 of the Family Law (Scotland) Act 1985; and

(b) reasonable having regard to the resources of the parties.[57]

Paragraphs (a) and (b) above are cumulative with the result that unless both are satisfied, the court has no power to make an order.[58] Accordingly, paragraph (b) can only operate to cut down any sum otherwise justified by the principles set out in section 9 of the Act, having regard to the resources of the parties.[59] However, the nature and value of the assets comprised in the matrimonial property or partnership property at the relevant date are assumed to remain substantially the same at the date of proof unless and until the contrary is averred and proved.[60]

Section 9(1) of the Act[61] specifies the principles that the court must apply in deciding what order for financial provision, if any, to make. These are —

(a) the net value of the matrimonial property should be shared fairly between the parties to the marriage or as the case may be the net value of the partnership property should be so shared between the partners in the civil partnership;

---

[54] *Dorrian v. Dorrian*, 1991 S.C.L.R. 661 at p. 663.

[55] *Ibid.*

[56] r. 33.48(1)(a) and (2)(a) or r. 33A.45(1)(a) and (2)(a). *C.f. Muir v. Muir,* 1994 S.C.L.R. 178 (application not entertained in absence of crave).

[57] 1985 Act, s. 8(2). "Resources" means present and foreseeable resources (s. 27(1)) and are not limited to capital resources — *Cunniff v. Cunniff,* 1999 S.C. 537 at p. 541. See also App. VIII, *infra.*

[58] *Wallis v. Wallis*, 1993 S.C. (H.L.) 49 at p. 56. See, *e.g., Sweeney v. Sweeney (No. 2)*, 2006 S.C. 82.

[59] *Latter v. Latter*, 1990 S.L.T. 805 at p. 807. *C.f. McVinnie v. McVinnie (No. 2),* 1997 S.L.T. (Sh. Ct.) 12.

[60] *Fulton v. Fulton*, 2000 Fam. L.R. 8. *C.f. Fraser v. Fraser,* 2002 Fam. L.R. 53.

[61] As amended by the Civil Partnership Act 2004, Sched. 28, para. 15(2) and the Human Fertilisation and Embryology Act 2008, Sched. 6, para. 46.

(b) fair account should be taken of any economic advantage derived by either person from contributions from the other, and of any economic disadvantage suffered by either person in the interests of the other person or of the family;

(c) any economic burden of caring should be shared fairly between the persons—
  (i) after divorce, for a child of the marriage under the age of 16 years;
  (ii) after dissolution of civil partnership, for a child under that age who has been accepted by both partners as a child of the family or in respect of whom they are, by virtue of sections 33 and 42 of the Human Fertilisation and Embryology Act 2008, the parents;

(d) a person who has been dependent to a substantial degree on the financial support of the other person should be awarded such financial provision as is reasonable to enable him to adjust, over a period of not more than three years from,
  (i) the date of the decree of divorce, to the loss of that support on divorce;
  (ii) the date of the decree of dissolution of the civil partnership, to the loss of that support on dissolution;

(e) a person who at the time of the divorce or the dissolution of the civil partnership seems likely to suffer serious financial hardship as a result of the divorce or dissolution should be awarded such financial provision as is reasonable to relieve him of hardship over a reasonable period.

These five principles are now considered in more detail.

Section 9(1)(a):

> "the net value of the matrimonial property should be shared fairly between the parties to the marriage or as the case may be the net value of the partnership property should be so shared between the partners in the civil partnership."[62]

It is convenient to break down this principle into its component parts, as follows:

(1) "the matrimonial property/the partnership property";
(2) "the net value";
(3) "shared fairly".

---

[62] Cases in which the principle in s. 9(1)(a) was considered are listed in App. VII, *infra.*

(1) *The matrimonial property* or *the partnership property* is all the property belonging to the parties or either of them at the relevant date which was acquired by them or him (otherwise than by way of gift or succession from a third party)—

(a) before the marriage, or the registration of the civil partnership, for use by them as a family home[63] or as furniture or plenishings for such a home, or

(b) during the marriage, or civil partnership, but before the relevant date.[64]

"Property", as used in the principle, may be heritable or moveable in nature.[65] It must fall within paragraph (a) or (b) above to be classed matrimonial property or partnership property.

Thus, for example, a claim for damages in respect of an accident occurring during the marriage or civil partnership but before the relevant date is matrimonial property or partnership property.[66] A claim for a refund in respect of income tax deducted during the marriage or civil partnership but before the relevant date is matrimonial property or partnership property.[67] The proportion of any rights or interests of either person—

(a) under a life policy or similar arrangement; and

(b) in any benefits under a pension arrangement[68] which either person has or may have (including such benefits payable in respect of the death of either person),

which is referable to the period specified in section 10(4)(b) of the 1985 Act (*i.e.* during the marriage, or civil partnership, but before 'the relevant date), is taken to form part of the matrimonial property or partnership property.[69] Where either person is entitled to PPF compensation,[70] the proportion of the compensation which is referable

---

[63] *C.f. Maclellan v. Maclellan,* 1988 S.C.L.R. 399 (croft tenancy); *Mitchell v. Mitchell,* 1994 S.C. 601 (matrimonial home in parties' previous marriage).

[64] 1985 Act, s. 10(4), and (4A), as inserted by the Civil Partnership Act 2004, Sched. 28, para. 16(5) and amended by the Family Law (Scotland) Act 2006, s. 17(3)(a).

[65] *Petrie v. Petrie,* 1988 S.C.L.R. 390

[66] *Skarpaas v. Skarpaas,* 1993 S.L.T. 343; *Carrol v. Carrol,* 2003 Fam. L.R. 108. *C.f. Petrie v. Petrie,* 1988 S.C.L.R. 390.

[67] *MacRitchie v. MacRitchie,* 1994 S.L.T. (Sh. Ct.) 72.

[68] "Benefits under a pension arrangement" includes any benefits by way of pension, including relevant state scheme rights, whether under a pension arrangement or not—1985 Act, s. 27(1), as inserted by the Welfare Reform and Pensions Act 1999, Sched. 12, para. 12.

[69] 1985 Act, s. 10(5), as amended by the Pensions Act 1995, s. 167(2)(a), the Welfare Reform and Pensions Act 1999, Sched. 12, para. 8(1) and (2), the Civil Partnership Act 2004, Sched. 28, para. 16(6) and the Family Law (Scotland) Act 2006, s. 17(3)(b).

[70] "PPF compensation" means compensation payable under the pension compensation

to the aforesaid period is taken to form part of the matrimonial property or partnership property.[71] The assets of a trust operated as a means of managing assets for the sole benefit of a party to the action may be regarded as matrimonial property or partnership property.[72]

On the other hand, property belonging to a company in which a party to the action has a controlling interest does not fall within the definition of matrimonial property or partnership property.[73] Heritable property of a firm, even where held in the name of individual partners of the firm ostensibly as individuals, also falls outwith the definition.[74] A hypothetical interest in the goodwill of a firm's business that could not be realised at the party's own hand is not matrimonial property or partnership property.[75] A bonus issue of shares issued after the marriage or civil partnership in proportion to existing holdings that predated the marriage or civil partnership is not matrimonial property or partnership property.[76] The uplift in value after the marriage or civil partnership of a shareholding that predated the marriage or civil partnership is not matrimonial property or partnership property.[77] An entitlement under a single farm payment scheme that did not come into force until after the relevant date is not matrimonial property or partnership property.[78] A redundancy payment received after the relevant date is not matrimonial property or partnership property.[79]

In relation to the phrase "acquired by them or him", when funds that represent one party's pre-matrimonial property or pre-partnership property, or a gift or succession from a third party, are paid into a joint bank account, this does not mean that the funds are "acquired" during the marriage; the funds remain pre-matrimonial property or pre-partnership property or property acquired by gift or succession from a third party, as the case may be.[80]

---

provisions (*viz.* Chap. 3 of Pt. 2 of the Pensions Act 2004 and any regulations or order made under it, Chap. 1 of Pt. 3 of the Pensions Act 2008 and any regulations or order made under it, or any provision corresponding to the foregoing in force in Northern Ireland)—1985 Act, s. 27(1C), as inserted by the Pensions Act 2008, Sched. 7, para. 9.

[71]　1985 Act, s. 10(5A), as inserted by the Family Law (Scotland) Act 2006, s. 17(3)(c), and amended by the Pensions Act 2008, Sched. 7, para. 4(a).

[72]　*AB v. CD*, 2007 Fam. L.R. 53.

[73]　*Wilson v. Wilson*, 1999 S.L.T. 249.

[74]　*Marshall v. Marshall*, 2007 Fam. L.R. 48.

[75]　*Rose v. Rose*, 1998 S.L.T. (Sh. Ct.) 56.

[76]　*Whittome v. Whittome (No. 1)*, 1994 S.L.T. 114. *C.f. Latter v. Latter,* 1990 S.L.T. 805 (shares issued on company reconstruction derived from gifted shares whereby party's proportionate interest in underlying assets was altered were matrimonial property).

[77]　*Whittome v. Whittome (No. 1)*, 1994 S.L.T. 114.

[78]　*Simpson v. Simpson*, 2007 Fam. L.R. 134.

[79]　*Smith v. Smith*, 1989 S.L.T. 668; *Tyrrell v. Tyrrell*, 1990 S.L.T. 406.

[80]　*Willson v. Willson*, 2009 Fam. L.R. 18.

With respect to the phrase "by way of gift or succession from a third party", the onus of proof in relation to any claim that a particular item of property was so acquired lies on the party so claiming.[81] A gift is "a transfer of property in a thing, voluntarily and without any valuable consideration" and may therefore include a gift effected through the medium of a trust.[82] Property may be matrimonial property or partnership property notwithstanding that it was acquired wholly or partly by means of a gift of money or shares from a third party.[83]

As regards the term "the relevant date", section 10(3) and (7) of the 1985 Act[84] defines it as whichever is the earlier of—

  (a) the date on which the persons ceased to cohabit (but no account is to be taken of any cessation of cohabitation where the persons thereafter resumed cohabitation except where the persons ceased to cohabit for a continuous period of 90 days or more before resuming cohabitation for a period of less than 90 days in all); or

  (b) the date of service of the summons in the action for divorce or for dissolution of civil partnership.

The question of when the parties ceased to cohabit is one of fact to be determined, at least in divorce actions, under reference to section 27(2) of the Act, which provides:

> "For the purposes of this Act, the parties to a marriage shall be held to cohabit with one another only when they are in fact living together as man and wife."[85]

(2) *The net value* of the matrimonial property or the partnership property is the value of the property at the relevant date after deduction of any debts incurred by one or both of the parties to the marriage or as the case may be of the partners—

  (a) before the marriage so far as they relate to the matrimonial property or before the registration of the civil partnership so far as they relate to the partnership property; and

  (b) during the marriage or partnership,

which are outstanding at that date.[86]

---

[81] *Wilson v. Wilson*, 1999 S.L.T. 249; *MacLean v. MacLean*, 2001 Fam. L.R. 118.

[82] *Whittome v. Whittome (No 1)*, 1994 S.L.T. 114 at p. 122.

[83] *Latter v. Latter*, 1990 S.L.T. 805; *Fulton v. Fulton*, 2000 Fam. L.R. 8.

[84] As amended by the Civil Partnership Act 2004, Sched. 28, para. 16(4) and (8).

[85] See, *e.g., Buczynska v. Buczynski*, 1989 S.L.T. 558; *Brown v. Brown*, 1998 Fam. L.R. 81; *Banks v. Banks*, 2005 Fam. L.R. 116; *Bain v. Bain*, 2008 Fam. L.R. 81.

[86] 1985 Act, s. 10(2), as amended by the Civil Partnership Act 2004, Sched. 28, para. 16(3) and the Family Law (Scotland) Act 2006, s. 16.

With regard to debts incurred by one or both of the parties to the marriage or as the case may be of the partners, the onus of proof in relation to any claim that a particular debt was outstanding at the relevant date lies on the party so claiming.[87] Income tax due on income earned up to the relevant date but not payable until after that date is a debt outstanding at the relevant date.[88] A contingent tax liability should not however be brought into account by way of deduction from the net value of matrimonial property or partnership property.[89] Likewise, a contingent liability to repay a proportion of the discount of the purchase price of the matrimonial home or family home should be disregarded in ascertaining the net value of the parties' matrimonial property or partnership property.[90] A foreign tax debt that the party did not intend to pay and was unenforceable in the United Kingdom is not a "debt" for the purpose of the 1985 Act.[91]

When calculating the net value of matrimonial property or partnership property, one does not require to be concerned with the question of which party owns which items or which party is liable for which debts.[92] Any changes in value after the relevant date must be left out of account.[93] If there is no net value to be shared, the principle is not applicable.[94]

A claim for damages that is yet to be quantified and admitted may be valued on the basis that it will attract less if offered for sale in the market place than the amount awarded by the decree that is obtained at the end of the day.[95] A business may be valued on a going concern basis.[96] However, valuation on a net asset basis or by reference to a person's capital account may be more appropriate.[97] Shares in a

---

[87] *Fulton v. Fulton,* 2000 Fam. L.R. 8; *Lessani v. Lessani,* 2007 Fam. L.R. 81.

[88] *McConnell v. McConnell,* 1997 Fam. L.R. 97; *Jackson v. Jackson,* 2000 S.C.L.R. 81; *Buchan v. Buchan,* 1992 S.C.L.R. 766; *MacRitchie v. MacRitchie,* 1994 S.L.T. (Sh. Ct.) 72.

[89] *Sweeney v. Sweeney,* 2004 S.C. 372; *Sweeney v. Sweeney (No. 2),* 2006 S.C. 82. Any such contingent liability could however be brought into account in determining the proportions in which matrimonial property or partnership property would be shared fairly, and in determining what was reasonable having regard to the parties' resources—*ibid.*

[90] *Stuart v. Stuart,* 2001 S.L.T. (Sh. Ct.) 20; *Sweeney v. Sweeney,* 2004 S.C. 372.

[91] *Cunniff v. Cunniff,* 1999 S.L.T. 992 at p. 996.

[92] *Russell v. Russell,* 2005 Fam. L.R 96. The position is different when one gets to the stage of deciding what order should be made so as to achieve a fair division of that net value—*ibid.*

[93] *Wallis v. Wallis,* 1993 S.C. (H.L.) 49.

[94] *Graham v. Graham,* 1997 Fam. L.R. 117.

[95] *Skarpaas v. Skarpaas,* 1993 S.L.T. 343. *C.f. Carrol v. Carrol,* 2003 Fam. L.R. 108 (broad brush approach adopted).

[96] *McKenzie v. McKenzie,* 1991 S.L.T. 461; *Savage v. Savage,* 1997 Fam. L.R. 132.

[97] *Bye v. Bye,* 1998 Fam. L.R. 103; *Brown v. Brown,* 1998 Fam. L.R. 81; *Rose v. Rose,* 1998 S.L.T. (Sh. Ct.) 56.

private company may be valued on a dividend basis or an earnings basis or an asset basis, depending on what information is available to a willing buyer at the relevant date.[98] Valuation of such shares on an asset basis may be made by reference to a hypothetical liquidation of the company.[99] It may be appropriate to discount the value of a minority shareholding to reflect its minority nature.[100] Household contents may be valued at auction prices or on a willing seller/willing buyer basis, adjusted as appropriate to the circumstances of the case.[101] Alternatively, they may be accounted for by way of their insurance value less an amount reflecting the excess over their probable true and fair value.[102] The rights or interests of a party under a life policy may be valued on the basis of its surrender value.[103] A debt due to a party may be valued at less than its book value.[104]

Calculation and verification in relation to the valuation of benefits under a pension arrangement and relevant state scheme rights fall to be carried out as prescribed.[105] The person responsible for the pension arrangement or the Secretary of State, as the case may be, requires to supply pension information as prescribed relevant to any power with respect to orders for financial provision.[106] Calculation and verification, and apportionment, of PPF compensation also fall to be carried out as prescribed.[107] The Board of the Pension Protection Fund requires to

---

[98] See, *e.g., Crockett v. Crockett*, 1992 S.C.L.R. 591; *McConnell v. McConnell*, 1997 Fam. L.R. 97; *Fulton v. Fulton*, 2000 Fam. L.R. 8; *Cordiner v. Cordiner*, 2003 Fam. L.R. 39; *L v. L*, 2003 Fam. L.R. 101; *W v. W*, 2004 Fam. L.R. 54; *M v. M, W Estate Trustees Ltd and Another*, 2011 Fam. L.R. 24.

[99] *Latter v. Latter*, 1990 S.L.T. 805.

[100] *Jackson v. Jackson*, 2000 S.C.L.R. 81; *L v. L*, 2003 Fam. L.R. 101; *W v. W*, 2004 Fam. L.R. 54; *Hodge v. Hodge*, 2008 Fam. L.R. 51; *Watt v. Watt*, 2009 S.L.T. 931.

[101] *Latter v. Latter*, 1990 S.L.T. 805.

[102] *McConnell v. McConnell*, 1997 Fam. L.R. 97. *C.f. Cahill v. Cahill*, 1998 S.L.T. (Sh. Ct.) 96.

[103] *Muir v. Muir*, 1989 S.L.T. (Sh. Ct.) 20.

[104] *Shipton v. Shipton*, 1992 S.C.L.R. 23.

[105] 1985 Act, s. 10(8) and (8A), as inserted by the Pensions Act 1995, s. 167(2)(b) and substituted by the Welfare Reform and Pensions Act 1999, Sched. 12, para. 8(3). Applicable regulations are the Divorce etc. (Pensions) (Scotland) Regulations 2000 (S.S.I. 2000 No. 112) and the Occupational Pension Schemes (Transfer Values) Regulations 1996 (S.I. 1996 No. 1847), reproduced in App. X, *infra*.

[106] Welfare Reform and Pensions Act 1999, s. 23(1)(a)(ii). Applicable regulations are the Pensions on Divorce etc. (Provision of Information) Regulations 2000 (S.I. 2000 No. 1048) and the Sharing of State Scheme Rights (Provision of Information and Valuation) (No. 2) Regulations 2000 (S.I. 2000 No. 2914), reproduced in App. X, *infra*.

[107] 1985 Act, s. 10(8B) and (8C), as inserted by the Welfare Reform and Pensions Act 1999, Sched. 12, para. 8(3) and substituted by the Pensions Act 2008, Sched. 7, para. 4(b). Applicable regulations are the Divorce and Dissolution etc. (Pension Protection Fund) (Scotland) Regulations 2006 (S.S.I. 2006 No. 254) and the Pension Protection Fund (Pension Compensation Sharing and Attachment on Divorce etc) Regulations 2011

supply pension compensation information as prescribed relevant to any power with respect to orders for financial provision.[108] The prescribed method of valuation in each case is mandatory.[109]

The court may derive assistance from a table of matrimonial property or partnership property showing values.[110]

(3) In applying the principle set out in section 9(1)(a), the net value of the matrimonial property or partnership property must be taken to be *shared fairly* between the persons when it is shared equally or in such other proportions as are justified by special circumstances.[111]

By virtue of section 10(6) of the 1985 Act,[112] "special circumstances", without prejudice to the generality of the words, may include—

(a) the terms of any agreement between the persons on the ownership or division of any of the matrimonial property or partnership property;[113]

(b) the source of the funds or assets used to acquire any of the matrimonial property or partnership property where those funds or assets were not derived from the income or efforts of the persons during the marriage or partnership;[114]

(S.I. 2011 No. 731), reproduced in App. X, *infra*. For the definition of "PPF compensation", see n. 70, *supra*.

[108] Pensions Act 2008, s. 118(1)(a)(iv). Applicable regulations are the Pension Protection Fund (Pension Compensation Sharing and Attachment on Divorce etc.) Regulations 2011 (S.I. 2011 No. 731), reproduced in App. X, *infra*.

[109] *Miller v. Miller*, 2000 Fam. L.R. 19; *Stewart v. Stewart*, 2001 S.L.T. (Sh. Ct.) 114; *Burnside v. Burnside*, 2007 Fam. L.R. 144.

[110] See *Crockett v. Crockett*, 1992 S.C.L.R. 591 and App. IX.

[111] 1985 Act, s. 10(1), as amended by the Civil Partnership Act 2004, Sched. 28, para. 16(2). *C.f.* 1985 Act, ss. 25 and 26 (presumption of equal shares in household goods and in money and property derived from housekeeping allowance).

[112] As amended by the Civil Partnership Act 2004, Sched. 28, para. 16(6).

[113] An agreement may be relevant whether it is to share property equally or unequally— *Jacques v. Jacques*, 1997 S.C. (H.L.) 20 at p. 25; *Jackson v. Jackson*, 2000 S.C.L.R. 81 at p. 95.

[114] Examples of relevant "sources" are pre-marriage or pre-partnership property (*Phillip v. Phillip*, 1988 S.C.L.R. 427; *Budge v. Budge*, 1990 S.L.T. 319; *Jesner v. Jesner*, 1992 S.L.T. 999; *MacLean v. MacLean*, 2001 Fam. L.R. 118; *Cordiner v. Cordiner*, 2003 Fam. L.R. 39); a damages award (*Petrie v. Petrie*, 1988 S.C.L.R. 390); an inheritance (*Davidson v. Davidson*, 1994 S.L.T. 506; *Cunningham v. Cunningham*, 2001 Fam. L.R. 12); a parental gift (*Kerrigan v. Kerrigan*, 1988 S.C.L.R. 603; *Buczynska v. Buczynski*, 1989 S.L.T. 558; *Latter v. Latter*, 1990 S.L.T. 805; *Gray v. Gray*, 2001 S.C.L.R. 681; *Buchan v. Buchan*, 2001 Fam. L.R. 48; *MacLean v. MacLean*, 2001 Fam. L.R. 118); and a family trust (*Jesner v. Jesner*, 1992 S.L.T. 999). "Assets" and "funds" denote some form of economic wealth that is realizable and usable for any purpose—*Lawson v. Lawson*, 1996 S.L.T. (Sh. Ct.) 83 (entitlement to discount in purchase of local authority house not "asset" within the meaning of s. 10(6)(b)).

(c) any destruction, dissipation or alienation of property by either person;[115]
(d) the nature of the matrimonial property or partnership property, the use made of it (including use for business purposes or as a family home) and the extent to which it would be reasonable to expect it to be realised or divided or used as security;[116]
(e) the actual or prospective liability for any expense of valuation or transfer of property in connection with the divorce or the dissolution of the civil partnership.

The words "special circumstances" do not have any technical meaning but refer to any circumstances that are special to the case.[117] Thus special circumstances may be found to exist, for example, where the parties' marriage or civil partnership was brief;[118] where one party needed to purchase a dwelling house and was too old to qualify for a mortgage;[119] where a party had a contingent liability to capital gains tax;[120] and where a party exhibited a lack of candour with the court regarding his assets.[121] A post-separation increase in the value of the matrimonial home or family home is not a special circumstance however.[122]

It is for the court of first instance in each case to determine whether an event amounts to special circumstances in the case in question and, if so, whether it justifies a division of the matrimonial property or partnership property in proportions other than equal; the court is not required to effect an unequal division whenever special circumstances are found to exist.[123]

The court may adopt a global approach in assessing and dividing matrimonial property or partnership property, or it may pursue a piecemeal approach, allowing it to divide a particular item from the rest to meet a special circumstance which bears on it primarily; there is room for the scheme of the 1985 Act to be applied in different ways in different situations as a matter of discretion.[124] Subparagraphs (b) and

---

[115] See, *e.g., Short v. Short*, 1994 G.W.D. 21-1300 (encumbering matrimonial home by forging husband's signature was dissipation). Mere non-payment of the mortgage is not dissipation (*Park v. Park*, 1988 S.C.L.R. 584; *Buchan v. Buchan*, 2001 Fam. L.R. 48). See also *Russell v. Russell*, 1996 G.W.D. 15-895 (failed business ventures not dissipation).
[116] For examples, see nn. 126–132 and accompanying text, *infra*.
[117] *Jacques v. Jacques*, 1997 S.C. (H.L.) 20.
[118] *Kerrigan v. Kerrigan*, 1988 S.C.L.R. 603; *White v. White*, 1992 S.C.L.R. 769.
[119] *Marshall v. Marshall*, 2007 Fam. L.R. 48.
[120] *Sweeney v. Sweeney (No. 2)*, 2006 S.C. 82.
[121] *Burchell v. Burchell*, 1997 Fam. L.R. 137; *Lessani v. Lessani*, 2007 Fam. L.R. 81.
[122] *Wallis v. Wallis*, 1993 S.C. (H.L.) 49.
[123] *Jacques v. Jacques*, 1997 S.C. (H.L.) 20.
[124] *Crockett v. Crockett*, Extra Division, 30 June 1993, unreported.

(d) of section 10(6) might be thought to invite the latter approach: some items of matrimonial property or partnership property might thus, for example, be treated differently from others according to their nature or the use to which they are put.[125] The matrimonial home or family home is one of the clearest examples of a particular item of matrimonial property or partnership property for which special arrangements may be justified.[126] Other examples might be a damages claim,[127] a damages award,[128] a criminal injuries compensation award,[129] a company shareholding,[130] a farm[131] and a pension.[132]

The court must not take account of the conduct of either party to the marriage or as the case may be of either partner unless the conduct has adversely affected the financial resources which are relevant to the decision of the court on a claim for financial provision.[133] Thus, for example, account may be taken of conduct having an adverse effect on the health of a spouse or partner and rendering him unfit for work;[134] of failure to meet mortgage commitments regularly notwithstanding receipt of a good salary, with no satisfactory explanation of what happened to the money;[135] or of failure to meet financial responsibilities after separation with respect to maintenance, mortgage and insurance payments notwithstanding court orders.[136]

Section 9(1)(b):

> *"fair account should be taken of any economic advantage derived by either person from contributions from the other, and*

---

[125] *Ibid.*

[126] *Little v. Little,* 1990 S.L.T. 785. See, *e.g., Cooper v. Cooper,* 1989 S.C.L.R. 347; *Budge v. Budge,* 1990 S.L.T. 319; *Farrell v. Farrell,* 1990 S.C.L.R. 717; *Peacock v. Peacock,* 1993 S.C. 88; *Murphy v. Murphy,* 1996 S.L.T. (Sh. Ct.) 91; *Collins v. Collins,* 1997 Fam. L.R. 50; *Cunniff v. Cunniff,* 1999 S.C. 537; *Trotter v. Trotter,* 2001 S.L.T. (Sh. Ct.) 42; *Gray v. Gray,* 2001 S.C.L.R. 681.

[127] *Skarpaas v. Skarpaas,* 1993 S.L.T. 343; *Carrol v. Carrol,* 2003 Fam. L.R. 108.

[128] *Petrie v. Petrie,* 1988 S.C.L.R. 390.

[129] *McGuire v. McGuire's Curator Bonis,* 1991 S.L.T. (Sh. Ct.) 76.

[130] *McConnell v. McConnell (No. 2),* 1997 Fam. L.R. 108.

[131] *Davidson v. Davidson,* 1994 S.L.T. 506.

[132] *Muir v. Muir,* 1989 S.L.T. (Sh. Ct.) 20; *Carpenter v. Carpenter,* 1990 S.L.T. (Sh. Ct.) 68; *Little v. Little,* 1990 S.L.T. 785; *Symon v. Symon,* 1991 S.C.L.R. 414; *Bannon v. Bannon,* 1993 S.L.T. 999; *Stephen v. Stephen,* 1995 S.C.L.R. 175; *Crosbie v. Crosbie,* 1996 S.L.T. (Sh. Ct.) 86; *Murphy v. Murphy,* 1996 S.L.T. (Sh. Ct.) 91. *C.f. Brooks v. Brooks,* 1993 S.L.T. 184 (fair and reasonable to treat actuarial value of pension as an immediately realizable capital sum as there were other assets capable of realisation).

[133] 1985 Act, s. 11(7)(a), as amended by the Civil Partnership Act 2004, Sched. 28, para. 17(7).

[134] *Bremner v. Bremner,* 2000 S.C.L.R. 912.

[135] *Buchan v. Buchan,* 2001 Fam. L.R. 48.

[136] *Gray v. Gray,* 2001 S.C.L.R. 681.

of any economic disadvantage suffered by either person in the interests of the other person or of the family."[137]

"Economic advantage" means advantage gained whether before or during the marriage or civil partnership and includes gains in capital, in income and in earning capacity; and "economic disadvantage" is construed accordingly.[138] An economic advantage may be "gained" before the benefit of that advantage has been realised, as where improvements are carried out to a property which is later sold; and so economic advantage and economic disadvantage may fall to be evaluated by reference to an extended period of time part of which may be after the dissolution of the marriage or civil partnership.[139]

"Contributions" are contributions made whether before or during the marriage or civil partnership, including indirect and non-financial contributions and, in particular, any such contribution made by looking after the family home or caring for the family.[140]

In applying the principle set out in section 9(1)(b), the court must have regard to the extent to which—

(a) the economic advantages or disadvantages sustained by either person have been balanced by the economic advantages or disadvantages sustained by the other person; and

(b) a resulting imbalance has been or will be corrected by a sharing of the value of the matrimonial property or the partnership property or otherwise.[141]

For a claim under section 9(1)(b) to succeed, therefore, it is not enough to show that a contribution by the claimant enabled the other spouse or partner to gain an economic advantage; it must also be shown that such an advantage was not balanced by an economic advantage which the claimant had gained.[142] The court has therefore to identify all the economic advantages derived by either party from the contributions of the other and all the economic disadvantages suffered by either party in the interests of the other party or of the family, and only if there is an imbalance can the court then go on further to consider what order is called for.[143]

---

[137] Cases in which the principle in s. 9(1)(b) was considered are listed in App. VII, *infra*.

[138] 1985 Act, s. 9(2), as amended by the Civil Partnership Act 2004, Sched. 28, para. 15(3).

[139] *Cahill v. Cahill*, 1998 S.L.T. (Sh. Ct.) 96, doubting *Dougan v. Dougan*, 1998 S.L.T. (Sh. Ct.) 27. *C.f. Porter v. Porter*, 2010 Fam. L.R. 68.

[140] 1985 Act, s. 9(2), as amended by the Civil Partnership Act 2004, Sched. 28, para. 15(3).

[141] 1985 Act, s. 11(2), as amended by the Civil Partnership Act 2004, Sched. 28, para. 17(2).

[142] *Petrie v. Petrie*, 1988 S.C.L.R. 390 at p. 394.

[143] *De Winton v. De Winton*, 1998 Fam. L.R. 110 at p. 114. See, *e.g.*, *Sutherland v. Sutherland*, 2008 Fam. L.R. 151.

Section 9(1)(b) considerations should not be taken into account in determining the fair sharing of matrimonial property; section 9(1)(b) comes into play as a separate justification for a different order for financial provision from the one which would have been justified if regard had only been had to section 9(1)(a).[144] There is no difficulty in applying section 9(1)(b) where the economic advantage does not bear on matrimonial property or partnership property; where it does so bear, however, while in some circumstances section 9(1)(b) might be capable of being invoked, there is a serious risk of undermining the section 9(1)(a) principle, the presumption that equal sharing is fair, and the need for special circumstances to displace the presumption, if in any case in which a party fails to displace the presumption of equal sharing, the same ground can then be traversed again in the guise of applying the section 9(1)(b) principle.[145]

In applying this principle, the court must not take account of the conduct of either party to the marriage or as the case may be either partner unless the conduct has adversely affected the financial resources which are relevant to the decision of the court on a claim for financial provision.[146]

Section 9(1)(c):

> "*any economic burden of caring should be shared fairly between the persons—*
> (i) *after divorce, for a child of the marriage under the age of 16 years;*
> (ii) *after dissolution of civil partnership, for a child under that age who has been accepted by both partners as a child of the family or in respect of whom they are, by virtue of sections 33 and 42 of the Human Fertilisation and Embryology Act 2008, the parents.*"[147]

In applying the principle set out in section 9(1)(c), the court must have regard to—

(a) any decree or arrangement for aliment for the child;
(b) any expenditure or loss of earning capacity caused by the need to care for the child;

---

[144] *Jackson v. Jackson*, 2000 S.C.L.R. 81 at p. 96. See, *e.g., Hodge v. Hodge*, 2008 Fam. L.R. 51.
[145] *Ibid.*
[146] 1985 Act, s. 11(7)(a), as amended by the Civil Partnership Act 2004, Sched. 28, para. 17(7).
[147] Cases in which the principle in s. 9(1)(c) was considered are listed in App. VII, *infra.*

(c) the need to provide suitable accommodation for the child;
(d) the age and health of the child;
(e) the educational, financial and other circumstances of the child;
(f) the availability and cost of suitable child-care facilities or services;
(g) the needs and resources of the persons; and
(h) all the other circumstances of the case, in having regard to which the court may, if it thinks fit, take account of any support, financial or otherwise, given by the person who is to make the financial provision to any person whom he maintains as a dependant in his household whether or not he owes an obligation of aliment to that person.[148]

Expenditure on the child after his or her sixteenth birthday should not be taken into account.[149] Future expenditure on school fees should be omitted from consideration also.[150]

In applying this principle, the court must not take account of the conduct of either party to the marriage or as the case may be either partner unless the conduct has adversely affected the financial resources which are relevant to the decision of the court on a claim for financial provision.[151]

Section 9(1)(d):

> *"a person who has been dependent to a substantial degree on the financial support of the other person should be awarded such financial provision as is reasonable to enable him to adjust, over a period of not more than three years from*
>
> (i) *the date of the decree of divorce, to the loss of that support on divorce;*
>
> (ii) *the date of the decree of dissolution of the civil partnership, to the loss of that support on dissolution."*[152]

In applying the principle set out in section 9(1)(d), the court must have regard to —

(a) the age, health and earning capacity of the person who is claiming the financial provision;

---

[148] 1985 Act, s. 11(3) and (6), as amended by the 2004 Act, Sched. 28, para. 17(3) and (6).
[149] *Monkman v. Monkman*, 1988 S.L.T. (Sh. Ct.) 37.
[150] *Maclachlan v. Maclachlan*, 1998 S.L.T. 693.
[151] 1985 Act, s. 11(7)(a), as amended by the Civil Partnership Act 2004, Sched. 28, para. 17(7).
[152] Cases in which the principle in s. 9(1)(d) was considered are listed in App. VII, *infra*.

(b) the duration and extent of the dependence of that person prior to divorce or to the dissolution of the civil partnership;

(c) any intention of that person to undertake a course of education or training;

(d) the needs and resources of the persons; and

(e) all the other circumstances of the case, in having regard to which the court may, if it thinks fit, take account of any support, financial or otherwise, given by the person who is to make the financial provision to any person whom he maintains as a dependant in his household whether or not he owes an obligation of aliment to that person.[153]

Dependence prior to the marriage or civil partnership may be taken into account.[154] The level of support afforded to the claimant between the date of separation and the date of divorce or dissolution of the civil partnership may be critical.[155] Failure to seek any financial support after separation may disentitle the claimant to an award under this principle.[156]

In applying this principle, the court must not take account of the conduct of either party to the marriage or as the case may be either partner unless either—

(a) the conduct has adversely affected the financial resources which are relevant to the decision of the court on a claim for financial provision; or

(b) it would be manifestly inequitable to leave the conduct out of account.[157]

Section 9(1)(e):

> "*a person who at the time of the divorce or the dissolution of the civil partnership seems likely to suffer serious financial hardship as a result of the divorce or dissolution should be awarded such financial provision as is reasonable to relieve him of hardship over a reasonable period.*"[158]

In applying the principle set out in section 9(1)(e), the court must have regard to—

---

[153] 1985 Act, s. 11(4) and (6), as amended by the 2004 Act, Sched. 28, para. 17(4) and (6).

[154] *Petrie v. Petrie*, 1988 S.C.L.R. 390.

[155] *Millar v. Millar*, 1990 S.C.L.R. 666 at p. 671.

[156] *Gray v. Gray*, 1991 S.C.L.R. 422.

[157] 1985 Act, s. 11(7), as amended by the Civil Partnership Act 2004, Sched. 28, para. 17(7).

[158] Cases in which the principle in s. 9(1)(e) was considered are listed in App. VII, *infra*.

(a) the age, health and earning capacity of the person who is claiming the financial provision;

(b) the duration of the marriage or of the civil partnership;

(c) the standard of living of the persons during the marriage or civil partnership;

(d) the needs and resources of the persons; and

(e) all the other circumstances of the case, in having regard to which the court may, if it thinks fit, take account of any support, financial or otherwise, given by the person who is to make the financial provision to any person whom he maintains as a dependant in his household whether or not he owes an obligation of aliment to that person.[159]

Failure to seek financial support after separation does not disentitle the claimant to an award under this principle.[160]

In applying this principle, the court must not take account of the conduct of either party to the marriage or as the case may be either partner unless either—

(a) the conduct has adversely affected the financial resources which are relevant to the decision of the court on a claim for financial provision; or

(b) it would be manifestly inequitable to leave the conduct out of account.[161]

Despite all the foregoing detail, the matter of financial provision on divorce or dissolution of civil partnership is essentially one of discretion, aimed at achieving a fair and practicable result in accordance with common sense.[162] It remains as important as it always was that the details of financial provision should be left in the hands of the court of first instance and not opened up for reconsideration on appeal.[163] It is only in very special circumstances that the appellate court is entitled to interfere.[164] It must be shown that the sheriff misdirected himself in law or failed to take into account a relevant and material factor or reached a result that is manifestly inequitable or plainly wrong.[165] In the event that the sheriff has made an error of fact, the matter is at large

---

[159] 1985 Act, s. 11(5) and (6), as amended by the 2004 Act, Sched. 28, para. 17(5) and (6).

[160] *Haughan v. Haughan*, 2002 S.C. 631.

[161] 1985 Act, s. 11(7), as amended by the Civil Partnership Act 2004, Sched. 28, para. 17(7).

[162] *Little v. Little*, 1990 S.L.T. 785 at p. 787. Note that there must be material before the court in the light of which that discretion can be exercised, even where the application is not contested—*Ali v. Ali*, 2001 S.C. 618. See, *e.g., AB v. CD*, 2007 Fam. L.R. 53.

[163] *Little v. Little*, 1990 S.L.T. 785 at p. 787; *Jacques v. Jacques*, 1997 S.C. (H.L.) 20 at p. 25.

[164] *Peacock v. Peacock*, 1993 S.C. 88 at p. 92.

[165] *Little v. Little*, 1990 S.L.T. 785 at p. 786.

for the appellate court so that it can take account of matters that were not before the sheriff at the stage of the proof such as the consequences of the sheriff's subsequent interlocutor on the matter of expenses.[166]

Where any parties have reached agreement in relation to an order for financial provision, a joint minute may be entered into expressing that agreement; and the court may grant decree in respect of those parts of the joint minute in relation to which he could otherwise make an order, whether or not such a decree would include a matter for which there was no crave.[167] A joint minute is binding on the parties.[168] The court cannot set aside the agreement that the joint minute expresses unless —

    (a) the interests of third parties, such as a child of the marriage or a child of the family, are affected;

    (b) it is void or voidable on some ground applicable to the general law of contract; or

    (c) there is specific statutory provision to that effect.[169]

Capital sum orders: pension lump sums

Where the court makes a capital sum order against a party to a marriage or a partner in a civil partnership ("the liable person") in circumstances where —

    (a) the matrimonial property or the partnership property includes any rights or interests in benefits under a pension arrangement[170] which the liable person has or may have (whether such benefits are payable to him or in respect of his death); and

    (b) those benefits include a lump sum payable to him or in respect of his death,

the court may, on making the capital sum order, make an order under

---

[166] *Cameron v. Cameron*, 2002 S.L.T. (Sh. Ct.) 23.

[167] r. 33.26(c) or r. 33A.27(c).

[168] *Jongejan v. Jongejan*, 1993 S.L.T. 595. *C.f. Methven v. Methven*, 1999 S.L.T. (Sh. Ct.) 117 (actings of parties consistent with joint intention to revoke agreement).

[169] *Anderson v. Anderson*, 1989 S.C.L.R. 475 (*c.f. Davidson v. Davidson*, 1989 S.L.T. 466). As to (c), see "Orders setting aside or varying agreements on financial provision", *infra*.

[170] "Pension arrangement" means (a) any occupational pension scheme within the meaning of the Pension Schemes Act 1993; (b) a personal pension scheme within the meaning of that Act; (c) a retirement annuity contract; (d) an annuity or insurance policy purchased or transferred for the purpose of giving effect to rights under an occupational pension scheme or a personal pension scheme; (e) an annuity purchased or entered into for the purpose of discharging liability in respect of a credit under s. 29(1)(b) of the Welfare Reform and Pensions Act 1999 or under corresponding Northern Ireland legislation — 1985 Act, s. 27(1), as inserted by the 1999 Act, Sched. 12, para. 12.

section 12A(2) or (3) of the 1985 Act in respect of such pension lump sum.[171]

Where the aforesaid benefits include a lump sum payable to the liable person, the court, on making the capital sum order, may make an order under section 12A(2) requiring the person responsible for the pension arrangement in question to pay the whole or part of that sum, when it becomes due, to the other party to the marriage or, as the case may be, to the other civil partner ("the other person").[172] Where the aforesaid benefits include a lump sum payable in respect of the death of the liable person, the court, on making the capital sum order, may make an order under section 12A(3) —

(a) if the person responsible for the pension arrangement in question has power to determine the person to whom the sum, or any part of it, is to be paid, requiring them to pay the whole or part of that sum, when it becomes due, to the other person;

(b) if the liable person has power to nominate the person to whom the sum, or any part of it, is to be paid, requiring the liable person to nominate the other person in respect of the whole or part of that sum;

(c) in any other case, requiring the person responsible for the pension arrangement in question to pay the whole or part of that sum, when it becomes due, to the other person instead of to the person to whom, apart from the order, it would be paid.[173]

However, the court must not, in the same proceedings, make both an order under section 12A(2) or (3) in respect of a pension lump sum and a pension sharing order in relation to the same pension arrangement.[174]

---

[171] 1985 Act, s. 12A(1), (2) and (3), as inserted by the Pensions Act 1995, s. 167(3) and amended by the Welfare Reform and Pensions Act 1999, Sched. 12, para. 9(2)–(4) and the Civil Partnership Act 2004, Sched. 28, para. 19.

[172] 1985 Act, s. 12A(2), as inserted by the Pensions Act 1995, s. 167(3) and amended by the Welfare Reform and Pensions Act 1999, Sched. 12, para. 9(3) and the Civil Partnership Act 2004, Sched. 28, para. 19(3).

[173] 1985 Act, s. 12A(3), as inserted by the Pensions Act 1995, s. 167(3) and amended by the Welfare Reform and Pensions Act 1999, Sched. 12, para. 9(4) and the Civil Partnership Act 2004, Sched. 28, para. 19(4). Such an order does not take effect until any assessment period (within the meaning of s. 132 of the Pensions Act 2004) comes to an end for a reason other than the giving of a transfer notice under s. 160 of that Act — 1985 Act, s. 12A(7ZA) and (7ZB), as inserted by the Family Law (Scotland) Act 2006 (Consequential Modifications) Order 2006 (S.S.I. 2006 No. 384), art. 8.

[174] 1985 Act, s. 8(4), as inserted by the Welfare Reform and Pensions Act 1999, Sched. 12, para. 6.

Where, as regards a pension arrangement, the parties to a marriage or the partners in a civil partnership have in effect a qualifying agreement which contains a term relating to pension sharing, the court must not make an order under section 12A(2) or (3) in respect of a pension lump sum relating to the arrangement unless it also sets aside the agreement or term under section 16(1)(b) of the 1985 Act.[175] A "term relating to pension sharing" is a term corresponding to provision which may be made in a pension sharing order and satisfying the requirements set out in sections 28(1)(f) or 48(1)(f) of the Welfare Reform and Pensions Act 1999,[176] namely provision which—

(a) is contained in a qualifying agreement between the parties to a marriage or between persons who are civil partners of each other;

(b) is in such form as the Secretary of State may prescribe by regulations;[177] and

(c) takes effect on the grant, in relation to the marriage, of decree of divorce under the Divorce ((Scotland) Act 1976 or (as the case may be) on the grant, in relation to the civil partnership, of decree of dissolution.[178]

A "qualifying agreement" is one which—

(a) has been entered into in such circumstances as the Secretary of State may prescribe by regulations;[179] and

(b) is registered in the Books of Council and Session.[180]

Where—

(a) an order imposes any requirement on the person responsible for a pension arrangement ("the first arrangement") and the liable person acquires transfer credits[181] under another

---

[175] 1985 Act, s. 8(5), as inserted by the Welfare Reform and Pensions Act 1999, Sched. 12, para. 6.

[176] As amended by the Civil Partnership Act 2004, Sched. 27, paras. 159 and 161.

[177] The regulations are the Pensions on Divorce etc. (Pension Sharing) (Scotland) Regulations 2000 (S.I. 2000 No. 1051), reproduced in App X, *infra*.

[178] 1985 Act, ss. 8(7)(a) and 16(2A), as inserted by the Welfare Reform and Pensions Act 1999, Sched. 12, paras. 6 and 11(3).

[179] The regulations are the Pensions on Divorce etc. (Pension Sharing) (Scotland) Regulations 2000 (S.I. 2000 No. 1051), reproduced in App X, *infra*.

[180] 1985 Act, s. 8(7)(b), as inserted by the Welfare Reform and Pensions Act 1999, Sched. 12, para. 6, and 1999 Act, s. 28(3).

[181] "Transfer credits" has the same meaning as in the Pension Schemes Act 1993—1985 Act, s. 12A(6), as inserted by the Pensions Act 1995, s. 167(4) and amended by the Welfare Reform and Pensions Act 1999, Sched. 12, para. 9(7) and the Civil Partnership Act 2004, Sched. 28, para. 19(4).

arrangement ("the new arrangement") which are derived (directly or indirectly) from a transfer from the first arrangement of all his accrued rights under that arrangement; and

(b) the person responsible for the new arrangement has been given notice in accordance with regulations,[182]

the order shall have effect as if it has been made instead in respect of the person responsible for the new arrangement.[183]

Any payment under an order in respect of a pension lump sum by the person responsible for the pension arrangement in question—

(a) shall discharge so much of the liability of the person responsible for the pension arrangement to or in respect of the liable person as corresponds to the amount of the payment; and

(b) shall be treated for all purposes as a payment by the liable person in or towards discharge of his liability under the capital sum order.[184]

Where—

(a) the court makes an order under section 12A(2) (lump sum payable to liable party) imposing requirements on the trustees or managers of an occupational pension scheme; and

(b) after the making of the order the Board of the Pension Protection Fund gives the trustees or managers of the scheme a notice under section 160 of the Pensions Act 2004 or the corresponding provision in force in Northern Ireland, in relation to the scheme,

the order shall have effect from the time when the notice is given—

(a) as if—

(i) references to the trustees or managers of the scheme were references to the Board; and

(ii) references to any lump sum to which the person with benefits under a pension arrangement is or might become entitled under the scheme were references to the amount of any compensation payable under Chapter 3

---

[182] The regulations are the Divorce etc. (Notification and Treatment of Pensions) (Scotland) Regulations 2000 (S.I. 2000 No. 1050), reproduced in App. X, *infra*.

[183] 1985 Act, s. 12A(6) as inserted by the Pensions Act 1995, s. 167(3) and amended by the Welfare Reform and Pensions Act 1999, Sched. 12, para. 9(7) and the Civil Partnership Act 2004, Sched. 28, para. 19(4). The court may nevertheless make an order after decree in terms of s. 12A(7), as to which see text accompanying nn. 305–306 *infra*.

[184] 1985 Act, s. 12A(4) as inserted by the Pensions Act 1995, s. 167(3) and amended by the Welfare Reform and Pensions Act 1999, Sched. 12, para. 9(5) and the Civil Partnership Act 2004, Sched. 28, para. 19(4).

of Part 2 of the Pensions Act 2004, or the corresponding provision in force in Northern Ireland, to which that person is or might become entitled in respect of that lump sum; and

(b) subject to such other modifications as may be prescribed.[185]

Where—

(a) the court makes an order under section 12A(3) (lump sum payable in respect of death of liable party); and
(b) after the making of the order the Board of the Pension Protection Fund gives the trustees or managers of the scheme a notice under section 160 of the Pensions Act 2004 or the corresponding Northern Ireland provision, in relation to the scheme,

the order shall, on the giving of such notice, be recalled.[186]

Application for such an order must be made by the pursuer by a crave in the initial writ, intimated to the person responsible for the pension arrangement.[187] The defender must apply for the order by a crave in the defences, intimated to the person responsible for the pension arrangement.[188]

Capital sum orders: pension compensation

Where the court makes a capital sum order against a party to a marriage or a partner to a civil partnership ("the liable person") in circumstances where the matrimonial property or the partnership property includes any rights to PPF compensation (*i.e.* compensation payable under the pension compensation provisions),[189] the court may, on making the capital sum order, make an additional order under section 12B(2) of the 1985 Act requiring the Board of the Pension Protection Fund, if at any time any payment in respect of PPF compensation becomes due to the liable person, to pay the whole or

---

[185] 1985 Act, s. 12A(7B) and (7C), as inserted by the Family Law (Scotland) Act 2006, s. 17. The court may nevertheless make an order after decree in terms of s. 12A(7) and (7ZC), as to which see text accompanying nn. 305–307, *infra*.

[186] 1985 Act, s. 12A(7A), as inserted by the Family Law (Scotland) Act 2006, s. 17.

[187] rr. 33.7(1)(l) and 33.48(1)(a) and (2)(a) or rr. 33A.7(1)(j) and 33A.45(1)(a) and (2)(a).

[188] rr. 33.15(3) and 33.34(1)(b)(ii) and (2)(b) or 33.48(1)(a) and (2)(a) or rr. 33A.15(3) and 33A.34(1)(b)(ii) and (2)(b) or 33A.45(1)(a) and (2)(a).

[189] 1985 Act, s. 27(1C), as inserted by the 2008 Act, Sched. 7, para. 9. "The pension compensation provisions" are (a) Chap. 3 of Pt. 2 of the Pensions Act 2004 and any regulations or order made under it, (b) Chap. 1 of Pt. 3 of the Pensions Act 2008 and any regulations or order made under it, (c) any provision corresponding to the foregoing in force in Northern Ireland—*ibid*.

part of that payment to the other party to the marriage or (as the case may be) to the other civil partner ("the other person").[190]

However, the court must not, in the same proceedings, make both an additional order under section 12B(2) of the 1985 Act in respect of PPF compensation and a pension compensation sharing order in relation to the same PPF compensation.[191] The court must not either make an additional order under section 12B(2) of the 1985 Act in relation to rights to PPF compensation that—

    (a)   derive from rights under a pension scheme which is subject to an order under section 12A(2) or (3) of the 1985 Act in respect of a pension lump sum in relation to the marriage or (as the case may be) civil partnership or a previous one between the same persons,

    (b)   derive from rights under a pension scheme which were at any time the subject of a pension sharing order in relation to the marriage or (as the case may be) civil partnership or a previous one between the same persons,

    (c)   are or have been the subject of a pension compensation sharing order in relation to the marriage or (as the case may be) civil partnership or a previous one between the same persons, or

    (d)   are the subject of an additional order under section 12B(2) of the 1985 Act in relation to the marriage or (as the case may be) civil partnership or a previous one between the same persons.[192]

Where, as regards PPF compensation, the parties to a marriage or the partners in a civil partnership have in effect a qualifying agreement which contains a term relating to pension compensation sharing, the court must not make an order relating to the compensation unless it also sets aside the agreement or term under section 16(1)(b) of the 1985 Act.[193] A "term relating to pension compensation sharing" is a term corresponding to provision which may be made in a pension compensation sharing order and satisfying the requirements set out in section 109(g) of the Pensions Act 2008, namely provision which—

    (a)   is contained in a qualifying agreement between the parties to a marriage or between the partners in a civil partnership,

---

[190] 1985 Act, s. 12B(1) and (2), as inserted by the Pensions Act 2008, Sched. 7, para. 6.

[191] 1985 Act, s. 8(8), as inserted by the Pensions Act 2008, Sched. 7, para. 2.

[192] 1985 Act, s. 12B(5), as inserted by the Pensions Act 2008, Sched. 7, para. 6.

[193] 1985 Act, s. 8(10), as inserted by the Pensions Act 2008, Sched. 7, para. 2.

(b) is in such form as the Secretary of State may prescribe by regulations;[194] and

(c) takes effect on the grant, in relation to the marriage, of decree of divorce or (as the case may be) on the grant, in relation to the civil partnership, of decree of dissolution,

except where the provision relates to the same rights to PPF compensation as are the subject of an additional order under section 12B(2) of the 1985 Act in respect of PPF compensation.[195] A "qualifying agreement" is one which—

(a) has been entered into in such circumstances as the Secretary of State may prescribe by regulations;[196] and

(b) is registered in the Books of Council and Session.[197]

Any such payment in respect of PPF compensation by the Board of the Pension Protection Fund—

(a) shall discharge so much of its liability to the liable person as corresponds to the amount of the payment; and

(b) shall be treated for all purposes as a payment made by the liable person in or towards the discharge of the person's liability under the capital sum order.[198]

Application for such an order is made by the pursuer by a crave in the initial writ, intimated to the Board of the Pension Protection Fund.[199] The defender may apply for the order by a crave in the defences, intimated to the Board of the Pension Protection Fund.[200]

Transfer of property orders

The court may make an order for the transfer of property to one party to a marriage, or one civil partner, by the other under section 8(2) of the 1985 Act—

(a) on granting decree of divorce or of dissolution of a civil partnership; or

---

[194] The regulations are the Pension Protection Fund (Pension Compensation Sharing and Attachment on Divorce etc.) Regulations 2011 (S.I. No. 731), reproduced in App X, *infra*.

[195] 1985 Act, ss. 8(11)(a) and 16(2AA), as inserted by the Pensions Act 2008, Sched. 7, paras. 2 and 8(d).

[196] The regulations are the Pension Protection Fund (Pension Compensation Sharing and Attachment on Divorce etc.) Regulations 2011 (S.I. No. 731), reproduced in App X, *infra*.

[197] 1985 Act, s. 8(11)(b), as inserted by the Pensions Act 2008, Sched. 7, para. 2, and 2008 Act, s. 110(1).

[198] 1985 Act, s. 12B(3), as inserted by the Pensions Act 2008, Sched. 7, para. 6.

[199] rr. 33.7(1)(o) and 33.48(1)(a) and (2)(a) or rr. 33A.7(1)(m) and 33A.45(1)(a) and (2)(a).

[200] rr. 33.15(3) and 33.34(1)(b)(ii) and (2)(b) or 33.48(1)(a) and (2)(a) or rr. 33A.15(3) and 33A.34(1)(b)(ii) and (2)(b) or 33A.45(1)(a) and (2)(a).

(b) within such period as the court on granting decree may specify.[201]

A transfer of property order does not itself transfer property but is no more than an order that the spouse or partner having the title to the property should transfer it to the other spouse or partner.[202] A sufficient description of the property should be included in the transfer of property order to satisfy the requirement of the common law, which is to distinguish the subjects from all other lands, and the court will expect to be provided with sufficient information from the party who seeks the order to enable this to be done.[203] In most instances a brief description will be all that is needed; in more complex cases it may be necessary for a more detailed description to be given.[204]

A transfer of property order may be made subject to payment of a sum of money in exchange, even where the non-applicant does not crave any such order for payment.[205] The applicant may formulate his crave for the transfer of property order such that the transfer is stated to be conditional upon the payment by him of a counterbalancing sum, or he may crave an ancillary order for a balancing payment to be made by him to the non-applicant as a condition of transfer of the property.[206] It may well be that the court can make the order for a balancing payment to be made in the absence of any crave for payment at the instance of either party.[207]

The court must not however make a transfer of property order if the consent of a third party that is necessary under any obligation, enactment or rule of law has not been obtained.[208] Where no such consent to a transfer of property is necessary under any obligation, enactment or rule of law, an order for the transfer of property subject to security can be made without the consent of the creditor but only if he has been given an opportunity of being heard by the court.[209]

Application for a transfer of property order must be made by the pursuer by a crave in the initial writ, intimated to any such third party or

---

[201] 1985 Act, ss. 8(1) and (2) and 12(1), as amended by the Civil Partnership Act 2004, Sched. 28, paras. 14(2) and 18(2). As to s. 12(1)(b), see nn. 297–300 and accompanying text, *infra*.

[202] *Walker v. Walker*, 1991 S.L.T. 157.

[203] *Ibid.*

[204] *Ibid.*

[205] *Wallis v. Wallis*, 1993 S.C. (H.L.) 49; *Collins v. Collins*, 1997 Fam. L.R. 50; *Murdoch v. Murdoch*, 2012 Fam. L.R. 2.

[206] *Murdoch v. Murdoch*, 2012 Fam. L.R. 2 at p. 6.

[207] *Ibid.* at p. 7.

[208] 1985 Act, s. 15(1).

[209] 1985 Act, s. 15(2); *MacNaught v. MacNaught*, 1996 S.C.L.R. 151.

creditor.[210] The defender must apply for a transfer of property order by a crave in the defences, intimated to any such third party or creditor.[211] Where any application for a transfer of property order has been made, the court must make such order, if any, as is:

(a) justified by the principles set out in section 9 of the Family Law (Scotland) Act 1985; and

(b) reasonable having regard to the resources of the parties.[212]

In its application to property transferred by virtue of a transfer of property order, section 10 of the 1985 Act (sharing of value of matrimonial property or partnership property) has effect as if for "relevant date" there were substituted "appropriate valuation date."[213]

The "appropriate valuation date" is—

(a) where the parties to the marriage or, as the case may be, the partners agree on a date, that date;

(b) where there is no such agreement, the date of the making of the transfer of property order.[214]

This deals only with the value of property being transferred and has no application to property retained whether or not the transfer is of one-half of an asset where the recipient owns the other half.[215] In the case of jointly owned property in respect of which a transfer of property order is sought, therefore, the proper method is to value all the assets at the relevant date and then require the applicant to pay (actually or notionally) one-half of current value to the non-applicant for a transfer to the applicant of his one-half share.[216]

If the court considers that, because of the exceptional circumstances of the case, the date in paragraph (b) above should not apply, the appropriate valuation date shall be such other date (being a date as near as may be to the date of the making of the transfer of property order) as the court may determine.[217] The word "exceptional" should be given its ordinary meaning, that is if there is something unusual or out of the ordinary or special which justified departing from the normal rule of

---

[210] r. 33.48(1)(a) and (2)(a) or r. 33A.45(1)(a) and (2)(a). As to intimation, see Chap. 1, text accompanying n. 14.

[211] r. 33.34(1)(b)(ii) and (2)(b) or r. 33A.34(1)(b)(ii) and (2)(b) or r. 33.48(1)(a) and (2)(a) or r. 33A.45(1)(a) and (2)(a). As to intimation, see Chap. 1, text accompanying n. 14.

[212] 1985 Act, s. 8(2).

[213] 1985 Act, s. 10(3A)(a) and (c), as inserted by the Family Law (Scotland) Act 2006, s. 16.

[214] 1985 Act, s. 10(3A)(b), as inserted by the Family Law (Scotland) Act 2006, s. 16.

[215] *Watt v. Watt*, 2009 S.L.T. 931 at p. 954.

[216] *Ibid.*

[217] 1985 Act, s. 10(3A)(b), as inserted by the Family Law (Scotland) Act 2006, s. 16.

adopting the date of the making of the transfer of property order as the appropriate valuation date.[218] A pre-litigation agreement (or at any rate a genuine belief held by one party and acted upon with the other party's consent) regarding the division of heritable property may be regarded as amounting to exceptional circumstances.[219] A delay in the making of a transfer of property order attributable to the non-applicant's conduct of the litigation may be seen as exceptional circumstances.[220] However, the making of payments in respect of the parties' mortgages and endowment policies after separation by one party on behalf of the other does not constitute exceptional circumstances.[221]

Pension sharing orders

The court may make a pension sharing order under section 8(2) of the 1985 Act on granting decree of divorce or of dissolution of a civil partnership.[222] If the order relates to rights under a pension arrangement, the court may include in the order provision about the apportionment between the parties of any charge under section 41 of the Welfare Reform and Pensions Act 1999 (charges in respect of pension sharing costs) or under corresponding Northern Ireland legislation.[223]

A "pension sharing order" is an order which—

    (a)   provides that one party's—
          (i)   shareable rights under a specified pension arrangement;
              or

---

[218] *Maxwell v. Maxwell,* 2008 Fam. L.R. 76.

[219] *Ibid.*

[220] *Willson v. Willson,* 2009 Fam. L.R. 18.

[221] *Sutherland v. Sutherland,* 2008 Fam. L.R. 151.

[222] 1985 Act, s. 8(1) and (2), as amended by the Civil Partnership Act 2004, Sched. 28, para. 14(1). See, *e.g., Galloway v. Galloway,* 2003 Fam. L.R. 10 and *Burnside v. Burnside,* 2007 Fam. L.R. 144. In *Burnside* the sheriff suggested completion of the following schedule for inclusion in the order for pension sharing: "1. All names by which the defender [or pursuer] as transferor has been known; 2. The transferor's date of birth; 3. The transferor's national insurance number; 4. All names by which the pursuer [or defender] as transferee has been known; 5. The transferee's date of birth; 6. The transferee's national insurance number; 7. Details of the pension arrangement and policy reference number of the transferor; 8. The specified amount or percentage value of the cash equivalent of the relevant benefits on the valuation day of the pension arrangement to be transferred; 9. Details of the pension arrangement and policy reference number of the transferee to which the amount or percentage is to be transferred; 10. The pension sharing charges are to be paid in full by the transferor [or the pension sharing charges are to be apportioned between the parties as follows:]."

[223] 1985 Act, s. 8A, as inserted by the Welfare Reform and Pensions Act 1999, Sched. 12, para. 7. Applicable regulations made under s. 41 of the Welfare Reform and Pensions Act 1999 are the Pensions on Divorce etc. (Charging) Regulations 2000 (S.I. 2000 No. 1049), reproduced in App. X, *infra.*

    (ii) shareable state scheme rights, be subject to pension sharing for the benefit of the other party; and

(b) specifies the percentage value, or the amount, to be transferred.[224]

The reference to shareable rights under a pension arrangement is to rights in relation to which pension sharing is available under Chapter I of Part IV of the Welfare Reform and Pensions Act 1999, or under corresponding Northern Ireland legislation.[225] Pension sharing is available under that Chapter in relation to a person's shareable rights under any pension arrangement other than excepted public service pension scheme.[226] For the purposes of the Chapter, a person's shareable rights under a pension arrangement are any rights of his under the arrangement, other than rights of a description specified by regulations.[227] The reference to shareable state scheme rights is to rights in relation to which pension sharing is available under Chapter II of Part IV of the Welfare Reform and Pensions Act 1999, or under corresponding Northern Ireland legislation.[228] For the purposes of the Chapter, a person's shareable state scheme rights are—

(a) his entitlement, or prospective entitlement, to a Category A retirement pension by virtue of section 44(3)(b) of the Social Security Contributions and Benefits Act 1992 (earnings-related additional pension), and

(b) his entitlement, or prospective entitlement, to a pension under section 55A of that Act (shared additional pension).[229]

However, the court must not, in the same proceedings, make both a pension sharing order and an order under section 12A(2) or (3) of the 1985 Act in respect of a pension lump sum in relation to the same pension arrangement.[230] The court must not either make a pension

---

[224] 1985 Act, s. 27(1), as inserted by the Welfare Reform and Pensions Act 1999, s. 20(3). In relation to the pension sharing mechanism, see further the 1999 Act, Part IV, Chapters I and II, and the Pension Sharing (Implementation and Discharge of Liability) Regulations 2000 (S.I. 2000 No. 1053), reproduced in App. X, *infra*.

[225] 1985 Act, s. 27(1A), as inserted by the Welfare Reform and Pensions Act 1999, s. 20(4).

[226] Welfare Reform and Pensions Act 1999, s. 27(1). For the purposes of subs. (1), a public service pension scheme is excepted if it is specified by order made by such Minister of the Crown or government department as may be designated by the Treasury as having responsibility for the scheme—*ibid*, s. 27(3).

[227] 1999 Act, s. 27(2). The regulations are the Pension Sharing (Valuation) Regulations 2000 (S.I. 2000 No. 1052), reproduced in App. X, *infra*.

[228] 1985 Act, s. 27(1A), as inserted by the Welfare Reform and Pensions Act 1999, s. 20(4).

[229] 1999 Act, s. 47(2).

[230] 1985 Act, s. 8(4), as inserted by the Welfare Reform and Pensions Act 1999, Sched. 12, para. 6.

sharing order in relation to the rights of a person under a pension arrangement if there is in force an order under section 12A(2) or (3) of the 1985 Act with respect to a pension lump sum which relates to benefits or future benefits to which he is entitled under the pension arrangement.[231]

Where, as regards a pension arrangement, the parties to a marriage or the partners in a civil partnership have in effect a qualifying agreement which contains a term relating to pension sharing, the court must not make a pension sharing order relating to the arrangement unless it also sets aside the agreement or term under section 16(1)(b) of the 1985 Act.[232]

Application for a pension sharing order must be made by the pursuer by a crave in the initial writ, intimated to the person responsible for the pension arrangement.[233] The defender must apply for a pension sharing order by a crave in the defences, intimated to the person responsible for the pension arrangement.[234] Where any such application has been made, the court must make such order, if any, as is:

(a) justified by the principles set out in section 9 of the Family Law (Scotland) Act 1985; and

(b) reasonable having regard to the resources of the parties.[235]

Any pension sharing order is deemed never to have taken effect if the person responsible for the arrangement to which the order relates does not receive before the end of the period of 2 months beginning with the relevant date (*i.e.* the date of the extract of the decree responsible for the divorce or dissolution of civil partnership to which the order relates)—

(a) copies of the relevant documents (*i.e.* copies of the pension sharing order and the decree responsible for the divorce or dissolution of civil partnership to which the order relates),

(b) such information relating to the transferor and transferee as the Secretary of State may prescribe by regulations.[236]

---

[231] 1985 Act, s. 8(6), as inserted by the Welfare Reform and Pensions Act 1999, Sched. 12, para. 6.

[232] 1985 Act, s. 8(5), as inserted by the Welfare Reform and Pensions Act 1999, Sched. 12, para. 6. As to qualifying agreements and terms relating to pension sharing, see text accompanying nn. 176–180, *supra*.

[233] rr. 33.7(1)(m) and 33.48(1)(a) and (2)(a) or rr. 33A.7(1)(k) and 33A.45(1)(a) and (2)(a).

[234] rr. 33.15(3) and 33.34(1)(b)(ii) and (2)(b) or 33.48(1)(a) and (2)(a) or rr. 33A.15(3) and 33A.34(1)(b)(ii) and (2)(b) or 33A.45(1)(a) and (2)(a).

[235] 1985 Act, s. 8(2).

[236] Welfare Reform and Pensions Act 1999, s. 28(7)–(9), as amended by the Civil Partnership Act 2004, Sched. 27, para. 159(8)–(10). As to the sheriff's power to extend the period or otherwise allow further time for compliance, see text accompanying nn. 316–319, *infra*.

Pension compensation sharing orders

The court may make a pension compensation sharing order under section 8(2) of the 1985 Act on granting decree of divorce or of dissolution of a civil partnership.[237] The court may include in the order provision about apportionment between the parties of any charge under section 117 of the Pensions Act 2008 or corresponding Northern Ireland legislation.[238]

A "pension compensation sharing order" is a an order which—

(a) provides that one party's shareable rights to PPF compensation that derive from rights under a specified compensation scheme (that is, specified in the order) are to be subject to pension compensation sharing for the benefit of the other party; and

(b) specifies the percentage value or amount to be transferred.[239]

The reference to shareable rights to PPF compensation is to rights in relation to which pension compensation sharing is available under Chapter 1 of Part 3 of the Pensions Act 2008 or under corresponding Northern Ireland legislation.[240] For the purposes of the Chapter, a right of a person to PPF compensation is "shareable" unless it is of a description specified by regulations.[241]

However, the court must not, in the same proceedings, make both a pension compensation sharing order and an additional order under section 12B(2) of the 1985 Act in respect of PPF compensation in relation to the same PPF compensation.[242] The court must not either make a compensation sharing order in relation to rights to PPF compensation that—

(a) derive from rights under a pension scheme which is subject to

---

[237] 1985 Act, s. 8(1) and (2), as amended by the Civil Partnership Act 2004, Sched. 28, para. 14(1).

[238] 1985 Act, s. 8B, as inserted by the Pensions Act 2008, Sched. 7, para. 3. Applicable regulations made under s. 117 of the Pensions Act 2008 are the Pension Protection Fund (Pension Compensation Sharing and Attachment on Divorce etc.) Regulations 2011 (S.I. 2011 No. 731), reproduced in App. X, *infra*.

[239] 1985 Act, s. 27(1), as inserted by the Pensions Act 2008, Sched. 7, para. 9. In relation to the pension compensation sharing mechanism, see further the 2008 Act, Pt. 3, Chaps. 1 and 2; the Pension Protection Fund (Pension Compensation Sharing and Attachment on Divorce etc.) Regulations 2011 (S.I. 2011 No. 731); the Pension Protection Fund (Pensions on Divorce etc. Charges) Regulations 2011 (S.I. 2011 No. 726), reproduced in App. X, *infra*.

[240] 1985 Act, s. 27(1B), as inserted by the Pensions Act 2008, Sched. 7, para. 9.

[241] Pensions Act 2008, s. 107(2). The regulations are the Pension Protection Fund (Pension Compensation Sharing and Attachment on Divorce etc.) Regulations 2011 (S.I. 2011 No. 731), reproduced in App. X, *infra*.

[242] 1985 Act, s. 8(8), as inserted by the Pensions Act 2008, Sched. 7, para. 2.

an order under section 12A(2) or (3) of the 1985 Act in respect
of a pension lump sum in relation to the marriage or (as the
case may be) civil partnership or a previous one between the
same persons,

(b) derive from rights under a pension scheme which were at
any time the subject of a pension sharing order in relation
to the marriage or (as the case may be) civil partnership or a
previous one between the same persons,

(c) are or have been the subject of a pension compensation sharing
order in relation to the marriage or (as the case may be) civil
partnership or a previous one between the same persons, or

(d) are the subject of an additional order under section 12B(2)
of the 1985 Act in respect of PPF compensation in relation
to the marriage or (as the case may be) civil partnership or a
previous one between the same persons.[243]

Where, as regards PPF compensation, the parties to a marriage or
the partners in a civil partnership have in effect a qualifying agreement
which contains a term relating to pension compensation sharing, the
court must not make an order relating to the compensation unless it
also sets aside the agreement or term under section 16(1)(b) of the
1985 Act.[244]

Application for a pension compensation sharing order must be
made by the pursuer by a crave in the initial writ, intimated to the
Board of the Pension Protection Fund.[245] The defender must apply
for a pension compensation sharing order by a crave in the defences,
intimated to the Board of the Pension Protection Fund.[246] Where any
such application has been made, the court must make such order, if any,
as is:

(a) justified by the principles set out in section 9 of the Family
Law (Scotland) Act 1985; and

(b) reasonable having regard to the resources of the parties.[247]

Any pension sharing compensation order is deemed never to have
taken effect if the Board of the Pension Protection Fund does not
receive before the end of the period of 2 months beginning with the

---

[243] 1985 Act, s. 8(9), as inserted by the Pensions Act 2008, Sched. 7, para. 2.

[244] 1985 Act, s. 8(10), as inserted by the Pensions Act 2008, Sched. 7, para. 2. As to qualifying
agreements and terms relating to pension compensation sharing, see text accompanying
nn. 194–197, *supra*.

[245] rr. 33.7(1)(n) and 33.48(1)(a) and (2)(a) or rr. 33A.7(1)(l) and 33A.45(1)(a) and (2)(a).

[246] rr. 33.15(3) and 33.34(1)(b)(ii) and (2)(b) or 33.48(1)(a) and (2)(a) or rr. 33A.15(3) and
33A.34(1)(b)(ii) and (2)(b) or 33A.45(1)(a) and (2)(a).

[247] 1985 Act, s. 8(2).

relevant date (*i.e.* the date of the extract of the decree responsible for the divorce or dissolution of civil partnership to which the order relates)

(a)   copies of the relevant documents (*i.e.* copies of the pension sharing order and the decree responsible for the divorce or dissolution of civil partnership to which it relates);

(b)   such information relating to the transferor and transferee as the Secretary of State may prescribe by regulations.[248]

Periodical allowance orders

The court may make an order for the making of a periodical allowance to one party to a marriage, or one civil partner, by the other under section 8(2) of the 1985 Act—

(a)   on granting decree of divorce or of dissolution of a civil partnership; or

(b)   within such period as the court on granting the decree may specify.[249]

An order for a periodical allowance may be for a definite or an indefinite period or until the happening of a specified event.[250] A party is entitled to argue for a restriction in the duration of an order without having given advance notice of his intention so to contend.[251]

---

[248] Pensions Act 2008, s. 110(2)–(4). As to the sheriff's power to extend the period or otherwise allow further time for compliance, see text accompanying nn. 320–321, *infra*.

[249] 1985 Act, ss. 8(1) and (2) and 13(1)(a) and (b), as amended by the Civil Partnership Act 2004, Sched. 28, paras. 14(1) and 20(2). As to s. 13(1)(b), see text accompanying nn. 322–324, *infra*. Cases in which a periodical allowance has been awarded include *Monkman v. Monkman*, 1988 S.L.T. (Sh. Ct.) 37 (for 10 years); *Dever v. Dever*, 1988 S.C.L.R. 352 (for 6 months); *Petrie v. Petrie*, 1988 S.C.L.R. 390 (for 1 year); *Atkinson v. Atkinson*, 1988 S.C.L.R. 396 (for 3 years); *Bell v. Bell*, 1988 S.C.L.R. 457 (until pursuer's death or remarriage or defender's 60th birthday); *Park v. Park*, 1988 S.C.L.R. 584 (for 1 year with an award at a reduced rate for a further year); *McDevitt v. McDevitt*, 1988 S.C.L.R. 206 (for 3 years); *Muir v. Muir*, 1989 S.L.T. (Sh. Ct.) 20 (for 1 year); *Tyrrell v. Tyrrell*, 1990 S.L.T. (Sh. Ct.) 406 (for 1 year); *Johnstone v. Johnstone*, 1990 S.L.T. (Sh. Ct.) 79 (until death or remarriage); *Barclay v. Barclay*, 1991 S.C.L.R. 205 (for 3 years); *Toye v. Toye*, 1992 S.C.L.R. 95 (for 3 years); *Loudon v. Loudon*, 1994 S.L.T. 381 (for 1 year); *McConnell v. McConnell (No. 2)*, 1997 Fam. L.R. 108 (for 6 months); *Gribb v. Gribb*, 1996 S.L.T. 719 (until death or remarriage); *Buckle v. Buckle*, 1995 S.C.L.R. 590 (for 1 year); *Haughan v. Haughan*, 1996 S.L.T. 321 (until death or remarriage); *Wilson v. Wilson*, 1999 S.L.T. 249 (for 30 months); *Galloway v. Galloway*, 2003 Fam. L.R. 10 (for 6 years); *L v. L*, 2003 Fam. L.R. 101 (for 3 years or until capital sum fully paid, whichever sooner); *Burnside v. Burnside*, 2007 Fam. L.R. 144 (for 3 years); *Sutherland v. Sutherland*, 2008 Fam. L.R. 151 (for 2 years); *Smith v. Smith*, 2010 S.L.T. 372 (for 3 years, with an additional amount until sale of matrimonial home, followed by an award at a reduced rate until defender's retirement).

[250] 1985 Act, s. 13(3).

[251] *Robertson v. Robertson*, 1989 S.C.L.R. 71.

Application for a periodical allowance order must be made by a crave in the initial writ or defences, as the case may be.[252] The pleadings of the applicant must contain an averment stating whether and, if so, when and by whom a maintenance order (within the meaning of section 106 of the Debtors (Scotland) Act 1987) has been granted in favour of or against that party or of any other person in respect of whom the order is sought.[253] Where an application for a periodical allowance order has been made, the court must not make the order unless—

(a) the order is justified by a principle set out in paragraph (c), (d) or (e) of section 9(1) of the Family Law (Scotland) Act 1985; and

(b) it is satisfied that an order for payment of a capital sum or for transfer of property or a pension sharing order or pension compensation sharing order would be inappropriate or insufficient to satisfy the requirements of section 8(2) of the 1985 Act (*viz.* that the court should make such order, if any, as is justified by the principles set out in section 9(1) of the Act and reasonable having regard to the resources of the parties).[254]

The claimant must aver and prove that these conditions are satisfied, for otherwise the principle of the "clean break" embodied in the Family Law (Scotland) Act 1985 prevents the court from considering the question of periodical allowance at all.[255]

An order for a periodical allowance—

(a) shall, if subsisting at the death of the person making the payment, continue to operate against the person's estate, but without prejudice to the making of an order after decree for variation or recall of the order for a periodical allowance order or for its conversion into an order for payment of a capital sum or for a transfer of property;

(b) shall cease to have effect on the person receiving payment—
    (i) marrying,
    (ii) entering into a civil partnership, or
    (iii) dying,

except in relation to any arrears due under it.[256]

---

[252] r. 33.48(1)(a) and (2)(a) or r. 33A.45(1)(a) and (2)(a).

[253] r. 33.5 or r. 33A.5.

[254] 1985 Act, s. 13(2), as amended by the Welfare Reform and Pensions Act 1999, Sched. 12, para. 10 and the Pensions Act 2008, Sched. 7, para. 7. See, *e.g., Savage v. Savage,* 1997 Fam. L.R. 132; *McConnell v. McConnell (No. 2),* 1997 Fam. L.R. 108.

[255] *Mackin v. Mackin,* 1991 S.L.T. (Sh. Ct.) 22 at p. 24.

[256] 1985 Act, s. 13(7), as amended by the Civil Partnership Act 2004, Sched. 28, para. 20(4).

Incidental orders

The court may make an incidental order under section 8(2) of the 1985 Act on the granting or refusal of decree of divorce or of dissolution of a civil partnership.[257]

Section 14(2) of the 1985 Act[258] provides that in the Act, "an incidental order" means one or more of the following orders—

(a)   an order for the sale of property;

(b)   an order for the valuation of property;

(c)   an order determining any dispute between the parties to the marriage, or as the case may be the partners, as to their respective property rights by means of a declarator thereof or otherwise;

(d)   an order regulating the occupation of—

　　(i)   the matrimonial home; or

　　(ii)   the family home of the partnership,

or the use of furniture or plenishings therein or excluding either person from such occupation;

(e)   an order regulating liability, as between the persons, for outgoings in respect of—

　　(i)   the matrimonial home; or

　　(ii)   the family home of the partnership,

or furniture or plenishings therein;

(f)   an order that security shall be given for any financial provision;

(g)   an order that payments shall be made or property transferred to any curator bonis or trustee or other person for the benefit of the person by whom or on whose behalf application has been made under section 8(1) of the 1985 Act for an incidental order;

(h)   an order setting aside or varying any term in an antenuptial or postnuptial marriage settlement or in any corresponding settlement in respect of the civil partnership;[259]

(j)   an order as to the date from which any interest on any amount awarded shall run;

---

[257] 1985 Act, ss. 8(1) and (2) and 14(1), as amended by the Civil Partnership Act 2004, Sched. 28, paras. 14(2) and 21(2).

[258] As amended by the Civil Partnership Act 2004, Sched. 28, para. 21(3) and as inserted by the Family Law (Scotland) Act 2006, s. 20.

[259] "Settlement" includes a settlement by way of a policy of assurance to which s. 2 of the Married Women's Policies of Assurance (Scotland) Act 1880 relates—1985 Act, s. 14(6). A co-partnery contract relative to the parties' farming business was held not to be a "marriage settlement" in *Robertson v. Robertson*, 2003 S.L.T. 208.

(ja) in relation to a deed relating to moveable property, an order dispensing with the execution of the deed by the grantor and directing the sheriff clerk to execute the deed;

(k) any ancillary order which is expedient to give effect to the principles set out in section 9 of the 1985 Act or to any order made under section 8(2) of the Act.[260]

Section 14 gives the court a discretionary power to be exercised in the circumstances of each case.[261] The phrase "incidental order" means what it says, namely something done by way of order incidental or ancillary to the making of an order under section 8(2) of the Act (orders for financial provision).[262] Incidental orders therefore exist to facilitate the making of the main orders of capital payment, transfer of property, periodical allowance and pension sharing.[263]

An incidental order under section 14(2)(a) for the sale of property thus requires to be, at least principally, aimed at financial provision on divorce or dissolution of civil partnership and cannot be made just to save the applicant the trouble of raising a separate action for division and sale.[264] Where the parties to the action are the whole partners in a firm, an incidental order for the sale of the firm's property is competent where both agree to the sale.[265]

For so long as an incidental order in terms of section 14(2)(d) regulating occupation of the matrimonial home or family home remains in force, the former spouse or civil partner is deemed to be, except to the extent that the order otherwise provides, a non-entitled spouse or non-entitled partner with occupancy rights in the property as regards (i) certain general powers of management in relation thereto; and (ii) protection against certain arrangements intended to defeat those rights.[266]

---

[260] See, *e.g.*, *Little v. Little*, 1990 S.L.T. 785 at p. 792 (order made regarding conveyancing expenses).

[261] *McKeown v. McKeown*, 1988 S.C.L.R. 355.

[262] *Demarco v. Demarco*, 1990 S.C.L.R. 635.

[263] *Amin v. Amin*, 2000 S.L.T. (Sh. Ct.) 115.

[264] *Reynolds v. Reynolds*, 1991 S.C.L.R. 175 at p. 176; *MacClue v. MacClue*, 1994 S.C.L.R. 933. An incidental order under s. 14(2)(a) was granted in *Reynolds*; *Lewis v. Lewis*, 1993 S.C.L.R. 32; *Jacques v. Jacques*, 1995 S.C. 327; *Crosbie v. Crosbie*, 1996 S.L.T. (Sh. Ct.) 86; *Thomson v. Thomson*, 2003 Fam. L.R. 22; *Cordiner v. Cordiner*, 2003 Fam. L.R. 39; *McCaskill v. McCaskill*, 2004 Fam. L.R. 123; *Connolly v. Connolly*, 2005 Fam. L.R. 106; *Sutherland v. Sutherland*, 2008 Fam. L.R. 151; *Smith v. Smith*, 2010 S.L.T. 372; *Porter v. Porter*, 2010 Fam. L.R. 68.

[265] *Clark v. Clark (No. 2)*, 2007 Fam. L.R. 34.

[266] 1985 Act, s. 14(5), (5A) and (5B), as amended by the Bankruptcy (Scotland) Act 1985, Sched. 7, para. 23 and inserted by the Civil Partnership Act 2004, Sched. 28, para. 21(5). An incidental order under s. 14(2)(d) was made in *Little v. Little*, 1990 S.L.T. 785 and *Symon v. Symon*, 1991 S.C.L.R. 414.

An incidental order may be granted under section 14(2)(e) for mortgage payments to be made for a period.[267] Such an order is incompetent as regards mortgage payments already made.[268]

The security required by an incidental order under section 14(2)(f) may take the form of a standard security over the property of a party found liable to pay a capital sum.[269] It is incompetent to order security for alimentary payments however.[270]

An incidental order under section 14(2)(j) relative to the date from which interest on any amount awarded should run must be seen as an integral part of the order for financial provision, and not as something added on afterwards once all the exercises to arrive at this provision are complete.[271] Thus, where a party has had the sole use or possession of an asset since the relevant date, the whole or part of the value of which is to be shared with the other party on divorce or dissolution of civil partnership, he may be required to pay interest as consideration for the use or possession which he has had between the relevant date and the date of decree.[272] Backdating of interest may be refused where the liable party has cared for the parties' children since separation.[273] In any case where a party seeks interest from a date prior to the date of decree, principles of fair notice require the case for such interest to be outlined in averments.[274] Any interest to date of decree may be awarded in the form of a lump sum.[275]

An incidental order for the discharge of a loan heritably secured over the matrimonial home may be made as an ancillary order under section 14(2)(k).[276] A party may seek a principal order for financial provision in his favour and an ancillary order in favour of the other party.[277] Such might include, for example, an order for payment of a counterbalancing sum by the applicant as a condition of transfer of a property to him or an order requiring the applicant to secure variation of a standard security whereby the other party may be freed of all liability thereunder.[278]

---

[267] *McCormick v. McCormick*, 1994 G.W.D. 35-2078 (order granted for a period until transfer of property order given effect to).

[268] *Macdonald v. Macdonald*, 1995 S.L.T. 72.

[269] *Ibid.*

[270] *Ibid.*

[271] *Geddes v. Geddes,* 1993 S.L.T. 494.

[272] *Ibid.*; *Welsh v. Welsh*, 1994 S.L.T. 828.

[273] *MacLean v. MacLean*, 2001 Fam. L.R. 118.

[274] *Watt v. Watt,* 2009 S.L.T. 931.

[275] *Savage v. Savage*, 1997 Fam. L.R. 132.

[276] *McConnell v. McConnell*, 1997 Fam. L.R. 97.

[277] *Murdoch v. Murdoch*, 2012 Fam. L.R. 2.

[278] *Ibid.*

Application for an incidental order must be made by a crave in the initial writ or defences, as the case may be.[279] Where any such application has been made, the court must make such order, if any, as is:

(a) justified by the principles set out in section 9 of the Family Law (Scotland) Act 1985; and
(b) reasonable having regard to the resources of the parties.[280]

Neither an incidental order, nor any rights conferred by such an order, shall prejudice any rights of any third party insofar as those rights existed immediately before the making of the order.[281]

Orders setting aside or varying agreements on financial provision

Where the parties to a marriage or the partners in a civil partnership have entered into an agreement[282] as to financial provision to be made on divorce or on dissolution of civil partnership, the court has power to make certain orders under section 16(1)(b) and (3) of the Family Law (Scotland) Act 1985.

The court may make an order under section 16(1)(b) of the Act[283] setting aside or varying the agreement or any term of it where the agreement was not fair and reasonable at the time it was entered into. The court may make an order under this provision—

(a) if the agreement contains neither a term relating to pension sharing[284] nor a term relating to pension compensation sharing,[285] on granting decree of divorce or of dissolution of civil

---

[279] r. 33.48(1)(a) and (2)(a) or r. 33A.45(1)(a) and (2)(a). *C. f. Trotter v. Trotter*, 2001 S.L.T. (Sh. Ct.) 42 (application not entertained in absence of crave).

[280] 1985 Act, s. 8(2); *Geddes v. Geddes*, 1993 S.L.T. 494 at p. 499.

[281] 1985 Act, s. 15(3).

[282] Such an agreement could include an antenuptial agreement (*Kibble v. Kibble*, 2010 S.L.T. (Sh. Ct.) 5), an agreement recorded in a joint minute (*Jongejan v. Jongejan*, 1993 S.L.T. 595) or an agreement contained in minutes of tender and acceptance of tender (*Young v. Young (No. 2)*, 1991 S.L.T. 869).

[283] As amended by the Civil Partnership Act 2004, Sched. 28, para. 22(1) and (2).

[284] A term relating to pension sharing is a term corresponding to provision which may be made in a pension sharing order and satisfying the requirements set out in s. 28(1)(f) or s. 48(1)(f) of the Welfare Reform and Pensions Act 1999—1985 Act, s. 16(2A), as inserted by the 1999 Act, Sched. 12, para. 11(2). See text accompanying nn. 176–180, *supra*.

[285] A term relating to pension compensation sharing is a term corresponding to provision which may be made in a pension compensation sharing order and satisfying the requirements set out in s. 109(g) of the Pensions Act 2008—1985 Act, s. 16(2AA), as inserted by the 2008 Act, Sched. 7, para. 8(d). See text accompanying nn. 194–197, *supra*.

partnership or within such time as the court may specify on granting decree of divorce or of dissolution of civil partnership;

(b) if the agreement contains a term relating to pension sharing or pension compensation sharing—

    (i) where the order sets aside the agreement or sets aside or varies the term relating to pension sharing or (as the case may be) the term relating to pension compensation sharing, on granting decree of divorce or of dissolution of civil partnership; or

    (ii) where the order sets aside or varies any other term of the agreement, on granting decree of divorce or of dissolution of civil partnership or within such time thereafter as the court may specify on granting decree of divorce or of dissolution of civil partnership.[286]

Where the agreement includes provision in respect of a person's rights or interest or benefits under an occupational pension scheme, the Board of the Pension Protection Fund's subsequently assuming responsibility for that scheme in accordance with Chapter 3 of Part 2 of the Pension Act 2004 or any provision in force in Northern Ireland corresponding to that Chapter shall not affect—

(a) the power of the court under section 16(1)(b) to make an order setting aside or varying the agreement or any term of it;

(b) on an appeal, the powers of the appeal court in relation to the order.[287]

For the purposes of section 16(1)(b), in considering whether or not an agreement was fair and reasonable at the time it was entered into, the court may have regard to the following principles:

(1) It is necessary to examine the agreement from the point of view of both fairness and reasonableness;

(2) Such examination must relate to all the relevant circumstances leading up to and prevailing at the time of the execution of the agreement, including among other things the nature and quality of any legal advice given to either party;

(3) Evidence that some unfair advantage was taken by one party of the other by reason of circumstances prevailing at the time of negotiations may have a cogent bearing on the determination of the issue;

---

[286] 1985 Act, s. 16(2)(b) and (c), as amended by the Family Law (Scotland) Act 2006, Sched. 2, para. 5(3).

[287] 1985 Act, s. 16(2B) and (2C), as inserted by the Family Law (Scotland) Act 2006, s. 17.

(4) The court should not be unduly ready to overturn agreements validly entered into; and

(5) The fact that it transpires that an agreement has led to an unequal and possibly a very unequal division of assets does not by itself necessarily give rise to any inference of unfairness and unreasonableness.[288]

Thus, for example, an agreement may be set aside where relevant information was withheld during negotiations,[289] where the parties were in error as to the existence or value of an important asset,[290] or where there was coercion inducing signature of the agreement.[291] It is not necessary for the applicant to establish both unfairness and unreasonableness.[292]

Without prejudice to the foregoing, the court may, on granting decree of divorce or dissolution of civil partnership, make an order under section 16(3) of the Act[293] setting aside or varying any term of an agreement relating to a periodical allowance where—

(a) the estate of the person by whom any periodical allowance is payable under the agreement has, since the date when the agreement was entered into, been sequestrated, the award of sequestration has not been recalled, and the person has not been discharged;

(b) an analogous remedy within the meaning of section 10(5) of the Bankruptcy (Scotland) Act 1985 has, since that date, come into force and remains in force in respect of that person's estate;

(c) that person's estate is being administered by a trustee acting under a voluntary trust deed granted since that date by the person for the benefit of his creditors generally or is subject to an analogous arrangement; or

(d) by virtue of the making of a maintenance calculation, child support maintenance has become payable by either party to

---

[288] *McAfee v. McAfee*, 1990 S.C.L.R. 805 at p. 808; *Gillon v. Gillon (No. 1)*, 1994 S.L.T. 978 at p. 982; *Gillon v. Gillon (No. 3)*, 1995 S.L.T. 678 at p. 681; *Clarkson v. Clarkson*, 2008 S.L.T. (Sh. Ct.) 2 at p. 6. The applicant was unsuccessful in *Anderson v. Anderson*, 1991 S.L.T. (Sh. Ct.) 11; *Gillon v. Gillon (No. 3)*, 1995 S.L.T. 678; *Inglis v. Inglis*, 1999 S.L.T. (Sh. Ct.) 59; *Turner v. Turner*, 2009 Fam. L.R. 124.

[289] *McKay v. McKay*, 2006 S.L.T. (Sh. Ct.) 149; *MacDonald v. MacDonald*, 2009 S.C.L.R. 520.

[290] *Worth v. Worth*, 1994 S.L.T. (Sh. Ct.) 54; *Clarkson v. Clarkson*, 2008 S.L.T. (Sh. Ct.) 2.

[291] *MacDonald v. MacDonald*, 2009 S.C.L.R. 520.

[292] *Clarkson v. Clarkson*, 2008 S.L.T. (Sh. Ct.) 2 at p. 6.

[293] As amended by the Child Support, Pensions and Social Security Act 2000, Sched. 3, para. 5(5), the Child Support (Amendments to Primary Legislation) (Scotland) Order 1993 (S.I. 1993 No. 660), art. 2(5) and the Civil Partnership Act 2004, Sched. 28, para. 22(3).

the agreement with respect to a child to whom or for whose benefit periodical allowance is paid under that agreement.

Application for an order under section 16(1)(b) or (3) of the Act must be made by a crave in the initial writ or defences, as the case may be.[294] A preliminary proof on such a crave is competent, so long as the court confines itself to sustaining and repelling pleas-in-law relative thereto and does not take the additional step of pronouncing an order setting aside or varying the agreement or any term of it, or any term relating to a periodical allowance, as the case may be, at the preliminary stage, such order being competent only on granting decree of divorce or dissolution of civil partnership.[295]

Any term of an agreement purporting to exclude the right to apply for an order under section 16(1)(b) or (3) is void.[296]

ORDERS MADE AFTER THE GRANTING OF DECREE

After decree of divorce or dissolution of civil partnership has been granted, the court may make certain orders for financial provision in the process of the original action. These are considered in turn.

Capital sum orders

By virtue of section 12(1)(b) of the 1985 Act,[297] the court may make an order for payment of a capital sum to one party to a marriage, or one civil partner, by the other under section 8(2) of the 1985 Act within such period as the court on granting decree of divorce or dissolution of civil partnership may specify.[298]

No such period can be extended using the provisions of the 1985 Act.[299] However, where the court on granting decree of divorce or dissolution of civil partnership specifies a period within which a capital sum order may be granted and proof in relation to the application for

---

[294] r. 33.48(1)(a) and (2)(b) or r. 33A.45(1)(a) and (2)(b). *C.f. Stewart v. Stewart*, 1990 S.C.L.R. 360 (application not entertained in absence of crave).

[295] *Gillon v. Gillon*, 1994 S.C. 162.

[296] 1985 Act, s. 16(4).

[297] As amended by the Civil Partnership Act 2004, Sched. 28, para. 18(2).

[298] See, *e.g., M v. M, W Estate Trustees Ltd and Another*, 2011 Fam. L.R. 24 (order for capital sum and periodical payments to be made within 13 months of divorce). Note that O.C.R 33.51(1)(a)(ii) or 33.48(1)(a)(ii) envisages that such a period may be specified by the court even where no application for an order for financial provision has yet been made, enacting that an application after final decree under s. 12(1)(b) of the Act (payment of capital sum) shall be made by minute in the process of the action to which the application relates.

[299] *Lindsay v. Lindsay*, 2005 S.L.T. (Sh. Ct.) 81 and 2007 Fam. L.R. 18.

that order commences but does not conclude within that period, the court has an inherent jurisdiction to extend the period in order to allow the proof to be concluded and justice done between the parties.[300]

In terms of section 12(4) of the 1985 Act,[301] where a capital sum order has been made, the court may, on an application by either party to the marriage, or either partner, on a material change of circumstances, vary the date or method of payment of the capital sum. Application after final decree for any such variation must be made by minute in the process of the action to which the application relates.[302]

Capital sum orders: pension lump sums

Section 12A(5) of the 1985 Act[303] enacts that where the liability of the liable person under a capital sum order has been discharged in whole or in part, other than by a payment by the person responsible for the pension arrangement under an order under section 12A(2) or (3) in respect of a pension lump sum, the court may, on an application by any person having an interest, recall any such order or vary the amount specified in such an order, as appears to the court appropriate in the circumstances. Application for such recall or variation must be made by minute in the process of the action to which the application relates.[304]

In terms of section 12A(7) of the Act,[305] the court may, on an application by any person having an interest, vary an order in respect of a pension lump sum by substituting for the person responsible for the pension arrangement specified in the order the person responsible for any other pension arrangement under which any lump sum referred to in section 12A(1) of the Act is payable to the liable person or in respect of his death. Application for such variation must be made by minute in the process of the action to which the application relates.[306]

For the purpose only of giving effect to section 12A(7), the court may deal with an order in respect of a pension lump sum so that it—

    (a)   is addressed to the Board of the Pension Protection Fund

---

[300] *Ibid.*

[301] As amended by the Civil Partnership Act 2004, Sched. 28, para. 18(3).

[302] r. 33.51(1)(a)(iii) or r. 33A.48(1)(a)(iii).

[303] As inserted by the Pensions Act 1995, s. 167(3) and amended by the Welfare Reform and Pensions Act 1999, Sched. 12, para. 9(6) and the Civil Partnership Act 2004, Sched. 28, para. 19(4).

[304] r. 33.51(3)(a) or r. 33A.48(3)(a).

[305] As inserted by the Pensions Act 1995, s. 167(3) and amended by the Welfare Reform and Pensions Act 1999, Sched. 12, para. 9(8) and the Civil Partnership Act 2004, Sched. 28, para. 19(4).

[306] r. 33.51(3)(b) or r. 33A.48(3)(b).

instead of the person responsible for the pension arrangement; and

(b) takes effect in respect of an entitlement to compensation payable under Chapter 3 of Part 2 of the Pensions Act 2004, or any corresponding provision in force in Northern Ireland, instead of rights in relation to any lump sum referred to in section 12A(1) of the 1985 Act which is payable to the liable party.[307]

Capital sum orders: pension compensation

Section 12B(4) of the 1985 Act[308] provides that where the liability of the liable person under the capital sum order has been discharged in whole or in part, other than by a payment by the Board of the Pension Protection Fund, the court may, on an application by any person having an interest, recall the order or vary the amount specified in such an order as appears to the court appropriate in the circumstances.

Application for such recall or variation must be made by minute in the process of the action to which the application relates.[309]

Transfer of property orders

In terms of section 12(1)(b) of the 1985 Act,[310] the court may make an order for transfer of property to one party to a marriage, or one civil partner, by the other under section 8(2) of the 1985 Act within such period as the court on granting decree may specify.[311]

No such period can be extended using the provisions of the 1985 Act.[312] However, where the court on granting decree of divorce or dissolution of civil partnership specifies a period within which a transfer of property order may be granted and proof in relation to the application for that order commences but does not conclude within that period, the court has an inherent jurisdiction to extend the period

---

[307] 1985 Act, s. 12A(7ZC) as inserted by the Family Law (Scotland) Act 2006 (Consequential Modifications) Order 2006 (S.S.I. 2006 No. 384), art. 8 and amended by the Pensions Act 2008, Sched. 7, para. 5.

[308] As inserted by the Pensions Act 2008, Sched. 7, para. 6.

[309] r. 33.51(3)(ba) or r. 33A.48(3)(ba).

[310] As amended by the Civil Partnership Act 2004, Sched. 28, para. 18(2).

[311] O.C.R. 33.51(1)(a)(ii) or 33A.48(1)(a)(ii) envisages that such a period may be specified by the court even where no application for an order for financial provision has yet been made, enacting that an application after final decree under s. 12(1)(b) of the Act (transfer of property) shall be made by minute in the process of the action to which the application relates.

[312] *Lindsay v. Lindsay*, 2005 S.L.T. (Sh. Ct.) 81 and 2007 Fam. L.R. 18.

in order to allow the proof to be concluded and justice done between the parties.[313]

In terms of section 12(4) of the 1985 Act,[314] where a transfer of property order has been made, the court may, on an application by either party to the marriage, or either partner, on a material change of circumstances, vary the date of transfer of property. Application after final decree for any such variation must be made by minute in the process of the action to which the application relates.[315]

Pension sharing orders

By virtue of sections 28(10) and 48(9) of the Welfare Reform and Pensions Act 1999, the sheriff may make an order relating to the activation of pension sharing in relation to pension sharing orders.

In terms of sections 28(7) and 48(6) of the 1999 Act,[316] if the person responsible for the pension arrangement to which the order relates or the Secretary of State, as the case may be, does not receive before the end of the period of 2 months beginning with the relevant date copies of the matrimonial documents and such information relating to the transferor and transferee as the Secretary of State may prescribe by regulations, the pension sharing order shall be deemed never to have taken effect.[317] The sheriff may in such circumstances, on the application of any person having an interest, make an order—

(a) extending the aforesaid period of 2 months; and
(b) if that period has already expired, providing that, if the person responsible for the pension arrangement receives the documents and information concerned before the end of the period specified in the order, section 28(7) or 48(6) of the 1999 Act, as the case may be, is to be treated as never having applied.[318]

Application for any such order must be made by minute in the process of the action to which the application relates.[319]

---

[313] *Ibid.*
[314] As amended by the Civil Partnership Act 2004, Sched. 28, para. 18(3).
[315] r. 33.51(1)(a)(iii) or r. 33A.48(1)(a)(iii).
[316] As amended by the Civil Partnership Act 2004, Sched. 27, paras. 159(8) and 161(8).
[317] See, further, text accompanying n. 236 *supra*.
[318] Welfare Reform and Pensions Act 1999, ss. 28(10) and 48(9).
[319] r. 33.51(3)(c) or r. 33A.48(3)(c).

Pension compensation sharing orders

In terms of section 110(5) of the Pensions Act 2008, the sheriff may make an order relating to the activation of pension compensation sharing in relation to pension compensation sharing orders.

By virtue of section 110(2) of the 2008 Act, if the Board of the Pension Protection Fund does not receive before the end of the period of 2 months beginning with the relevant date a copy of the relevant documents and such information relating to the transferor and transferee as the Secretary of State may prescribe by regulations, the pension compensation sharing order is to be regarded as never having taken effect.[320] The sheriff may in such circumstances, on the application of any person having an interest, make an order—

(a) extending the aforesaid period of 2 months; and
(b) if that period has already expired, providing that, if the person responsible for the pension arrangement receives the documents and information concerned before the end of the period specified in the order, section 110(2) of the 2008 Act is to be treated as never having applied.[321]

Periodical allowance orders

Section 13(1) of the 1985 Act[322] *inter alia* provides that an order under section 8(2) for a periodical allowance may be made:

"(b) within such period as the court on granting decree of divorce or of dissolution of civil partnership may specify; or
(c) after the granting of decree of divorce or of dissolution of civil partnership where—
  (i) no such order has been made previously;
  (ii) application for the order has been made after the date of decree; and
  (iii) since the date of decree there has been a change of circumstances."

As regards section 13(1)(b), no such period can be extended using the provisions of the 1985 Act.[323] However, where the court on granting decree of divorce or dissolution of civil partnership specifies a period within which a periodical allowance order may be granted and proof in relation to the application for that order commences but does not

---

[320] See, further, text accompanying n. 248, *supra*.
[321] Pensions Act 2008, s. 110(5).
[322] As amended by the Civil Partnership Act 2004, Sched. 28, para. 20(2).
[323] *Lindsay v. Lindsay*, 2005 S.L.T. (Sh. Ct.) 81 and 2007 Fam. L.R. 18.

conclude within that period, the court has an inherent jurisdiction to extend the period in order to allow the proof to be concluded and justice done between the parties.[324]

An order for a periodical allowance may be for a definite or an indefinite period or until the happening of a specified event.[325] A party is entitled to argue for a restriction in the duration of an order without having given advance notice of his intention so to contend.[326]

Application after final decree for an order for a periodical allowance must be made by minute in the process of the action to which the application relates.[327] The pleadings of the applicant must contain an averment stating whether and, if so, when and by whom a maintenance order (within the meaning of section 106 of the Debtors (Scotland) Act 1987) has been granted in favour of or against that party or of any other person in respect of whom the order is sought.[328] Where such a minute is lodged, any party may lodge a motion for any interim order which may be made pending the determination of the application.[329] Where an application for a periodical allowance order has been made, the court must not make the order unless—

(a) the order is justified by a principle set out in paragraph (c), (d) or (e) of section 9(1) of the Family Law (Scotland) Act 1985; and

(b) it is satisfied that an order for payment of a capital sum or for transfer of property or a pension sharing order or pension compensation sharing order would be inappropriate or insufficient to satisfy the requirements of section 8(2) of the 1985 Act (*viz.* that the court should make such order, if any, as is justified by the principles set out in section 9(1) of the Act and reasonable having regard to the resources of the parties).[330]

An order for a periodical allowance—

(a) shall, if subsisting at the death of the person making the payment, continue to operate against the person's estate, but without prejudice to the making of an order after decree for

---

[324] *Ibid.*

[325] 1985 Act, s. 13(3).

[326] *Robertson v. Robertson*, 1989 S.C.L.R. 71.

[327] r. 33.51(1)(a)(i) or r. 33A.48(1)(a)(i).

[328] r. 33.5 or r. 33A.5.

[329] r. 33.51(2) or r. 33A.48(2).

[330] 1985 Act, s. 13(2), as amended by the Welfare Reform and Pensions Act 1999, Sched. 12, para. 10 and the Pensions Act 2008, Sched. 7, para. 7. See, *e.g., Savage v. Savage*, 1997 Fam. L.R. 132; *McConnell v. McConnell (No. 2)*, 1997 Fam. L.R. 108.

variation or recall of the order for a periodical allowance order
or for its conversion into an order for payment of a capital
sum or for a transfer of property;
  (b) shall cease to have effect on the person receiving payment —
      (i) marrying,
      (ii) entering into a civil partnership, or
      (iii) dying,

except in relation to any arrears due under it.[331]

Section 13(4) of the 1985 Act[332] states that where an order for a
periodical allowance has been made under section 8(2), and since the
date of the order there has been a material change of circumstances,
the court shall, on an application by or on behalf of either party to the
marriage or his executor,[333] or as the case may be either partner or his
executor, have power by subsequent order —

  (a) to vary or recall the order for a periodical allowance;
  (b) to backdate such variation or recall to the date of the
      application therefor or, on cause shown, to an earlier date;
  (c) to convert the order into an order for payment of a capital
      sum or for a transfer of property.

Without prejudice to the generality of section 13(4), the making of
a maintenance calculation with respect to a child who has his home
with a person to whom the periodical allowance is made (being a
child to whom the person making the allowance has an obligation
of aliment) is a material change of circumstances for the purposes of
that subsection.[334] The death and resultant loss of earning capacity of
the former spouse or partner against whom the periodical allowance
order was made amounts to a material change of circumstances.[335] On
the other hand, a material change of circumstances is not constituted
merely by showing that the court at the time of the earlier award
proceeded upon a particular hypothesis which has turned out to be
incorrect.[336]

---

[331] 1985 Act, s. 13(7), as amended by the Civil Partnership Act 2004, Sched. 28, para. 20(4).

[332] As amended by the Civil Partnership Act 2004, Sched. 28, para. 20(3).

[333] See, *e.g., Sandison's Exrx. v. Sandison*, 1984 S.L.T. 111 and *Finlayson v. Finlayson's Exrx.*, 1986 S.L.T. 19.

[334] 1985 Act, s. 13(4A), as inserted by the Child Support (Amendments to Primary Legislation) (Scotland) Order 1993 (S.I. 1993 No. 660 (S. 98)), art. 2(4) and amended by the Child Support, Pensions and Social Security Act 2000, Sched. 3, para. 5(4).

[335] *Sandison's Exrx. v. Sandison*, 1984 S.L.T. 111 and *Finlayson v. Finlayson's Exrx.*, 1986 S.L.T. 19.

[336] *Walker v. Walker*, 1994 S.C. 482.

Where the court backdates an order under paragraph (b) above, the court may order any sums paid by way of periodical allowance to be repaid.[337] The provisions of the 1985 Act apply to applications under section 13(4) as they apply to applications for periodical allowance and orders on such applications.[338]

Application after final decree for any order under section 13(4) of the Act must be made by minute in the process of the action to which the application relates.[339] The pleadings of the applicant must contain an averment stating whether and, if so, when and by whom a maintenance order (within the meaning of section 106 of the Debtors (Scotland) Act 1987) has been granted in favour of or against that party or of any other person in respect of whom the order is sought.[340] Where such a minute is lodged, any party may lodge a motion for any interim order which may be made pending the determination of the application.[341]

Incidental orders

In terms of section 14(1) of the Family Law (Scotland) Act 1985,[342] incidental orders may be made under section 8(2) of the Act after the granting or refusal of decree of divorce or dissolution of civil partnership.

Incidental orders are listed in section 14(2) of the Act, detailed above. These orders exist however to facilitate the making of the main orders of capital payment, transfer of property, periodical allowance and pension sharing.[343] Accordingly, an application after decree of divorce or dissolution of civil partnership for an incidental order for the sale of property in terms of section 14(2)(a) is incompetent.[344] On the other hand, section 14(3) of the Act[345] provides that an incidental order referred to in section 14(2)(d) and (e) (regulation of occupation and liability for outgoings in respect of the matrimonial home or family home) may be made only on or after the granting of decree of divorce or dissolution of civil partnership. Thus, the court has power after decree to deal with a situation where one party continues to occupy the matrimonial home or family home while it stands in the name of the other.[346] An incidental order in the form of an ancillary order that

---

[337] 1985 Act, s. 13(6).
[338] 1985 Act, s. 13(5).
[339] r. 33.51(1)(a)(iv) or r. 33A.48(1)(a)(iv).
[340] r. 33.5 or r. 33A.5.
[341] r. 33.51(2) or r. 33A.48(2).
[342] As amended by the Civil Partnership Act 2004, Sched. 28, para. 21(2).
[343] *Amin v. Amin*, 2000 S.L.T. (Sh. Ct.) 115; *Williams v. Williams*, 2008 S.L.T. (Sh. Ct.) 134.
[344] *Amin v. Amin*, 2000 S.L.T. (Sh. Ct.) 115.
[345] As amended by the Civil Partnership Act 2004, Sched. 28, para. 21(4).
[346] *Amin v. Amin*, 2000 S.L.T. (Sh. Ct.) 115 at p. 116.

is expedient to give effect to an order for financial provision may be granted after decree.[347]

Section 14 of the 1985 Act gives the court a discretionary power to be exercised in the circumstances of each case.[348] Application after final decree for an incidental order must be made by minute in the process of the action to which the application relates.[349] Where such a minute is lodged, any party may lodge a motion for any interim order which may be made pending the determination of the application.[350]

In terms of section 14(4), an incidental order may be varied or recalled by subsequent order on cause shown. An application after the grant or refusal of an application under —

(i)   section 8(1) or 14(3) of the 1985 Act for an incidental order, or

(ii) section 14(4) of the Act (variation or recall of incidental order)

must be made by minute in the process of the action to which the application relates.[351] Where such a minute is lodged, any party may lodge a motion for any interim order which may be made pending the determination of the application.[352]

Orders setting aside or varying agreements on financial provision

Where the parties to a marriage or the partners in a civil partnership have entered into an agreement[353] as to financial provision to be made on divorce or on dissolution of civil partnership, the court has power, at any time after granting decree of divorce or of dissolution of civil partnership, to make an order under section 16(1)(a) of the Family Law (Scotland) Act 1985[354] setting aside or varying any term of the agreement relating to a periodical allowance where the agreement expressly provides for the subsequent setting aside or variation of that

---

[347] *C.f. Walker v. Walker,* 1994 G.W.D. 8-496 (former wife ordained to sign and deliver necessary forms of indemnity and disclaimer in connection with 3 joint insurance policies that had formed part of the matrimonial property).

[348] *McKeown v. McKeown,* 1988 S.C.L.R. 355.

[349] r. 33.51(1)(a)(v) or r. 33A.48(1)(a)(v).

[350] r. 33.51(2) or r. 33A.48(2).

[351] r. 33.51(1)(b) or r. 33A.48(1)(b).

[352] r. 33.51(2) or r. 33A.48(2).

[353] Such an agreement could include an antenuptial agreement (*Kibble v. Kibble*, 2010 S.L.T. (Sh. Ct.) 5), an agreement recorded in a joint minute (*Jongejan v. Jongejan*, 1993 S.L.T. 595) or an agreement contained in minutes of tender and acceptance of tender (*Young v. Young (No. 2)*, 1991 S.L.T. 869).

[354] As amended by the Civil Partnership Act 2004, Sched. 28, para. 22(2).

term.[355] In the absence of such express provision in the agreement, the court does not have this power.[356]

The court has power, at any time after granting decree of divorce or dissolution of civil partnership, to make an order under section 16(3) of the Act[357] setting aside or varying any term of an agreement relating to a periodical allowance where —

(a) the estate of the person by whom any periodical allowance is payable under the agreement has, since the date when the agreement was entered into, been sequestrated, the award of sequestration has not been recalled, and the person has not been discharged;

(b) an analogous remedy within the meaning of section 10(5) of the Bankruptcy (Scotland) Act 1985 has, since that date, come into force and remains in force in respect of that person's estate;

(c) that person's estate is being administered by a trustee acting under a voluntary trust deed granted since that date by the person for the benefit of his creditors generally or is subject to an analogous arrangement; or

(d) by virtue of the making of a maintenance calculation, child support maintenance has become payable by either party to the agreement with respect to a child to whom or for whose benefit periodical allowance is paid under that agreement.

An application for an order under section 16(1)(a) or (3) of the 1985 Act made after final decree must be made by minute in the process of the action to which the application relates.[358]

---

[355] 1985 Act, s. 16(2)(a). See, *e.g., Mills v. Mills*, 1990 S.C.L.R. 213.

[356] *Ellerby v. Ellerby*, 1991 S.C.L.R. 608.

[357] As amended by the Child Support, Pensions and Social Security Act 2000, Sched. 3, para. 5(5), the Child Support (Amendments to Primary Legislation) (Scotland) Order 1993 (S.I. 1993 No. 660), art. 2((5) and the Civil Partnership Act 2004, Sched. 28, para. 22(3).

[358] r. 33.52(a) or r. 33A.49(a).

SPECIMEN CRAVES AND ASSOCIATED PLEAS-IN-LAW

1. MERITS

C—   (i)   To divorce the defender from the pursuer on the ground that the marriage has broken down irretrievably as established by the defender's adultery.

      (ii)   To divorce the defender from the pursuer on the ground that the marriage has broken down irretrievably as established by the defender's behaviour.

      (iii)   To divorce the defender from the pursuer on the ground that the marriage has broken down irretrievably as established by the parties' non-cohabitation for a continuous period of one year or more and the defender's consent to the granting of decree of divorce.

      (iv)   To divorce the defender from the pursuer on the ground that the marriage has broken down irretrievably as established by the parties' non-cohabitation for a continuous period of two years or more.

P—   The marriage of the parties having broken down irretrievably, the pursuer is entitled to decree of divorce as first craved.

C—   (i)   To dissolve the civil partnership between the pursuer and the defender on the ground that the civil partnership has broken down irretrievably as established by the defender's behaviour.

      (ii)   To dissolve the civil partnership between the pursuer and the defender on the ground that the civil partnership has broken down irretrievably as established by the parties' non-cohabitation for a continuous period of one year or more and the defender's consent to the granting of decree of dissolution of the civil partnership.

      (iii)   To dissolve the civil partnership between the pursuer and the defender on the ground that the civil partnership has broken down irretrievably as established by the parties' non-cohabitation for a continuous period of two years or more.

P—   The civil partnership of the parties having broken down irretrievably, the pursuer is entitled to decree of dissolution of civil partnership as first craved.

C—   To divorce the defender from the pursuer on the ground that an interim gender recognition certificate under the Gender Recognition Act 2004 has, after the date of the marriage, been issued to the pursuer.

P—   An interim gender recognition certificate having after the date of the marriage been issued to the pursuer, the pursuer is entitled to decree of divorce as first craved.

C—   To dissolve the civil partnership between the pursuer and the defender on the ground that an interim gender recognition certificate under the Gender Recognition Act 2004 has, after the date of registration of the civil partnership, been issued to the pursuer.

P—   An interim gender recognition certificate having after the date of the registration of the civil partnership been issued to the pursuer, the pursuer is entitled to decree of dissolution of civil partnership as first craved.

C—   To divorce the defender from the pursuer on the ground that an interim gender recognition certificate under the Gender Recognition Act 2004 has, after the date of the marriage, been issued to the defender.

P—   An interim gender recognition certificate having after the date of the marriage been issued to the defender, the pursuer is entitled to decree of divorce as first craved.

C—   To dissolve the civil partnership between the pursuer and the defender on the ground that an interim gender recognition certificate under the Gender Recognition Act 2004 has, after the date of registration of the civil partnership, been issued to the defender.

P—   An interim gender recognition certificate having after the date of registration of the civil partnership been issued to the defender, the pursuer is entitled to decree of dissolution of civil partnership as first craved.

C—   To postpone the grant of decree of divorce until the defender has given consent to the pursuer's remarriage.

P—   The pursuer being prevented from entering into a religious marriage by virtue of a requirement of that religion and the defender being able to act so as to remove, or enable or contribute to the removal of, the impediment which prevents that marriage, and it being just and reasonable to do so, the grant of decree of divorce should be postponed as   craved.

2. PROTECTIVE MEASURES

C—   (1)   To interdict the defender from abusing the pursuer by means of violence, harassment, threatening conduct, or any other conduct giving rise, or likely to give rise, to physical or mental injury, fear, alarm or distress; to make a determination, in pursuance of section 3(1) of the Domestic Abuse (Scotland) Act 2011, that the said interdict is a domestic abuse interdict; and to attach a power of arrest to the said interdict; and

(2)   To interdict the defender from entering or remaining in the pursuer's place of work at "George's Salon", 35 Leven Street, Geetown; to make a determination, in pursuance of section 3(1) of the Domestic Abuse (Scotland) Act 2011, that the said interdict is a domestic abuse interdict; and to attach a power of arrest to the said interdict.

P—   The defender having abused the pursuer in the manner condescended on, and having shown an intention to persist therein, the pursuer is entitled to interdict as   craved.

P—   The interdicts   craved being domestic abuse interdicts, a determination to that effect should be made as craved.

P—   A power of arrest being necessary to protect the pursuer from a risk of abuse in breach of the interdicts, should be attached to each of the said interdicts as   craved.

C—   To ordain the defender to appear personally before the court on such day and at such hour as the court may appoint to answer to the charge against him of being guilty of contempt of court and breach of the interdict granted by the Sheriff of North Strathclyde at Oban on 5 February 2012, whereby the defender was interdicted from abusing the pursuer by *inter alia* using violence towards her; and failing his appearance before the court as aforesaid, to grant warrant to officers of the court to apprehend the defender and bring him before the court to answer as aforesaid; and, on the charge being admitted or proved, to find that the defender has been guilty of contempt of court and breach of interdict and in respect thereof to visit him with such punishment as to the court shall seem just; and to find the defender liable in expenses.

P— The defender, being in breach of interdict as condescended on, should be found guilty and punished as craved.

C— (1) To grant an exclusion order suspending the defender's occupancy rights in the matrimonial home at 1 High Street, Seatown;

(2) To grant warrant for the summary ejection of the defender from the matrimonial home at 1 High Street, Seatown;

(3) To interdict the defender from entering the matrimonial home at 1 High Street, Seatown without the express permission of the pursuer; and to attach a power of arrest to the said interdict;

(4) To interdict the defender from entering or remaining in High Street, Seatown; and to attach a power of arrest to the said interdict;

(5) To make a determination, in pursuance of section 3(1) of the Domestic Abuse (Scotland) Act 2011, that each of the foregoing interdicts is a domestic abuse interdict; and

(6) To interdict the defender from removing, except with the written consent of the pursuer or by a further order of the court, any furniture or plenishings in the matrimonial home at 1 High Street, Seatown.

P— An exclusion order being necessary for the protection of the pursuer from reasonably apprehended conduct of the defender which would be injurious to her health, and the pursuer being entitled to the ancillary orders craved, an exclusion order suspending the defender's occupancy rights in the matrimonial home and orders ancillary thereto should be granted as craved.

P– The interdicts craved being domestic abuse interdicts, a determination to that effect should be made.

C— (1) To grant an exclusion order suspending the defender's occupancy rights in the family home at 15 Low Street, Efftown;

(2) To grant warrant for the summary ejection of the defender from the family home at 15 Low Street, Efftown;

(3) To interdict the defender from entering the family home at 15 Low Street, Efftown without the express permission of the pursuer; and to attach a power of arrest to the said interdict;

(4)   To interdict the defender from entering or remaining in Low Street, Efftown; and to attach a power of arrest to the said interdict;

(5)   To make a determination, in pursuance of section 3(1) of the Domestic Abuse (Scotland) Act 2011, that each of the foregoing interdicts is a domestic abuse interdict; and

(6)   To interdict the defender from removing, except with the written consent of the pursuer or by a further order of the court, any furniture or plenishings in the family home at 15 Low Street, Efftown.

P—   An exclusion order being necessary for the protection of the pursuer from reasonably apprehended conduct of the defender which would be injurious to her health, and the pursuer being entitled to the ancillary orders craved, an exclusion order suspending the defender's occupancy rights in the family home and orders ancillary thereto should be granted as   craved.

P –   The interdicts   craved being domestic abuse interdicts, a determination to that effect should be made.

C—   To interdict the defender from effecting any transfer of, or transaction involving, any redundancy payment received or to be received by him from Rosebank Ltd, 15 Gold Street, Seatown, which has the effect of defeating in whole or in part the pursuer's claim for financial provision as   craved; and to grant such other order as the court thinks fit.

P—   The defender being liable to effect a transfer of, or transaction involving, his property which is likely to have the effect of defeating the pursuer's claim for financial provision in whole or in part, interdict should be granted as   craved.

3. PROPERTY ORDERS

C—   To find and declare that the pursuer is entitled to occupy the matrimonial home at 110 High Street, Seatown.

P—   The pursuer being a non-entitled spouse and the said dwelling house being a matrimonial home, the pursuer is entitled to declarator as   craved.

C—   To find and declare that the pursuer is entitled to occupy the family home at 14 Dover Road, Enntown.

P— The pursuer being a non-entitled partner and the said dwelling house being a family home, the pursuer is entitled to declarator as   craved.

C— To grant leave to the pursuer to enter and occupy the matrimonial home at 110 High Street, Seatown.

P— The pursuer being a non-entitled spouse and it being just and reasonable for the occupancy rights of the pursuer to be enforced, leave to enter and occupy the matrimonial home should be granted as   craved.

C— To grant leave to the pursuer to enter and occupy the family home at 14 Dover Road, Enntown.

P The pursuer being a non-entitled partner and it being just and reasonable for the occupancy rights of the pursuer to be enforced, leave to enter and occupy the family home should be granted as   craved.

C— To grant to the pursuer the possession and use of the items of furniture and plenishings specified in the schedule hereto in the matrimonial home at 110 High Street, Seatown.

P— The pursuer being a non-entitled spouse and it being just and reasonable for the pursuer to be granted the possession and use of the specified items owned by the defender in the matrimonial home, decree therefor should be granted as   craved.

C— To grant to the pursuer the possession and use of the items of furniture and plenishings specified in the schedule hereto in the family home at 14 Dover Road, Enntown.

P The pursuer being a non-entitled partner and it being just and reasonable for the pursuer to be granted the possession and use of the specified items owned by the defender in the family home, decree therefor should be granted as   craved.

C— To grant decree for the transfer of the tenancy of the matrimonial home at 22 High Street, Seatown from the defender to the pursuer.

P— The pursuer being a non-entitled spouse and it being just and reasonable that the tenancy of the matrimonial home be transferred from the defender to the pursuer, decree therefor should be granted as   craved.

C— To grant decree for the transfer of the tenancy of the family home at 14 Dover Road, Enntown from the defender to the pursuer.

P The pursuer being a non-entitled partner and it being just and reasonable that the tenancy of the family home be transferred from the defender to the pursuer, decree therefor should be granted as craved.

C— To grant decree for the vesting of the joint tenancy of the matrimonial home the dwelling house at 22 Low Street, Seatown in the pursuer solely.

P— The pursuer being a joint tenant of the matrimonial home and it being just and reasonable that the said joint tenancy should be vested in the pursuer solely, decree should be granted as craved.

C— To grant decree for the vesting of the joint tenancy of the family home at 14 Dover Road, Enntown in the pursuer solely.

P The pursuer being a joint tenant of the family home and it being just and reasonable that the said joint tenancy should be vested in the pursuer solely, decree should be granted as craved.

4. CHILDREN

C— To make a residence order in respect of John Smith, born 28 March 2007, whereby he is to live with the pursuer.

P— It being in the best interests of the child that the residence order sought be made, decree should be granted as craved.

C— To make a contact order in respect of Alexander Robertson, born 2 October 2010, whereby he is to be with the pursuer each Saturday from 10 a.m. until 6 p.m. and every fourth weekend from 6 p.m. on Friday until 6 p.m. on Sunday.

P— It being in the best interests of the child that the contact order sought be made, decree should be granted as craved.

C— To make a specific issue order in respect of Thomas Thompson, born 11 July 2001, whereby he is to attend

Millerstone Academy for the academic year commencing 16 August 2012.

P— It being in the best interests of the child that the specific issue order sought be made, decree should be granted as craved.

5. MONEY

C— (i) To grant decree against the defender for payment to the pursuer of a capital sum of twenty thousand pounds (£20,000), payable on such date and by such method as the court thinks fit, with interest on the said sum or such proportion thereof as the court thinks fit at the rate of eight per cent a year or such other rate as the court thinks fit from 11 September 2008 or such other date as the court thinks fit until payment.

(ii) To grant decree requiring The Standard Assurance Company plc, 1 George Street, Alva, as persons responsible for the defender's personal pension Scheme, reference number A467045/23, to pay the whole or part of any pension lump sum payable to the defender or in respect of the death of the defender, when it becomes due, to the pursuer.

(iii) To grant decree requiring The Board of the Pension Protection Fund, if at any time any payment in respect of Pension Protection Fund compensation relating to the occupational pension scheme of Artis Ltd, 31 Pearl Street, Glasgow, becomes due to the defender, to pay the whole or part of that payment to the pursuer.

(iv) To grant decree, subject to payment of such sum (if any) to the defender by the pursuer as the court thinks fit, for the transfer of the defender's right title and interest in the heritable property at 4 Old Street, Avebury to the pursuer; to ordain the defender to make, execute and deliver to the pursuer a valid disposition of the said subjects and such other deeds as may be necessary to give the pursuer a valid title to the subjects, and that within one month of the date of decree to follow hereon; and in the event of the defender failing to make, execute and deliver such disposition and other deeds, to authorise and ordain the sheriff clerk to subscribe on behalf of the defender a disposition of the subjects and such other deeds as may be necessary to give the pursuer a valid title to the subjects, all as adjusted at the sight of the sheriff clerk.

(v) To grant decree providing that the defender's shareable

rights under his personal pension scheme with Prudential Life Co. Ltd, 23 Albert Square, Edinburgh, reference number 3544667/23, shall be subject to pension sharing for the benefit of the pursuer and that the sum of one hundred and fifty thousand pounds (£150,000), with interest accrued at eight per cent a year from 1 July 2009 or at such other rate and from such other date as the court thinks fit until the date of transfer of the appropriate pension credit into a qualifying scheme for the pursuer, be so transferred.

(vi) To grant decree providing that the defender's shareable rights to Pension Protection Fund compensation relating to the occupational pension scheme of Trainspotters Limited, 12 Calvin Drive, Edinburgh shall be subject to pension compensation sharing for the benefit of the pursuer and that fifty per cent (50%) of any such rights shall be transferred to the pursuer.

P— The order craved being justified by the principles set forth in section 9(1) of the Family Law (Scotland) Act 1985 and reasonable having regard to the resources of the parties, should be granted.

C— (i) To grant an incidental order for the sale of the parties' heritable property at 6 Abbey Street, Perth and for that purpose to grant warrant to such person as the court shall think proper to dispose of the subjects, heritably and irredeemably, by public roup or private bargain, in such manner and under such conditions as the court shall direct; to ordain the pursuer and the defender to execute and deliver to the purchaser or purchasers of the subjects such dispositions and other deeds as shall be necessary for constituting full right thereto in their persons, failing which to dispense with such execution and delivery and to direct the sheriff clerk to execute such dispositions and other deeds all as adjusted at his sight as shall be necessary aforesaid; and to make such order regarding the price of the subjects when sold, after deduction of any debts or burdens affecting the same and all other expenses attending the sale, as to the court seems proper.

(ii) To grant an incidental order declaring that the pursuer is the sole owner of the Ford Escort motor car, registration number R123 ABC.

(iii) To grant an incidental order entitling the pursuer to reside in the heritable property at 5 Low Street, Aberdeen and excluding the defender therefrom for three years or such other period following upon the granting of decree as to the court seems proper.

(iv) To grant an incidental order declaring the defender liable, as between the parties, for a period of three years or such other period following upon the granting of decree as to the court seems proper, to make all the mortgage payments, as they fall due, to the National Building Society, 1 Ervine Road, Carlops, in respect of the loan secured by the standard security granted by the parties in favour of the said National Building Society on 5 August 2002 over the heritable property at 4 Princess Road, Carlops.

(v) To grant an incidental order ordaining the defender to grant a standard security over his heritable property at 6 Royal Mews, Ayr in favour of the pursuer for all sums due and to become due to her in respect of the order for financial provision craved and failing his doing so within such time as the court may specify to authorise and direct the sheriff clerk to execute such standard security, as adjusted at his sight.

P— The order craved being justified by the principles set forth in section 9(1) of the Family Law (Scotland) Act 1985 and reasonable having regard to the resources of the parties, should be granted.

C— To grant decree against the defender for payment to the pursuer of a periodical allowance of fifty pounds (£50) per week for a period of three years, or such lesser period as the court thinks fit, from the date of decree of divorce or until the death or remarriage of the pursuer, if sooner.

C— To grant decree against the defender for payment to the pursuer of a periodical allowance of ninety pounds (£90) per week for a period of three years, or such lesser period as the court thinks fit, from the date of dissolution of the civil partnership of the parties or until the death of, or the entering into a civil partnership by, the pursuer, if sooner.

P— The order craved being justified by the principle set forth in section 9(1)(d) of the Family Law (Scotland) Act 1985 and reasonable having regard to the resources of the parties and an order for payment of a capital sum or for transfer of property or a pension sharing order being insufficient *et separatim* inappropriate to satisfy the requirements of section 8(2) of the Family Law (Scotland) Act 1985, the order craved as aforesaid should be granted.

C— To grant decree against the defender for payment to the pursuer of a periodical allowance of seventy-five pounds (£75) per week until the death or remarriage of the pursuer or for such lesser period as the court thinks fit.

C— To grant decree against the defender for payment to the pursuer of a periodical allowance of one hundred and twenty pounds (£120) per week until the death of, or entering into a civil partnership by, the pursuer or for such lesser period as the court thinks fit.

P— The order   craved being justified by the principle detailed in section 9(1)(e) of the Family Law (Scotland) Act 1985 and reasonable having regard to the resources of the parties, and an order for payment of a capital sum or for transfer of property or a pension sharing order being insufficient *et separatim* inappropriate to satisfy the requirements of section 8(2) of the Family Law (Scotland) Act 1985, the order craved as aforesaid should be granted.

C— To grant an order setting aside the agreement as to financial provision on divorce between the parties entered into on 13 March 2009.

P— The agreement as to financial provision on divorce between the parties not being fair and reasonable at the time it was entered into, should be set aside as   craved.

C— To vary the decree dated 7 April 2011 insofar as providing for payment by the defender to the pursuer of a capital sum and that by substituting for the date of payment specified therein the date "7 August 2013".

P— There having been a material change of circumstances, the interlocutor should be varied as craved.

C— To recall the decree dated 15 July 2009, insofar as it ordains the defender to make payment to the pursuer of a periodical allowance, with effect from such date as to the court seems appropriate, and to ordain the repayment by the pursuer to the defender of such sum or sums as the court thinks fit.

P— There having been a material change of circumstances the said order should be recalled as craved.

6. MISCELLANEOUS

C— To grant warrant to intimate this initial writ to Mrs Jane

Jackson, residing at 2 Park Grove, Aytown, mother and one of the next of kin of the defender; and to Mamie Jackson, residing at 52 Maple Terrace, Beetown, daughter of the defender who has reached the age of 16 years.

C— To grant warrant to intimate this initial writ to Mary Black, residing at 2 Glebe Street, Seatown, as a person with whom the defender is alleged to have committed adultery.

C— To grant warrant to intimate this initial writ to Alan Smith, 23 Broad Street, Edinburgh, as guardian of the defender under or by virtue of the Adults with Incapacity (Scotland) Act 2000.

C— To grant warrant to intimate this initial writ to Mrs Indira Banda, 5 Calcutta Road, Bombay, as an additional spouse of the defender.

C— To grant warrant to intimate this initial writ to Beetown Council, Central Avenue, Beetown, as a local authority having care of Mark White.

C— To grant warrant to intimate this initial writ to Roger Allan, residing at 1 Main Street, Beetown, as a person liable to maintain Peter Jones.

C— To grant warrant to intimate this initial writ to Henry Smith, residing at 4 Jeffrey Street, Deetown, as a parent of Peter Smith.

C— To grant warrant to intimate to Alan Smith, 101 High Road, Efftown, as a child to whom any section 11 order made as craved would relate.

C— To grant warrant to intimate this initial writ to The Huddersfield Building Society, 123 High Street, Jaytown, as holders of a security in respect of the heritable property at 1 Johnson Terrace, Jaytown.

C— To grant warrant to intimate this initial writ to Peter Evans, 1 Forth Road, Geetown, as a person in whose favour the transfer of the property referred to in the fourth crave was made.

C—   To grant warrant to intimate this initial writ to Seatown Council, Main Square, Seatown, as landlords of the matrimonial home at 1 High Street, Seatown.

C—   To grant warrant to intimate this initial writ to Hugh White, residing at 4 George Place, Seatown, as landlord of the family home at 110 High Street, Seatown.

C—   To grant warrant to intimate this initial writ to the Scottish Amicable Pension Co. Ltd, 23 Lyons Place, Edinburgh, as persons responsible for the defender's personal pension scheme, reference no 24566/765/23.

C—   To grant warrant to intimate this initial writ to the Board of The Pension Protection Fund, Knollys House, 17 Addiscombe Road, Croydon.

C—   To dispense with intimation to George Banks in respect that his address is not known and cannot reasonably be ascertained.

C—   To dispense with intimation to Alan Jones, child under the age of 16 years.

C—   To find the defender liable in expenses.

SPECIMEN MOTIONS

1. MERITS

The pursuer moves the court to allow proof by affidavit evidence.

The pursuer moves the court to allow proof by affidavit evidence in relation to the merits of the action.

The pursuer moves the court to allow the action to proceed as undefended.

The defender moves the court to prorogate the time for implementing the order of the sheriff dated 24 May 2013 by a further 14 days.

The pursuer moves the court to prorogate the time for lodging a record by a further seven days.

The defender moves the court to grant decree of absolvitor, which failing to dismiss the action, with expenses.

The pursuer moves the court to sist the cause for negotiations.

The pursuer moves the court to recall the sist and re-enrol the cause for further procedure.

2. PROTECTIVE MEASURES

The pursuer moves the court to grant interim interdict against the defender from abusing the pursuer by means of violence, harassment, threatening conduct, or any other conduct giving rise, or likely to give rise, to physical or mental injury, fear, alarm or distress.

The pursuer moves the court to make a determination, in pursuance of section 3(1) of the Domestic Abuse (Scotland) Act 2011, that the interim interdict dated 5 June 2013 is a domestic abuse interdict; and to attach a power of arrest to the said interim interdict.

The pursuer moves the court to ordain the defender to appear at the bar to explain his failure to obtemper the interlocutor dated 14 February 2013.

The pursuer moves the court (1) to grant an interim order suspending the defender's occupancy rights in the matrimonial home at 33 Low Street, Enntown; (2) to grant warrant for the summary ejection of the defender therefrom; (3) to grant interim interdict against the defender from entering the said matrimonial home without the express permission of the pursuer; (4) to make a determination, in pursuance of section 3(1) of the Domestic Abuse (Scotland) Act 2011, that the said interim interdict is a domestic abuse interdict; (5) to attach a power of arrest to the said interim interdict; and (6) to grant interim interdict against the defender from removing, except with the written consent of the pursuer or by a further order of the court, any furniture or plenishings in the matrimonial home.

The pursuer moves the court (1) to grant an interim order suspending the defender's occupancy rights in the family home at 16 Parr Street, Eggtown; (2) to grant warrant for the summary ejection of the defender therefrom; (3) to grant interim interdict against the defender from entering the said family home without the express permission of the pursuer; (4) to make a determination, in pursuance of section 3(1) of the Domestic Abuse (Scotland) Act 2011, that the said interim interdict is a domestic abuse interdict; (5) to attach a power of arrest to the said interim interdict; and (6) to grant interim interdict against the defender from removing, except with the written consent of the pursuer or by a further order of the court, any furniture or plenishings in the family home.

The pursuer moves the court to grant interim interdict against the defender from effecting any transfer of, or transaction involving, his Mercedes motor vehicle, registration number A75 GNT, or such other order as the court thinks fit.

The pursuer moves the court to grant warrant for diligence by arrestment on the dependence of the action.

The pursuer moves the court to grant warrant for diligence by inhibition on the dependence of the action.

The defender moves the court (1) to recall the warrant for diligence by arrestment on the dependence of the action granted by the court on 12 January 2013; and (2) to recall the arrestment on the dependence of the action executed in pursuance of the said warrant by way of service of a schedule of arrestment upon Chartered Bank plc, 18 Nova Scotia Street, Leven.

The defender moves the court to restrict the warrant for diligence by inhibition on the dependence of the action granted by interlocutor dated 26 March 2013, and any inhibition executed and registered in pursuance of the said warrant, to the defender's heritable property at 13 Glebe Road, Marchbank.

3. PROPERTY ORDERS

The pursuer moves the court to grant leave to the pursuer to enter the matrimonial home at 63 George Road, Kaytown.

The pursuer moves the court to grant leave to the pursuer to enter the family home at 12 Lennox Street, Enntown.

The pursuer moves the court to dispense with the defender's consent to the sale of the heritable subjects at 56 Andrews Road, Peatown by the pursuer to George Smith, residing at 359 Albert Avenue, Teetown, in terms of missives dated 3, 5 and 6 March 2012.

4. CHILDREN

The pursuer moves the court to grant interim interdict against the defender from removing Joyce Jones, born 23 March 2007, out of the control of the pursuer or furth of the sheriffdom.

The pursuer moves the court to ordain Mrs Eve Stewart to appear at the bar to disclose to the court such information as she has which is relevant to the whereabouts of Alison Brown, born 16 November 2009.

The pursuer moves the court to appoint a local authority or a reporter to investigate and report to the court on the circumstances of Violet Jones, born 4 April 2006, and on proposed arrangements for the care and upbringing of the child.

The pursuer moves the court to make an interim residence order in respect of John Green, born 1 May 2005, whereby he is to reside with the pursuer.

The defender moves the court to make an interim contact order in respect of Mary Jones, born 26 August 2011, whereby she is to be with the defender each Saturday from 10 a.m. until 6 p.m.

5. MONEY

The pursuer moves the court to ordain the defender to make payment to her of interim aliment at the rate of £150 per week.

The defender moves the court to vary the interlocutor dated 13 June 2013 by reducing the interim aliment payable thereunder to the sum of £70 per week.

The pursuer moves the court to ordain the defender to provide details of his resources to the court within 21 days.

The pursuer moves the court to grant an incidental order *pendente lite* for the sale of the heritable property at 21 Black Street, Geetown; to that end, to grant warrant to Allan Jones, Solicitor and Estate Agent, 654 Main Street, Geetown, or such other person as the court thinks fit, to dispose of the subjects in such manner and under such conditions as the court shall direct; and to ordain the parties to execute and deliver such disposition and other deeds as shall be necessary to give a valid title to the subjects to the purchaser or purchasers thereof, which failing to authorise the sheriff clerk to execute such disposition and deeds, as adjusted at his sight.

6. MISCELLANEOUS

The pursuer moves the court to grant warrant to intimate the initial writ to John Jones, 12 High Street, Deetown, as a person with whom the defender is alleged to have had an association.

APPENDIX III

SPECIMEN WRITS[1]

1. HUME v. HUME

A. Initial Writ

SHERIFFDOM OF NORTH STRATHCLYDE AT PAISLEY

INITIAL WRIT

in the cause

MRS KATHLEEN ALICIA ANDREWS
or HUME (Assisted Person), 331 Main
Street, Paisley

PURSUER

against

EDWARD HUME, 52 Great Queen Street,
Manchester

DEFENDER

The pursuer craves the court:

1. To divorce the defender from the pursuer on the ground that the marriage has broken down irretrievably as established by the defender's adultery.
2. To grant warrant to intimate this initial writ to Racquel Smith, residing at 52 Great Queen Street, Manchester, as a person with whom the defender is alleged to have committed adultery.
3. To find the defender liable in expenses.

---

[1] These are drawn from five fictitious sheriff court processes.

180

CONDESCENDENCE

1. The pursuer resides at 331 Main Street, Paisley. The defender resides at 52 Great Queen Street, Manchester. The parties were married in Glasgow 1 July 2000. They have two children: Sheila Amy Alicia Hume, born 5 July 2001, and George Hume, born 22 November 2002. Relative marriage and birth certificates are produced.
2. The pursuer has been habitually resident in Scotland throughout the period of one year immediately preceding the raising of this action. She has been resident within the Sheriffdom of North Strathclyde for a period exceeding 40 days immediately preceding the raising of this action. She is unaware of any proceedings continuing in Scotland or elsewhere which are in respect of the marriage or capable of affecting its validity or subsistence.
3. After their marriage the parties lived together until about 4 May 2012. Since then they have not lived together. The defender has formed an adulterous relationship with Racquel Smith, designed in the third crave. Since the said date they have resided together at 52 Great Queen Street, Manchester and have there committed adultery. The marriage has broken down irretrievably. There is no prospect of a reconciliation. The pursuer now seeks decree of divorce.
4. The said children reside with the pursuer. They are happy and well cared for. The pursuer is willing and able to devote her whole time and attention to them and provide them with a good home.

PLEA-IN-LAW

The marriage of the parties having broken down irretrievably, the pursuer is entitled to decree of divorce as first craved.

IN RESPECT
WHEREOF

Enrolled Solicitor
503 Bank Street, Paisley
Solicitor for Pursuer

2. SMART v. SMART

A. Initial Writ, including Minute for Decree

SHERIFFDOM OF GLASGOW AND STRATHKELVIN AT
GLASGOW

INITIAL WRIT

in the cause

JOANNA WYSE or SMART
(Assisted Person), 4 Gardeners Crescent,
Springboig, Glasgow
PURSUER

against

HENRY JOSEPH SMART, 14 Grove
Place, Dennistoun, Glasgow
DEFENDER

The pursuer craves the court:

1. To divorce the defender from the pursuer on the ground that the marriage has broken down irretrievably as established by the defender's behaviour.
2. To interdict the defender from abusing the pursuer by means of violence, harassment, threatening conduct, and any other conduct giving rise, or likely to give rise, to physical or mental injury, fear, alarm or distress; to make a determination, in pursuance of section 3(1) of the Domestic Abuse (Scotland) Act 2011, that the said interdict is a domestic abuse interdict; and to attach a power of arrest to the said interdict.
3. To find the defender liable in expenses.

CONDESCENDENCE

1. The pursuer resides at 4 Gardeners Crescent, Springboig, Glasgow. The defender resides at 14 Grove Place, Dennistoun, Glasgow. The parties were married at Glasgow on 20 November 2009. They have no children. Relative marriage certificate is produced.
2. The parties are habitually resident in Scotland. The pursuer has been resident in the Sheriffdom of Glasgow and Strathkelvin for a period exceeding 40 days immediately preceding the raising of

this action. She knows of no proceedings continuing in Scotland or elsewhere which are in respect of the marriage or capable of affecting its validity or subsistence.

3. The marriage has broken down irretrievably as established by the defender's behaviour. He developed an alcohol problem. Latterly he drank every day. He would regularly return home drunk late at night. He would become heavily intoxicated at social events to the embarrassment and humiliation of the pursuer. He spent little time at home. He did little to assist in the management of the household. The defender's said behaviour adversely affected the pursuer's health. On or about 6 June 2012, the parties separated. Since then they have not lived together. The pursuer cannot reasonably be expected to cohabit with the defender. There is no prospect of a reconciliation. The pursuer now seeks decree of divorce.

4. Following the parties' separation aforesaid the defender has persistently abused the pursuer. He has frequently abused her by telephone. He has threatened to assault her if she does not resume cohabitation with him. He has followed her in the street demanding a reconciliation. In particular, on or about 5 August 2012, the defender shouted abuse and threats at the pursuer from the street outside her house. The pursuer is apprehensive that he will continue so to act. She is fearful lest he carry out his threats. She accordingly seeks the protection of the interdict and power of arrest second craved.

PLEAS-IN-LAW

1. The marriage of the parties having broken down irretrievably, the pursuer is entitled to decree of divorce as first craved.

2. The defender having abused the pursuer in the manner condescended on, and having shown an intention to persist therein, the pursuer is entitled to interdict as second craved.

3. The interdict second craved being a domestic abuse interdict, a determination to that effect should be made as craved.

4. A power of arrest being necessary to protect the pursuer from a risk of abuse in breach of interdict, should be attached to the said interdict as second craved.

IN RESPECT
WHEREOF

Enrolled Solicitor
692 West George Street,
Glasgow
Solicitor for Pursuer

WADDELL having considered the evidence contained in the affidavits and the other documents all as specified in the schedule hereto and being satisfied that upon the evidence a motion for decree in terms of the first and third craves of the initial writ may properly be made, moves the court accordingly.

IN RESPECT
WHEREOF

Solicitor for Pursuer

SCHEDULE

1. Affidavit of pursuer.
2. Affidavit of Glenda Parkes or Wilson.
3. Marriage certificate, no. 5 of process.

B. Affidavit of Pursuer

SHERIFFDOM OF GLASGOW AND STRATHKELVIN AT
GLASGOW

AFFIDAVIT

of the pursuer

in the cause

JOANNA WYSE or SMART
(Assisted Person), 4 Gardeners Crescent,
Springboig, Glasgow
PURSUER

against

HENRY JOSEPH SMART, 14 Grove
Place, Dennistoun, Glasgow
DEFENDER

At Glasgow, the Fifteenth day of December Two Thousand and Twelve, in the presence of ALLAN WADDELL, Solicitor and Notary Public,

692 West George Street, Glasgow, Compeared: JOANNA WYSE or SMART, residing at 4 Gardeners Crescent, Springboig, Glasgow, who being solemnly sworn, Depones as follows:

1. My full name is Joanna Wyse or Smart. I am 25 years of age, a part-time teller at Citibank, and I reside at 4 Gardeners Crescent, Springboig, Glasgow.
2. I married my husband, Henry Joseph Smart, at present residing at 14 Grove Place, Dennistoun, Glasgow, at Glasgow on 20 November 2009. We have no children. I produce an extract of the entry in the Register of Marriages, no. 5 of process, which I have signed as relative hereto.
3. My husband and I are habitually resident in Scotland. I was resident in the Sheriffdom of Glasgow and Strathkelvin for at least 40 days prior to raising this action of divorce. I do not know of any proceedings continuing in Scotland or elsewhere concerning my marriage or capable of affecting its validity or subsistence.
4. My marriage has broken down irretrievably. I believe that my husband had a drinking problem when we got married but it became progressively worse. Eventually he would never come home without calling in at the pub on the way. When he returned home, he would stay for a short time only before going back out to the pub, where he would stay drinking until closing time. He would then come home drunk. He worked as a TV engineer with Johnsons of Edinburgh Road, Glasgow until he was sacked on account of his drinking.

   My husband's drinking caused me humiliation and embarrassment at the few social events that we attended. My husband behaved so badly at these, because he was hopelessly drunk, that I had to spend almost the entire evening apologising. On one particular occasion, at a disco for a charity held after the death of a friend of mine, I felt particularly bad because my husband had been rude and unpleasant to everybody and had embarrassed and humiliated me in front of a good number of my friends.

   My husband also did virtually nothing to assist with running the house, although I cannot say that he kept me short of money. It was only grudgingly that he ever helped in the decoration of our home, and apart from that he never did anything at all, not even drying the dishes.

   Although my husband never assaulted me, his behaviour certainly affected my health and nerves. I would often get asthmatic attacks because of the stress I felt. Eventually, I felt that I could no longer tolerate his behaviour. On 6 June 2012, I left him and we have not lived together since. I confirm that there is no prospect of a reconciliation between us.

5. Following our separation my husband pestered me by telephone and in the streets, making various threats to hurt me if I did not go back to him. Since I obtained an interim interdict against him to stop him molesting me, I have heard nothing more from him.

All of which is truth as the deponent shall answer to God.

.... Deponent

..... Notary Public

C. Affidavit of Glenda Parkes or Wilson

SHERIFFDOM OF GLASGOW AND STRATHKELVIN AT GLASGOW

AFFIDAVIT

of Mrs Glenda Parkes or Wilson

in the cause

JOANNA WYSE or SMART (Assisted Person), 4 Gardeners Crescent, Springboig, Glasgow

PURSUER

against

HENRY JOSEPH SMART, 14 Grove Place, Dennistoun, Glasgow

DEFENDER

At Glasgow, the Fifteenth day of December Two Thousand and Twelve, in the presence of ALLAN WADDELL, Solicitor and Notary Public, 692 West George Street, Glasgow, Compeared GLENDA PARKES or WILSON, residing at 43 Queen's Road, Springboig, Glasgow, who being solemnly sworn, Depones as follows:

1. My full name is Glenda Parkes or Wilson. I am 27 years of age, a part-time sales assistant and reside at 43 Queen's Road, Springboig, Glasgow.
2. I have been a friend of Joanna Smart, the pursuer in this action, for several years. I came to know her husband pretty well and am able to speak to events during their marriage from my own per-

sonal knowledge. I am aware that Mrs Smart and her husband have been separated since about June of this year. I also know why their relationship broke down: it was solely as a result of the defender's increasing addiction to drink. He seemed to drink virtually every day. He often came round to my house to try to persuade my husband to go drinking with him. Usually he had already had a few and was quite drunk.

I would say that there was a definite effect on Mrs Smart's health. She has asthma and his behaviour affected her asthmatic condition. Before the separation she had to use her inhaler far more than ever before. There were days also when I went to her house and found her sitting in the kitchen in floods of tears. The whole marital relationship slid to rock-bottom as a result of his drinking and its effect on her. I have been at a number of social occasions which they attended before they separated at which he was drunk and I know that she was embarrassed by his behaviour at them. I do not see them ever getting back together again.

All of which is truth as the deponent shall answer to God.

. . . . Deponent

. . . . . Notary Public

3. ANDERSON v. JAMIESON

A. Initial Writ, including Minute for Decree

SHERIFFDOM OF GRAMPIAN, HIGHLAND AND
ISLANDS AT STONEHAVEN

INITIAL WRIT

in the cause

BARBARA ANDERSON, 4 Dundas
Street, Stonehaven
PURSUER

against

OLIVE HANSON or JAMIESON, 4
Nursery Street, Stonehaven
DEFENDER

The pursuer craves the court:

1. To dissolve the civil partnership between the pursuer and the defender on the ground that the civil partnership has broken down irretrievably as established by the parties' non-cohabitation for a continuous period of one year or more and the defender's consent to the granting of decree of dissolution of civil partnership.
2. To grant warrant to intimate this initial writ to Hamish Wilson Robertson, 1 Forge Park, Brechin, as a person who is liable to maintain Peter Robertson.

CONDESCENDENCE

1. The pursuer resides at 4 Dundas Street, Stonehaven. The defender resides at 4 Nursery Street, Stonehaven. The parties registered as civil partners at Edinburgh on 5 December 2011. The defender has a child treated as one of the family by the pursuer: Peter Robertson, born 5 July 2000. Extracts of the relevant entries in the civil partnership register and the register of births are produced. The natural father of the aforesaid child is Hamish Wilson Robertson, designed in the second crave.
2. The parties are habitually resident in Scotland. The pursuer has been resident within the Sheriffdom of Grampian, Highland and Islands

for a period exceeding 40 days immediately preceding the raising of this action. She is unaware of any proceedings continuing in Scotland or elsewhere which are in respect of the civil partnership or capable of affecting its validity or subsistence.

3. After the date of registration of their civil partnership the parties lived together until about 4 January 2012. Since then they have not lived together. The defender is prepared to consent to the granting of decree of dissolution of civil partnership. The civil partnership has broken down irretrievably. There is no prospect of a reconciliation. The pursuer seeks decree of dissolution of civil partnership.

4. The said child resides with the defender and is well looked after. The present arrangements for his care and upbringing are satisfactory.

PLEA-IN-LAW

The civil partnership between the pursuer and the defender having broken down irretrievably, the pursuer is entitled to decree of dissolution of civil partnership as first craved.

IN RESPECT
WHEREOF

Enrolled Solicitor
10 Main Square,
Stonehaven
Solicitor for Pursuer

THOMSON having considered the evidence contained in the affidavits and the other documents all as specified in the schedule hereto and being satisfied that upon the evidence a motion for decree in terms of the first crave of the initial writ may properly be made, moves the court accordingly.

IN RESPECT
WHEREOF

Solicitor for Pursuer

SCHEDULE

1. Affidavit of pursuer.
2. Affidavit of defender.
3. Affidavit of Mrs Jeannie Hogg or Hanson.
4. Certificate of civil partnership, no. 5 of process.
5. Birth certificate, no. 6 of process.
6. Notice of Consent, no. 7 of process.

B. Affidavit of Pursuer

SHERIFFDOM OF GRAMPIAN, HIGHLAND AND
ISLANDS AT STONEHAVEN

AFFIDAVIT

of the pursuer

in the cause

BARBARA ANDERSON, 4 Dundas
Street, Stonehaven

PURSUER

against

OLIVE HANSON JAMIESON, 4
Nursery Street, Stonehaven

DEFENDER

At Stonehaven, the Seventh day of September Two Thousand and
Thirteen, in the presence of JOHN THOMSON, Notary Public, 10
Main Square, Stonehaven, Compeared: residing at 4 Dundas Street,
Stonehaven, who being solemnly sworn, Depones as follows:

1. My full name is Barbara Anderson. I am aged 42 years and I reside
   at 4 Dundas Street, Stonehaven. I am unemployed.
2. I registered as a civil partner of Olive Hanson Jamieson, presently residing at 4 Nursery Street, Stonehaven at Edinburgh on
   5 December 2011. She has a child from a previous marriage: Peter
   Robertson, born 5 July 2000, whose natural father is Hamish Wilson
   Robertson, residing at 1 Forge Park, Brechin, Angus. I treated Peter
   Robertson as one of the family. I produce extracts of the relevant
   entries in the civil partnership and birth registers, numbers 5 and
   6 of process, which I have docqueted as relative hereto.

3. Olive Hanson Jamieson and I are habitually resident in Scotland. I have been resident within the Sheriffdom of Grampian, Highland and Islands for a period exceeding 40 days immediately preceding the raising of this action. I am not aware of any proceedings continuing in Scotland or elsewhere which are in respect of the civil partnership or capable of affecting its validity or subsistence.

4. After registration of our civil partnership Olive Hanson Jamieson and I lived together until about 4 January 2012. Since then we have not lived together. There is no prospect of a reconciliation. Olive Hanson Jamieson consents to the granting of decree of dissolution of civil partnership. I identify her signature on the Form of Consent, no. 7 of process, which I have docqueted as relative hereto.

5. Since the separation I have seen very little of the child, Peter. I am not in a position to speak to the present arrangements for his care and upbringing.

All of which is truth as the Deponent shall answer to God.

.... Deponent

..... Notary Public

C. Affidavit of Amy Anderson

SHERIFFDOM OF GRAMPIAN, HIGHLAND AND
ISLANDS AT STONEHAVEN

AFFIDAVIT

of Amy Anderson

in the cause

BARBARA ANDERSON, 4 Dundas
Street, Stonehaven

PURSUER

against

OLIVE HANSON JAMIESON,
4 Nursery Street, Stonehaven

DEFENDER

At Stonehaven, the Seventh day of September Two Thousand and Thirteen, in the presence of JOHN THOMSON, Notary Public, 10 Main Square, Stonehaven, Compeared: Amy Anderson, residing at 4 Dundas Street, Stonehaven, who being solemnly sworn, Depones as follows:

1. My full name is Amy Anderson, I am aged 67 years. I reside at 4 Dundas Street, Stonehaven. I am retired. I am the mother of Barbara Anderson, the pursuer in this action.
2. My daughter lives with me. I am aware that she separated from Olive Hanson Jamieson, her civil partner, on 4 January 2012. She did in fact come to stay with me at that time and has lived with me ever since. I therefore know that she has not lived with Olive Hanson Jamieson since then.

All of which is truth as the Deponent shall answer to God.

. . . . Deponent

. . . . . Notary Public

D. Affidavit of Defender

SHERIFFDOM OF GRAMPIAN, HIGHLAND AND ISLANDS AT STONEHAVEN

AFFIDAVIT

of the defender

in the cause

BARBARA ANDERSON, 4 Dundas Street, Stonehaven

PURSUER

against

OLIVE HANSON JAMIESON, 4 Nursery Street, Stonehaven

DEFENDER

At Stonehaven, the Twenty-First day of September Two Thousand and Thirteen, in the presence of ALAN MARSH, Notary Public, 11 New Street, Stonehaven, Compeared: OLIVE HANSON JAMIESON, residing at 4 Nursery Street, Stonehaven, who being solemnly sworn, Depones as follows:

1. My full name is Olive Hanson Jamieson. I am aged 32 years and reside at 4 Nursery Street, Stonehaven. I am unemployed.
2. I separated from my civil partner, Barbara Anderson on 4 January 2012. My son Peter Robertson has lived with me since the separation. He stays with me in the former family home at 4 Nursery

Street, Stonehaven. The property is a Scottish Homes house and is well furnished. It comprises a livingroom, two bedrooms, kitchenette and bathroom. Peter has one bedroom and I have the other. I always do my best to keep the house clean and tidy. Peter attends St Mark's Primary School near my house and is getting on well there. The school is a ten minute walk from my home. I accompany my son to and from the school each day. His attendance record is excellent. He has lots of friends with whom he plays regularly.

3. I am unemployed and in receipt of state benefits. I am able to devote my whole time and attention to Peter's care and wellbeing. My mother visits almost every day and helps out where necessary. She also babysits him to allow me to go out from time to time during the evenings. Peter is a happy and healthy boy. He has no contact with my civil partner and does not seem to miss her.

All of which is truth as the Deponent shall answer to God.

. . . . Deponent

. . . . . Notary Public

E. Affidavit of Mrs Jeannie Hogg or Hanson

SHERIFFDOM OF GRAMPIAN, HIGHLAND AND
ISLANDS AT STONEHAVEN

AFFIDAVIT

of Mrs Jeannie Hogg or Hanson

in the cause

BARBARA ANDERSON, 4 Dundas
Street, Stonehaven

PURSUER

against

OLIVE HANSON JAMIESON,
4 Nursery Street, Stonehaven

DEFENDER

At Stonehaven, the Twenty-First day of September, Two Thousand and Seven in the presence of ALAN MARSH, Notary Public, 11 New Street, Stonehaven, Compeared: MRS JEANNIE HOGG or HANSON, residing at 66 Nursery Street, Stonehaven, who being solemnly sworn,

Depones as follows:

1. My full name is Jeannie Hogg or Hanson. I am 55 years of age and reside at 66 Nursery Street, Stonehaven. I am a housewife. I am the mother of the defender, Mrs Olive Hanson Jamieson.
2. My daughter and her civil partner, Barbara Anderson, separated on 4 January 2012. Since then my grandson Peter has lived with my daughter in the former family home at 4 Nursery Street, Stonehaven. I visit them virtually every day and usually spend a couple of hours in their presence. We sit around talking or go out to the shops together. My daughter does not work and devotes all her time to looking after Peter. He is always healthy and happy. He adores his mother and is always relaxed and at ease in her company. He is also happy and carefree when with me. He enjoys staying with me whenever I babysit him, which I do to allow my daughter to go out from time to time during the evenings. He does not see Ms Anderson and never asks after her. He does not appear to miss her at all.
3. My daughter and Peter live in a Scottish Homes house which has a livingroom, two bedrooms, kitchenette and bathroom. Peter has his own bedroom and my daughter has the other. The house is always immaculate. My daughter never allows her home to be anything other than extremely clean and tidy.
4. Peter now attends St Mark's Primary School, Stonehaven. The school is only about ten minutes away by foot. My daughter takes her son to and from school herself every day. If she were for any reason unable to do so, I am always available to step in and help out. His attendance record is excellent and I know he enjoys it. He is forever off to play with some new friend or other.

All of which is truth as the Deponent shall answer to God.

. . . . Deponent

. . . . . Notary Public

4. SCOTT v. SCOTT

A. Initial Writ

SHERIFFDOM OF LOTHIAN AND BORDERS AT
EDINBURGH

INITIAL WRIT

in the cause

MRS ANN GEORGE or SCOTT
(Assisted Person), 5 Merton Grove,
Edinburgh

PURSUER

against

PHILIP SCOTT, 14 Elm Grove, Dalkeith
DEFENDER

The pursuer craves the court:

1. To divorce the defender from the pursuer on the ground that the marriage has broken down irretrievably as established by the parties' non-cohabitation for a continuous period of two years or more.
2. To make a residence order in respect of Daphne Scott, born 25 June 2006, whereby she is to live with the pursuer.
3. Failing an order in terms of the second crave, to make a contact order in respect of Daphne Scott, born 25 June 2006, whereby she is to be with the pursuer each Saturday from 10 a.m. until 6 p.m. and every fourth weekend from 6 p.m. on Friday until 6 p.m. on Sunday.
4. To grant warrant to intimate this initial writ to Mrs Elspeth Scott, residing at 22 George Place, Dalkeith as a person in fact exercising care or control in respect of Daphne Scott.
5. To grant warrant to intimate to Daphne Scott, 22 George Place, Dalkeith, as a child to whom any section 11 order made as craved would relate.
6. To find the defender liable in expenses.

CONDESCENDENCE

1. The pursuer resides at 5 Merton Grove, Edinburgh. The defender resides at 14 Elm Grove, Dalkeith. The parties were married at Edinburgh on

1 March 2001. They have one child, Daphne Scott born 25 June 2006. Relative marriage and birth certificates are produced.

2. The parties are habitually resident in Scotland. The pursuer has been resident within the Sheriffdom of Lothian and Borders for a period exceeding 40 days immediately preceding the raising of this action. She is unaware of any proceedings continuing in Scotland or elsewhere which are in respect of the marriage or capable of affecting its validity or subsistence. She is unaware of any proceedings continuing or concluded in Scotland or elsewhere which relate to the said child.

3. After the marriage the parties lived together until about June 2010. Since then the parties have not lived together. The marriage has broken down irretrievably. There is no prospect of a reconciliation. The pursuer now seeks decree of divorce.

4. After the parties' separation the child resided with the pursuer. On or about 4 March 2012, at or about 7 p.m., the defender came to the pursuer's house. He demanded to see the child forthwith. The pursuer declined to accede. The defender thereupon assaulted her. He forcibly entered the house and seized the child. He removed the child to the house of his mother, Mrs Elspeth Scott, designed in the third crave. The child remains in the care or control of Mrs Scott. It is not in the best interests of the child to live with Mrs Scott or with the defender. The child was well settled and happy with the pursuer. She attended the local school where she performed well. The child wishes to live with the pursuer. It is in her best interests so to do. It is better for her that the residence order which failing the contact order be made than that no order be made at all.

PLEAS-IN-LAW

1. The marriage of the parties having broken down irretrievably, the pursuer is entitled to decree of divorce as first craved.

2. It being in the best interests of the child that the residence order which failing the contact order sought be made, decree should be granted as second or third craved.

IN RESPECT
WHEREOF

Enrolled Solicitor
42 St Charlotte Street,
Edinburgh
Solicitor for Pursuer

B. Defences

SHERIFFDOM OF LOTHIAN AND BORDERS AT
EDINBURGH

DEFENCES

in the cause

MRS ANN GEORGE or SCOTT
(Assisted Person), 5 Merton Grove,
Edinburgh
PURSUER

against

PHILIP SCOTT, 14 Elm Grove, Dalkeith
DEFENDER

The defender craves the court:

1. To make a residence order in respect of Daphne Scott, born 25 June 2006, whereby she is to live with the defender.
2. To grant warrant to intimate to Daphne Scott, 22 George Place, Dalkeith, as a child to whom any section 11 order made as craved would relate.

ANSWERS TO CONDESCENDENCE

1. Admitted under explanation that the defender now resides at 22 George Place, Dalkeith.
2. Believed to be true. The defender knows of no such proceedings.
3. Admitted.
4. Admitted that after the parties' separation the child resided with the pursuer. Admitted that on 4 March 2012, at about 7 p.m. the defender came to the pursuer's house. Admitted that he requested access to the child. Admitted that he removed the child to the house of his mother, Mrs Elspeth Scott. Admitted that the child attended the local school. Not known and not admitted how she performed there. *Quoad ultra* denied. Explained and averred that on the said date, when the defender called at the pursuer's house, he requested access to the child. The pursuer thrust the child into the defender's arms. She told him to keep her for good. The pursuer was drunk at the time. The defender believes and avers that the pursuer is frequently under the influence of alcohol. Her house is

dirty. The child was not being properly looked after. Her clothing was torn and filthy. She required to be thoroughly scrubbed at the defender's mother's house where she now lives. There is ample accommodation there for her. She is well looked after by both the defender and his mother. She is happy living with them. She is settling well at her new school. It is in her best interests to live with the defender. It is better for her that the residence order be made than that no order be made at all. The defender believes and avers that it is further in the best interests of the child not to stay overnight with the pursuer.

Pleas-in-law

1. It being in the best interests of the child that the residence order sought by the defender be made, decree therefor should be pronounced as first craved.
2. It not being in the best interests of the child that the residence order sought by the pursuer be made, decree therefor should not be pronounced as second craved by the pursuer.
3. It not being in the best interests of the child that the contact order sought by the pursuer be made, decree therefor should not be pronounced as third craved by the pursuer.

IN RESPECT
WHEREOF

Enrolled Solicitor
4 Market Street,
Dalkeith
Solicitor for Defender

5. BANKS v. BANKS

A. Initial Writ

SHERIFFDOM OF TAYSIDE, CENTRAL AND FIFE AT DUNDEE

INITIAL WRIT

in the cause

JOHN BANKS, 4 Almond Place,
Liverpool

PURSUER

against

MRS ANNIE ALLISON or BANKS,
1 Park Street, Dundee

DEFENDER

The pursuer craves the court:

1. To divorce the defender from the pursuer on the ground that the marriage has broken down irretrievably as established by the parties' non-cohabitation for a continuous period of two years or more.
2. To grant warrant to intimate this initial writ to Dundee City Council, City Chambers, 21 City Square, Dundee, as a local authority having care of Peter Banks.

CONDESCENDENCE

1. The pursuer resides at 4 Almond Place, Liverpool. The defender resides at 1 Park Street, Dundee. The parties were married at Hamilton on 5 June 1985. There is one child of the marriage under the age of 16 years: Peter Banks, born 5 June 2001. Relative marriage and birth certificates are produced.
2. The defender is habitually resident in Scotland. She has been resident within the Sheriffdom of Tayside, Central and Fife for a period exceeding 40 days immediately preceding the raising of this action. The pursuer is unaware of any proceedings continuing in Scotland or elsewhere which are in respect of the marriage or capable of affecting its validity or subsistence.

3. After their marriage the parties lived together until about 9 January 2010. Since then they have not lived together. The marriage has broken down irretrievably. There is no prospect of a reconciliation. The pursuer seeks decree of divorce.
4. The said child is at present in the care of Dundee City Council, designed in the second crave.

PLEA-IN-LAW

The marriage of the parties having broken down irretrievably, the pursuer is entitled to decree of divorce as first craved.

IN RESPECT
WHEREOF

Enrolled Solicitor,
1 Fleet Street, Glasgow
Solicitor for Pursuer

B. Defences

SHERIFFDOM OF TAYSIDE, CENTRAL AND
FIFE AT DUNDEE

DEFENCES

in the cause

JOHN BANKS, 4 Almond Place,
Liverpool

PURSUER

against

MRS ANNIE ALLISON or BANKS,
1 Park Street, Dundee

DEFENDER

The defender craves the court:

1. To grant decree against the pursuer for payment to the defender of a capital sum of ten thousand pounds (£10,000), payable at such date and by such method as the court thinks fit, with interest on the said sum or such proportion thereof as the court thinks fit at the rate of eight per cent a year or such other rate as the court thinks fit from 9 January 2010 or such other date as the court thinks fit until payment.
2. To grant decree against the pursuer for payment to the defender of a periodical allowance of one hundred pounds (£100) per week for a period of three years, or such lesser period as the court thinks fit, from the date of decree of divorce or until the death or remarriage of the defender, if sooner.

ANSWERS TO CONDESCENDENCE

1. Admitted.
2   Admitted. The defender knows of no such proceedings. The defender knows of no relevant maintenance order within the meaning of section 106 of the Debtors (Scotland) Act 1987.
3. Admitted.
4. Admitted.
5. The defender seeks orders for financial provision on divorce as first and second craved. As at the date of separation the pursuer had savings of £20,000 and the defender had no capital. The defender is in employment as a clerkess and earns about £220 per week. She is in receipt of maintenance from the pursuer at the rate of £100 per week. She has no capital. She has been dependent on the pursuer for financial support throughout the marriage. The pursuer has a substantial income and is well able to make payment of a periodical allowance as craved. In all the circumstances, the sums first and second craved represent, respectively, a fair sharing of the matrimonial property and reasonable financial provision enabling the defender to adjust to the loss of support upon divorce. In these circumstances decree should be granted as first and second craved.

PLEAS-IN-LAW

1. The order first craved being justified by the principle set forth in section 9(1)(a) of the Family Law (Scotland) Act 1985 and reasonable having regard to the parties' resources, should be granted.
2. The order second craved being justified by the principle set forth

in section 9(1)(d) of the Family Law (Scotland) Act 1985 and reasonable having regard to the parties' resources and an order for payment of a capital sum being insufficient to satisfy the requirements of section 8(2) of the Act, the order second craved should be granted.

IN RESPECT
WHEREOF

Enrolled Solicitor,
42 Ainslie Street,
Dundee
Solicitor for Defender

C. Joint Minute for Parties

SHERIFFDOM OF TAYSIDE, CENTRAL AND
FIFE AT DUNDEE

JOINT MINUTE

for the parties

in the cause

JOHN BANKS, 4 Almond Place,
Liverpool

PURSUER

against

MRS ANNIE ALLISON or BANKS,
1 Park Street, Dundee

DEFENDER

JONES for the pursuer and
ADAMS for the defender concurred and hereby concur in stating to the court that in the event of decree of divorce being granted and subject to the approval of the court the parties have agreed and hereby agree as follows:

1. The pursuer shall pay to the defender a capital sum of eight thousand pounds (£8,000), payable upon the granting of decree of divorce, with interest thereon at the rate of eight per cent a year from the date of decree to follow hereon until payment; and
2. The pursuer shall pay to the defender a periodical allowance of one hundred pounds (£100) per week for a period of two years from the date of decree of divorce or until the death or remarriage of the defender, if sooner.

The parties therefore craved and hereby crave the court to interpone authority hereto and grant decree in terms hereof.

IN RESPECT
WHEREOF

Enrolled Solicitor,
1 Fleet Street, Glasgow
Solicitor for Pursuer

Enrolled Solicitor,
42 Ainslie Street,
Dundee
Solicitor for Defender

PRACTICE NOTE RE AFFIDAVITS IN FAMILY ACTIONS[1]

When affidavits may be lodged

1. Once the period within which a notice of intention to defend requires to be lodged has expired without such notice having been lodged, affidavits may be prepared and lodged without any order of the court.

Person before whom sworn or affirmed

2. An affidavit is admissible if it is sworn (or affirmed) before a notary public, justice of the peace, or any person having authority to administer oaths for the place where the affidavit is sworn, such as a commissioner for oaths or a British diplomatic officer or consul abroad. A solicitor acting for a party to the action may act in a notarial capacity when an affidavit is sworn. Any person before whom an affidavit is sworn (referred to below as "the notary") must observe all the normal rules in this connection and must satisfy himself or herself as to the capacity of the witness to swear an affidavit.

Importance of affidavits

3. The witness should be made to appreciate the importance of the affidavit and that the affidavit constitutes his or her evidence in the case. The possible consequences of giving false evidence should be explained to the witness. Before the witness signs the affidavit he or she must have read it or the notary must have read it over to the witness.

Oath or affirmation

4. The witness must be placed on oath or must affirm.

Form and signature of the affidavit

5. The document should be on A4 paper. The affidavit should commence with the words "At   the   day of   20   , in the presence of
I   having been solemnly sworn/having affirmed give evidence as follows:". The affidavit should be drafted in the first person and should take the form of numbered paragraphs. The full name, age, address and occupation of the witness should be given in the first paragraph. The affidavit should end with the

[1] This Practice Note has been issued in each of the Sheriffdoms.

204

words "All of which is the truth as I shall answer to God" or "All of which is affirmed by me to be true", as appropriate. Any blanks in the affidavit must be filled in. Any insertion, deletion or other amendment to the affidavit requires to be initialled by the witness and the notary. Each page must be signed by both the witness and the notary. It is not necessary for the affidavit to be sealed by the notary.

Drafting the affidavit

6. An affidavit should be based on a reliable and full precognition of the witness.

7. The drafter of an affidavit should provide himself or herself, before drawing it, with an up-to-date copy of the pleadings, a copy of the appropriate precognition and the relative productions. The affidavit should be drawn so as to follow the averments in the pleadings to the extent that these are within the knowledge of that particular witness and in the same order.

8. Affidavits should be expressed in the words of the person whose affidavit it is, should be accurate as at the date of the affidavit and should not consist of a repetition of passages in the pleadings. It should be clear from the terms of the affidavit whether the witness is speaking from his or her own knowledge, as when the witness was present and saw what happened, or whether the witness is relying on what he or she was told by a particular person.

Productions

9. Productions already lodged in process must be borrowed up, and put to the party or to the witness who refers to them in his or her affidavit. Each production will require to be referred to in the affidavit by its number of process and must be docqueted and signed by the witness and the notary. If a production has not yet been lodged when the affidavit is sworn, it will require to be identified by the witness in the affidavit, should be docqueted with regard to the affidavit and signed by the witness and the notary. It must then be lodged as a production. Some productions will necessarily be docqueted with regard to more than one affidavit.

10. In consent cases, the defender's written consent form will have to be put to the pursuer in his or her affidavit, and be identified, docqueted and signed in the same way as other productions.

11. In adultery cases, photographs of both the pursuer and the defender may require to be produced, put to the appropriate witnesses and be identified, docqueted and signed in the manner already described.

Date of affidavit

12. All affidavits lodged must be of recent date. This factor is particularly important in cases involving children, cases in which financial craves are involved and in any other circumstances where the evidence of a witness or circumstances to which the wit-

ness speaks are liable to change through the passage of time. The notary must take particular care in such cases to ensure that the affidavit evidence as to such matters is correct as at the time the affidavit is sworn. Affidavits relating to the welfare of children which have been sworn more than three months prior to lodging a minute for decree are likely to be rejected by the court as out of date.

Applications relating to parental responsibilities and rights (See OCR 33.28)

13. In actions in which an application in terms of section 11 of the Children (Scotland) Act 1995 is before the court not fewer than two affidavits dealing with the welfare of the child(ren) should be provided, at least one of them from a person who is neither a parent nor a party to the action. These affidavits should present the court with a full picture of the arrangements for the care of the child(ren) along the lines set out in paragraph 15, adapted to suit the circumstances of the particular case. The affidavits should set out reasons why it is better that the section 11 order be made than not. The pursuer's affidavit should deal fully with the arrangements which have been made for their care, so far as within his or her knowledge. If the pursuer cannot give substantial evidence as to that it is likely to be necessary to obtain such evidence from the person who is responsible for their care.

14. In actions of divorce or judicial separation in which there are children of the marriage or children treated by the parties as a child of their family but in which no order in terms of section 11 in terms of the Children (Scotland) Act 1995 is sought, the court, in terms of section 12, requires to consider whether to exercise the powers set out in section 11 or 54 of that Act in light of the information before it as the arrangements for the child(ren)'s upbringing. Information accordingly requires to be before the court as to these arrangements. As a minimum, the affidavits of the witnesses should include the information set out in paragraphs 15 (*a*) to (*e*) below.

15. An affidavit dealing with the arrangements for the care of children should, where relevant, include the following:

(*a*) the qualifications of the witness, if not a parent, to speak about the child; how often, and in what circumstances the witness normally sees the child;

(*b*) the ability of those with whom the child lives to provide proper care for him or her;

(*c*) observations as to the relationship between the child and the other members of the household, the child's general appearance, interests, state of health and well-being;

(*d*) a description of the home conditions in which the child lives;

(*e*) the arrangements for contact between the child and any parent (and siblings) who do not live in the same household as the child;

(*f*) information about the school the child attends; whether the child attends school regularly; and

(*g*) details of child care arrangements during working hours, including the arrangements for such care outwith school hours.

Affidavit relating to disclosure of the whereabouts of children

16. An affidavit sworn or affirmed in compliance with an order to disclose the whereabouts of children (in terms of the Family Law Act 1986, section 33 and Ordinary Cause Rule 33.23) will require to be drafted in such a way as to meet the requirements of the court in the circumstances of the particular case. The form of the affidavit should be as above.

Financial and other ancillary craves

17. Affidavit evidence in support of financial craves is necessary in an undefended action. (See *Ali v Ali,* 2001 S.C. 618; 2001 S.L.T. 602; 2001 S.C.L.R. 485.) Where financial craves are involved, the evidence should be as full, accurate and up to date as possible. If the evidence is insufficient the court may require supplementary evidence to be provided. If, after an affidavit has been sworn and the solicitor concerned has parted with it, a material change of circumstances occurs before decree has been granted the court must be informed forthwith. A further affidavit may have to be sworn.

18. The pursuer should give evidence as to his or her own financial position at the date of the affidavit. Where the pursuer gives evidence in an affidavit as to the financial position of the defender, the affidavit should state the date, as precisely as possible, at which the information was valid. The court must be provided with information which is as up to date as possible as to the defender's ability to pay the sums the pursuer is seeking. Where the pursuer cannot obtain recent information as to the defender's means the affidavit should state that that is the case but should contain as much material information relating to the defender's means as possible. If the pursuer is unable to provide sufficient evidence to justify the orders craved in full, in the minute for decree, after the words "in terms of crave(s) (number(s)...) of the initial writ", there may be added words such as "or such other sum (or sums) as the court may think proper".

19. Where the pursuer has craved a capital sum, an order for the sale of the matrimonial home, a periodical allowance, interdict or expenses, for example, and in the minute for decree does not seek decree for one or more of these, the reasons for that should be given in his or her affidavit.

Joint minutes

20. When parties record their agreement in a joint minute as to how financial and other ancillary craves should be dealt with by the court, the pursuer's affidavit

should refer to the joint minute and indicate that he or she is content that the agreement set out in it should be given effect.

Minute for decree

21. The minute for decree must be signed by a solicitor who has examined the affidavits and other documents. That solicitor takes responsibility therefor, whether or not he or she is the person who drew the initial writ or affidavits. The minute for decree should not be signed seeking decree of divorce or separation unless the evidence consists of or includes evidence other than that of a party to the marriage (Civil Evidence (Scotland) Act 1988, s. 8(3); *Taylor v Taylor,* 2000 S.L.T. 1419; 2001 S.C.L.R. 16).

CONVENTION ON THE RIGHTS OF THE CHILD

Adopted by the General Assembly of the United Nations on 20
November 1989

PREAMBLE

The States Parties to the present Convention,

Considering that, in accordance with the principles proclaimed in
the Charter of the United Nations, recognition of the inherent dignity
and of the equal and inalienable rights of all members of the human
family is the foundation of freedom, justice and peace in the world,

Bearing in mind that the peoples of the United Nations have, in
the Charter, reaffirmed their faith in fundamental human rights and in
the dignity and worth of the human person, and have determined to
promote social progress and better standards of life in larger freedom,

Recognizing that the United Nations has, in the Universal Declaration of Human Rights and in the International Covenants on Human
Rights, proclaimed and agreed that everyone is entitled to all the rights
and freedoms set forth therein, without distinction of any kind, such as
race, colour, sex, language, religion, political or other opinion, national
or social origin, property, birth or other status,

Recalling that, in the Universal Declaration of Human Rights, the
United Nations has proclaimed that childhood is entitled to special
care and assistance,

Convinced that the family, as the fundamental group of society
and the natural environment for the growth and well-being of all its
members and particularly children, should be afforded the necessary
protection and assistance so that it can fully assume its responsibilities
within the community,

Recognizing that the child, for the full and harmonious development
of his or her personality, should grow up in a family environment, in
an atmosphere of happiness, love and understanding.

Considering that the child should be fully prepared to live an
individual life in society, and brought up in the spirit of the ideals
proclaimed in the Charter of the United Nations, and in particular in
the spirit of peace, dignity, tolerance, freedom, equality and solidarity,

Bearing in mind that the need to extend particular care to the child has been stated in the Geneva Declaration of the Rights of the Child of 1924 and in the Declaration of the Rights of the Child adopted by the General Assembly on 20 November 1959 and recognized in the Universal Declaration of Human Rights, in the International Covenant on Civil and Political Rights (in particular in articles 23 and 24), in the International Covenant on Economic, Social and Cultural Rights (in particular in article 10) and in the statutes and relevant instruments of specialized agencies and international organizations concerned with the welfare of children,

Bearing in mind that, as indicated in the Declaration of the Rights of the Child, "the child, by reason of his physical and mental immaturity, needs special safeguards and care, including appropriate legal protection, before as well as after birth",

Recalling the provisions of the Declarations on Social and Legal Principles relating to the Protection and Welfare of Children, with Special Reference to Foster Placement and Adoption Nationally and Internationally; the United Nations Standard Minimum Rules for the Administration of Juvenile Justice (The Beijing Rules); and the Declaration on the Protection of Women and Children in Emergency and Armed Conflict,

Recognizing that, in all countries in the world, there are children living in exceptionally difficult conditions, and that such children need special consideration,

Taking due account of the importance of the traditions and cultural values of each people for the protection and harmonious development of the child,

Recognizing the importance of international co-operation for improving the living conditions of children in every country, in particular in the developing countries,

Have agreed as follows:

PART I

ARTICLE I

For the purposes of the present Convention, a child means every human being below the age of eighteen years unless, under the law applicable to the child, majority is attained earlier.

ARTICLE 2

1. States Parties shall respect and ensure the rights set forth in the present Convention to each child within their jurisdiction without discrimination of any kind, irrespective of the child's or his or her

parent's or legal guardian's race, colour, sex, language, religion, political or other opinion, national, ethnic or social origin, property, disability, birth or other status.

2. States Parties shall take all appropriate measures to ensure that the child is protected against all forms of discrimination or punishment on the basis of the status, activities, expressed opinions, or beliefs of the child's parents, legal guardians, or family members.

ARTICLE 3

1. In all actions concerning children, whether undertaken by public or private social welfare institutions, courts of law, administrative authorities or legislative bodies, the best interests of the child shall be a primary consideration.

2. States Parties undertake to ensure the child such protection and care as is necessary for his or her well-being, taking into account the rights and duties of his or her parents, legal guardians, or other individuals legally responsible for him or her, and, to this end, shall take all appropriate legislative and administrative measures.

3. States Parties shall ensure that the institutions, services and facilities responsible for the care or protection of children shall conform with the standards established by competent authorities, particularly in the areas of safety, health, in the number and suitability of their staff, as well as competent supervision.

ARTICLE 4

States Parties shall undertake all appropriate legislative, administrative, and other measures for the implementation of the rights recognized in the present Convention. With regard to economic, social and cultural rights, States Parties shall undertake such measures to the maximum extent of their available resources and, where needed, within the framework of international co-operation.

ARTICLE 5

States Parties shall respect the responsibilities, rights and duties of parties or, where applicable, the members of the extended family or community as provided for by local custom, legal guardians or other persons legally responsible for the child, to provide, in a manner consistent with the evolving capacities of the child, appropriate direction and guidance in the exercise by the child of the rights recognized in the present Convention.

ARTICLE 6

1. States Parties recognize that every child has the inherent right to life.
2. States Parties shall ensure to the maximum extent possible the survival and development of the child.

ARTICLE 7

1. The child shall be registered immediately after birth and shall have the right from birth to a name, the right to acquire a nationality and, as far as possible, the right to know and be cared for by his or her parents.
2. States Parties shall ensure the implementation of these rights in accordance with their national law and their obligations under the relevant international instruments in this field, in particular where the child would otherwise be stateless.

ARTICLE 8

1. States Parties undertake to respect the right of the child to preserve his or her identity, including nationality, name and family relations as recognized by law without unlawful interference.
2. Where a child is illegally deprived of some or all of the elements of his or her identity, States Parties shall provide appropriate assistance and protection, with a view to speedily re-establishing his or her identity.

ARTICLE 9

1. States parties shall ensure that a child shall not be separated from his or her parents against their will, except when competent authorities subject to judicial review determine, in accordance with applicable law and procedures, that such separation is necessary for the best interests of the child. Such determination may be necessary in a particular case such as one involving abuse or neglect of the child by the parents, or one where the parents are living separately and a decision must be made as to the child's place of residence.
2. In any proceedings pursuant to paragraph 1 of the present article, all interested parties shall be given an opportunity to participate in the proceedings and make their views known.
3. States Parties shall respect the right of the child who is separated from one or both parents to maintain personal relations and direct contact with both parents on a regular basis, except if it is contrary to the child's best interests.
4. Where such separation results from any action initiated by a State Party, such as the detention, imprisonment, exile, deportation

or death (including death arising from any cause while the person is in the custody of the State) of one or both parents or of the child, that State Party shall, upon request, provide the parents, the child or, if appropriate, another member of the family with the essential information concerning the whereabouts of the absent member(s) of the family unless the provision of the information would be detrimental to the well-being of the child. States Parties shall further ensure that the submission of such a request shall of itself entail no adverse consequences for the person(s) concerned.

ARTICLE 10

1. In accordance with the obligation of States Parties under article 9, paragraph 1, applications by a child or his or her parents to enter or leave a State Party for the purposes of family reunification shall be dealt with by States Parties in a positive, humane and expeditious manner. States Parties shall further ensure that the submission of such a request shall entail no adverse consequences for the applicants and for the members of their family.
2. A child whose parents reside in different States shall have the right to maintain on a regular basis, save in exceptional circumstances personal relations and direct contacts with both parents. Towards that end and in accordance with the obligation of States Parties under article 9, paragraph 1, States Parties shall respect the right of the child and his or her parents to leave any country, including their own, and to enter their own country. The right to leave any country shall be subject only to such restrictions as are prescribed by law and which are necessary to protect the national security, public order (*ordre public*), public health or morals or the rights and freedoms of others and are consistent with the other rights recognized in the present Convention.

ARTICLE 11

1. States Parties shall take measures to combat the illicit transfer and non-return of children abroad.
2. To this end, States Parties shall promote the conclusion of bilateral or multilateral agreements or accession to existing agreements.

ARTICLE 12

1. States Parties shall assure to the child who is capable of forming his or her own views the right to express those views freely in all matters affecting the child, the views of the child being given due weight in accordance with the age and maturity of the child.

2. For this purpose, the child shall in particular be provided the opportunity to be heard in any judicial and administrative proceedings affecting the child, either directly, or through a representative or an appropriate body, in a manner consistent with the procedural rules of national law.

ARTICLE 13

1. The child shall have the right to freedom of expression; this right shall include freedom to seek, receive and impart information and ideas of all kinds, regardless of frontiers, either orally, in writing or in print, in the form of art, or through any other media of the child's choice.
2. The exercise of this right may be subject to certain restrictions, but these shall only be such as are provided by law and are necessary:
(a) For respect of the rights or reputations of others; or
(b) For the protection of national security or of public order (*ordre public*), or of public health or morals.

ARTICLE 14

1. States Parties shall respect the right of the child to freedom of thought, conscience and religion.
2. States Parties shall respect the rights and duties of the parents and, when applicable, legal guardians, to provide direction to the child in the exercise of his or her right in a manner consistent with the evolving capacities of the child.
3. Freedom to manifest one's religion or beliefs may be subject only to such limitations as are prescribed by law and are necessary to protect public safety, order, health or morals, or the fundamental rights and freedom of others.

ARTICLE 15

1. States Parties recognize the rights of the child to freedom of association and to freedom of peaceful assembly.
2. No restrictions may be placed on the exercise of these rights other than those imposed in conformity with the law and which are necessary in a democratic society in the interests of national security or public safety, public order (*ordre public*), the protection of public health or morals or the protection of the rights and freedoms of others.

ARTICLE 16

1. No child shall be subjected to arbitrary or unlawful interference with his or her privacy, family, home or correspondence, nor to unlawful attacks on his or her honour and reputation.

2. The child has the right to the protection of the law against such interference or attacks.

ARTICLE 17

States Parties recognize the important function performed by the mass media and shall ensure that the child has access to information and material from a diversity of national and international sources, especially those aimed at the promotion of his or her social, spiritual and moral well-being and physical and mental health. To this end, States Parties shall:

(a) Encourage the mass media to disseminate information and material of social and cultural benefit to the child and in accordance with the spirit of article 29;

(b) Encourage international co-operation in the production, exchange and dissemination of such information and material from a diversity of cultural, national and international sources;

(c) Encourage the production and dissemination of children's books;

(d) Encourage the mass media to have particular regard to the linguistic needs of the child who belongs to a minority group or who is indigenous;

(e) Encourage the development of appropriate guidelines for the protection of the child from information and material injurious to his or her well-being, bearing in mind the provisions of articles 13 and 18.

ARTICLE 18

1. States Parties shall use their best efforts to ensure recognition of the principle that both parents have common responsibilities for the upbringing and development of the child. Parents or, as the case may be, legal guardians, have the primary responsibility for the upbringing and development of the child. The best interests of the child will be their basic concern.

2. For the purpose of guaranteeing and promoting the rights set forth in the present Convention, States Parties shall render appropriate assistance to parents and legal guardians in the performance of their child-rearing responsibilities and shall ensure the development of institutions, facilities and services for the care of children.

3. States Parties shall take all appropriate measures to ensure that children of working parents have the right to benefit from child-care services and facilities for which they are eligible.

ARTICLE 19

1. States Parties shall take all appropriate legislative, administrative, social and educational measures to protect the child from all forms of physical or mental violence, injury or abuse, neglect or negligent treatment, maltreatment or exploitation, including sexual abuse, while in the care of parent(s), legal guardian(s) or any other person who has the care of the child.
2. Such protective measures should, as appropriate, include effective procedures for the establishment of social programmes to provide necessary support for the child and for those who have the care of the child, as well as for other forms of prevention and for identification, reporting, referral, investigation, treatment and follow-up of instances of child maltreatment described heretofore, and, as appropriate, for judicial involvement.

ARTICLE 20

1. A child temporarily or permanently deprived of his or her family environment, or in whose own best interests cannot be allowed to remain in that environment, shall be entitled to special protection and assistance provided by the State.
2. States Parties shall in accordance with their national laws ensure alternative care for such a child.
3. Such care could include, *inter alia*, foster placement, *kafalah* of Islamic law, adoption or if necessary placement in suitable institutions for the care of children. When considering solutions, due regard shall be paid to the desirability of continuity in a child's upbringing and to the child's ethnic, religious, cultural and linguistic background.

ARTICLE 21

States Parties that recognize and/or permit the system of adoption shall ensure that the best interests of the child shall be the paramount consideration and they shall:
(a) Ensure that the adoption of a child is authorized only by competent authorities who determine, in accordance with applicable law and procedures and on the basis of all pertinent and reliable information, that the adoption is permissible in view of the child's status concerning parents, relatives and legal guardians and that, if required, the persons concerned have given their informed consent to the adoption on the basis of such counselling as may be necessary;
(b) Recognize that inter-country adoption may be considered as an

alternative means of child's care, if the child cannot be placed in a foster or an adoptive family or cannot in any suitable manner be cared for in the child's country of origin;

(c) Ensure that the child concerned by inter-country adoption enjoys safeguards and standards equivalent to those existing in the case of national adoption;

(d) Take all appropriate measures to ensure that, in inter-country adoption, the placement does not result in improper financial gain for those involved in it;

(e) Promote, where appropriate, the objectives of the present article by concluding bilateral or multilateral arrangements or agreements, and endeavour, within this framework, to ensure that the placement of the child in another country is carried out by competent authorities or organs.

ARTICLE 22

1. States Parties shall take appropriate measures to ensure that a child who is seeking refugee status or who is considered a refugee in accordance with applicable international or domestic law and procedures shall, whether unaccompanied or accompanied by his or her parents or by any other person, receive appropriate protection and humanitarian assistance in the enjoyment of applicable rights set forth in the present Convention and in other international human rights or humanitarian instruments to which the said States are Parties.

2. For this purpose, States Parties shall provide, as they consider appropriate, co-operation in any efforts by the United Nations and other competent intergovernmental organizations or non-governmental organizations co-operating with the United Nations to protect and assist such a child and to trace the parents or other members of the family of any refugee child in order to obtain information necessary for reunification with his or her family. In cases where no parents or other members of the family can be found, the child shall be accorded the same protection as any other child permanently or temporarily deprived of his or her family environment for any reason, as set forth in the present Convention.

ARTICLE 23

1. States Parties recognize that a mentally or physically disabled child should enjoy a full and decent life, in conditions which ensure dignity, promote self-reliance and facilitate the child's active participation in the community.

2. States Parties recognize the right of the disabled child to special care and shall encourage and ensure the extension, subject to available

resources, to the eligible child and those responsible for his or her care, of assistance for which application is made and which is appropriate to the child's condition and to the circumstances of the parents or others caring for the child.

3. Recognizing the special needs of a disabled child, assistance extended in accordance with paragraph 2 of the present article shall be provided free of charge, whenever possible, taking into account the financial resources of the parents or others caring for the child, and shall be designed to ensure that the disabled child has effective access to and receives education, training, health care services, rehabilitation services, preparation for employment and recreation opportunities in a manner conducive to the child's achieving the fullest possible social integration and individual development, including his or her cultural and spiritual development.

4. States Parties shall promote, in the spirit of international co-operation, the exchange of appropriate information in the field of preventive health care and of medical, psychological and functional treatment of disabled children, including dissemination and access to information concerning methods of rehabilitation, education and vocational services, with the aim of enabling States Parties to improve their capabilities and skills and to widen their experience in these areas. In this regard, particular account shall be taken of the needs of developing countries.

ARTICLE 24

1. States Parties recognize the right of the child to the enjoyment of the highest attainable standard of health and to facilities for the treatment of illness and rehabilitation of health. States Parties shall strive to ensure that no child is deprived of his or her right of access to such health care services.

2. States Parties shall pursue full implementation of this right and, in particular, shall take appropriate measures:

(a)   To diminish infant and child mortality;

(b)   To ensure the provision of necessary medical assistance and health care to all children with emphasis on the development of primary health care;

(c)   To combat disease and malnutrition, including within the frame-work of primary health care, through, *inter alia*, the application of readily available technology and through the provision of adequate nutritious foods and clean drinking-water, taking into consideration the dangers and risks of environmental pollution;

(d)   To ensure appropriate pre-natal and post-natal health care for mothers;

(e)   To ensure that all segments of society, in particular parents and children, are informed, have access to education and are supported in the use of basic knowledge of child health and nutrition, the advantages of breast-feeding, hygiene and environmental sanitation and the prevention of accidents;

(f) To develop preventive health care, guidance for parents and family planning education and services.

3. States Parties shall take all effective and appropriate measures with a view to abolishing traditional practices prejudicial to the health of children.

4. States Parties undertake to promote and encourage international co-operation with a view to achieving progressively the full realization of the right recognized in the present article. In this regard, particular account shall be taken of the needs of developing countries.

ARTICLE 25

States Parties recognize the right of a child who has been placed by the competent authorities for the purposes of care, protection or treatment of his or her physical or mental health, to a periodic review of the treatment provided to the child and all other circumstances relevant to his or her placement.

ARTICLE 26

1. States Parties shall recognize for every child the right to benefit from social security, including social insurance, and shall take the necessary measures to achieve the full realization of this right in accordance with their national law.

2. The benefits should, where appropriate, be granted, taking into account the resources and the circumstances of the child and persons having responsibility for the maintenance of the child, as well as any other consideration relevant to an application for benefits made by or on behalf of the child.

ARTICLE 27

1. States Parties recognize the right of every child to a standard of living adequate for the child's physical, mental, spiritual, moral and social development.

2. The parent(s) or others responsible for the child have the primary responsibility to secure, within their abilities and financial capacities, the conditions of living necessary for the child's development.

3. States Parties, in accordance with national conditions and within their means, shall take appropriate measures to assist parents and others

responsible for the child to implement this right and shall in case of need provide material assistance and support programmes, particularly with regard to nutrition, clothing and housing.
4. States Parties shall take all appropriate measures to secure the recovery of maintenance for the child from the parents or other persons having financial responsibility for the child, both within the State Party and from abroad. In particular, where the person having financial responsibility for the child lives in a State different from that of the child, States Parties shall promote the accession to international agreements or the conclusion of such agreements, as well as the making of other appropriate arrangements.

ARTICLE 28

1. States Parties recognize the right of the child to education, and with a view to achieving this right progressively and on the basis of equal opportunity, they shall, in particular:
(a) Make primary education compulsory and available free to all;
(b) Encourage the development of different forms of secondary education, including general and vocational education, make them available and accessible to every child, and take appropriate measures such as the introduction of free education and offering financial assistance in case of need;
(c) Make higher education accessible to all on the basis of capacity by every appropriate means;
(d) Make educational and vocational information and guidance available and accessible to all children;
(e) Take measures to encourage regular attendance at schools and the reduction of drop-out rates.
2. States Parties shall take all appropriate measures to ensure that school discipline is administered in a manner consistent with the child's human dignity and in conformity with the present Convention.
3. States Parties shall promote and encourage international co-operation in matters relating to education, in particular with a view to contributing to the elimination of ignorance and illiteracy throughout the world and facilitating access to scientific and technical knowledge and modern teaching methods. In this regard, particular account shall be taken of the needs of developing countries.

ARTICLE 29

1. States Parties agree that the education of the child shall be directed to:
(a) The development of the child's personality, talents and mental and physical abilities to their fullest potential;
(b) The development of respect for human rights and fundamental

freedoms, and for the principles enshrined in the Charter of the United Nations;

(c) The development of respect for the child's parents, his or her own cultural identity, langauge and values, for the national values of the country in which the child is living, the country from which he or she may originate, and for civilizations different from his or her own;

(d) The preparation of the child for responsible life in a free society, in the spirit of understanding, peace, tolerance, equality of sexes, and friendship among all peoples, ethnic, national and religious groups and persons of indigenous origin;

(e) The development of respect for the natural environment.

2. No part of the present article or article 28 shall be construed so as to interfere with the liberty of individuals and bodies to establish and direct educational institutions, subject always to the observance of the principles set forth in paragraph 1 of the present article and to the requirements that the education given in such institutions shall conform to such minimum standards as may be laid down by the State.

ARTICLE 30

In those States in which ethnic, religious or linguistic minorities or persons of indigenous origin exist, a child belonging to such a minority or who is indigenous shall not be denied the right, in community with other members of his or her group, to enjoy his or her own culture to profess and practise his or her own religion, or to use his or her own language.

ARTICLE 31

1. States Parties recognize the right of the child to rest and leisure, to engage in play and recreational activities appropriate to the age of the child and to participate freely in cultural life and the arts.

2. States Parties shall respect and promote the right of the child to participate fully in cultural and artistic life and shall encourage the provision of appropriate and equal opportunities for cultural, artistic, recreational and leisure activity.

ARTICLE 32

1. States Parties recognize the right of the child to be protected from economic exploitation and from performing any work that is likely to be hazardous or to interfere with the child's education, or to be harmful to the child's health or physical, mental, spiritual, moral or social development.

2. States Parties shall take legislative, administrative, social and educational measures to ensure the implementation of the present article. To this end, and having regard to the relevant provisions of other international instruments, States Parties shall in particular:

(a) Provide for a minimum age or minimum ages for admission to employment;

(b) Provide for appropriate regulation of the hours and conditions of employment;

(c) Provide for appropriate penalties or other sanctions to ensure the effective enforcement of the present article.

ARTICLE 33

States Parties shall take all appropriate measures, including legislative, administrative, social and educational measures, to protect children from the illicit use of narcotic drugs and psychotropic substances as defined in the relevant international treaties, and to prevent the use of children in the illicit production and trafficking of such substances.

ARTICLE 34

States Parties undertake to protect the child from all forms of sexual exploitation and sexual abuse. For these purposes, States Parties shall in particular take all appropriate national, bilateral and multilateral measures to prevent:

(a) The inducement or coercion of a child to engage in any unlawful sexual activity;

(b) The exploitative use of children in prostitution or other unlawful sexual practices;

(c) The exploitative use of children in pornographic performances and materials.

ARTICLE 35

States Parties shall take all appropriate national, bilateral and multilateral measures to prevent the abduction of, the sale of or traffic in children for any purpose or in any form.

ARTICLE 36

States Parties shall protect the child against all other forms of exploitation prejudicial to any aspects of the child's welfare.

ARTICLE 37

States Parties shall ensure that:

(a) No child shall be subjected to torture or other cruel, inhuman or degrading treatment or punishment. Neither capital punishment nor life imprisonment without possibility of release shall be imposed for offences committed by persons below eighteen years of age;

(b) No child shall be deprived of his or her liberty unlawfully or arbitrarily. The arrest, detention or imprisonment of a child shall be in conformity with the law and shall be used only as a measure of last resort and for the shortest appropriate period of time;

(c) Every child deprived of liberty shall be treated with humanity and respect for the inherent dignity of the human person, and in a manner which takes into account the needs of persons of his or her age. In particular, every child deprived of liberty shall be separated from adults unless it is considered in the child's best interest not to do so and shall have the right to maintain contact with his or her family through correspondence and visits, save in exceptional circumstances;

(d) Every child deprived of his or her liberty shall have the right to prompt access to legal and other appropriate assistance, as well as the right to challenge the legality of the deprivation of his or her liberty before a court or other competent, independent and impartial authority, and to a prompt decision on any such action.

ARTICLE 38

1. States Parties undertake to respect and to ensure respect for rules of international humanitarian law applicable to them in armed conflicts which are relevant to the child.

2. States Parties shall take all feasible measures to ensure that persons who have not attained the age of fifteen years do not take a direct part in hostilities.

3. States Parties shall refrain from recruiting any person who has not attained the age of fifteen years into their armed forces. In recruiting among those persons who have attained the age of fifteen years but who have not attained the age of eighteen years, States Parties shall endeavour to give priority to those who are oldest.

4. In accordance with their obligations under international humanitarian law to protect the civilian population in armed conflicts, States Parties shall take all feasible measures to ensure protection and care of children who are affected by an armed conflict.

ARTICLE 39

States Parties shall take all appropriate measures to promote physical and psychological recovery and social reintegration of a child victim of: any form of neglect, exploitation, or abuse; torture or any other form of cruel, inhuman or degrading treatment or punishment; or armed conflicts. Such recovery and reintegration shall take place in an environment which fosters the health, self-respect and dignity of the child.

ARTICLE 40

1. States Parties recognize the right of every child alleged as, accused of, or recognized as having infringed the penal law to be treated in a manner consistent with the promotion of the child's sense of dignity and worth, which reinforces the child's respect for the human rights and fundamental freedoms of others and which takes into account the child's age and the desirability of promoting the child's reintegration and the child's assuming a constructive role in society.
2. To this end, and having regard to the relevant provisions of international instruments, States Parties shall, in particular, ensure that:
(a) No child shall be alleged as, be accused of, or recognized as having infringed the penal law by reason of acts or omissions that were not prohibited by national or international law at the time they were committed;
(b) Every child alleged as or accused of having infringed the penal law has at least the following guarantees:
   (i) To be presumed innocent until proven guilty according to law;
   (ii) To be informed promptly and directly of the charges against him or her, and, if appropriate, through his or her parents or legal guardians, and to have legal or other appropriate assistance in the preparation of presentation of his or her defence;
   (iii) To have the matter determined without delay by a competent, independent and impartial authority or judicial body in a fair hearing according to law, in the presence of legal or other appropriate assistance and, unless it is considered not to be in the best interests of the child, in particular, taking into account his or her age or situation, his or her parents or legal guardians;
   (iv) Not to be compelled to give testimony or to confess guilt; to examine or have examined adverse witnesses and to obtain the participation and examination of witnesses on his or her behalf under conditions of equality;

(v) If considered to have infringed the penal law, to have this decision and any measures imposed in consequence thereof reviewed by a higher competent, independent and impartial authority or judicial body according to law;

(vi) To have the free assistance of an interpreter if the child cannot understand or speak the language used;

(vii) To have his or her privacy fully respected at all stages of the proceedings.

3. States Parties shall seek to promote the establishment of laws, procedures, authorities and institutions specifically applicable to children alleged as, accused of, or recognized as having infringed the penal law, and, in particular:

(a) The establishment of a minimum age below which children shall be presumed not to have the capacity to infringe the penal law;

(b) Whenever appropriate and desirable, measures for dealing with such children without resorting to judicial proceedings, providing that human rights and legal safeguards are fully respected.

4. A variety of dispositions, such as care, guidance and supervision orders; counselling; probation; foster care; education and vocational training programmes and other alternatives to institutional care shall be available to ensure that children are dealt with in a manner appropriate to their well-being and proportionate both to their circumstances and the offence.

ARTICLE 41

Nothing in the present Convention shall affect any provisions which are more conducive to the realization of the rights of the child and which may be contained in:

(a) The law of a State Party; or

(b) International law in force for that State.

PART II

ARTICLE 42

States Parties undertake to make the principles and provisions of the Convention widely known, by appropriate and active means, to adults and children alike.

ARTICLE 43

1. For the purpose of examining the progress made by States Parties in achieving the realization of the obligations undertaken in the present

Convention, there shall be established a Committee on the Rights of the Child, which shall carry out the functions hereinafter provided.

2. The Committee shall consist of ten experts of high moral standing and recognized competence in the field covered by this Convention. The members of the Committee shall be elected by States Parties from among their nationals and shall serve in their personal capacity, consideration being given to equitable geographical distribution, as well as to the principal legal systems.

3. The members of the Committee shall be elected by secret ballot from a list of persons nominated by States Parties. Each State Party may nominate one person from among its own nationals.

4. The initial election to the Committee shall be held no later than six months after the date of the entry into force of the present Convention and thereafter every second year. At least four months before the date of each election, the Secretary-General of the United Nations shall address a letter to States Parties inviting them to submit their nominations within two months. The Secretary-General shall subsequently prepare a list in alphabetical order of all persons thus nominated, indicating States Parties which have nominated them and shall submit it to the States Parties to the present Convention.

5. The elections shall be held at meetings of States Parties convened by the Secretary-General at United Nations Headquarters. At those meetings, for which two-thirds of States Parties shall constitute a quorum, the persons elected to the Committee shall be those who obtain the largest number of votes and an absolute majority of the votes of the representatives of States Parties present and voting.

6. The members of the Committee shall be elected for a term of four years. They shall be eligible for re-election if renominated. The term of five of the members elected at the first election shall expire at the end of two years; immediately after the first election, the names of these five members shall be chosen by lot by the Chairman of the meeting.

7. If a member of the Committee dies or resigns or declares that for any other cause he or she can no longer perform the duties of the Committee, the State Party which nominated the member shall appoint another expert from among its nationals to serve for the remainder of the term, subject to the approval of the Committee.

8. The Committee shall establish its own rules of procedure.

9. The Committee shall elect its officers for a period of two years.

10. The meetings of the Committee shall normally be held at United Nations Headquarters or at any other convenient place as determined by the Committee. The Committee shall normally meet annually. The duration of the meetings of the Committee shall be determined, and reviewed, if necessary, by a meeting of the States Parties to the present Convention, subject to the approval of the General Assembly.

11. The Secretary-General of the United Nations shall provide the

necessary staff and facilities for the effective performance of the functions of the Committee under the present Convention.

12. With the approval of the General Assembly, the members of the Committee established under the present Convention shall receive emoluments from United Nations resources on such terms and conditions as the Assembly may decide.

ARTICLE 44

1. States Parties undertake to submit to the Committee, through the Secretary-General of the United Nations, reports on the measures they have adopted which give effect to the rights recognized herein and on the progress made on the enjoyment of those rights:

(a) Within two years of the entry into force of the Convention for the State Party concerned;

(b) Thereafter every five years.

2. Reports made under the present article shall indicate factors and difficulties, if any, affecting the degree of fulfilment of the obligations under the present Convention. Reports shall also contain sufficient information to provide the Committee with a comprehensive understanding of the implementation of the Convention in the country concerned.

3. A State Party which has submitted a comprehensive initial report to the Committee need not, in its subsequent reports submitted in accordance with paragraph 1(b) of the present article, repeat basic information previously provided.

4. The Committee may request from States Parties further information relevant to the implementation of the Convention.

5. The Committee shall submit to the General Assembly, through the Economic and Social Council, every two years, reports on its activities.

6. States Parties shall make their reports widely available to the public in their own countries.

ARTICLE 45

In order to foster the effective implementation of the Convention and to encourage international co-operation in the field covered by the Convention:

(a) The specialised agencies, the United Nations Children's Fund, and other United Nations organs shall be entitled to be represented at the consideration of the implementation of such provisions of the present Convention as fall within the scope of their mandate. The Committee may invite the specialized agencies, the United Nations Children's Fund and other competent bodies as it may consider appropriate to provide expert advice on the implementation of the Convention in areas falling within the scope of their respective mandates. The Committee may invite the specialized agencies, the United Nations Children's Fund, and other United Nations organs to submit reports on the implementation of the Convention in areas falling within the scope of their activities;

(b) The Committee shall transmit, as it may consider appropriate, to the specialized agencies, the United Nations Children's Fund and other competent bodies, any reports from States Parties that contain a request, or indicate a need, for technical advice or assistance, along with the Committee's observations and suggestions, if any, on these requests or indications;

(c) The Committee may recommend to the General Assembly to request the Secretary-General to undertake on its behalf studies on specific issues relating to the rights of the child;

(d) The Committee may make suggestions and general recommendations based on information received pursuant to articles 44 and 45 of the present Convention. Such suggestions and general recommendations shall be transmitted to any State Party concerned and reported to the General Assembly, together with comments, if any, from States Parties.

PART III

ARTICLE 46

The present Convention shall be open for signature by all States.

ARTICLE 47

The present Convention is subject to ratification. Instruments of ratification shall be deposited with the Secretary-General of the United Nations.

ARTICLE 48

The present Convention shall remain open for accession by any State. The instruments of accession shall be deposited with the Secretary-General of the United Nations.

ARTICLE 49

1. The present Convention shall enter into force on the thirtieth day following the date of deposit with the Secretary-General of

the United Nations of the twentieth instrument of ratification or accession.

2. For each State ratifying or acceding to the Convention after the deposit of the twentieth instrument of ratification or accession, the Convention shall enter into force on the thirtieth day after the deposit by such State of its instrument of ratification or accession.

ARTICLE 50

1. Any State Party may propose an amendment and file it with the Secretary-General of the United Nations. The Secretary-General shall thereupon communicate the proposed amendment to States Parties, with a request that they indicate whether they favour a conference of States Parties for the purpose of considering and voting upon the proposals. In the event that, within four months from the date of such communication, at least one-third of the States Parties favour such a conference, the Secretary-General shall convene the conference under the auspices of the United Nations. Any amendment adopted by a majority of States Parties present and voting at the conference shall be submitted to the General Assembly for approval.

2. An amendment adopted in accordance with paragraph 1 of the present article shall enter into force when it has been approved by the General Assembly of the United Nations and accepted by a two-thirds majority of States Parties.

3. When an amendment enters into force, it shall be binding on those States Parties which have accepted it, other States Parties still being bound by the provisions of the present Convention and any earlier amendments which they have accepted.

ARTICLE 51

1. The Secretary-General of the United Nations shall receive and circulate to all States the text of reservations made by States at the time of ratification or accession.

2. A reservation incompatible with the object and purpose of the present Convention shall not be permitted.

3. Reservations may be withdrawn at any time by notification to that effect addressed to the Secretary-General of the United Nations, who shall then inform all States. Such notification shall take effect on the date on which it is received by the Secretary-General.

ARTICLE 52

A State Party may denounce the present Convention by written notification to the Secretary-General of the United Nations. Denunciation becomes effective one year after the date of receipt of the notification by the Secretary-General.

ARTICLE 53

The Secretary-General of the United Nations is designated as the depositary of the present Convention.

ARTICLE 54

The original of the present Convention, of which the Arabic, Chinese, English, French, Russian and Spanish texts are equally authentic, shall be deposited with the Secretary-General of the United Nations.

In witness thereof the undersigned plenipotentiaries, being duly authorized thereto by their respective Governments, have signed the present Convention.

REPORTED CASES INVOLVING SECTION 11 ORDERS

(1) *McGhee v. McGhee*, 1998 Fam.L.R. 122 (Sheriff T. Scott)

Parties married in January 1988 and living apart at date of proof (June 1998)—Husband accepting wife's child (F, born April 1983)—Parties having two children (RAM, born November 1988, and RVM, born June 1990)—Wife always principal carer and having children with her during periods of separation—Husband awarded custody of children on 16 April 1996 on joint motion after parties' reconciliation—Parties having another child (M, born 13 May 1996)—Parties separating finally about one year later, wife leaving matrimonial home with M and being prevented from taking the other three children by husband relying upon his award of custody—Wife seeking variation of custody award, claiming husband assaulted her while she was pregnant, drove while unfit through drink, encouraged children to consume alcohol, kept RAM up late talking until the early hours and gave RAM (when aged nine) a box of matches to play with—Husband arguing that many of wife's complaints were historical and that she was obliged to show a change of circumstances since granting of joint motion for custody—Wife held entitled to residence order, it being of little value where interlocutor sought to be varied was not the product of a full judicial investigation to look for a change of circumstances since agreement was made.

(2) *Fourman v. Fourman*, 1998 Fam. L.R. 98 (Sheriff N.M.P. Morrison Q.C.)

Parties married in November 1982 and living apart at date of proof (September 1998)—Parties having three children (PF, born July 1984, MF, born September 1989 and RF, born May 1992)—Parties separating in February 1998, wife leaving matrimonial home with children—Children living with each parent for equal amount of time ever since separation and wanting to spend equal time with both parents—Wife an Australian with dual nationality—Wife seeking specific issue order to be allowed to remove children to Australia to live there, claiming that life for her and the children would be cheaper, easier and better than in Scotland and that she would be more capable there of pursuing her career ambition to train and practise in acupuncture—Wife held not entitled to specific issue order, her wanting to take the children to Australia really because she wanted to go rather than because it was in their best interests to go; and it not seeming that stability, security and predictability were more apparent or more likely in Australia than they were in Scotland.

(3) *G v. G,* 1999 Fam. L.R. 30 (Sheriff Principal C. G. B. Nicholson Q.C.)

Parties married in August 1995 and living apart at date of motion (January 1999)—Parties having a child (K, born January 1997)—Parties separating in April 1997, husband leaving matrimonial home—Child living with wife in happy and settled environment ever since separation—Husband granted a variety of contact orders—Wife failing to comply with orders and as a result being found guilty of contempt of court on three occasions—Husband seeking interim residence order—Husband held not entitled to interim residence order, it being better for K that no order be made at all in respect that the ordering of a change in a child's residence would always be something which should be approached with care particularly where, as here, the existing arrangements appeared to be above reproach; and even greater care had to be exercised when it was proposed to remove a child from a happy and settled environment.

(4) *Dosoo v. Dosoo (No. 2),* 1999 Fam.L.R. 130 (Sheriff J. M. S. Horsburgh Q.C.)

Parties married in October 1980 and living apart at date of proof (October 1999)—Parties having three children (K, born May 1984, F, born November 1986, and B, born July 1994)—Parties living separate lives within matrimonial home from April 1998 and husband thereafter removing—Children living with wife ever since separation—Husband seeking contact order in relation to B only, K and F being unwilling to see him—Husband arguing that B had good relationship with him, that loss of contact could harm B's development and that as the product of a mixed race marriage contact with him was particularly important to B—Husband held not entitled to contact order, the evidence of a strong relationship with B not being convincing; husband seeming uninterested in imparting knowledge to his children about their Ghanaian background; his interest in the two older children having waned as they grew older; and B being likely to acquire from him negative influences.

(5) *H v. H,* 2000 Fam.L.R. 73 (Sheriff Principal D. J. Risk Q.C.)

Parties married in 1992 and living apart at date of proof (July 1998)—Husband accepting wife's child (A, born August 1986)—Parties having a child (N, born January 1995) after separation in March 1993—Husband seeking orders relating to N in separate proceedings conjoined with divorce action—Husband seeking contact order in relation to A, who suffered from attention deficit disorder, Asperger's syndrome and Tourette's syndrome—Motion granted to allow A to be sisted as a party and A allowed to lead evidence from professionals that he was of sufficient understanding to be competent witness and to lodge affidavit stating his opposition to contact—Husband held not entitled to contact order, there being expert evidence that affidavit a true representation of A's views rather than an echo of his mother with whom he lived.

(6) *M v. M,* 2000 Fam.L.R. 84 (Lord Kingarth)

Parties divorced in January 1996 and living apart at date of proof (June 2000)—Parties having three children (AM, born January 1988, HM, born February 1990, and EM, born February 1992)—Children living with wife in Ross-shire ever since separation—Husband residing in Edinburgh and having contact with children two out of three weekends in summer and alternate weekends in winter, in addition to half the school holidays, the parties driving to a halfway point to transfer children for each visit—Wife seeking residence and specific issue orders to allow her to remove children from Scotland to reside with her in the United States, wishing to live in the US to look after her elderly mother, to protect her stake in the family property business (which stake would increase upon her mother's death) and to take up a well remunerated post within the business—Wife held entitled to residence and specific issue orders, she having good reason to make the proposed move to the United States and making her plans over a substantial period (though there was nothing approaching an absolute need for her to go there); there being a reasonable expectation that she and her new husband would be able to provide a materially better life for the children in the US; the children being better able to generally grow in a stable environment compared with their life in Scotland which was punctuated by weekend contact visits and long travel to Edinburgh; their inheritance being likely to be better protected by wife living in the US; AM expressing a clear desire to go to the US; and there being a clear risk that if wife and her new husband's plans were thwarted it would leave a strong sense of regret affecting family atmosphere—Husband held entitled to contact order allowing nine weeks' residential contact in the UK every summer and two further weeks in Scotland each Christmas, it being desirable to maintain a degree of regularity in contact.

(7) *White v. White*, 2001 S.C. 689 (First Division; Sheriff C. G. B. Nicholson Q.C.; Sheriff K. A. Ross)

Parties divorced in August 1997 and living apart at date of proof (May 1999)—Parties having two children (K, born November 1985, and V, born July 1991)—Children living with wife ever since parties' separation in 1995—Husband having good relationship with children prior to separation and no evidence that his relationship with them was in any way detrimental or harmful to them—Husband having contact with children after separation, although K sometimes reluctant to see him, until early 1997 when relations between parties broke down and wife took steps to prevent contact taking place—Husband seeking contact with children every alternate Saturday—Husband dropping application for contact with K after her expressing desire not to see him—Husband held entitled to contact with V every alternate Saturday, it generally being conducive to welfare of children if their absent parents maintain personal relations and direct contact with them on a regular basis.

(8) *Cunningham v. Cunningham*, 2001 Fam.L.R. 12 (Lord Macfadyen)

Parties married and living apart at date of proof (November 2000)—Parties having a child (M, born July 1988)—Child living with wife ever since parties' separation—Husband having regular contact with child but on occasions exhibiting argumentative and aggressive behaviour in relation to contact, thereby upsetting and frightening M—Parties agreed that arrangements relating to M should continue but husband opposing residence order in wife's favour lest he thereby be excluded to some extent from his proper parenting role—Wife held entitled to residence order, it being better for M that an order be made than that there be no such order in respect that (i) order would put on a formal basis the agreed arrangement; (ii) it would reassure M that she was to stay with her mother and alleviate feelings of insecurity and uncertainty; and (iii) it would provide a secure platform for development of contact between husband and M.

(9) *Bailey v. Bailey*, 2001 Fam.L.R. 133 (Sheriff Principal J. C. McInnes Q.C.)

Parties divorced in 1998 and living apart at date of proof (July 2001)—Parties having three children (C, L and D)—Children living with wife ever since separation in 1995—Husband having contact with children until October 1999—Wife rarely making children available thereafter, despite court orders—Children, though upset and confused as a result of the anxiety seemed to have developed in relation to contact, appearing to have enjoyed and benefited from contact on the few occasions when it had taken place—Reporter appointed by court to supervise and report on period of contact between husband and children on 4 November 2000 in order to assist court in reaching a decision as to whether there should be an order for contact—Report wholly favourable to husband but not available until after proof concluded and not taken into consideration—Husband held at first instance not entitled to contact but, after appeal, cause remitted back to sheriff to hear submissions in relation to report.

(10) *S v. S*, 2002 S.C. 246 (Extra Division)

Parties married and living apart at date of proof (May 2001)—Parties having a child (D, born April 1992)—Parties separating in 1999—Child living with wife ever since separation and husband having generous overnight contact—Wife wishing to further her career by taking promoted post in Australia for three years—Wife seeking residence order and specific issue order to allow her to take D to Australia—Court dispensing with intimation by way of Form F9 to child when action raised in November 1999 and not subsequently taking steps to ascertain views of child—Appeal court obtaining report which concluded that child did not want to go to Australia—Wife held not entitled to residence order or specific issue order.

(11) *G v. G*, 2002 Fam.L.R. 120 (Extra Division; Lord Hardie of Blackford)

Parties married and living apart at date of motion (May 2002)—Parties having two children (EJ and A)—Children living with wife ever since parties' separation—Parties not having made any clear decision about children's education at time of separation—Wife seeking interim specific issue order in relation to EJ, aged 12 at date of motion, providing that she attend a boarding school and ordaining husband to make payment of all school fees and outlays save insofar as met by scholarship award or relating to riding expenses and stabling costs—EJ attending day school but awarded scholarship for boarding school, meeting 50 per cent of annual school fees and livery for horse for period of six years from autumn term of 2002—Entrance to school under award able to be deferred for one year on same terms—EJ, who had a talent for horseriding, wished to go to the boarding school—Husband not consulted prior to application being made on EJ's behalf for scholarship and disputing appropriateness of boarding school education—Husband's financial circumstances not straightforward as he was presently living off capital—Wife held not entitled to interim specific issue order, there not being a sufficient basis to make it reasonable to disturb the status quo; the husband's views as to which school was more appropriate being entitled to be taken into account; and the proper weight to be given to EJ's views and the relevance of any decision for A's future schooling being matters which had to be considered, best done at proof.

(12) *M v C,* 2002 S.L.T. (Sh. Ct.) 82 (Sheriff A.L. Stewart Q.C.)

Parties married in July 1994 and living apart at date of proof (March 2002)—Parties having a child (M, born August 1996)—Parties separating in July 1999—Child living with wife ever since separation—Wife reverting to using maiden name after parties' separation, wishing M to use that name also and enrolling him at school under changed name—Wife a practising Roman Catholic and wanting M to be brought up in that faith, attending catechism classes—Husband seeking specific issue orders (1) that wife could not alter M's surname; and (2) that M should not be required to attend classes in religious instruction, in each case without husband's consent—Husband held entitled to specific issue order that wife could not alter M's surname without his consent, it being as a general rule quite inappropriate for either parent to take a unilateral decision to change a child's name and there being no overwhelming reasons why M's surname should be changed without husband's consent, even though eight months had elapsed since M registered at school under changed name—Husband held not entitled to specific issue order that M should not be required to attend classes in religious instruction, the catechism classes being a normal part of the education of a child brought up as a Catholic who did not attend a denominational school for which husband's consent was not required or, in any event, able reasonably to be withheld.

(13) *Ellis v. Ellis,* 2003 Fam.L.R. 77 (Sheriff G. J. Evans)

Parties married and living apart at date of proof (November 2002)—Parties having two children (J, born July 1994, and R, born January 1997)—Parties separating in September 1997, with J residing primarily with husband and R with wife until summer 2000 when children's residence shared between parties—Children residing primarily from April 2001 with wife, who showed level of commitment to children which had initially been absent from husband in persevering with pregnancies despite strong opposition from him and had been consistent in her willingness to give full consideration to them—J's behaviour at school showing marked improvement once wife had become his primary carer—Parties' relationship acrimonious—Husband awarded interim contact on two nights each week, on weekends from Friday at 5.30 p.m. until 10 a.m. on Sunday and residential contact of at least one week during school holidays—Husband living with new Finnish partner (K) with whom he had child aged 7-8 months, but future of their relationship uncertain and possibility of their moving to Finland—Husband seeking residence order in relation to children—J expressing wish to live with him but view based on transitory circumstances such as the effect on wife of post natal depression and the fact that she was a stronger disciplinarian than husband, his house was materially better equipped than wife's and he had promised rewards to J if he was awarded residence—Wife held entitled to residence order, the fact that wife the primary carer of J and R being a very strong factor in wife's favour; there being a greater degree of certainty about wife's circumstances; and children's residing with her not being so detrimental to their welfare that the advantages that they had gained from continuity and stability in their circumstances should be sacrificed to unknown and untested future with husband and K—Husband held entitled to contact on basis of existing interim arrangements.

(14) *G v. G,* 2003 Fam.L.R. 118 (Sheriff W. Holligan)

Parties divorced and living apart at date of proof (July 2003)—Parties having a child (G, born April 1997)—Parties separating in June 1999, husband leaving matrimonial home—Husband initially having overnight contact with child twice a week, midweek and at weekend, subsequently stopping overnight midweek contact and, in September 2002, ceasing midweek contact altogether—Child not making as much progress at school as he ought to although no cause had been identified and his difficulties might resolve with time or might require learning support— Husband seeking residence order—Child's views not sought, having regard to opinion of psychologist that not practicable to seek child's views in relation to residence—Husband held not entitled to residence order, it being in child's best interests to continue to reside with wife and it being better that no order for residence be made than that an order be made.

(15) *J v. J,* 2004 Fam.L.R. 20 (Second Division)

Parties divorced and living apart at date of proof (February 2003)—Parties having two children (N, born July 1992, and R, born July 1995)—Parties separating in March 1995—

Children living with wife ever since separation—Husband having contact with children on an informal basis with both children—Husband obtaining new job, his hours of work tending to conflict with contact arrangements which were often cancelled at short notice—Parties' relationship becoming acrimonious and informal contact arrangements breaking down—Husband ceasing from late 1997 to attempt to maintain contact with children—Children expressing wishes in 2001 not to have contact—Husband held entitled to contact order in relation to children in terms providing for gradual resumption of contact, consideration being given to weight to be attached to children's wishes, their being liable to be upset at the outset if contact were resumed and the long term considerations which worked entirely to their benefit.

(16) *K v. K*, 2004 Fam.L.R. 25 (Sheriff A. M. Bell)

Parties married in July 1993 and living apart at date of proof (August 2003)—Parties having three children (M, born December 1993, K, born July 1995, and X, born December 1998)—Parties separating in July 2001—Children living with wife until January 2002 when they went to live with husband—Wife suffering from depression for many years and abusing alcohol and drugs—Husband initially willing to allow wife to have contact but she having no contact for nearly 18 months during which time she underwent psychiatric treatment and alcohol detoxification—Wife twice taking drugs overdose in 2002—Wife beginning a relationship with a man in July 2002 and living with him at date of proof—Wife on probation and subject to community service order and sentence deferred for good behaviour—Wife attempting suicide in December 2002—Wife re-establishing contact with children at contact centre in May 2003, seeing them twice—M expressing a wish to continue to see her, K being obviously unhappy at present and unsure whether she wanted to see her, and X not expressing any wish to give a view as to whether he wished to see her—Wife held entitled to contact order in relation to M and X, contact to take place for one hour per week at a contact centre.

(17) *S v. FD*, 2010 S.L.T. (Sh. Ct.) 107 (Sheriff N.M.P. Morrison Q.C.)

Parties married in February 2003 and living apart at date of proof (April 2010)—Parties having two children (Z, born May 2003, and N, born December 2007)—Parties separating in October 2008—Children thereafter living with wife in Edinburgh—Separation following upon claim by wife that Z, a girl, had alleged that husband had tickled and kissed her vagina—Wife making further claims of sexual abuse of daughter by husband, albeit her original police statement did not mention such abuse—Husband denying allegations—No suggestion that husband had abused N, a boy—Husband seeking unsupervised contact with both children—Wife seeking a specific issue order to allow her to take the children on holiday to Spain (her home country) for six weeks each year—Husband held entitled to unsupervised contact on the basis that he had not in fact sexually abused his daughter—Wife held not entitled to specific issue order, there being a real and present risk that she would not return with children to Scotland from holiday in Spain, given the fact that she had made false allegations against the husband and had received unsolicited advice from a Spanish lawyer to use a dirty trick to obtain jurisdiction of Spanish courts.

(18) *H v. H,* 2010 S.L.T. 395 (Lord Woolman)

Parties married in April 1992 and living apart at date of proof (March 2010)—Parties having two children (LH, born November 1996, and AH, born February 1999)—Parties separating in October 2008—Parties both Australian citizens living in Glasgow—Husband intending to return to work in Australia whereas wife wishing to remain in Scotland—LH, described as a mature and confident young woman, had written to the court expressing her wish to remain with her mother—AH, described as an introspective boy who would be distressed and anxious about his father if they were separated, had written to the court stating that he thought it would be better for his future if he lived in Australia—Children also interviewed more than once by two psychologists to similar effect—Daughter having many friends in Glasgow and primary emotional bond with wife—Son enjoying outdoor pursuits—Husband having extended family in Australia and son would be able to engage in cricket, tennis and golf as part of outdoor lifestyle in Australia—Mother held entitled to residence order in respect of daughter—Husband held entitled to residence order in respect of son.

(19) *M v. M,* 2012 S.L.T. 428 (Extra Division; Sheriff Principal E.F. Bowen Q.C.)

Parties married in April 2003 and living apart at date of proof (June 2010)—Parties having two children (D, born February 2004, and A, born in about 2006)—Elder child having complications at birth leaving him with degree of deafness and requirement to wear special glasses to correct squint—Parties residing in Scotland until August 2008 when wife attempted to remove children to England in order to live with another man in Berkshire — Court order required to secure their return — Children then living with wife in former matrimonial home with husband having regular contact — Wife granted residence order in respect of children, of consent, in November 2008 — Children in familiar, settled and happy surroundings — Wife deciding in 2009 that she wished to live with other man in Berkshire and seeking specific issue order to allow her to relocate to England with children — Potentially significant risks arising for the children, especially D, from what was in contemplation — Wife held not entitled to specific issue order as she had not shown that relocation was in best interests of children.

(20) *S v. S*, 2012 Fam. L.R. 32 (Extra Division)

Parties divorced in 2010 and living apart at date of proof (November 2011) — Parties having child (B, born in about 2005) — Wife primary carer and "bedrock" of life of child, a boy — Husband enjoying extensive day and residential contacts and activities covering a minimum of some 5 days in each fortnight together with extra assistance when required — Both parties employed at senior management level within major international companies providing services to oil and gas industry — Wife suddenly offered significant promoted post at employers' principal base in Houston, Texas — Wife having to resign existing position and, in the event of not taking up promoted post, would require to seek alternative employment — Wife unwilling to contemplate separation from B — Tensions arising between husband and wife as a result of proposed move — Wife seeking residence order and specific issue order to allow her to relocate to Houston with B — Wife held entitled to residence order and specific issue order permitting her to relocate to Houston with B as being in best interests of child, bearing in mind that old status quo had now gone and could never be regained and also that child's relationship with husband was already strong and well established and could realistically be maintained in a variety of ways.

REPORTED CASES INVOLVING
SECTION 9(1) PRINCIPLES

Cases in which section 9(1)(a) of the Family Law (Scotland) Act 1985 was considered include the following:

(1) *Petrie v. Petrie*, 1988 S.C.L.R. 390 (Sheriff D. J. Risk)
Parties married in June 1983 and separated in November 1985 — Husband seriously injured in March 1983 and receiving damages in October 1986 — Damages held not to be matrimonial property — Opinion that, having regard to the special circumstances mentioned in s. 10(6)(b) and (d), wife's share of the compensation payment would probably have been discounted to a very great extent, if not entirely.

(2) *Phillip v. Phillip*, 1988 S.C.L.R. 427 (Sheriff E. F. Bowen)
Parties married in December 1952 and separated in summer 1976 — Matrimonial property at relevant date comprising husband's savings, life policy and retirement gratuity together with reduced pension rights as well as matrimonial home owned by husband — Proportion of matrimonial home's purchase price (assessed at £4,000 as at the date of separation) coming from property which husband owned prior to the marriage — Value of matrimonial property at relevant date held to be £39,200 — Held that, having regard to the special circumstances mentioned in s. 10(6)(b), the sum of £4,000 should be deducted from net value of matrimonial property at relevant date and that resulting balance, namely £35,200, should be shared equally.

(3) *Bell v. Bell*, 1988 S.C.L.R. 457 (Sheriff J. C. M. Jardine)
Parties married in July 1960 and separated in June 1986 — Matrimonial property at relevant date comprising (i) jointly owned matrimonial home and household goods therein; (ii) wife's savings; and (iii) husband's savings, insurance policies and occupational pension — Matrimonial home valued on basis of actual sale price shortly after relevant date — Household goods and husband's interest in occupational pension scheme referable to the period of the marriage up to relevant date valued on broad axe basis — Matrimonial

property at relevant date valued at £99,484, comprising £70,692 (husband) and £28,792 (wife) — Wife receiving payments and goods from husband after separation valued at £38,584 — Wife held entitled to equal division of matrimonial property, namely (after deduction of £38,584) to capital sum of £11,158, restricted to £10,000 to comply with the terms of her crave.

(4) *Park v. Park*, 1988 S.C.L.R. 584 (Sheriff D. Kelbie)

Parties married in December 1980 and separated in October 1985 — Matrimonial property at relevant date comprising (i) jointly owned matrimonial home (subject to mortgage), insurance policies and household furniture and furnishings; and (ii) husband's interest in occupational pension scheme — Arrears of mortgage payments accumulating — Husband keeping household furniture and furnishings — Wife held entitled to capital sum representing one-half of agreed value of furniture and furnishings and one-half of husband's probable interest in occupational pension scheme — Failure to make mortgage payments held not to amount to special circumstances in terms of s. 10(6)(c).

(5) *Kerrigan v. Kerrigan*, 1988 S.C.L.R. 603 (Sheriff G. J. Evans)

Parties married in August 1984 and separated in September 1985 — Matrimonial property at relevant date comprising jointly owned matrimonial home — Matrimonial home purchased in contemplation of marriage with building society loan and gift of money from husband's mother — Husband making mortgage payments — Husband held entitled to transfer of property order in respect of wife's one-half *pro indiviso* share of matrimonial home.

(6) *Buczynska v. Buczynski*, 1989 S.L.T. 558 (Lord Morton of Shuna)

Parties married in July 1969 and separated in May 1987 — Separation held to have occurred when husband's solicitor sent a letter requesting wife to leave the house by which time parties had ceased to share a bedroom and wife had ceased to cook for the husband — Wife owning flat at relevant date — Husband owning matrimonial home valued at £80,000 at relevant date — Wife acquiring flat with building society loan and gift from mother — Held that if wife's flat was matrimonial property, special circumstances existed as provided for in s. 10(6)(b) — Wife held entitled to capital sum of £35,000.

(7) *Little v. Little*, 1989 S.C.L.R. 613; 1990 S.L.T. 785 (First Division; Lord Cameron of Lochbroom)

Parties married in October 1961 and separated in April 1986 — Matrimonial property at relevant date comprising matrimonial home owned by husband (valued at £66,500 and subject to mortgage of £20,800), furniture and furnishings therein (valued at £2,500), timeshares held in joint names, contents of joint bank account (£840), personal possessions, two cars (used for professional purposes), speedboat owned by husband (valued at £600), six endowment policies in husband's name (valued at £27,501) and interests held by each party in certain other policies and pension schemes — Husband's pension interests exceeding wife's in value by £70,996 — Husband keeping contents of joint bank account — Husband making payment of £2,616 towards timeshare after separation — Wife held entitled to (i) transfer of property order in respect of a one-half *pro indiviso* share of matrimonial home and furniture and furnishings therein; and (ii) an award of capital sum of £38,260, comprising (a) the sum of £35,498, representing the difference in value of parties' interests in their respective pension schemes at relevant date; and (b) the sum of £2,763, representing one-half of the value of endowment policies, speedboat and joint bank account (£14,470) less one-half of mortgage outstanding at relevant date and one-half of timeshare payment made after separation (£11,708) — Extract superseded in respect of one-half of capital sum for a period of six years.

(8) *Walker v. Walker*, 1989 S.C.L.R. 625; 1991 S.L.T. 157 (First Division; Lord Morton of Shuna)

Parties married in July 1960 and separated in October 1986 — Matrimonial property at relevant date comprising (i) jointly owned matrimonial home; and (ii) other substantial heritable and moveable assets owned by husband — Wife held entitled to transfer of property orders reflecting one-half of net value of the matrimonial property at relevant date as well as husband's advantage and wife's disadvantage in terms of future income arising from business built up by contributions made by both parties during the marriage.

(9) *Muir v. Muir*, 1989 S.L.T. (Sh. Ct.) 20 (Sheriff I. A. Macmillan)

Parties married in September 1964 and separated in November 1984 — Matrimonial property at relevant date comprising matrimonial home owned by husband and his interest in insurance policies and pension fund — Wife held entitled to capital sum reflecting one-half of net value of matrimonial home, one-half of surrender value of insurance policies and two-fifths of value of pension fund, all as valued as at relevant date.

(10) *Cooper v. Cooper*, 1989 S.C.L.R. 347 (Sheriff Principal R. D. Ireland Q.C.; Sheriff N. McPartlin)

Parties separated in 1987 after several years of marriage

— Matrimonial property at relevant date comprising jointly owned matrimonial home, household contents and cash — Husband keeping cash and sharing household contents — Wife living in matrimonial home with children of marriage and husband living in sheltered accommodation — Wife assuming responsibility for repaying loans on house — Wife held entitled to transfer of property order with respect to husband's one-half share, having regard to the special circumstances specified in s. 10(6)(d).

(11) *Morrison v. Morrison*, 1989 S.C.L.R. 574 (Sheriff G. H. Gordon Q.C.)

Parties married in March 1971 and separated in September 1987 — Matrimonial property at relevant date comprising (i) jointly owned matrimonial home, household contents and endowment policy; (ii) taxi business owned by husband; and (iii) car owned by wife — Wife contributing to taxi business — Children of marriage living with wife — Wife held entitled to capital sum reflecting (a) two-thirds of total value of matrimonial home and contents less husband's share of wife's car and wife's half-share of matrimonial home as joint owner; and (b) one-half of net value of taxi business.

(12) *Budge v. Budge*, 1990 S.L.T. 319 (Lord Cameron of Lochbroom)

Parties married in April 1980 and separated in July 1985 — Matrimonial property at relevant date comprising caravan owned by wife (valued at £100) and lease of croft owned by husband (valued at £9,500) — Lease originally acquired by husband with £7,000 obtained from sale of property owned by him before marriage — Wife assisting husband in maintaining and improving croft during the parties' cohabitation — Wife held entitled to capital sum of £1,200, assessing fair sharing of the matrimonial property in croft at £1,250 less £50 for value of wife's caravan.

(13) *Tyrrell v. Tyrrell*, 1990 S.L.T. 406 (Lord Sutherland)

Parties married in September 1964 and separated in October 1982 — Matrimonial property at relevant date comprising (i) assets distributed by agreement between parties upon separation; (ii) husband's cash, shares, life assurance policies and interest in pension fund (valued at £67,496); and (iii) wife's jewellery and fur (valued at £12,432) — Net value of total matrimonial property at relevant date therefore £79,928 — Wife held entitled to capital sum of £27,532, reflecting an equal division of the undistributed assets less those retained by her — Wife held not entitled to any share of husband's redundancy payment received by him in June 1986.

(14) *Latter v. Latter*, 1990 S.L.T. 805 (Lord Marnoch)

Parties separated in March 1987 after several years of marriage — Matrimonial property at relevant date comprising (a) husband's pension rights (valued at £169,000); (b) husband's interest in insurance policies (valued at £2,050); (c) husband's shares in Marks & Spencer plc (valued at £2,670); (d) debt due to husband by family trust (£4,655); (e) furniture and contents of matrimonial home (valued at £12,000 on a basis close to willing buyer/willing seller); (f) husband's shareholding of 4,150 shares in private family company, M & H Latter (Holdings) Ltd (valued at £626,650 on a net asset basis without any deduction for notional capital gains tax liability); and (g) various undisclosed assets (valued at about £229,000) — Debts at relevant date comprising (i) debt due by husband to family company of £5,000; and (ii) arrears of tax amounting to £41,000 — Net value of matrimonial property at relevant date therefore about £1,000,000 — Matrimonial home, purchased with funds paid by wife's parents direct to solicitors as gift to wife, held not to be matrimonial property — Shareholding in M & H Latter (Holdings) Ltd deriving from series of shareholdings gifted to, or inherited or purchased with gifted funds by, husband in what were now subsidiary companies following on an overall company reconstruction — Special circumstances relied on by wife (for which husband debited with figure of £25,000) were that (a) some of capital of wife's family trust had been lent unprofitably by husband to his companies; (b) husband's conduct had resulted in unnecessary financial hardship to wife; and (c) some of parties' furniture replaced furniture originally donated by wife's parents — Special circumstances relied on by husband were that (a) substantial sums were spent by husband's family on matrimonial home (for which husband credited with sum of £90,000); (b) pension was not realisable (for which no credit given, standing availability of other liquid assets); and (c) shareholding emanated in substance if not in form from donation or inheritance (for which net value of matrimonial property discounted by around half the value of those shares, namely by sum of £320,000) — Wife held entitled to capital sum of £275,000, representing (i) one-half of discounted net value of matrimonial property, namely £340,000 (50% of £680,000), less (ii) net credit due to husband, namely £65,000 (£90,000 less £25,000), with extract superseded for two months.

(15) *Carpenter v. Carpenter*, 1990 S.L.T. (Sh. Ct.) 68 (Sheriff R.H. Dickson)

Parties married in June 1964 and separated in October 1983

    — Matrimonial property at relevant date comprising husband's interest in pension fund and life policies — Wife held entitled to capital sum reflecting one-half of value of life policies and three-eighths of value of interest in pension fund at relevant date.

(16) *Main v. Main*, 1990 S.C.L.R. 165 (Sheriff Principal Sir Frederick O'Brien Q.C.)

    Parties married in April 1967 and separated in September 1986 — Matrimonial property at relevant date comprising jointly owned matrimonial home and other assets in respect of which a payment of £1,400 by husband to wife would produce an equal sharing — Wife making payments of about £2,000 in respect of parties' joint mortgage since date of separation — Wife not wishing to sell matrimonial home where she had resided with her daughters for many years — Held that wife was entitled to capital sum of £5,400, comprising (i) £1,400 to produce an equal sharing; (ii) £1,000 in respect of the mortgage payments; and (iii) £3,000 to facilitate purchase of matrimonial home, having regard to the special circumstances mentioned in s. 10(6)(d).

(17) *Farrell v. Farrell*, 1990 S.C.L.R. 717 (Sheriff C. N. Stoddart)

    Parties married in August 1981 and separated in July 1986 — Matrimonial property at relevant date comprising jointly owned matrimonial home (with low net value) and furniture and plenishings therein — Wife continuing to occupy matrimonial home — Husband leaving wife with burden of keeping up mortgage after separation — Wife held entitled to transfer of property order in respect of husband's one-half share of matrimonial home and furniture and plenishings therein so far as not in her sole ownership, there being special circumstances present.

(18) *Thomson v. Thomson*, 1991 S.L.T. 126 (Lord Cameron of Lochbroom)

    Parties separated in May 1986 after several years of marriage — Matrimonial property at relevant date comprising husband's life insurance policies and shares in two private companies with total value of £15,000 — Husband subsequently transferring the shares to his brother purportedly for value — Transfer held to be collusive arrangement to defeat the wife's claim in which no money actually changed hands and husband's resources therefore assessed on the basis that he had as yet received no payment for shares — Wife held entitled to capital sum of £7,500.

(19) *McKenzie v. McKenzie*, 1991 S.L.T. 461 (Lord Prosser)

    Parties married in 1971 and separated in December 1987

— Matrimonial property at relevant date comprising jointly owned matrimonial home, husband's interest in pension fund valued at £70,900 and wife's business valued on a going concern basis at £16,000 — Wife held entitled to capital sum representing the difference between one-half of value of husband's pension and one-half of value of her business, namely £27,450.

(20) *Anderson v. Anderson*, 1991 S.L.T. (Sh. Ct.) 11 (Sheriff W. C. Henderson)

Parties married in July 1967 and separated in April 1987 — Matrimonial property at relevant date comprising household contents, cash, shares, personal items and car — Husband taking personal items and signing document narrating "I sign everything over to my wife i.e. household contents, money in bank, shares" upon separation — Husband subsequently claiming capital sum, conceding wife's entitlement to car — Held that husband had effectively ousted the jurisdiction of the court; and that, in any event, even if the matter fell to be approached from the standpoint of an agreement between the parties, s. 10(6)(a) entitled the court to make no award.

(21) *Skarpaas v. Skarpaas*, 1991 S.L.T. (Sh. Ct.) 15; 1993 S.L.T. 343 (First Division; Sheriff Principal R.A. Bennett Q.C.; Sheriff A. L. Stewart)

Parties married in August 1984 and separated in July 1988 — Matrimonial property at relevant date comprising husband's claim for damages for personal injuries sustained during the course of the marriage less certain debts — Decree granted in husband's favour after relevant date for such damages, including sums for solatium, past loss of earnings, interest and loss of future earning capacity — No evidence led as to value of damages claim if offered for sale in the market place at relevant date — Held that in the absence of such evidence value of damages claim as quantified by the court less debts should be shared, under deduction of interest on sums for solatium and past loss of earnings referable to period after relevant date and, having regard to the special circumstances mentioned in s. 10(6)(d), under further deduction of sums for solatium and loss of future earning capacity.

(22) *Pryde v. Pryde*, 1991 S.L.T. (Sh. Ct.) 26 (Sheriff A .M. Bell)

Parties married in August 1980 and separated in August 1987 — Matrimonial property at relevant date comprising husband's interest in pension fund, valued at £550 — Wife held entitled to capital sum of £200, it being clear that sole item of matrimonial property was something which was not easily realised and husband having no other resources — Husband's contention that certain furniture was also matrimonial property rejected, there being in any event no evidence led as to the value thereof.

(23) *McGuire v. McGuire's Curator Bonis*, 1991 S.L.T. (Sh. Ct.) 76 (Sheriff W.C. Henderson)

Parties married in November 1955 and separated in November 1987 — Matrimonial property at relevant date comprising the sum of at least £40,000 held by husband's curator bonis, being residue of husband's original award of criminal injuries compensation in total sum of £45,000, including £25,000 for solatium — Husband requiring permanent residential care — £32,000 still held by curator bonis at date of proof — Husband entitled to state assistance for cost of his care if and when his capital fell below £8,000 — Wife held entitled to capital sum of £20,000, with some, albeit fairly slight regard to personal element of solatium factor in the award as a special circumstance in terms of s. 10(6)(d).

(24) *Wallis v. Wallis*, 1991 S.C.L.R. 192; 1992 S.C. 455; 1993 S.C. (H.L.) 49 (House of Lords; First Division; Sheriff A. B. Wilkinson)

Parties married in March 1986 and separated in March 1987 — Matrimonial property at relevant date comprising (i) jointly owned matrimonial home (valued at £17,400 net) and furniture and plenishings therein (valued at £13,500); and (ii) husband's car (valued at £8,000) — Matrimonial home increasing in value by £24,000 by date of proof — Husband held entitled to transfer of property order in respect of wife's one-half share of matrimonial home and furniture and plenishings therein, subject to payment by him of capital sum of £19,450, representing (i) one-half of net value of matrimonial home at relevant date (£8,700); (ii) one-half of value of furniture and plenishings therein (£6,750); and (iii) one-half of value of motor car (£4,000).

(25) *Symon v. Symon*, 1991 S.C.L.R. 414 (Sheriff A. M. G. Russell Q.C.)

Parties married in 1976 and separated in October 1987 — Matrimonial property at relevant date comprising (i) jointly owned property, namely matrimonial home, household contents (valued at £3,000) and contents of building society account; and (ii) property owned by husband, namely car, insurance policies and pension rights (valued at £27,000) — Husband removing some of household contents after separation — Wife held entitled to one-half of value of car and insurance policies, the sum of £6,000 as her share of husband's

pension rights and the sum of £500 to balance the division of household contents — Order granted for sale of matrimonial home.
(26) *Jesner v. Jesner*, 1992 S.L.T. 999 (Lord Osborne)

Parties separated after several years of marriage — Matrimonial property at relevant date comprising (i) jointly owned property, namely a derelict farmhouse with adjoining land (valued at £30,000), household furnishings, a 60% share of an area of surrounding farmland (valued at £24,000) and three motor cars (valued at £4,500); and (ii) shares in a private company owned by husband (valued at £12,000) — Husband contriving to lose household furnishings — Farmhouse with adjoining land purchased with loan of £30,000, which was still outstanding at relevant date, and the proceeds of sale of house owned by husband prior to marriage — Assets of husband's company purchased by the use of money put in trust for husband by his father — Husband held entitled to transfer of property order in respect of wife's one-half share of the farmhouse with adjoining land, thus leaving wife with marginally under 30% of net value of matrimonial property.
(27) *Crockett v. Crockett*, 1992 S.C.L.R. 591; 30 June 1993, unreported (Extra Division; Lord McCluskey)

Parties married in August 1984 and separated in August 1988 — Matrimonial property at relevant date comprising jointly owned matrimonial home, insurance policy in joint names, husband's shares in private company (valued by reference to future maintainable earnings), wife's 38.03% interest in company's pension fund, husband's 61.97% interest therein, husband's interest in other insurance and pension policies and husband's cash — Parties each liable for bank debt at relevant date — Net value of matrimonial property at relevant date amounting to £390,387.90, comprising £142,175.29 (wife) and £248,212.61 (husband) — Husband's company insolvent by date of proof — Husband accepting substantial liability to aliment child of marriage — Wife held entitled to capital sum of £17,500, having regard to need for husband to apply remaining resources to try to save business or give it marketability.
(28) *Gulline v. Gulline*, 1992 S.L.T. (Sh. Ct.) 71 (Sheriff G. J. Evans)

Parties married in August 1973 and separated in July 1984 — Matrimonial property at relevant date comprising (i) assets distributed by agreement between parties upon separation and (ii) husband's interest in pension fund (valued at £34,590) — Joint debt of about £1,000 met by husband after separation

— Wife held entitled to capital sum reflecting one-half of husband's interest in pension fund less about half of joint debt, namely £17,000, payable on date of husband's retirement, with interest at the rate of 7.5 per cent per annum (the projected rate of return on investment) from date of decree of divorce.

(29) *Shipton v. Shipton*, 1992 S.C.L.R. 23 (Sheriff N.E.D. Thomson)

Parties married in September 1978 and separated in September 1987 — Matrimonial property at relevant date comprising (i) jointly owned matrimonial home (valued at £53,000) and furnishings therein (valued at £1,375); and (ii) husband's interest in pensions and insurance policy, shares and loan outstanding to him as director (valued at £17,195, discounting book value of loan by £27,000) — Matrimonial home purchased with assistance from husband's father by way of gift or loan of £4,800 — Matrimonial property at relevant date valued at £66,770, after deduction of the sum of £4,800 — Wife held entitled to capital sum of £9,285, payable within four weeks of date of sale of the matrimonial home.

(30) *Toye v. Toye*, 1992 S.C.L.R. 95 (Sheriff A. S. Jessop)

Parties married in March 1969 and separated in December 1988 — Matrimonial property at relevant date comprising (i) jointly owned matrimonial home and furniture and plenishings therein; (ii) jointly owned endowment policies; and (iii) husband's interest in pension policies — Total net value of matrimonial property at date of proof amounting to £149,542, comprising £86,000 (net value of matrimonial home); £11,000 (endowment policies); and £52,542 (pension policies) — Wife living in matrimonial home with child of marriage — Wife held entitled to transfer of property order in respect of husband's one-half share of (a) matrimonial home and furniture and plenishings therein; and (b) endowment policies, subject to taking responsibility for mortgage payments and insurance premiums and relinquishing in exchange all right, title and interest in husband's pension policies, there being special circumstances justifying an unequal division of matrimonial property and economic disadvantage suffered by wife.

(31) *White v. White*, 1992 S.C.L.R. 769 (Temporary Sheriff J. Gilmour)

Parties married in January 1991 and separated in February 1991 — Matrimonial property at relevant date comprising matrimonial home purchased shortly before marriage by husband in own name with his own funds and a loan obtained by him — Parties only cohabiting for a few weeks — Wife held not entitled to any financial provision.

(32) *Peacock v. Peacock*, 1993 S.C. 88 (Second Division)

Parties separated in August 1989 after several years of marriage — Matrimonial property at relevant date comprising matrimonial home and life assurance policy jointly owned by parties — Matrimonial home valued at relevant date at £29,000, subject to mortgage of £13,949, and at date of proof at £32,000, subject to a mortgage of £14,562 — Life assurance policy having surrender value of £643.75 — Wife in employment and continuing to occupy matrimonial home with parties' children after separation and making all but one of mortgage payments — Husband unemployed and making no financial contribution to children's maintenance — Wife held entitled, subject to assignation to husband of her share of life assurance policy, to transfer of property order in respect of husband's one-half share of matrimonial home, having regard to the special circumstances mentioned in s. 10(6)(d), in particular that transfer was necessary for children's welfare.

(33) *Brooks v. Brooks*, 1993 S.L.T. 184 (Lord Marnoch)

Parties separated in November 1988 after several years of marriage — Matrimonial property at relevant date comprising (i) jointly owned heritable properties; (ii) wife's assets (valued at £48,626); and (iii) husband's assets (valued at £100,974, inclusive of pension entitlement valued at £86,974) — Debt outstanding by husband to wife's mother amounting to £4,580 — Wife held entitled to capital sum of £23,884, representing one-half of difference in value between parties' respective matrimonial property less the debt, with extract superseded for a period of four months.

(34) *Bannon v. Bannon*, 1993 S.L.T. 999 (Lord Cameron of Lochbroom)

Parties married in September 1971 and separated in August 1988 — Matrimonial property at relevant date comprising husband's interest in pension fund, valued at £46,000 — Husband without resources — Wife held entitled to capital sum of £32,000, with extract superseded until date upon which husband would be entitled to retire on full pension, over six years thence.

(35) *Macdonald v. Macdonald*, 1993 S.C.L.R. 132 (Lord Caplan)

Parties separated in May 1990 after several years of marriage — Matrimonial property at relevant date comprising (i) jointly owned matrimonial home (valued at £247,000 and subject to mortgage of £39,000) and joint building society account (£900); (ii) wife's pension (valued at £22,000); and (iii) husband's pension (valued at £14,708) and endowment policies (valued at £38,203) less his bank debt of £7,000 — Matrimonial property owned by wife at relevant date therefore valued at £126,450 and husband's at £150,361 — Matrimonial property of parties at relevant date accordingly valued in total at £276,811 — Wife held entitled to equalisation payment of about £12,000 (being one-half of total matrimonial property less wife's share) under s. 9(1)(a).

(36) *Lewis v. Lewis*, 1993 S.C.L.R. 32 (Sheriff Principal J. S. Mowat Q.C.)

Parties separated in November 1985 after several years of marriage — Matrimonial property at relevant date comprising (i) jointly owned matrimonial home; (ii) husband's savings of £4,300; and (iii) wife's savings of £6,800 — Order made for sale of matrimonial home — Husband held entitled to capital sum of £700.

(37) *Loudon v. Loudon,* 1994 S.L.T. 381 (Lord Milligan)

Parties married in 1973 and separated in February 1991 — Matrimonial property at relevant date comprising assets valued at £834,119, although high degree of suspicion that husband had not disclosed all relevant assets — Wife arguing for unequal division on that basis and for her economic disadvantage — Wife held entitled to capital sum of £308,765, being the balance left after allowance made for sum of £150,000 already advanced to her by husband, the total (£458,765.45) representing 55% of the value of matrimonial property at relevant date.

(38) *Shand v. Shand*, 1994 S.L.T. 387 (Lord Coulsfield)

Parties married in August 1969 and separated in March 1985 — Matrimonial property at relevant date comprising assets valued at £259,951 but husband subsequently sequestrated — Both parties in receipt of income support at date of proof, but suspicions that husband in one way or another enjoyed some supplement to that income — Sole identified asset not falling under sequestration a pension policy in which husband had an interest with present transfer value of £12,207 — Pension policy capable of being realised forthwith to produce capital sum of £3,000 and income of £900 per annum or, if allowed to mature for a further period of seven or eight years, possible capital sum of £6,000 with income of £2,400 per annum to follow — Wife held entitled to capital sum of £12,000, with extract superseded until the likely date of conclusion of the sequestration, a period of almost two years.

(39) *Davidson v. Davidson*, 1994 S.L.T. 506 (Lord MacLean)

Parties married in July 1988 and separated in September 1991 — Matrimonial property at relevant date comprising farm valued at £177,000 — Farm purchased with money realised by wife from her substantial inherited shareholdings to enable her to carry on a farming business — Husband likely to suffer considerable financial hardship as a result of divorce — Husband held entitled to capital sum of £60,000, there being special circumstances why the matrimonial property should not be shared equally.

(40) *Welsh v. Welsh*, 1994 S.L.T. 828 (Lord Osborne)

Parties married in April 1969 and separated in December 1987 — Matrimonial property at relevant date comprising jointly owned matrimonial home (valued at £29,000 and subject to mortgage of £19,280), furniture and plenishings (valued at £1,500), husband's interest in a superannuation scheme (valued at £15,850), motor car (valued at £500), cash in bank (£71.91) and an endowment policy (valued at £321.20) — Total net value of matrimonial property at relevant date therefore £27,963.11 — Wife consenting to transfer of property order in respect of her one-half share of matrimonial home — Wife held entitled to balancing capital payment of £13,981, representing an equal sharing of the matrimonial property as at the relevant date.

(41) *Whittome v. Whittome (No. 1)*, 1994 S.L.T. 114 (Lord Osborne)

Parties married in October 1970 and separated in November 1985 — Husband owning 502,438 shares in public limited company with total value of £678,291 at relevant date — Company originally a private family company — Husband's shareholding originally acquired variously by way of gift, advances of trust capital and from the trust upon its effective determination — Husband's shareholding subsequently increasing twice by bonus issue of shares, the latter forming part of reorganisation of company involving increase in share capital, division of each ordinary £1 share into four ordinary 25p shares, reflected in new share certificates issued, and re-registration of company as public limited company with new articles of association — Husband's proportionate share of company unaffected by reorganisation — Husband's shareholding at relevant date held not to be matrimonial property — Uplift in value of husband's shareholding between date of acquisition and relevant date not matrimonial property — Wife held not entitled to award of a capital sum.

(42) *Gribb v. Gribb*, 1994 S.L.T. (Sh. Ct.) 43; 1996 S.L.T. 719 (Second Division; Sheriff J. C. McInnes Q.C.)

Parties married in March 1953 and separated in February 1991 — Matrimonial property at relevant date comprising jointly owned matrimonial home (valued at £52,000), the contents thereof (valued at £6,195) and husband's interest in his pension scheme (valued at £100,800) — Wife held entitled to transfer of property order in respect of husband's one-half share of matrimonial home.

(43) *Jacques v. Jacques*, 1995 S.C. 327; 1997 S.C. (H.L.) 20 (House of Lords; First Division)

Parties married in January 1987 and separated in September 1990 — Matrimonial property at relevant date comprising jointly owned matrimonial home (valued at £55,000) and various other items — Matrimonial home purchased for £30,000, the source of funds being the sale proceeds of house owned by husband and occupied by parties before their marriage — Matrimonial home requiring certain repairs, financed by balance of sale proceeds and bank loan taken out by husband, with both parties giving up employment to renovate the property, thus contributing to increase in value of property — Husband still liable as at relevant date in respect of loan in the sum of £5,000 but retaining after separation items of matrimonial property of broadly equivalent value — Husband using matrimonial home for unsuccessful bed and breakfast business — Husband held not entitled to transfer of property order, there being no special circumstances present justifying departure from equal sharing — Wife held entitled to order for sale of matrimonial home, with extract superseded for six months.

(44) *Tahir v. Tahir (No. 2)*, 1995 S.L.T. 451 (Lord Clyde)

Parties married in 1979 and separated in August 1985 — Matrimonial property at relevant date comprising matrimonial home (valued at £13,500), the contents thereof (valued at £200), certain other items (valued at £2,385) and funds of £17,000 — Debts at relevant date comprising £10,000 in respect of mortgage and £2,526.59 in respect of repairs bill — Debt alleged to be due by husband to third party for which a sheriff court decree existed held to be fictitious and sheriff court decree accordingly reduced — Net value of matrimonial property at relevant date therefore a round total of £20,000 — Wife held entitled to one-half thereof in terms of s. 9(1)(a), namely £10,000.

(45) *Mayor v. Mayor*, 1995 S.L.T. 1097 (Lord Marnoch)

Parties separated in 1983 after several years of marriage — Matrimonial property at relevant date comprising (i) wife's savings of £1,000; and (ii) husband's interest in family business (valued at £4,358), ownership of premises thereof (valued at £65,000) and cash (£3,252) — Husband transferring other properties into name of his mother, who had since died, his entitlement on her intestacy amounting to £31,000 — Wife held entitled to capital sum of £50,000, with extract superseded for six months, it being unavoidable that family business premises be sold in order to do justice between the parties.

(46) *Buckle v. Buckle*, 1995 S.C.L.R. 590 (Sheriff N. McPartlin)

Parties married for thirty years — Matrimonial property at relevant date comprising husband's pension rights, valued at £76,000 — Wife held entitled to capital sum of £15,000, payable by monthly instalments of £250 over five years.

(47) *Lawson v. Lawson*, 1996 S.L.T. (Sh. Ct.) 83 (Sheriff Principal C. G. B. Nicholson Q.C.)

Parties married in September 1987 and separated in December 1988 — Matrimonial property at relevant date comprising matrimonial home, valued at £29,000 and burdened with mortgage of £15,000 — Matrimonial home formerly belonging to local authority and tenanted by husband's parents and then by husband prior to marriage — History of tenancy entitling husband to purchase house (market value £25,500) just before marriage at substantially discounted price, namely £11,960 — Held that there were no special circumstances relating to the source of the funds or assets used to acquire the matrimonial property since entitlement to discount on the purchase of a particular thing is not an "asset" within the meaning of s. 10(6)(b).

(48) *Crosbie v. Crosbie*, 1996 S.L.T. (Sh. Ct.) 86 (Sheriff Principal G. L. Cox Q.C.)

Parties married in 1957 and separated in October 1991 — Matrimonial property at relevant date comprising (i) jointly owned matrimonial home; and (ii) husband's interest in pension fund (valued at £78,000) and certain assets retained by him (valued at £40,000) less debt of £1,832; and (iii) certain assets retained by wife (valued at £23,230) — Wife held entitled to capital sum of £36,469 (of which £7,469 payable within seven days, £19,000 within six months and the balance of £10,000 by monthly instalments of £416), comprising (i) £7,469, representing equal sharing of matrimonial property except for the pension interest; and (ii) £29,000, representing fair sharing of pension interest having regard to its non-realisability.

(49) *Murphy v. Murphy*, 1996 S.L.T. (Sh. Ct.) 91 (Sheriff A. M. Bell)

Parties married in October 1969 and separated in January 1991 — Matrimonial property at relevant date comprising (i) jointly owned matrimonial home; and (ii) husband's interest in pensions (valued at £28,301.13), insurance policy (valued at £354), car (valued at £1,000) and cash (£3,147.13) — Wife receiving about £2,500 after separation — Wife living in matrimonial home with children of marriage — Matrimonial home having net value of £36,370.19 at date of proof — Wife held entitled to transfer of property order in respect of husband's one-half share of matrimonial home.

(50) *Cunniff v. Cunniff*, 1997 Fam.L.R. 42; 1999 S.C. 537 (Extra Division; Lord Abernethy)

Parties married in May 1971 and separated after divorce proceedings were raised in March 1991 — Matrimonial property at relevant date comprising jointly owned matrimonial home (valued at £80,000), family car (valued at £2,500), husband's pension interest (valued at £8,600), cash held by wife (£1,272) and cash held by husband (£9) — Total value of matrimonial property at relevant date therefore £92,381 — Debts at relevant date comprising mortgage of £39,500 and matrimonial debts of £11,460, not including Irish tax debt which husband did not intend to pay and which was unenforceable — Net value of matrimonial property at relevant date accordingly £41,421 — Wife retaining family car — Husband unemployed and unable to pay matrimonial debts for which he alone was liable — Wife living in matrimonial home with child under 16 (and being visited by older children), paying mortgage, unable to afford alternative accommodation and prone to ill health — Sale of matrimonial home sought by husband liable to result in claim by Scottish Legal Aid Board against sale proceeds, not leaving husband necessarily better off — Wife held entitled to transfer of property order in respect of husband's one-half share of matrimonial home, there being special circumstances justifying unequal division of matrimonial property — Husband's earning capacity and increase in value of his pension fund held to be resources for the purposes of financial provision on divorce.

(51) *Graham v. Graham*, 1997 Fam.L.R. 117 (Second Division)

Parties separated in February 1993 after several years of marriage — Matrimonial property at relevant date comprising matrimonial home jointly owned by them along with third party — Matrimonial home valued at £28,000 and subject to mortgage of £14,000 at relevant date — Parties' combined interest in matrimonial home therefore valued at £9,332 — Parties also having debts at relevant date amounting to £9,278 for which husband had assumed responsibility — Wife held not entitled to transfer of property order in respect of husband's one-third share of matrimonial home.

(52) *McConnell v. McConnell*, 1997 Fam.L.R. 97; 1997 Fam.L.R. 108 (Second Division; Lord Osborne)

Parties separated in November 1990 after several years of

marriage — Matrimonial property at relevant date comprising jointly owned matrimonial home and contents therein (valued by discounting their insurance value) and various other assets held jointly or by one or other party (including husband's shares in private company valued under reference to company's net assets) — Total matrimonial property at relevant date valued at £1,450,044, whereof property valued at £331,622 in wife's hands and property valued at £1,118,422 in husband's — Debts at relevant date (excluding certain contingent tax liabilities but including tax liability arising in relation to income enjoyed during year preceding relevant date) amounting to £141,337, whereof wife liable for £18,728 (being one-half of outstanding mortgage over matrimonial home of £37,456) and husband for £122,609 — Net value of total matrimonial property at relevant date therefore £1,308,707, whereof £312,894 in wife's hands and £995,813 in husband's — Wife held entitled to (i) transfer of property order in respect of husband's one-half share of matrimonial home and contents therein (valued at £272,500); (ii) an incidental order for payment by husband of outstanding mortgage over matrimonial home (inclusive of wife's one-half liability in the sum of £18,728); and (iii) capital sum of £50,000, the total value of orders for financial provision thereby made in favour of wife being £341,228, representing in round figures one-half of net value of the matrimonial property at relevant date less net value of matrimonial property in wife's hands, there being no special circumstances justifying an unequal division of matrimonial property.

(53) *Adams v. Adams (No. 1)*, 1997 S.L.T. 144 (Lord Gill)

Parties married in September 1978 and separated in September 1991 — Matrimonial property at relevant date comprising jointly owned matrimonial home and insurance policy on joint lives and various other assets (valued at £44,380) — Wife living in matrimonial home with children — Order for sale of matrimonial home granted — Wife held entitled to capital sum of £22,190, representing an equal sharing of matrimonial property, payable on receipt by husband of his half share of sale proceeds.

(54) *Savage v. Savage,* 1997 Fam.L. R. 132 (Lord Sutherland)

Parties separated in June 1990 after several years of marriage — Matrimonial property at relevant date comprising (i) jointly owned matrimonial home; and (ii) husband's savings (£49,300) and business (valued on a going concern basis at £75,000) — Parties agreeing sale of matrimonial home and division of proceeds — Wife receiving proceeds of insurance policies amounting to £2,100 — Net value of undistributed matrimonial property therefore amounting to £122,200 — Wife held entitled to capital sum of £63,600 (with extract superseded *quoad* the sum of £18,600 for three months), comprising (i) £61,100, representing equal sharing of matrimonial property; and (ii) £2,500, representing interest thereon from relevant date.

(55) *Gracie v. Gracie*, 1997 S.L.T. (Sh. Ct.) 15 (Sheriff R. G. Craik Q.C.)

Parties married in February 1975 and separated in February 1994 — Matrimonial property at relevant date comprising jointly owned matrimonial home, joint endowment policy and husband's interest in pension scheme (valued at £30,000) — Wife held entitled to capital sum of £15,000, payable by 11 annual instalments of £1,000 until date of husband's entitlement to pension, when balance due.

(56) *Collins v. Collins*, 1997 Fam.L.R. 50 (Sheriff J. R. Smith)

Parties married in August 1980 and separated in January 1988 — Matrimonial property at relevant date comprising jointly owned matrimonial home (valued at £14,400 net), furniture (valued at £4,700) and cash (£911) — Husband retaining furniture and cash — Value of matrimonial property at relevant date therefore £20,011, whereof £12,811 retained by husband and £7,200 retained by wife — Debts at relevant date amounting to £858, paid by wife — Husband suffering from multiple sclerosis with reduced life expectancy and requiring constant professional care in matrimonial home (adapted into what resembled nursing home) — Wife's conduct adversely affecting parties' resources — Husband held entitled to transfer of property order in respect of wife's one-half share of matrimonial home, having regard to special circumstances mentioned in s. 10(6)(d) — Wife held entitled to capital sum of £9,927.54 (secured by standard security over matrimonial home and with extract superseded until date of husband's death, with no interest thereon), comprising (i) £3,234, representing an equal sharing of the net value of the matrimonial property; and (ii) £7,200, representing net value of wife's one-half share of matrimonial home at relevant date, restricted to £9,927.54 to comply with terms of wife's crave.

(57) *Maclachlan v. Maclachlan*, 1998 S.L.T. 693 (Lord Macfadyen)

Parties separated in March 1995 after several years of marriage — Matrimonial property at relevant date comprising jointly owned matrimonial home subject to a joint mortgage, household contents, parties' respective interests in pension funds and certain other assets, including funds in wife's hands derived from a redundancy payment — Parties sharing household contents by agreement — Parties' pension interests broadly comparable in value — Wife's other assets at relevant date valued at £25,294.60 and husband's at £5,523.13 — Husband held entitled to equal sharing of balance of matrimonial property, namely £9,885.74 (being one-half of £30,817.73, less £5,523.13), there being no special circumstances present to justify sharing other than equally.

(58) *Wilson v. Wilson*, 1999 S.L.T. 249 (Lord Marnoch)

Parties married in February 1979 and separated in February 1996 — Matrimonial property at relevant date comprising assets having net value of £804,122, whereof wife's assets valued at £93,452 — Husband failing to discharge onus of proof that certain monies inherited — Property held by husband's company held not to be matrimonial property — Wife held entitled to the sum of £308,609, representing equal division of matrimonial property.

(59) *Jackson v. Jackson*, 2000 S.C.L.R. 81 (Lord Macfadyen)

Parties married in 1986 and separated after divorce proceedings were raised in October 1996 — Matrimonial property at relevant date comprising various agreed items of property, valued at £163,190 (wife) and £232,906 (husband), and various other items of property, namely wife's jewellery (valued at £10,448), wife's share of contents of matrimonial home (valued at £9,460), husband's share thereof (valued at £780), wife's pension (valued at £6,039), husband's pension (valued at £51,744), wife's shareholding in private family company, P & B Enterprises Ltd (valued at £436,205) and husband's shareholding therein (valued at £440,942) — Total value of matrimonial property at relevant date therefore £1,351,714, comprising £625,342 (wife) and £726,372 (husband) — Husband's debts at relevant date, including tax debt subsequently paid by him, amounting to £23,532 — Total net value of matrimonial property at relevant date accordingly £1,328,182, comprising £625,342 (wife) and £702,840 (husband) — Funds used to acquire shareholding in P & B Enterprises Ltd to some extent derived from husband's efforts before marriage but unclear as to how much so derived and husband in any event choosing to invest those funds in that company on basis that shares taken almost equally between wife and himself — Wife held entitled to capital sum of £38,750, representing equal sharing of net value of matrimonial property, there being no special circumstances present justifying unequal sharing — Extract superseded until sale of shares in P & B Enterprises Ltd effected.

(60) *R v. R*, 2000 Fam.L.R. 43 (Lord Eassie)

Parties married in April 1988 and separated in March 1998 — Matrimonial property at relevant date comprising farm and other assets with total value of £1,204,635 (excluding furniture and plenishings divided by agreement), whereof husband owned everything except for three horses belonging to wife valued at £5,000 — Great bulk of matrimonial property stemming from assets inherited by or given to husband — Wife having care of children of marriage and suffering economic disadvantage — Wife held entitled to capital sum of £380,000, there being special circumstances in terms of s. 10(6)(b) justifying an unequal division of matrimonial property.

(61) *Fulton v. Fulton*, 2000 Fam. L.R. 8 (Lord Nimmo Smith)

Parties married in April 1984 and separated in June 1993 — Matrimonial property at relevant date valued at £986,356, comprising (i) matrimonial home and contents, valued at £206,015; (ii) husband's interest in pension scheme, valued at £300,086; and (iii) husband's minority shareholding in private company, valued (on an earnings basis) at £480,255 — Held that there were no special circumstances justifying unequal sharing — Wife retaining matrimonial property valued at £162,718 — Wife accordingly held entitled to capital sum of £330,460.

(62) *Stuart v. Stuart*, 2001 S.L.T. (Sh. Ct.) 20 (Sheriff Principal J.C. McInnes Q.C.)

Parties married in June 1989 and separated in July 1995 — Matrimonial property at relevant date comprising jointly owned matrimonial home and its contents, a car, husband's interest in an occupational pension scheme and an insurance policy with a negative value — Matrimonial home purchased at discount from development corporation in June 1995 for £26,840, funded by building society loan of £27,000, and valued at relevant date at £45,000 — Varying proportions of discount repayable in the event of resale within three years — Other assets valued at relevant date at £6,733.18 — Matrimonial home valued at £46,000 and subject to loan of £27,050.07 in May 1999 — Matrimonial home remaining unsold at date of proof, husband paying mortgage costs and policy premiums since separation — Wife held entitled to capital sum of £12,336.59, comprising (i) £9,000, being her share of the net proceeds of sale of the matrimonial home at relevant date (ignoring contingent liability to repay discount); and (ii) £3,366.59, representing equal sharing of the other assets.

(63) *Trotter v. Trotter*, 2001 S.L.T. (Sh. Ct.) 42 (Sheriff Principal C.G.B. Nicholson Q.C.)

Parties separated in December 1997 after several years of marriage—Matrimonial property date comprising jointly owned matrimonial home and contents, two endowment policies in joint names securing mortgage over matrimonial home, wife's interest in pension fund and husband's three pension policies and cash in bank—Net value of matrimonial property at relevant date amounting to just under £66,900—Wife occupying matrimonial home since separation with daughters of the marriage aged 16 and 18 at date of proof, maintaining the property and paying all mortgage costs and policy premiums, and requiring to provide a home for daughters for at least a few years; and liable to be left in very vulnerable position if house sold—Wife held entitled to transfer of property orders in respect of husband's interest in matrimonial home and contents and relative endowment policies (leaving wife with property to the value of just over £40,000 and husband with property worth a little over £26,000), there being special circumstances justifying an unequal division of net value of matrimonial property at relevant date.

(64) *Cunningham v. Cunningham*, 2001 Fam.L.R. 12 (Lord Macfadyen)

Parties separated in 1998 after several years of marriage—Matrimonial property at relevant date comprising assets with an aggregate value of £1,285,376, whereof £390,056 in hands of wife and £895,320 in hands of husband—Matrimonial property in wife's hands including assets acquired with inherited funds totalling £50,000—Husband using inherited capital of £214,100 to fund matrimonial property to the extent of (i) a holiday home in his own name, valued at £68,000; (ii) a contribution of £100,000 to the purchase price of the jointly owned matrimonial home; and (iii) an unidentified contribution of £50,000 to matrimonial property in his own hands—Wife held entitled to capital sum of £218,632 (less payment to account of £25,000), representing an equal division of value of matrimonial property after (i) deduction from matrimonial property in wife's hands of £50,000 (being the value of matrimonial property in her own hands acquired with her inherited funds); and (ii) deduction from matrimonial property in husband's hands of £118,000 (being the sum of (a) £68,000, being the value of his holiday home funded by his inherited capital; and (b) £50,000, being his contribution to matrimonial property in his own hands from his inherited capital), no credit being given to husband for contribution of £100,000 to purchase of matrimonial home.

(65) *McHugh v. McHugh*, 2001 Fam.L.R. 30 (Lord Macfadyen)
    Parties separated in July 1999 after several years of
marriage—Matrimonial property at relevant date comprising
matrimonial home in joint names, subject to secured loan,
and sundry items of incorporeal property—Husband held
beneficially entitled to only one-half of shares in limited
company issued in his name—Net value of matrimonial
property at relevant date accordingly amounting to £461,749,
whereof £112,992 held by wife and £348,757 held by
husband—Wife held entitled to (1) in return for discharge
of his whole liabilities under the standard security over the
matrimonial home and indemnification by wife of husband
in respect of all liabilities arising under standard security
after decree but before such discharge, transfer of property
order in respect of husband's one-half *pro indiviso* share in
matrimonial home, valued at £20,191; and (2) capital sum of
£97,700, with interest on unpaid balance thereof from time to
time outstanding at five per cent a year from date of decree,
all by the following instalments, *viz.* (i) one instalment of
£25,000 payable within one month of date of decree, and (ii)
annual instalments of £20,000 (or such lesser amount as shall
remain outstanding) on 1 May each year until the whole has
been paid.
(66) *Gray v. Gray*, 2001 S.C.L.R. 681 (Sheriff A.L. Stewart Q.C.)
    Parties separated in May 1999 after several years of
marriage—Matrimonial property at relevant date comprising
matrimonial home, with a net value of £24,023.09, and other
items valued at £9,814.95—Wife using £6,000 gifted by her
parents as deposit for parties' first home—Wife continuing
to reside in matrimonial home after separation along with the
two children of the marriage—Matrimonial home reasonably
close to wife's parents' house and to children's school, so that
it would be disruptive for children to move—Wife's parents
giving her financial assistance towards maintaining mortgage
payments whereas husband almost continuously failing to
meet financial responsibilities after separation with respect
to aliment for wife and children and mortgage and insurance
payments relative to matrimonial home, notwithstanding court
orders—Wife held entitled, subject to consent of mortgagor,
to transfer of property order in respect of husband's interest
in matrimonial home, there being special circumstances
justifying unequal sharing of net value of matrimonial property
at relevant date.
(67) *Buchan v. Buchan*, 2001 Fam.L.R. 48 (Sheriff A. Pollock)
    Parties separated in January 1995 after several years of

marriage—Matrimonial property at relevant date comprising jointly owned matrimonial home valued at £127,500 and relative endowment policy, wife's pension entitlement valued at £57,869.21 and husband's pension valued as at August 1995 at £11,223.46—Wife's parents gifting £20,000 towards cost of first matrimonial home in exchange for undertaking that they would be housed by parties for the rest of their lives—Wife keeping the family financially for five years through teaching post when husband lost his job; matrimonial home repossessed through husband failing to maintain mortgage payments, and wife contributing £13,000 towards deposit for new matrimonial home; and husband thereafter leading independent social life and having affairs, spending £22,000 in two years and providing little support for family other than sporadic payments towards mortgage and life insurance premiums, which were in arrears at relevant date—Wife held entitled to transfer of property orders in respect of husband's interest in matrimonial home and endowment policy associated therewith, wife's parents' gift amounting to special circumstances, husband deriving economic advantage from wife's various roles throughout marriage as joint breadwinner, housekeeper, mother and teacher, and husband's conduct adversely affecting parties' financial resources.

(68) *MacLean v. MacLean*, 2001 Fam.L.R. 118 (Lord Rodger of Earlsferry)

Parties married in October 1980 and separated in May 1993—Matrimonial property at relevant date comprising assets with an aggregate net value of £1,035,985, whereof £1,008,557 (including personal equity plan worth £27,897) owned by wife and £27,428 (a personal equity plan) owned by husband—Wife applying mother's gift of £40,000 to purchase of farm—Other matrimonial property deriving more or less directly from funds provided by wife out of property owned by her prior to marriage—Wife an extremely hard-working, able and dedicated farmer—Husband also contributing to farm work, being very able at what he did—Wife having sole responsibility for care and maintenance of children of marriage since separation—Husband held entitled to capital sum of £235,000, being 25% (rounded down) of net value of matrimonial property at relevant date after deduction of parties' personal equity plans and mother's gift (*i.e.* £940,660), but, having regard in particular to fact that wife had had all the responsibility for care and maintenance of children since separation, order for backdating of interest on capital sum to relevant date refused.

(69) *Fraser v. Fraser*, 2002 Fam.L.R. 53 (Extra Division)

Parties separated in September 1989 after several years of marriage — Matrimonial property at relevant date comprising husband's interest in occupational pension scheme valued at £105,395 — Husband's sole capital resource at date of proof held to be a one-half share in a joint bank account with cohabitant — Wife held entitled to capital sum of £1,000, being one-half of the sum at credit in the bank account, payment to be made six months from the date of decree with interest at the legal rate.

(70) *Pressley v. Pressley*, 2002 S.C.L.R. 804 (Sheriff Principal Sir Stephen S.T. Young Q.C.)

Parties married in November 1995 and separated in May 2000 — Matrimonial property at relevant date comprising wife's shares (acquired during marriage by way of employee sharesave accounts commenced prior to marriage), savings and pension interest, valued at £40,134 — Shares falling in value since relevant date — Wife having other readily realisable capital assets and house — Husband held entitled to capital sum of £20,067, there being no special circumstances justifying departure from principle of equal sharing.

(71) *Thomson v. Thomson*, 2003 Fam.L.R. 22 (Sheriff C. J. Harris Q.C.)

Parties married in June 1994, separated in April 1996 and divorced in September 2002 — Matrimonial property at relevant date comprising jointly owned matrimonial home, valued at £52,000 and subject to mortgage of £33,731.95, and husband's pension valued at £3,550 — Matrimonial home worth £57,500 and subject to mortgage of £27,370.96 at date of proof (December 2002) — Wife occupying matrimonial home since separation along with child of the marriage aged seven at date of proof and unable to afford to buy or rent property in locality — Husband paying half the mortgage since separation while living elsewhere — Husband held entitled to order for sale of matrimonial home, postponed for four and a half years until completion of child's primary education at local school, with net free proceeds of sale split equally in respect that husband's continuing liability to make mortgage payments offset any special circumstances supporting unequal division of proceeds.

(72) *Cordiner v. Cordiner*, 2003 Fam.L.R. 39 (Sheriff Principal Sir Stephen S.T. Young Q.C.)

Parties married in December 1985 and separated in late 1997 — Matrimonial property at relevant date comprising jointly owned matrimonial home with a net value of £126,000 and other assets with an aggregate value of £99,000 whereof savings of £5,000 (only) in wife's sole name—Husband owning assets at date of marriage worth £107,000—Wife held entitled to sale of matrimonial home and division of free proceeds into 126 parts with 69.5 parts to be paid to husband and 56.5 parts to wife, representing equal division of value of matrimonial property at relevant date after deduction of value of (i) husband's assets at date of marriage; and (ii) wife's only capital asset at date of separation.

(73) *L v. L*, 2003 Fam.L.R. 101 (Lord Bonomy)

Parties married in April 1985 and separated in June 1998—Matrimonial property at relevant date comprising matrimonial home valued at £220,000 and contents thereof and other assets—Net value of matrimonial property at relevant date amounting to £1,789,340, whereof husband owned assets worth £1,781,132 and wife owned £8,208—Wife held entitled to (i) transfer of property order, of consent, in respect of matrimonial home and contents thereof; and (ii) capital sum of £650,000, representing one-half of value of matrimonial property at relevant date (*i.e.* £894,670) less (a) £8,208, being wife's assets at relevant date; (b) £220,000, being value of matrimonial home at relevant date; and (c) £16,462 in respect of household contents.

(74) *Carrol v. Carrol*, 2003 Fam.L.R. 108 (Sheriff A. S. Jessop)

Parties separated in August 1997 after several years of marriage—Matrimonial property at relevant date comprising (i) jointly owned matrimonial home, with a net value of £39,969; (ii) jointly owned insurance policy, with a net value of £5,900; (iii) part of husband's personal injury damages claim arising from accident in the course of his employment in 1993 in which he was seriously injured, valued at £63,397.14; (iv) husband's personal pension policy, valued at £8,101; and (v) furniture, valued at £1,062, less debts totalling £39,308—Net value of matrimonial property at relevant date amounting to £79,121.14—Husband's damages claim settled on a global basis for £240,000 following upon tender for £210,000 broken down into various heads—Claim valued on a fairly broad brush approach, excluding *solatium* and loss of future earnings and deducting repayable benefits and fees but not discounting for assignation, there being no proof that claim had value if offered for sale in market place or what value such a claim would have—Husband's prospects of employment in the future remote—Wife residing in matrimonial home with children of marriage, it being in younger child's best interests to continue to live in same house and attend same school—Wife held entitled to (i) transfer of property order in respect of husband's interests in matrimonial home and insurance policy; and (ii) capital sum of £1,000, payable by monthly instalments of £25, an equal division of matrimonial property not being possible given husband's financial circumstances.

(75) *Coyle v. Coyle*, 2004 Fam. L.R. 2 (Lady Smith)

Parties married in February 1975 and separated in February 1995 — Matrimonial property at relevant date comprising matrimonial home, valued at £270,000, and other assets — Net value of matrimonial property at relevant date amounting to £1,157,913 or £1,182,913, whereof wife owned assets worth £21,053 — Matrimonial home subsequently valued at £500,000 but wife suffering economic disadvantage in interests of husband and children by refraining from pursuing her career — Wife held entitled to (i) transfer of property order in respect of matrimonial home; and (ii) capital sum of £295,000, there being no special circumstances justifying unequal sharing of net value of matrimonial property at relevant date.

(76) *Christie v. Christie*, 2004 S.L.T. (Sh. Ct.).95 (Sheriff Principal B. A. Kerr Q.C.)

Parties separated in November 2001 after several years of marriage — Matrimonial property at relevant date comprising jointly owned matrimonial home, endowment policies relative to the heritable loan secured over the house, pensions and other savings — Net value of matrimonial property at relevant date amounting to £73,260.74 — Matrimonial home increasing in value by 15% since separation during which period husband residing in matrimonial home and funding heritable loan while wife elsewhere with 15-year-old daughter — Wife held entitled to transfer of property orders in respect of husband's interest in matrimonial home and relative endowment policies (giving her £31,882 or 43.5% of the net value of the matrimonial property at relevant date), the need for the child and her mother to return as soon as possible to the matrimonial home being a powerful and compelling reason for granting the orders.

(77) *Kennedy v. Kennedy*, 2004 S.L.T. (Sh. Ct.) 102 (Sheriff Principal B. A. Kerr Q.C.)

Parties separated in June 1996 after several years of marriage — Matrimonial property at relevant date comprising (i) endowment policy in joint names worth £8,320; (ii) contents of matrimonial home retained by wife, valued at £1,000, wife's pension, valued at £1,910, and wife's savings of £760; and (iii) husband's pension, valued at £36,750 with additional voluntary contributions worth £3,540, husband's savings of £3,400 and husband's reversionary interest in matrimonial

home, valued at £17,000—Net value of matrimonial property
at relevant date accordingly £72,680—Wife held entitled to
(1) transfer of property orders in respect of matrimonial home
and husband's one-half share of endowment policy, valued at
£21,160 in total; and (2) capital sum of £7,350, with no order
made in respect of remaining matrimonial property, resulting in
equal sharing of net value of matrimonial property at relevant
date.

(78) *W v. W*, 2004 Fam.L.R. 54 (Lord Clarke)

Parties married in March 1981 and separated in May
1999—Matrimonial property at relevant date comprising
jointly owned matrimonial home, valued at £150,000, and
other assets—Net value of matrimonial property at relevant
date amounting to £460,649—Wife encashing after separation
bond for £20,000 forming part of matrimonial property —Wife
residing in matrimonial home with four children of marriage
whose best interests served by continuing to reside there—
Matrimonial home valued at £225,000 at date of proof—Wife
held entitled to (i) transfer of property order in respect of
husband's interest in matrimonial home; and (ii) capital sum
of £22,824.50, account being taken of bond encashed by
wife (£20,000) and increase in value of defender's interest
in matrimonial home since separation (£37,500), resulting in
equal sharing of net value of matrimonial property at relevant
date.

(79) *McCaskill v. McCaskill*, 2004 Fam.L.R. 123 (Sheriff Principal
I. D. Macphail Q.C.)

Parties separated in August 1998 after several years of
marriage—Matrimonial property at relevant date comprising
(i) jointly owned matrimonial home, valued at £45,000; and (ii)
husband's pension interest, valued at £21,460—Matrimonial
home valued at £100,000 at date of proof—Wife caring for
child of the marriage—Husband making certain payments in
relation to property—Wife held entitled to (1) capital sum of
£14,570, comprising (i) £10,820, being one-half of husband's
pension interest, and (ii) £3,750, to enable fair sharing of
economic burden of caring for child; and (2) order for sale of
matrimonial home and for equal division of proceeds of sale
after deduction of husband's payments.

(80) *Connolly v. Connolly,* 2005 Fam. L.R.106 (First Division)

Parties separated after several years of marriage—
Matrimonial property at relevant date *inter alia* comprising
jointly owned properties in Scotland and Ireland—Net value
of matrimonial property, excluding Irish property, at relevant
date amounting to £342,386, whereof wife owned assets

worth £238,742 and husband owned assets worth £103,644 —
Husband in arrears of aliment at date of proof — Continuing
hostility between parties creating potential difficulties in
achieving co-operation over sale of Irish property — Husband
held entitled to capital sum of £69,677, being one-half of the
differential between the parties' respective assets (apart from
the Irish property), subject to certain adjustments the effect
of which was to add the sum of £2,128 — Husband's capital
sum to be under deduction of outstanding arrears of aliment —
Wife held entitled to an order requiring husband to execute
a disposition in her favour of his one-half share of the Irish
property and husband held entitled to order for the sale of the
Irish property immediately thereafter with the sale proceeds
deposited at the disposal of the court.

(81) *Russell, v. Russell,* 2005 Fam. L.R. 96 (Sheriff Principal
R. A. Dunlop Q.C.)

Parties separated after several years of marriage — Net value of
matrimonial property at relevant date amounting to £24,272.88,
comprising matrimonial home owned by wife (valued at
£48,000 and subject to loan of £10,480.32) less husband's bank
debt of £12,500 and parties' joint debts of £746.80 — Husband
held entitled to capital sum of £24,400 in order that the parties
should be left with net assets of approximately the same value,
measured at the date of separation.

(82) *Sweeney v. Sweeney,* 2003 S.L.T. 892; 2004 S.C. 372; 2006
S.C. 82 (Extra Division; Lord Kingarth)

Parties married in October 1981 and separated in December
1998 — Net value of matrimonial property at relevant date
amounting to £4,432,419.43, whereof husband owned
assets valued at £3,316,728.16 (of which assets valued at
£1,037,622.16 were reasonable to realise and assets valued
at £2,279,106 were not reasonable to realise) and wife owned
assets valued at £1,115, 691.27 (of which assets valued at
£348,634 were reasonable to realise and assets valued at
£769,614 were not reasonable to realise) — Wife accepting that
husband's business interest should be apportioned otherwise
than equally, thus restricting her entitlement upon a fair sharing
of the net value of the matrimonial property to the sum of
£1,066,338, less advance payment of £350,000 — Wife held
entitled to capital sum of £950,000 (the outstanding balance
of £600,000 being payable in five instalments over a period
of just over three and a half years), having regard to the fact
that if the husband was required to pay the wife's entitlement
in full he would be left with no funds available to preserve or
develop his business if required.

(83) *Burnside v. Burnside*, 2007 Fam. L.R. 144 (Sheriff N. M. P. Morrison Q.C.)

Parties married in June 1981 and separated in July 2000 — Matrimonial property at relevant date comprising (i) the matrimonial home (valued at £270,051 net of mortgage and cost of completion certificate); (ii) the husband's police pension (valued at £179,446); and (iii) other assets (£47,747), with liabilities of £13,204 — Net value of matrimonial property at relevant date therefore £484,040 — Wife seeking transfer of husband's one-half share in matrimonial home to herself and pension sharing order — Held that wife should receive 60% of the net value of the matrimonial property — Wife therefore held entitled to transfer of property order in exchange for compensating payment by her to husband of £79,373 and pension sharing order for £107,667.

(84) *Lessani v. Lessani*, 2007 Fam. L.R. 81 (Sheriff Principal J. A. Taylor)

Parties separated in May 1996 some time after marriage — Wife awarded interim aliment in February 1997 — Husband sequestrated in January 2003 and obtaining discharge in January 2006 — Husband failing to prove existence of debt of £22,500 at relevant date — Husband also patently failing to make full disclosure of assets to court — Husband's lack of candour treated as special circumstances justifying unequal division of matrimonial property in wife's favour, entitling her to award of £61,500 under this principle.

(85) *AB v. CD*, 2007 Fam. L.R. 53 (Lord Brodie)

Parties married in May 1995 and separated in June 1999 — Substantial assets, including matrimonial home, cash and shares held by discretionary trust — Trust, on the face of trust instrument, constituted according to the laws of Jersey with husband's interest being no more than that of one potential beneficiary — Trust in fact operated as a means of managing assets for husband's benefit — Trust assets held to be matrimonial property — Matrimonial property at relevant date therefore comprising assets with an aggregate value of £2,854,000 (£79,000 in respect of wife's property and £2,775,000 in respect of husband's property) — Wife held entitled in undefended action to capital sum concluded for, namely £1,000,000.

(86) *Marshall v. Marshall*, 2007 Fam. L.R. 48 (Lord Hardie of Blackford)

Parties married in November 1972 and separated in November 2001 — Husband entering into farming partnership with brother before marriage — Husband and brother purchasing farms during marriage in own names — Matrimonial property at relevant date held to comprise (i) increase in balance on husband's capital account in farming partnership during marriage, valued at £102,833; (ii) sundry items of property, whereof husband's share valued at £63,954.07 and wife's at £6,824.82; (iii) household contents valued at £2,500 and (iv) motor vehicle valued at £5,500 — Farms held to be owned by farming partnership at relevant date and accordingly not matrimonial property — Net value of matrimonial property at relevant date therefore £181,611.89 — Increase in value of farming partnership's heritable property during marriage and wife's requirement for capital to purchase house outright (since at age 60 she would not qualify for a mortgage) held to be special circumstances justifying unequal division of matrimonial property in wife's favour — Wife held entitled to a capital sum equating to 75% of matrimonial property (£136,208.91) less her existing share (£6,824.82), namely £129,384.09, rounded up to £130,000.

(87) *Lindsay v. Lindsay*, 2007 Fam. L.R. 18 (Sheriff Principal B. A. Lockhart)

Parties separated after several years of marriage — Parties operating ice cream business during marriage — Matrimonial property at relevant date valued at £175,740.71, comprising (i) husband's farm and cars valued at £158,300; (ii) wife's pension and ice cream equipment valued at £15,440.71; and (iii) joint assets valued at £2,000 — Debts at relevant date valued at £118,786.24, comprising (i) husband's liabilities of £102,998.05; and (ii) joint liabilities of £15,788.10 — Net value of matrimonial property therefore £56,954.47 — Wife held entitled to capital sum of £19,930.63, being 50% of net value of matrimonial property at relevant date (£28,477.23) less net property already held (£8,546.61) — Payment of part of capital sum deferred for two years to enable property to be realised.

(88) *Simpson v. Simpson*, 2007 S.L.T. (Sh. Ct.) 43; 2007 Fam. L.R. 134 (Sheriff Principal Sir Stephen S. T. Young Q.C.; Sheriff D. J. Cusine)

Parties married in July 1995 and separated in January 2004 — Matrimonial property at relevant date comprising farm and other items valued at £176,618.76, with liabilities of £28,343 — Single farm payment entitlement under scheme not yet in force at relevant date held not to be matrimonial property — Net value of matrimonial property at relevant date therefore £148,275.76, whereof one-half £74,137.88 — Held that there were no special circumstances justifying unequal sharing — Wife taking property with her when leaving matrimonial home valued at £25,204.99 — Wife held entitled to capital sum of £48,932.89.

(89) *Maxwell v. Maxwell*, 2007 Fam. L.R. 76 (Lord Hardie of Blackford)

Parties married in August 1968 and separated in February 2001 — Parties jointly owning two heritable properties of approximately equal value, namely the matrimonial home and a Spanish property — Wife receiving entire sale proceeds of sale of Spanish property in 2002 amounting to £158,822 on understanding that husband would receive sole ownership of matrimonial home, then valued at £170,000 — Matrimonial home valued at £362,500 as at date of decree — Parties agreeing division of matrimonial property, including transfer of wife's interest in matrimonial home and insurance policies, in exchange for balancing payment to be decided by court — Held that there were exceptional circumstances as a result of which valuation at date of decree should not apply in relation to matrimonial home — Wife held entitled to balancing payment of £142,666, based on value of matrimonial home in 2002, including sum of £5,000 representing one-half of difference between gross values of matrimonial home and Spanish property, respectively, in 2002.

(90) *Hodge v. Hodge*, 2008 Fam. L.R. 51 (Sheriff Principal B. A. Lockhart)

Parties separated in July 2002 after several years of marriage — Matrimonial property at relevant date valued at £305,800, whereof assets valued at £252,432 (matrimonial home, husband's 25% shareholding in company and husband's director's loan) derived from non-matrimonial property, namely husband's family farming partnership — Husband's shareholding valued on basis of hypothetical sale of shareholding and not of whole company, with 30% discount applied to reflect minority nature of holding — Held that special circumstances justified unequal sharing of net value of matrimonial home, husband's 25% shareholding in company and husband's director's loan, with net value of matrimonial property otherwise shared equally — Wife accordingly held entitled to £90,000 less value of her own share of matrimonial property (£20,549), yielding award of £69,451.

(91) *McKinnon v. McKinnon*, 2008 Fam. L.R. 25 (Sheriff Principal J. A. Taylor)

Parties separated some time after marriage — Parties agreeing value of matrimonial property at relevant date and that husband would retain matrimonial home — Parties in dispute over holiday home in husband's name — Wife seeking transfer of title to holiday home in return for which she would pay £1,519.73 — Husband seeking to retain holiday home in exchange for balancing payment of £9,480.27 — Husband contending that order for payment of capital sum should always be first choice of the court — Wife held entitled to transfer property order in exchange for payment to husband of £1,519.73, whereby each party emerging from marriage with ownership of heritable property.

(92) *Sutherland v. Sutherland*, 2008 Fam. L.R. 151 (Sheriff D. A. Kinloch)

Parties married in 1991 and separated in December 2006 — Matrimonial property at relevant date comprising jointly held assets (matrimonial home and two other heritable properties, endowment policies and joint bank account) and assets held by husband and wife separately — Net value of matrimonial property at relevant date in the region of £475,000 — Husband paying whole cost of mortgages and endowment policies on the two heritable properties after separation — Properties valued at £30,000 and £35,000, respectively, at relevant date and, along with associated endowment policies, increasing slightly in value thereafter — Parties agreeing that each should retain assets in own name, with the two heritable properties and associated endowment policies being transferred to husband — Held that matrimonial property should be divided equally — Wife held entitled to balancing payment of £67,864, based on valuation of heritable properties at date of transfer, and order for sale of matrimonial home would be made.

(93) *Watt v. Watt*, 2009 S.L.T. 931 (Lady Smith)

Parties married in July 1977 and separated in August 2002 — Husband a fisherman and value of matrimonial property at relevant date arising largely from his fishing interests — Net value of matrimonial property at relevant date, including shareholdings in companies through which husband operated, amounting to £9,417,038.21 — Wife held entitled to 48% of net value of matrimonial property, namely £4,520,178.34 — Wife already having ownership of items of matrimonial property valued at £587,919 at relevant date — Wife retaining husband's share of cash at credit in bank accounts of £15,639 and seeking transfer of property orders for house, flat and bond with total current value of £264,801 — Wife therefore retaining or being about to receive further property with current value of £280,440 (£15,639 + £264,801) — Wife accordingly owning or retaining or being about to receive property valued at £868,359 (£587,919 + £280,440) — Wife held entitled to transfer of property orders sought and capital sum of £3,651,819.34 (£4,520,178.34 – £868,359).

(94) *Willson v. Willson*, 2009 Fam. L.R. 18 (Lord Drummond Young)

Parties married in April 2001 and separated in October 2005 — Matrimonial property at relevant date comprising matrimonial home and another heritable property in joint names, two cars and a Rolex watch — Total value of matrimonial property held to be £821,750, with matrimonial debts of £420,984 — Net value of matrimonial property therefore £400,766 — Held that this should be divided equally between parties, giving them £200,383 each — Parties also having funds amounting to £231,930 in bank accounts at date of separation, source of funds being pre-matrimonial property in the proportions 16% (husband) and 84% (wife) — Parties each taking one-half of funds (£115,965) following separation — Held that this sum should be shared in the same proportions, entitling wife to £194,821 and husband to £37,109 — Wife held entitled to transfer of husband's one-half share in matrimonial home, valued at £153,516, and husband held entitled to transfer of wife's one-half share in other heritable property and also cars and Rolex watch, valued at £247,250 — Wife also entitled to capital sum of £125,724, representing (i) equalisation payment of £78,857, being the difference between bank account funds received by husband (£115,965) and amount he should have received (£37,109); and (ii) balancing payment of £46,867, being difference between value of items retained by husband (£247,250) and his equal share of matrimonial property (£200,383).

(95) *Porter v. Porter*, 2010 Fam. L.R. 68 (Sheriff Principal Sir Stephen S. T. Young Q.C.)

Parties separated in April 2007 after several years of marriage — Parties in dispute over whether sum of £80,000 paid by company of which husband was sole shareholder and controlling mind to third party just before relevant date and repaid just afterwards on his instructions constituted matrimonial property — Held that funds must have been paid out as husband's remuneration or dividend and so being held by third party at relevant date on husband's behalf — Funds therefore matrimonial property — Wife held entitled to capital sum accordingly.

(96) *M v. M, W Estate Trustees Ltd and Another*, 2011 Fam. L.R. 24 (Lady Clark of Calton)

Parties married in August 1988 and separated in December 2008 — Matrimonial property at relevant date valued at £5,415,888, comprising £608,161 (wife) and £4,807,727 (husband), with husband's majority shareholding valued on break-up basis due to company's problems — Husband subsequently losing £2,220,729 in loan to company — Assets for purposes of division accordingly being taken to be £3,195,159 — Held that this sum should be shared equally, thereby valuing wife's share at £1,597,579 — Wife accordingly entitled to capital sum of £789,418 and pension sharing order for £200,000 in addition to retained property.

(97) *Murdoch v. Murdoch*, 2012 Fam. L.R. 2 (Extra Division)
Parties married in July 2003 and separated in August 2004 — Matrimonial property at relevant date comprising matrimonial home in husband's name valued at £35,000, burdened with a loan of £10,080, and other assets worth £3,088.58 — Matrimonial debts at relevant date amounting to £9,322.13 — Net value of matrimonial property at relevant date therefore £18,686 — Wife living in matrimonial home with child since separation and paying mortgage and all other bills associated with property since that date — Wife seeking transfer of property order in relation to matrimonial home, with father willing to make funds available to enable her to make balancing payment to husband — Serious doubt as to whether house would sell if placed on the market and whether most recent valuation of £65,000 was realizable — Parties with very limited resources — Wife held entitled to transfer of property order subject to balancing payment to husband of £20,600, based on value of matrimonial home at relevant date, and incidental order also made requiring her to secure variation of standard security whereby husband freed of all liability thereunder.

Cases in which section 9(1)(b) of the Family Law (Scotland) Act 1985 was considered include the following:

(1) *Petrie v. Petrie*, 1988 S.C.L.R. 390 (Sheriff D.J. Risk) (husband held not to have derived economic advantage from presence of wife in the home).
(2) *Kerrigan v. Kerrigan*, 1988 S.C.L.R. 603 (Sheriff G. J. Evans) (wife held to have derived economic advantage from husband's mortgage payments by increase in value of jointly owned matrimonial home).
(3) *Muir v. Muir*, 1989 S.L.T. (Sh. Ct.) 20 (Sheriff I. A. Macmillan) (husband held not to have derived economic advantage from wife's occupation of his house since separation).
(4) *Little v. Little*, 1989 S.C.L.R. 613 (Lord Cameron of Lochbroom) (wife held to have suffered economic disadvantage in the family interest by the interruption of her professional career in order to look after house and family for a period).

(5) *Walker v. Walker*, 1989 S.C.L.R. 625 (Lord Morton of Shuna) (wife held to have suffered an economic disadvantage and husband a corresponding economic advantage in terms of future income arising from the business built up by the contributions both parties made during the marriage).

(6) *Tyrrell v. Tyrrell*, 1990 S.L.T. 406 (Lord Sutherland) (husband held not to have derived any economic advantage from any contribution by wife by way of increase in value of his pension since separation).

(7) *Farrell v. Farrell*, 1990 S.C.L.R. 717 (Sheriff C. N. Stoddart) (wife held to have suffered an economic disadvantage and the husband a corresponding economic advantage from contributions made by her since the parties' separation in terms of mortgage, rates and insurance payments relative to the matrimonial home).

(8) *Skarpaas v. Skarpaas*, 1991 S.L.T. (Sh. Ct.) (Sheriff A. L. Stewart) (wife held to have suffered economic disadvantage in relation to her business because of need to look after injured husband).

(9) *Jesner v. Jesner*, 1992 S.L.T. 999 (Lord Osborne) (husband held to have derived economic advantage from wife's contribution in looking after family home and caring for family).

(10) *Shipton v. Shipton*, 1992 S.C.L.R. 23 (Sheriff N. E. D. Thomson) (wife held to have suffered economic disadvantage through her inability to work during the marriage).

(11) *Toye v. Toye*, 1992 S.C.L.R. 95 (Sheriff A. S. Jessop) (wife held to have suffered economic disadvantage by giving up work which she could not readily resume).

(12) *Macdonald v. Macdonald*, 1993 S.C.L.R. 132 (Lord Caplan) (wife held to have suffered economic disadvantage through having assumed greater economic burden of caring for children than husband hitherto).

(13) *Davidson v. Davidson*, 1994 S.L.T. 506 (Lord MacLean) (husband held to have derived economic advantage from gifts of money from wife).

(14) *Ranaldi v. Ranaldi*, 1994 S.L.T. (Sh. Ct.) 25 (Sheriff R. G. Craik Q.C.) (husband held to have derived economic advantage through wife having taken in lodgers throughout marriage).

(15) *Loudon v. Loudon*, 1994 S.L.T. 381 (Lord Milligan) (wife held to have suffered economic disadvantage by giving up work and losing earning potential).

(16) *Welsh v. Welsh*, 1994 S.L.T. 828 (Lord Osborne) (wife's economic disadvantage in giving up well-paid employment to look after husband and children held to have been balanced by economic advantage from being maintained by husband

and from enjoying the results of mortgage payments made exclusively by him in respect of jointly owned matrimonial home and by economic disadvantage suffered by him accordingly; but economic advantage held to have been enjoyed by husband in having exclusive use of house after separation with corresponding economic disadvantage to wife).

(17) *Tahir v. Tahir (No. 2)*, 1995 S.L.T. 451 (Lord Clyde) (husband held to have gained economic advantage, and the wife a corresponding economic disadvantage, by his forcibly dispossessing her of her jewellery).

(18) *Hunter v. Hunter*, 1996 S.C.L.R. 329 (Sheriff Principal D.J. Risk Q.C.) (wife held not to have suffered economic disadvantage during the course of the marriage through the husband's payment of aliment for his children by a previous marriage).

(19) *Adams v. Adams (No. 1)*, 1997 S.L.T. 144 (Lord Gill) (wife's economic disadvantage in prejudicing her career by bringing up the parties' children held to have been counterbalanced by husband's greater contribution to household finances).

(20) *McVinnie v. McVinnie (No. 2)* 1997 S.L.T. (Sh. Ct.) 12 (Sheriff Principal C.G.B. Nicholson Q.C.) (husband held to have derived economic advantage through child-caring contribution by wife and from portion of wife's receipts from sale of her interest in two houses).

(21) *De Winton v. De Winton*, 1998 Fam.L.R. 110 (Lord Cameron of Lochbroom) (husband held to have gained economic advantage from wife's financial investment in farming partnership which had allowed the firm overdraft to be lowered and certain improvements to be carried out at the expense of disabling her from dealing with her own money to her own profit — an advantage not cancelled out by her receiving her share of the partnership assets — and from her management of holiday cottages which had enhanced their revenue earning capacity to his financial benefit; but wife's contribution to the children's school fees not an economic disadvantage to wife nor, in any event, a corresponding economic advantage to husband).

(22) *Cahill v. Cahill*, 1998 S.L.T. (Sh. Ct.) 96 (Sheriff Principal E. F. Bowen Q.C.) (wife held to have derived economic advantage through improvements carried out to her cottage by the husband during the marriage).

(23) *Wilson v. Wilson*, 1999 S.L.T. 249 (Lord Marnoch) (husband's economic advantage gained through the wife's looking after the family home and the parties' children while he ploughed

back considerable profits into his company held not to have been balanced throughout the marriage by an economic advantage to her such as a better lifestyle).

(24) *Cunniff v. Cunniff*, 1997 Fam.L.R. 42; 1999 S.C. 537 (Extra Division; Lord Abernethy) (husband's economic advantage in working full time and gaining additional qualifications while wife had given up work and raised the family held to have resulted in an imbalance of economic advantage and disadvantage which warranted correction, albeit that the wife's economic disadvantage could not be quantified).

(25) *R v. R*, 2000 Fam.L.R. 43 (Lord Eassie) (wife held to have suffered economic disadvantage through being unable to pursue an independent economic activity because of her natural commitment to care of the children of marriage and organisation of family home, including in particular her design input and de facto superintendence of its refurbishment).

(26) *Cunningham v. Cunningham*, 2001 Fam.L.R. 12 (Lord Macfadyen) (wife held not to have suffered any quantifiable economic disadvantage in interrupting her career as a paediatric physiotherapist for some six years when children were young in order to care for them).

(27) *Buchan v. Buchan*, 2001 Fam.L.R. 48 (Sheriff A. Pollock) (wife held to have suffered economic disadvantage and husband to have derived an economic advantage from wife's various roles throughout marriage as joint breadwinner, housekeeper, mother and teacher).

(28) *Pressley v. Pressley*, 2002 S.C.L.R. 804 (Sheriff Principal Sir Stephen S. T. Young) (wife held not to have suffered economic disadvantage nor husband an economic advantage from fact that wife's earnings higher than husband's during marriage).

(29) *Carrol v. Carrol*, 2003 Fam.L.R. 108 (Sheriff A. S. Jessop) (wife held to have suffered economic disadvantage to a slight extent through having to give up her employment and losing career prospects and possible pension in order to look after parties' four children while husband at work).

(30) *Coyle v. Coyle*, 2004 Fam.L.R. 2 (Lady Smith) (husband held not to have gained economic advantage from wife's management of house and children, but wife held to have suffered economic disadvantage in interests of husband and children by refraining, at husband's request, from pursuing her career).

(31) *Symanski v. Symanski (No. 2)*, 2005 Fam. L.R. 2 (Sheriff Principal C. G. B. Nicholson Q.C.) (husband held to have gained economic advantage from wife's injections of capital into his failed businesses prior to the marriage).

(32) *Burnside v. Burnside*, 2007 Fam. L.R. 144 (Sheriff N. M.

P. Morrison Q.C.) (wife held to have suffered economic disadvantage in giving up work to look after children of the marriage).

(33) *Willson v. Willson*, 2009 Fam. L.R. 18 (Lord Drummond Young) (wife held to have derived no economic advantage from husband's contributions in respect of substandard work carried out by him on matrimonial home and no net economic advantage in any other respect).

(34) *Porter v. Porter*, 2010 Fam. L.R. 68 (Sheriff Principal Sir Stephen S. T. Young Q.C.) (wife held to have suffered economic disadvantage in family's interests in giving up work following marriage in order to look after home and children of the marriage, economic disadvantage in husband's interest in so far as she had not been paid salary due to her by husband's company, economic disadvantage from husband's failure to make agreed mortgage payments, and economic disadvantage from husband's removal of her car, requiring her to borrow money to buy another).

(35) *B v. B*, 2011 Fam. L.R. 91 (Lord Woolman) (husband held to have derived economic advantage from contributions by wife who ran the household, looked after the children and provided assistance around the farm).

Cases in which section 9(1)(c) of the Family Law (Scotland) Act 1985 was considered include the following:

(1) *Monkman v. Monkman*, 1988 S.L.T. (Sh. Ct.) 37 (Sheriff Principal P. I. Caplan Q.C.) (economic burden held to be shared fairly by periodical allowance under s. 9(1)(c) for wife until child about 20 years old).

(2) *Morrison v. Morrison*, 1989 S.C.L.R. 574 (Sheriff G. H. Gordon Q.C.) (economic burden held to be shared fairly by award to wife under s. 9(1)(c) of two-thirds of value of matrimonial home and contents).

(3) *Millar v. Millar*, 1990 S.C.L.R. 666 (Sheriff Principal C. G. B. Nicholson Q.C.; Sheriff R. G. Craik Q.C.) (economic burden held to be shared fairly under reference to alimentary award in child's favour).

(4) *Shipton v. Shipton*, 1992 S.C.L.R. 23 (Sheriff N. E. D. Thomson) (economic burden held to be shared fairly by award of greater share of matrimonial property).

(5) *Toye v. Toye*, 1992 S.C.L.R. 95 (Sheriff A. S. Jessop) (economic burden held to be shared fairly by award of periodical allowance for three years).

(6) *Macdonald v. Macdonald*, 1993 S.C.L.R. 132 (Lord Caplan) (economic burden held to be shared fairly by award of capital sum to enable need to provide accommodation for children to be met).

(7) *Adams v. Adams (No. 1)*, 1997 S.L.T. 144 (Lord Gill) (economic burden held to be shared fairly by resumption of alimentary payments by husband).

(8) *Maclachlan v. Maclachlan*, 1998 S.L.T. 693 (Lord Macfadyen) (economic burden held to be shared fairly by substantial adjustment of capital in wife's favour — cancelled out by husband's entitlement under s. 9(1)(a)).

(9) *McCaskill v. McCaskill*, 2004 Fam. L.R. 123 (Sheriff Principal I. D. Macphail Q.C.) (economic burden held to be shared fairly by enhanced award of capital sum).

10) *Lessani v. Lessani*, 2007 Fam. L.R. 81 (Sheriff Principal J. A. Taylor) (economic burden held to be shared fairly by award of capital sum sufficient to allow wife to maintain her existing level of income until child attained the age of 16).

(11) *B v. B*, 2011 Fam. L.R. 91 (Lord Woolman) (economic burden held to be shared fairly by award of capital sum).

(12) *Murdoch v. Murdoch*, 2012 Fam. L.R. 2 (Extra Division) (economic burden held to be shared fairly by order for transfer of property in exchange for counterbalancing payment).

Cases in which section 9(1)(d) of the Family Law (Scotland) Act 1985 was considered include the following:

(1) *Dever v. Dever*, 1988 S.C.L.R. 352 (Sheriff Principal S. E. Bell Q.C.) (wife aged 27 years and married living with husband for six years, no children, in receipt of state benefits, claimed no maintenance since separation 18 months prior to diet of proof, awarded periodical allowance under s. 9(1)(d) for six months from date of decree).

(2) *Petrie v. Petrie*, 1988 S.C.L.R. 390 (Sheriff D. J. Risk) (wife aged 42 years and married and living with husband for two years, one child, cohabited with husband for several years before marriage, in receipt of state benefits, no skills or qualifications but fit for work, claimed no maintenance since separation in belief that her adultery disentitled her, awarded periodical allowance under s. 9(1)(d) for one year from date of decree).

(3) *Atkinson v. Atkinson*, 1988 S.C.L.R. 396 (Sheriff Principal R. R. Taylor Q.C.) (wife earning salary insufficient for her upkeep in the standard of life she enjoyed during marriage,

awarded a periodical allowance under s. 9(1)(d) for three years from date of decree).

(4) *Park v. Park*, 1988 S.C.L.R. 584 (Sheriff D. Kelbie) (wife married and living with husband for five years, no children, earning one-fifth of the total amount earned by the parties, awarded a periodical allowance under s. 9(1)(d) to increase her "share" to one-third and allow her to adjust back to one-fifth, award being made for one year and at reduced rate for further year).

(5) *Muir v. Muir*, 1989 S.L.T. (Sh. Ct.) 20 (Sheriff I. A. Macmillan) (wife aged 47 years, no dependent children, in receipt of invalidity benefit, hoping to resume work as shop assistant, separated for four years and in receipt of maintenance during last of those years, awarded a periodical allowance under s. 9(1)(d) for one year from date of decree).

(6) *Tyrrell v. Tyrrell*, 1990 S.L.T. 406 (Lord Sutherland) (wife married and living with husband for 18 years, in part-time employment and in receipt of maintenance for seven years after separation until date of proof, awarded a periodical allowance under s. 9(1)(d) for one year from date of decree).

(7) *Sheret v. Sheret*, 1990 S.C.L.R. 799 (Sheriff N. McPartlin) (wife married and living with husband for two years, aged 42 years, with no immediate prospects of employment, supported only periodically by husband, awarded a periodical allowance under s. 9(1)(d) for 13 weeks from date of decree).

(8) *Millar v. Millar*, 1990 S.C.L.R. 666 (Sheriff Principal C. G. B. Nicholson Q.C.; Sheriff R. G. Craik Q.C.) (wife married and living with husband for 10 years, one child in joint custody, wife in part-time employment and in receipt of interim aliment for herself and child, awarded aliment in larger amount for child leaving small shortfall, held not entitled to a periodical allowance under s. 9(1)(d)).

(9) *Thomson v. Thomson*, 1991 S.L.T. 126 (Lord Cameron of Lochbroom) (wife dependent wholly for her financial support on husband for five years before separation, awarded interim aliment three years later against husband held to have taken every opportunity to avoid his financial responsibilities since separation, awarded a periodical allowance under s. 9(1)(d) for three years).

(10) *Barclay v. Barclay*, 1991 S.C.L.R. 205 (Sheriff I. C. Cameron) (wife aged 29 years, married and living with husband for some three years, no children, permanently disabled by multiple sclerosis and resident in a nursing home, not envisaged that she would ever be able to resume life in the community, awarded a periodical allowance under s. 9(1)(d) for three years).

(11) *Gray v. Gray*, 1991 S.C.L.R. 422 (Sheriff T. Russell) (wife dependent to substantial degree on husband's financial support prior to separation, since then not provided with, nor had she sought, financial support from husband, held to have adjusted to withdrawal of support and no award made).

(12) *Loudon v. Loudon*, 1994 S.L.T. 381 (Lord Milligan) (wife aged 45 years, married and living with husband for 17 years, one child (aged 17), wife unemployed and requiring to retrain to "get back on employment ladder", awarded a periodical allowance under s. 9(1)(d) for one year).

(13) *Whittome v. Whittome (No. 1)*, 1994 S.L.T. 114 (Lord Osborne) (wife married and living with husband for 15 years, two children, dependent on husband for financial support, awarded a periodical allowance under s. 9(1)(d) for three years).

(14) *Buckle v. Buckle*, 1995 S.C.L.R. 590 (Sheriff N. McPartlin) (wife financially dependent on husband after 30 years' marriage but undergoing one-year college course in office technology, held entitled to capital sum payable by instalments over five years, awarded a periodical allowance under s. 9(1)(d) for one year).

(15) *McConnell v. McConnell*, 1997 Fam.L.R. 97; 1997 Fam.L.R. 108 (Second Division; Lord Osborne) (wife married and living with husband for 16 years, three children, wife almost exclusively dependent upon income from husband, held reasonable for her to have period of time to adjust to new circumstances created by determination of the litigation, awarded a periodical allowance under s. 9(1)(d) for six months).

(16) *Wilson v. Wilson*, 1999 S.L.T. 249 (Lord Marnoch) (wife married and living with husband for 17 years, two children aged 18 and 16, dependent on husband for financial support, requiring to retrain in order to get back on employment ladder, awarded a periodical allowance under s. 9(1)(d) for 30 months).

(17) *L v. L*, 2003 Fam.L.R. 101 (Lord Bonomy) (wife married and living with husband for 13 years, three children (aged 17, 15 and six), dependent to a substantial degree on husband's financial support pending settlement of the capital sum awarded to her, held entitled to periodical allowance under s. 9(1)(d) for three years or until the capital sum fully paid, whichever was sooner).

(18) *Burnside v. Burnside*, 2007 Fam. L.R. 144 (Sheriff N. M. P. Morrison Q.C.) (wife married and living with husband for 19 years, two children, in full-time employment but with substantial dependency on husband in relation to mortgage, endowment and insurance payments for matrimonial home,

awarded a periodical allowance under s. 9(1)(d) for a period of three years).

(19) *Sutherland v. Sutherland*, 2008 Fam. L.R. 151 (Sheriff D. A. Kinloch) (wife, one child, in part-time employment, substantially dependent on husband's financial support, requiring to retrain, awarded a periodical allowance under s. 9(1)(d) for two years).

(20) *Smith v. Smith*, 2010 S.L.T. 372 (Lord Malcolm) (wife aged 57 with health problems, married and living with much younger husband for 24 years, very limited or no earning capacity and totally reliant on husband's financial support, husband with very substantial earnings, awarded a periodical allowance under s. 9(1)(d) for three years and thereafter under s. 9(1)(e), at a reduced rate, until husband's retirement from paid employment)

Cases in which section 9(1)(e) of the Family Law (Scotland) Act 1985 was considered include the following:

(1) *Atkinson v. Atkinson*, 1988 S.C.L.R. 396 (Sheriff Principal R. R. Taylor Q.C.) (wife with salary insufficient for her upkeep in the standard of life she enjoyed during marriage, but her income and substantial capital made it "quite out of the question" to make award under s. 9(1)(e)).

(2) *Bell v. Bell*, 1988 S.C.L.R. 457 (Sheriff J. C. M. Jardine) (wife aged 51 years, married and living with husband for 26 years, no dependent children, a qualified teacher but a full-time housewife and mother dependent on husband's support throughout the marriage, unlikely to find work affording reasonable remuneration, with sufficient capital to retain a nice house but with no income after divorce, awarded a periodical allowance under s. 9(1)(e) until husband's sixtieth birthday or her own death or remarriage).

(3) *Muir v. Muir*, 1989 S.L.T. (Sh. Ct.) 20 (Sheriff I. A. Macmillan) (wife aged 47 years, no dependent children, in receipt of invalidity benefit, hoping to resume work as shop assistant, separated for four years and in receipt of maintenance during last of those years, awarded a periodical allowance under s. 9(1)(d) for one year, but s. 9(1)(e) held inapplicable).

(4) *Tyrrell v. Tyrrell*, 1990 S.L.T. 406 (Lord Sutherland) (wife married and living with husband for 18 years, in part-time employment and in receipt of maintenance for seven years after separation until date of proof, had received substantial capital at time of separation, with further capital sum upon

decree, held entitled to award of a periodical allowance under s. 9(1)(d), but to no award under s. 9(1)(e)).

(5) *Johnstone v. Johnstone*, 1990 S.L.T. (Sh. Ct.) 79 (Sheriff R. D. Ireland Q.C.) (wife aged 35 years, married and living with husband for 13 years, one child, unfit for work because of epilepsy, awarded a periodical allowance under s. 9(1)(e) until her death or remarriage).

(6) *McKenzie v. McKenzie*, 1991 S.L.T. 461 (Lord Prosser) (wife aged nearly 60 years, married and living with husband for 16 years, no dependent children, ran small business with low income with possibility of income from lodger, entitled to small pension at 60, held liable to be "seriously short of money" notwithstanding award of capital sum if no maintenance awarded, awarded a periodical allowance under s. 9(1)(e) until death or remarriage).

(7) *Barclay v. Barclay*, 1991 S.C.L.R. 205 (Sheriff I. C. Cameron) (wife aged 29 years, married and living with husband for some three years, no children, permanently disabled by multiple sclerosis and resident in a nursing home, not envisaged that she would ever be able to resume life in the community, awarded a periodical allowance under s. 9(1)(d) for three years from date of decree but, requiring substantial support anyway from public funds, refused award under s. 9(1)(e)).

(8) *Davidson v. Davidson*, 1994 S.L.T. 506 (Lord MacLean) (husband aged 46 years with very restricted earning capacity and without sound mental health, wife a very wealthy woman, marriage of five years' duration, husband awarded capital sum under s. 9(1)(e) in respect of loss of home and "considerable financial comfort" of wife's money).

(9) *Gribb v. Gribb*, 1996 S.L.T. 719 (Second Division; Sheriff J. C. McInnes) (wife aged 62 years, married and living with her husband for 38 years, in part-time employment and in receipt of modest pension payments, awarded transfer of property order in respect of husband's interest in the matrimonial home and held entitled to award of a periodical allowance under s. 9(1)(e) until her death or remarriage).

(10) *Buckle v. Buckle*, 1995 S.C.L.R. 590 (Sheriff N. McPartlin) (wife financially dependent on husband after 30 years' marriage but undergoing one-year college course in office technology, awarded a capital sum payable by instalments over five years, held entitled to a periodical allowance under s. 9(1)(d) for one year but any financial hardship occasioned by the divorce held to be mitigated by capital award and so no award under s. 9(1)(e)).

(11) *Haughan v. Haughan*, 1996 S.L.T. 321; 2002 S.C. 631 (Extra Division; Lord Marnoch) (wife aged 51 years, married and living with husband for 26 years, suffering impaired hearing, chronic high blood pressure and fibrositis and moderate to severe depression, in penurious circumstances with very restricted earning capacity, held entitled to award of a periodical allowance under s. 9(1)(e) until her death or remarriage).

(12) *Savage v. Savage*, 1997 Fam.L.R. 132 (Lord Sutherland) (wife unfit for work and unlikely to find employment, but awarded a "not insubstantial" capital sum, husband's business drawings at very modest level, no award under s. 9(1)(e)).

(13) *Galloway v. Galloway*, 2003 Fam.L.R. 10 (Temporary Judge T. G. Coutts Q.C.) (wife aged 55 years, no dependent children, in part-time employment, husband with very substantial income, awarded a periodical allowance under s. 9(1)(e) until her sixtieth birthday or her death or remarriage, whichever was the earlier).

(14) *Smith v. Smith*, 2010 S.L.T. 372 (Lord Malcolm) (wife aged 57 with health problems, married and living with much younger husband for 24 years, very limited or no earning capacity and totally reliant on husband's financial support, husband with very substantial earnings, awarded a periodical allowance under s. 9(1)(d) for three years and thereafter under s. 9(1)(e), at a reduced rate, until husband's retirement from paid employment).

REPORTED CASES INVOLVING EXPENSES AWARDS

(1) *Little v. Little*, 1990 S.L.T. 785 (First Division; Lord Cameron of Lochbroom)

Wife seeking transfer of property order relating to matrimonial home and capital sum of £60,000, increased by amendment to £100,000 at the outset of the proof — After proof wife found entitled to transfer of property order concluded for and capital sum of £38,260 — Wife moving for the expenses of the action, arguing that husband had failed to make a sufficient offer, thereby requiring her to go to proof — The court found that husband's dilatory and unreasonable conduct in agreeing matters of valuation and in considering a proper basis for settlement in advance of the proof had caused the proceedings to have been more protracted than otherwise need have been the case — Wife accordingly awarded expenses of the proof and procedure following thereon, and *quoad ultra* no expenses found due to or by either party — The appellate court observed that the normal principle in petitory actions that expenses should follow success is not one that can be applied in its full rigour to cases of this type and it may be quite inappropriate to adopt it in a case where much trouble has been taken to achieve a fair division of the matrimonial property between the parties with the full co-operation of both sides; and so there was much to be said for the view that the parties' conduct rather than the result itself should be the principal criterion upon which to proceed, the whole matter being bound up intimately with the division of the matrimonial property itself and the effect of that division on the resources of the parties.

(2) *Whittome v. Whittome (No. 2)*, 1994 S.L.T. 130 (Lord Osborne)

Husband seeking capital sum of £100,000 — Wife seeking capital sum of £200,000, a periodical allowance of £200 per week and aliment of £100 per week for each of two children of the marriage — After proof wife found entitled to a periodical allowance of £50 per week for a period of three years from the date of decree and aliment of £90 for each child — Wife's claim for a capital sum was however refused, she having failed to persuade the court that husband's very substantial assets should be categorised as matrimonial property — Husband abandoning his own claim for capital sum during submissions at conclusion of evidence — Both parties moving for the expenses of the action, wife arguing that husband had made no offer of a periodical allowance at any time and that his best offer of aliment for each child had been £75 per week each — The court found that (i) while the wife had failed on the issue of categorisation, she had been successful on the several other matters in dispute; (ii) the wife's conduct of the litigation had been generally reasonable in that a great deal of factual material was the subject of agreement between the parties initiated by her legal advisers and that she was acting reasonably in seeking to obtain a decision of the court on the very difficult issue of categorisation of the husband's very considerable assets, there being little by way of authority to assist in the interpretation of the relevant legislation in relation to the various transactions to which husband's property had been subjected; and (iii) the practical effect on the resources of wife (who was assuming substantial responsibility, both practical and financial, for the care and upbringing of the two children) of granting husband's motion would be grave and would totally extinguish the benefit of the award of periodical allowance in her favour, whereas granting wife's motion, at least in part, would have comparatively little practical impact upon husband's financial circumstances — Wife accordingly awarded expenses of the action modified to 75%.

(3) *Macdonald v. Macdonald*, 1995 S.L.T. 72 (Extra Division; Lord Caplan)

Wife seeking transfer of property order relating to matrimonial home as well as orders for custody of children of the marriage and for their educational expenses — Husband opposing orders and seeking order for sale of matrimonial home — After proof wife found entitled to custody of children, payment of a lump sum in respect of their educational expenses and capital sum of £50,000, but transfer of property order refused and order for sale of matrimonial home granted instead — Wife moving for the expenses of the action — The court found that wife's claims had, for the major part, been successful and that husband had had no reasonable basis for contesting the issues which had generated much of the expense, the issues raised by the sale of the house occupying only a minor proportion of the time of the proof — Wife accordingly awarded expenses of the action modified to 60% — The court observed that matrimonial proceedings which involved custody questions and complex financial claims and counterclaims could not really be regarded as equivalent to a reparation or similar action for the purposes of regulating expenses, that sometimes there was more than one arrangement which could be described as reasonable though the court had to select a particular combination of remedies, that it might in certain circumstances be reasonable for a party to make claims designed to protect children even though the claimant eventually fails to secure their custody, and that accordingly in regard to expenses the equities of the situation needed careful analysis.

(4) *Adams v. Adams (No. 2)*, 1997 S.L.T. 150 (Lord Gill)

Wife seeking transfer of property order relating to matrimonial home and capital sum of £100,000 — Husband opposing orders and seeking order for sale of matrimonial home — After proof wife found entitled to capital sum of £22,190, but transfer of property order refused and order for sale of matrimonial home granted instead — Husband moving for expenses of the action — The court found that (i) husband had been successful on the two central questions in the proof, namely whether the matrimonial home should be transferred to wife or should be sold and whether wife should receive more than half of the matrimonial property; (ii) neither party could be faulted in respect of the disclosure of assets, the proof itself being conducted skilfully and expeditiously and counsel saving time and expense by reaching a realistic agreement on the valuation of the matrimonial property; (iii) the impact upon wife of an adverse award of expenses was not a decisive consideration in this case; (iv) wife's insistence upon the two points of principle upon which she failed necessitated the proof and the fact that husband made no extra-judicial offer on which he would found did not affect the matter since wife did not regard either of the two points of principle as negotiable; and (v) between the raising of the action and the date of the proof, both parties' personal and financial affairs were subject to uncertainty, so that neither could adopt a final position until full and up to date information had been exchanged shortly before the proof — Husband accordingly awarded expenses of the proof and ensuing procedure; *quoad ultra* no expenses found due to or by either party — The court observed that in cases under the Family Law (Scotland) Act 1985 success may not always be a straightforward matter; but even if one party is clearly successful the court may nevertheless take other considerations into account; and that in such cases the court's approach to expenses must be more flexible than it would be in a simple petitory action, so that in exercising its discretion as to expenses the court may take into account such matters as the reasonableness of the parties' claims, the extent to which they have co-operated in disclosing, and agreeing on the value of, their respective assets, the offers they have made to settle, the extent to which proof could have been avoided and, of course, the final outcome.

(5) *De Winton v. De Winton*, 1997 S.L.T. 1118 (Lord Cameron of Lochbroom)

Wife seeking capital sum of £150,000 — Husband opposing order — After proof wife held entitled to capital sum of £30,000 — Wife moving for expenses of the action — The court found that (i) neither party could be said to have been successful in the action, each putting the other to proof of their respective positions; (ii) wife's claim was based on an assessment of economic disadvantage to her which in correspondence was stated at £267,607.27 and at the end of the proof was set at £150,000; (iii) husband's position in correspondence, having initially been prepared to make an offer, was that parties should choose an appropriate forum for litigation as the points raised by wife were quite novel and the amount claimed not insubstantial, and that he was not prepared to settle matters except on the basis that there was no payment of capital by either party to the other except in relation to what was due by way of share of profit or capital from the farming partnership to wife; and (iv) there was no reason to criticise the conduct of either party in relation to the proceedings in court — No expenses found due to or by either party.

(6) *Cameron v. Cameron*, 2002 S.L.T. (Sh. Ct.) 23 (Sheriff Principal C.G.B. Nicholson Q.C.)

Wife seeking capital sum of £50,000 and a periodical allowance of £100 per week — Husband opposing order — After proof wife held entitled to capital sum of £10,370 (based on an arithmetical error) but no award of periodical allowance — Wife moving for expenses of the action — The appellate court found that husband had offered on two occasions to settle wife's claim for a capital sum, initially in the sum of £10,797 (mentioned in husband's pleadings by amendment shortly before the date of the proof) and then in the sum of £13,000 (at commencement of proof), the latter being in excess of the sum (£12,320) that the sheriff should have awarded — No expenses found due to or by either party.

(7) *Sweeney v. Sweeney (No. 3)*, 2007 S.C. 396 (First Division)

Wife seeking a capital sum of £2,000,000 and a periodical allowance of £6,250 per month — Husband opposing orders — After proof, and appeal, wife held entitled to capital sum of £950,000 and a periodical allowance of £4,000 per month for a period of one year from the date of decree — Wife moving for expenses of action and appeal — The court found that (i) at the early stages of the litigation husband had offered less than £115,000 in settlement; (ii) shortly before the proof he had offered a capital sum of £700,000 but without any award of a periodical allowance; (iii) during the appeal stages he had increased his offer to a capital sum of £850,000, again without a periodical allowance but with a contribution of £25,000 towards wife's expenses; (iv) no criticism could properly be made of the parties' conduct of matters prior to the proof, with both behaving responsibly and the proof being conducted efficiently and with co-operation between the parties; and (v) a number of issues remained to be resolved by the court, on some of which wife had been largely successful, either at first instance or in the appeal, resulting in a significant difference to capital sum award, with remaining matters on which she was unsuccessful taking up relatively small proportion of the time taken at proof and not of major significance to assessment of financial provision — Wife awarded expenses of proof and appeal; and *quoad ultra* no expenses found due to or by either party — The appellate court observed that the mere circumstance that a claimant has succeeded in obtaining an award modestly higher than what has been offered, judicially or extra-judicially, by the other party will not ordinarily entitle the successful party to an award of the expenses of process; that what has gone before will also be of importance; that parties were to be encouraged to make a full disclosure of assets and to agree, where possible, on valuations, thus narrowing as much as practicable the areas of remaining disputes; that where both parties have co-operated in such matters, the just disposal of expenses may well be of no expenses due to or by; that on the other hand where a party takes the other party to proof on an issue or issues on which he is unsuccessful to the extent of the other party's securing an award significantly greater than any outstanding offer, the expense caused to the successful party may well be recoverable by an award; and that while each party should be explicit as to what would be acceptable by way of settlement, it will be the relationship of the judicial award to the offer of the obligant, as prospective payee, which will ordinarily be of primary significance.

(8) *Lindsay v. Lindsay*, 2007 Fam. L.R. 18 (Sheriff Principal B. A. Lockhart)

Wife seeking capital sum of just under £62,000 during period specified by sheriff upon granting decree of divorce

— Husband opposing order — After proof, and appeal, wife held entitled to capital sum of £19,930.63 — Wife moving for expenses of action during post-divorce period — The court found that both sides had achieved success on certain arguments at the proof, husband's approach to valuation of his farm being upheld but wife's award being more than £9,000 higher than the figure calculated by husband to be due — No expenses found due to or by either party.

(9) *Hodge v. Hodge*, 2008 Fam. L.R. 51 (Sheriff Principal B. A. Lockhart)

Wife seeking capital sum and a periodical allowance — Husband opposing orders — After proof wife held entitled to capital sum of £79,451 and periodical allowance of £350 per month for six months (amounting to £2,100) — Husband moving for expenses of proof — The court found that (i) husband had made attempts to settle and avoid a proof, offering initially the sum of £95,368 (excluding wife's own items of matrimonial property valued at £20,549) and then the sum of £105,000 (again excluding wife's own items), the capital sum eventually awarded being substantially less than either of these offers; (ii) in the event, wife was unsuccessful in financial terms at the proof, seeking £26,000 for her claim for economic advantage/disadvantage and being awarded only £10,000, and seeking half the net value of the matrimonial property and being awarded only about one-third; (iii) husband had co-operated fully during the proceedings in meeting all requests for financial information made on behalf of wife; and (iv) husband had made offers prior to the proof to have parties' respective accountants negotiate on the question of business interests, which offers had not taken up by wife and evidence of expert accountants had taken up best part of a day at the proof — Husband awarded expenses of proof; *quoad ultra* no expenses found due to or by either party.

TABLE OF MATRIMONIAL PROPERTY AND RESOURCES[1]

PURSUER	£	DEFENDER	£
At relevant date:		*At relevant date:*	
(i) one-half interest in matrimonial home	96,937	(i) one-half interest in matrimonial home	96,937
(ii) one-half interest in Scottish Widows Insurance Policy . . .	3,684	(ii) one-half interest in Scottish Widows Insurance Policy . . .	3,684
(iii) 38.03% interest in C.C. Hornig & Son Ltd Executive Pension Fund . . .	43,318	(iii) 61.97% interest in C.C. Hornig & Son Ltd Executive Pension Fund . . .	70,588
		(iv) interest in Legal & General Pension Plan Policy . . .	4,000
		(v) interest in Liverpool and Victoria Insurance Policy . . .	2,200
		(vi) cash in Bank of Scotland . . .	3,567.32
		(vii) shares in C.C. Hornig & Son Ltd	69,000
SUBTOTAL	143,939	SUBTOTAL	249,976.32
Less		*Less*	
(a) one-half liability to Bank of Scotland . . .	1,763.71	(a) one-half liability to Bank of Scotland . . .	1,763.71
TOTAL	**142,175.29**	**TOTAL**	**248,212.61**

[1]This is the table (revised) presented to the court on behalf of the defender in *Crockett v. Crockett*, 1992 S.C.L.R. 591.

At present date:	£	At present date:	£
(i) 14 Glenorchy Terrace, Edinburgh . . .	100,000	(i) 10 Ventnor Terrace, Edinburgh . . .	90,000
(ii) one-half interest in Scottish Widows Insurance Policy . . .	6,449	(ii) one-half interest in Scottish Widows Insurance Policy . . .	6,449
[(iii) 38.03% interest in C.C. Hornig & Son Ltd Executive Pension Fund . . .	54,390]	[(iii) 61.97% interest in C.C. Hornig & Son Ltd Executive Pension Fund . . .	88,628]
[(iv) personal jewellery	8,000]	[(iv) interest in Legal & General Pension Plan Policy . . .	7,444]
		(v) interest in Liverpool and Victoria Insurance Policy	10,343
		(vi) shares in Abbey National . . .	2,000
		(vii) cash in Bank of Scotland . . .	3,567.22
		(viii) cash in Bank of Scotland . . .	41,136.52
		(ix) shares in C.C. Hornig & Son Ltd	nil
		[(x) personal jewellery	8,000)]
	--------------		--------------
SUBTOTAL	**106,449***	**SUBTOTAL**	**153,495.74***
Less (a) mortgage . . .	16,000	*Less* (a) mortgage . . .	30,312
(b) one-half liability to Bank of Scotland . . .	273.39	(b) one-half liability to Bank of Scotland . . .	273.39
(c) cheque account overdraft with Bank of Scotland . . .	2,000	(c) current account overdraft with Bank of Scotland . . .	8,620
(d) legal fees . . .	10,000	(d) legal fees . . .	10,000
	--------------		--------------
	28,273.39		49,205.39
TOTAL	**78,175.61**	**TOTAL**	**104,290.35**
*excludes (illiquid) pension(s) and personal jewellery			

PENSIONS ON DIVORCE REGULATIONS

A. The Occupational Pension Schemes (Transfer Values) Regulations 1996[1] (S.I. 1996 No. 1847)

The Secretary of State for Social Security, in exercise of the powers conferred upon him by sections 93(1), 93(1B), 93A(2) and (3),

---

[1] As amended by S.I. 2003 No. 1727, S.I. 2005 No. 72, S.I. 2005 No. 3377, S.I. 2008 No. 1050, S.I. 2008 No. 2450 and S.I. 2009 No. 615.

94(3), 95(2), (5) and (6), 97(1), (2), (3) and (4), 98(1), (1A), (2), (3) and (4), 99(4) and (7), 113(1) and (3), 153(1), 168(4), 181(1), 182(2) and (3) and 183(3) of the Pensions Schemes Act 1993 and sections 10(2) and 124(1) of the Pensions Act 1995 and of all other powers enabling him in that behalf . . . hereby makes the following Regulations:

PART I

GENERAL

Citation, commencement & interpretation

1.— (1) These Regulations may be cited as the Occupational Pension Schemes (Transfer Values) Regulations 1996 and shall come into force on 6th April 1997.

(2) In these Regulations, unless the context otherwise requires—

"the 1993 Act" means the Pension Schemes Act 1993;
"the 1995 Act" means the Pensions Act 1995;
"the 2004 Act" means the Pensions Act 2004;
"actuary" means—

(*a*) the actuary mentioned in section 47(1)(b) of the 1995 Act (professional advisers); or
(*b*) in relation to a scheme to which that section does not apply—
  (i) a Fellow of the Faculty of Actuaries;
  (ii) a Fellow of the Institute of Actuaries;
  (iii) a person with other actuarial qualifications who is approved, at the request of the trustees of the scheme in question, by the Secretary of State as being a proper person to act for the purposes of these Regulations in connection with that scheme;
"appropriate date" has the meaning given to that expression in section 97(3A) of the 1993 Act;
"base rate" has the meaning given to that expression in the Local Government Pension Scheme Regulations 1995;
"cash equivalent" means a cash equivalent or guaranteed cash equivalent mentioned in section 93A(1) or 94(1) of the 1993 Act;
"discount rates" means the interest rates used to discount future payments of benefit for the purposes of placing a current value on them;
"effective date" means the date as at which the assets and liabilities are valued for the purposes of the insufficiency report;

"guarantee date" has the meaning given to that expression in section 93A(2) of the 1993 Act;

"initial cash equivalent" means the amount calculated in accordance with regulation 7(1)(a);

"insufficiency report" means the actuary's last relevant report before the guarantee date prepared in accordance with Schedule 1B (insufficiency reports);

"insufficiency report liabilities" has the meaning given in paragraph 7 of Schedule 1B;

"insurance policy" means an insurance policy which is a contract on human life or a contract of annuity on human life, but excluding a contract which is linked to investment funds;

"member" has the meaning given in section 124(1) of the 1995 Act (interpretation);

"post-1997 protected rights" has the meaning given to that expression in the Protected Rights (Transfer Payment) Regulations 1996;

"relevant date" has the meaning given to that expression in section 94(2) of the 1993 Act;

"salary related benefits" means benefits that are not money purchase benefits;

"salary related scheme" means a scheme which is salary related within the meaning of section 93(1A) of the 1993 Act;

"scheme", except in the expressions "personal pension scheme" and "receiving scheme", means occupational pension scheme;

"section 9(2B) rights" has the meaning given to that expression in the Contracting-out (Transfer and Transfer Payment) Regulations 1996;

"statement of entitlement" has the meaning given in section 93A(1) of the 1993 Act (salary related schemes: right to statement of entitlement);

"trustees", in relation to a scheme which is not set up or established under a trust, means the managers of the scheme; and other expressions have the same meaning as in the 1993 Act.

. . .

PART III

GUARANTEED STATEMENTS OF ENTITLEMENT AND CALCULATION OF TRANSFER VALUES

Manner of calculation and verification of cash equivalents— general provisions

7.—(1) Subject to paragraphs (4) and (7), cash equivalents are to be calculated and verified—

(*a*) by calculating the initial cash equivalent—
    (i) for salary related benefits, in accordance with regulations 7A and 7B;
    or
    (ii) for money purchase benefits, in accordance with regulation 7C, and then making any reductions in accordance with regulation 7D; or
(*b*) in accordance with regulation 7E.

(2) The trustees must decide whether to calculate and verify the cash equivalent in accordance with paragraph (1)(a) or (b), but they can only choose paragraph (1)(b) if they have had regard to any requirement for consent to paying a cash equivalent which is higher than the amount calculated and verified in accordance with paragraph (1)(a).

(3) The trustees are responsible for the calculation and verification of cash equivalents and initial cash equivalents.

(4) Where a member, in relation to whom a cash equivalent is to be calculated and verified, is a member of a scheme modified by—

(*a*) the British Coal Staff Superannuation (Modification) Regulations 1994; or
(*b*) the Mineworkers' Pension Scheme (Modification) Regulations 1994, the cash equivalent of his bonus is to be calculated and verified by the trustees, having obtained the advice of the actuary, to reflect the fact that a reduced bonus, or no bonus, may become payable in accordance with the provisions governing the scheme in question.

(5) For the purposes of paragraph (4) "bonus" means any—

(*a*) augmentation of his benefits; or
(*b*) new, additional or alternative benefits, which the trustees of the scheme in question have applied to the member's benefits, or granted to him in accordance with the provisions governing that scheme, on the basis of findings as to that scheme's funding position.

(6) Paragraph (7) applies where the cash equivalent is calculated and verified in accordance with paragraph (1)(a).

(7) Where a portion of the cash equivalent relates to a salary related benefit and a portion relates to a money purchase benefit, the initial cash equivalent is to be calculated—

(*a*) for the salary related benefit portion, in accordance with regulations 7A and 7B; and (*b*) for the money purchase benefit portion, in accordance with regulation 7C.

Manner of calculation of initial cash equivalents for salary related benefits

7A.—(1) For salary related benefits, the initial cash equivalent is to be calculated—

(*a*) on an actuarial basis; and
(*b*) in accordance with paragraph (2) and regulation 7B.

(2) The initial cash equivalent is the amount at the guarantee date which is required to make provision within the scheme for a member's accrued benefits, options and discretionary benefits.

(3) For the purposes of paragraph (2), the trustees must determine the extent—

(*a*) of any options the member has which would increase the value of his benefits under the scheme;
(*b*) of any adjustments they decide to make to reflect the proportion of members likely to exercise those options; and
(*c*) to which any discretionary benefits should be taken into account, having regard to any established custom for awarding them and any requirement for consent before they are awarded.

Initial cash equivalents for salary related benefits: assumptions and guidance

7B.—(1) The trustees must calculate the initial cash equivalent for salary related benefits—

(*a*) by using the assumptions determined under this regulation; and
(*b*) where the scheme falls within paragraph (6), in accordance with the guidance referred to in that paragraph.

(2) Having taken the advice of the actuary, the trustees must determine the economic, financial and demographic assumptions.

(3) In determining the demographic assumptions, the trustees must have regard to—

(*a*) the main characteristics of the members of the scheme; or
(*b*) where the members of the scheme do not form a large enough group to allow demographic assumptions to be made,

the characteristics of a wider population sharing similar characteristics to the members.

(4) Except where the scheme falls within paragraph (6), the trustees must have regard to the scheme's investment strategy when deciding what assumptions will be included in calculating the discount rates in respect of the member.

(5) The trustees must determine the assumptions under this regulation with the aim that, taken as a whole, they should lead to the best estimate of the initial cash equivalent.

(6) A scheme falls within this paragraph if it is a public service scheme in respect of which guidance has been prepared, and from time to time revised, by the Treasury for calculating the discount rates.

Manner of calculation of initial cash equivalents for money purchase benefits

7C.—(1) For money purchase benefits, the initial cash equivalent is to be calculated in accordance with this regulation.

(2) The initial cash equivalent is the realisable value at the date of calculation of any benefits to which the member is entitled.

(3) The trustees must calculate that realisable value—

   (*a*) in accordance with the scheme rules; and
   (*b*) in a manner which is—
       (i)   approved by the trustees; and
      (ii) consistent with Chapter IV of Part IV of the 1993 Act.

(4) The realisable value must include any increases to the benefits resulting from a payment of interest made in accordance with the scheme rules.

Reductions to initial cash equivalents

7D.—(1) An initial cash equivalent may, or as the case may be must, be reduced in accordance with Schedule 1A (reductions in initial cash equivalents).

(2) The trustees may request an insufficiency report from the actuary in accordance with Schedule 1B.

(3) The trustees may treat the actuary's last relevant GN11 report as an insufficiency report.

Alternative manner of calculating and verifying cash equivalents

7E.—(1) This regulation applies where the trustees have decided to calculate and verify the cash equivalent in accordance with regulation 7(1)(b).

(2) The cash equivalent is to be calculated and verified in such manner as may be approved by the trustees.

(3) The cash equivalent must be higher than it would be if it was calculated and verified in accordance with regulation 7(1)(a).

(4) For the purposes of calculating and verifying the cash equivalent, the trustees may request an insufficiency report from the actuary in accordance with Schedule 1B.

(5) The trustees may treat the actuary's last relevant GN11 report as an insufficiency report.

. . .

Disclosure

11.—(1) Subject to paragraphs (1A) and (1B), an active member of any scheme, and a deferred member of a money purchase scheme, is entitled to receive from the trustees, on request, the information mentioned in Schedule 1 in writing.

(1A) Paragraph (1) does not apply where the request was made within 12 months of the last occasion that such information was provided to the member.

(1B) Information provided under paragraph (1) is to be provided by the trustees as soon as reasonably practicable, and in any event within three months after the date that the member makes the request.

(3) For the purposes of paragraph (1) "active member" and "deferred member" have the meaning given to those expressions by section 124 of the 1995 Act (interpretation).

(4) The trustees must ensure that a statement of entitlement to a guaranteed cash equivalent is accompanied by—

   (*a*) the information mentioned in Schedule 1 in relation to any cash equivalent of or transfer value in relation to the member's money purchase benefits (if any) under the scheme, calculated by reference to the guarantee date;

   (*b*) a statement in writing—

   (ii) indicating whether, and if so for what reasons and by what amount, the member's initial cash equivalent has been reduced under Schedule 1A and if any such reduction has been made the reduction shall indicate the paragraph of Schedule 1A which has been relied upon and shall give an estimate of the date (if any) by which it will be possible to make available a guaranteed cash equivalent which is not so reduced,

   (iii) explaining the terms and effects of regulation 6(3) (no right to make an application for a guaranteed statement of entitlement within 12 months of the last such application),

        (iv) explaining that if the member wishes to exercise his right to take the guaranteed cash equivalent the member must submit a written application to do so within three months beginning on the guarantee date,

        (v) explaining that in exceptional circumstances the guaranteed cash equivalent may be reduced and that the member will be informed if it is so reduced,

        (vi) where the scheme has begun to wind up, explaining that—

            (aa) the value of the member's guaranteed cash equivalent may be affected by the scheme's winding up; and

            (bb) a decision to take a guaranteed cash equivalent should be given careful consideration;

   (*c*) the information mentioned in paragraph 3 of Schedule 1.

(4A) For the purposes of paragraph (4)(b)(vi), the question whether a scheme has begun to wind up shall be determined in accordance with section 124(3A) to (3D) of the 1995 Act.

(5) Where a guaranteed cash equivalent is reduced or increased under regulation 9, the trustees must notify the member of that fact in writing within ten days (excluding Saturdays, Sundays, Christmas Day, New Year's Day and Good Friday) and such notification must—

   (*a*) state the reasons for and the amount of the reduction or increase;

   (*b*) indicate the paragraph of regulation 9 which has been relied upon; and

   (*c*) state that the member has a further three months, beginning with the date on which the member is informed of the reduction or increase, to make a written application to take the guaranteed cash equivalent as so reduced or increased.

(6) Where any person fails to comply with any requirement imposed upon that person by this regulation, the Regulatory Authority may by notice in writing require that person to pay, within 28 days, a penalty which

   (*a*) in the case of an individual, shall not exceed £1,000; and

   (*b*) in any other case, shall not exceed £10,000.

. . .

SCHEDULE 1   Regulation 11

INFORMATION TO BE MADE AVAILABLE TO MEMBERS

1. Whether any cash equivalent (within the meaning of Chapter IV of Part IV of the 1993 Act) is available to the member or would be

so available if the member's pensionable service were to terminate and if so—

(*a*) an estimate of its amount, calculated and verified in accordance with regulations 7 to 7E on the basis that the member's pensionable service terminated or will terminate on a particular date;

(*b*) the accrued rights to which it relates;

(*c*) whether any part of the estimated amount of the cash equivalent is attributable to additional benefits—

    (i) which have been awarded at their discretion if their established custom continues unaltered;

    (ii) which will be awarded at their discretion if their established custom continues unaltered and in either case whether that part is attributable to the whole or only part of those benefits; and

(*d*) if the estimated amount of the cash equivalent included a reduction of the initial cash equivalent under Schedule 1A—

    (i) a statement of that fact, a statement of the amount by which the initial cash equivalent has been reduced and an explanation of the reason for the reduction, which must refer to the paragraph of Schedule 1A relied upon,

    (ii) an estimate of the date (if any) by which it will be possible to make available a cash equivalent which is not so reduced; and

    (iii) a statement of the member's rights to obtain further estimates.

2. Whether any transfer value (not being a cash equivalent within the meaning of Chapter IV of Part IV of the 1993 Act) is available to the member or would be so available if the member's pensionable service were to terminate and if so—

(*a*) an estimate of its amount, calculated on the basis that the member's pensionable service terminated or will terminate on a particular date;

(*b*) the accrued rights to which it relates;

(*c*) whether any part of the estimated amount of the transfer value is attributable to additional benefits—

    (i) which have been awarded at the discretion of the trustees; or

    (ii) which will be awarded at their discretion if their established custom continues unaltered and in either case whether that part is attributable to the whole or only part of those benefits; and

(*d*) if the estimated amount of the transfer value has been reduced to an amount which is less than it otherwise would be because of an actuary's opinion that the scheme's assets are insufficient to meet its liabilities in full —
  (i)   a statement of that fact and an explanation;
  (ii) an estimate of the date (if any) by which it will be possible to make available a transfer value the amount of which is not so reduced; and
  (iii) a statement of the member's rights to obtain further estimates.

3. Where information is made available under paragraph 1 or 2 to a member of a salary related scheme, the information to be made available to such a member also includes —

(*a*) a statement that the Financial Services Authority, the Regulatory Authority and the Pensions Advisory Service provide information about transfers that may assist the member in deciding whether to transfer;
(*b*) if the scheme is an eligible scheme as defined in section 126 of the 2004 Act (eligible schemes), confirmation that the scheme is so eligible and that the Board of the Pension Protection Fund exists;
(*c*) a recommendation that the member should take financial advice before making decisions about transfers.

SCHEDULE 1A   Regulation 7D(1)

REDUCTIONS IN INITIAL CASH EQUIVALENTS

1. In a case where two or more paragraphs of this Schedule apply, they must be applied in the order in which they occur in this Schedule.
2. In the case of a scheme to which Part 3 of the 2004 Act (scheme funding) applies, the member's initial cash equivalent may be reduced by the trustees if —

(*a*) the insufficiency conditions are met;
(*b*) the insufficiency report has an effective date which is no earlier than the effective date of the most recent actuarial valuation received by the trustees in accordance with section 224(4) of the 2004 Act (scheme funding).

3. The insufficiency conditions are that the last insufficiency report shows that at the effective date of the report —

(*a*) the scheme had assets that were insufficient to cover the insufficiency report liabilities in respect of all the members; and

(*b*) the assets were insufficient to cover in full any category of insufficiency report liabilities that is an equivalent category of liabilities for benefits in respect of which the member's cash equivalent is being calculated.

4. If the insufficiency conditions are met the trustees may reduce, by a percentage not exceeding the deficiency percentage, any part of the member's initial cash equivalent that is payable in respect of such an equivalent category of liabilities as are mentioned in paragraph 3(b).

5. The deficiency percentage for any such part of a member's initial cash equivalent is the percentage by which the insufficiency report shows that the assets were insufficient to cover that category of liabilities.

6. If, by virtue of regulations made under section 232 of the 2004 Act (power to modify provisions of Part 3), Part 3 of that Act applies to a section of a scheme as if that section were a separate scheme, paragraphs 2 and 3 apply as if that section were a separate scheme and as if the reference to a scheme were accordingly a reference to that section.

7. In a case where a contributions equivalent premium has been paid in respect of a member in accordance with section 55 of the 1993 Act (payment of state scheme premiums on termination of certified status), the initial cash equivalent must be reduced (to nil if need be) to the extent that it represents the member's accrued rights which have been extinguished by virtue of section 60 of the 1993 Act (effect of payment of premiums on rights) by payment of that premium.

8. Where a member's cash equivalent is to be used for acquiring —

(*a*) transfer credits under the rules of another scheme; or

(*b*) rights under the rules of a personal pension scheme,

and the receiving scheme has undertaken to provide benefits at least equal to the benefits represented by that cash equivalent on payment of a lesser sum (including nil), the initial cash equivalent must be reduced so that the cash equivalent is that lesser sum.

9. Where effect has been given to protected rights in accordance with section 32A of the 1993 Act (discharge of protected rights on winding up: insurance policies), the initial cash equivalent of those rights must be reduced so that the cash equivalent is nil.

10. Where all or any of a member's benefits have been appropriately secured, the initial cash equivalent in respect of those benefits must be reduced so that the cash equivalent is nil.

11. For the purposes of paragraph 10, "appropriately secured" means the same as in section 19 of the 1993 Act (discharge of liability where guaranteed minimum pensions secured by insurance policies or annuity contracts), except that a policy of insurance or annuity contract which is taken out or entered into with an authorised friendly society (as defined for the purposes of regulation 6 of the Occupational Pension Schemes (Preservation of Benefit) Regulations 1991 (means of assuring short service benefit)), but which otherwise satisfies the conditions for being appropriate for the purposes of section 19 of that Act, is to be treated as if it were appropriate for the purposes of that section provided the terms of such policy or contract are not capable of being amended, revoked or rescinded.

12. Where a scheme has (in the case of a cash equivalent mentioned in section 93A of the 1993 Act, before the guarantee date) begun to be wound up, an initial cash equivalent may be reduced to the extent necessary for the scheme to comply with the winding up provisions (as defined in section 73B(10(a) of the 1995 Act) and regulations made under those provisions.

13. If, by virtue of regulations made under section 73B(4)(b)(i) of the 1995 Act (sections 73 and 73A: supplementary) by virtue of section 73B(5) of that Act, the winding up provisions (as so defined) apply to a section of a scheme as if that section were a separate scheme, paragraph 12 applies as if that section were a separate scheme and as if the references to a scheme were accordingly references to that section.

14. Where all or any of the benefits to which an initial cash equivalent relates have been surrendered, commuted or forfeited before the date on which the trustees do what is needed to carry out what the member requires, the initial cash equivalent of the benefits so surrendered, commuted or forfeited must be reduced so that the cash equivalent is nil.

15. The trustees may reduce an initial cash equivalent to reflect any reasonable administration costs were the member to leave the scheme and must offset against those costs any reasonable administrative savings.

SCHEDULE 1B   Regulations 7D(2)
and 7E(4)

INSUFFICIENCY REPORTS

1. Where the trustees have requested an insufficiency report under regulation 7D(2) or 7E(4), the actuary is responsible for the preparation of the report.

2. The insufficiency report must contain —

    (*a*) a comparison, as at the effective date of the report, between the insufficiency report liabilities of all members and the market value of the assets of the scheme; and

    (*b*) a statement of any allowance the actuary makes under paragraph 3.

3. The actuary may deduct from the assets of the scheme an allowance which —

    (*a*) is of such amount as he considers reasonable in the circumstances of the scheme; and

    (*b*) represents the expenses associated with wind up.

4. Where it appears to the actuary that the circumstances are such that it is appropriate, he may exclude any rights under an insurance policy from the scheme assets.

5. Where rights under an insurance policy are excluded under paragraph 4, the liabilities secured by the policy must be disregarded for the purposes of the insufficiency report.

6. The value of any rights under an insurance policy included in the scheme assets must be the value the actuary considers appropriate.

7. The insufficiency report liabilities are —

    (*a*) for active members with vested rights, calculated and verified in accordance with regulations 7 to 7E and Schedule 1A as appropriate, except that —
        (i)   paragraphs 2 to 6 of Schedule 1A are to be disregarded;
        (ii) references to "guarantee date" are to be taken to mean the effective date of the report; and
        (iii) it is to be assumed that the member ceases pensionable service on the effective date;

    (*b*) for deferred members, calculated and verified in accordance with regulations 7 to 7E and Schedule 1A as appropriate except that —
        (i)   paragraphs 2 to 6 of Schedule 1A are to be disregarded;
        (ii) references to "guarantee date" are to be taken to mean the effective date of the report;

    (*c*) for pensioner members, calculated and verified in accordance with regulations 7 to 7C as appropriate except that references to "guarantee date" are to be taken to mean the effective date of the report;

(*d*) for members over normal pension age not in receipt of a pension, calculated and verified —
  (i)   in the same way as those of pensioner members; and
  (ii) on the assumption that the member's pension comes into payment on the effective date of the report;
(*e*) for pension credit members, calculated and verified in accordance with regulations 7 to 7E and Schedule 1A as appropriate except that —
  (i)   paragraphs 2 to 6 of Schedule 1A are to be disregarded; and
  (ii) references to "guarantee date" are to be taken to mean the effective date of the report; and
(*f*) for members with unvested rights, equal to the amount of the unvested contributions and the actuary is to assume that the member ceases pensionable service on the effective date of the report.

8. When preparing the insufficiency report —

(*a*) the actuary must make estimates comparing the relevant assets with the relevant liabilities of the scheme in respect of each category of liability;
(*b*) for the purposes of sub-paragraph (a), the actuary may use one or more categories of liability;
(*c*) where the actuary uses more than one category, he must have regard to the priority order on winding up specified in section 73(3) of the 1995 Act (preferential liabilities on winding up); and
(*d*) in determining the extent and content of the category or categories of liability, the actuary may use such approximations as he considers reasonable.

9. In this Schedule —

"relevant assets" means, subject to paragraphs 2(b) to 6, for a particular category of liability, the market value of the scheme assets, less than the total of the relevant liabilities for all categories with greater priority under the priority order and are not to exceed the maximum of the relevant liabilities for that category.
"relevant liabilities" means, for a particular category of liability, the sum of all insufficiency report liabilities falling into that category.

B. The Divorce etc. (Pensions) (Scotland) Regulations 2000[2] (S.S.I. 2000 No. 112)

The Scottish Ministers, in exercise of the powers conferred upon them by section 10(8) and (8A) of the Family Law (Scotland) Act 1985 and of all other powers enabling them in that behalf, hereby make the following Regulations:

Citation, commencement and application

1.—(1) These Regulations may be cited as the Divorce etc. (Pensions) (Scotland) Regulations 2000 and shall come into force on 1st December 2000.

(2) These Regulations shall not affect any action for divorce commenced before 1st December 2000 or any action for declarator of nullity of marriage commenced before that date.

(3) For the purposes of these Regulations an action for divorce or action for declarator of nullity of marriage shall commence on the date of service of the summons.

Interpretation

2.—(1) In these Regulations —
"the Act" means the Family Law (Scotland) Act 1985;
"the 1993 Act" means the Pension Schemes Act 1993;
"the 1995 Act" means the Pensions Act 1995;
"the 1999 Act" means the Welfare Reform and Pensions Act 1999;
"active member" has the same meaning as in section 124(1) of the 1995 Act;
"benefits under a pension arrangement" has the same meaning as in section 27(1), subject to section 12A(10) and any reference to the rights or interests which a party has or may have in benefits under a pension arrangement includes a reference to the rights or interests which a party has or may have in such benefits which are payable in respect of the death of either party;
"deferred member" has the meaning given by section 124(1) of the 1995 Act;
"normal pension age" has the meaning given in section 180 (normal pension age) of the 1993 Act;
"a party" means a party to a marriage;

---

[2] As amended by S.S.I. 2000 No. 392, S.S.I. 2000 No. 438 and S.S.I. 2008 No. 293.

"occupational pension scheme" has the same meaning as in section 1 of the 1993 Act;

"pension arrangement" has the same meaning as in section 46(1) of the 1999 Act;

"person responsible for a pension arrangement" has the same meaning as in section 46(2) of the 1999 Act;

"personal pension scheme" has the same meaning as in section 1 of the 1993 Act but as if the reference to employed earners in that definition were to any earner;

"matrimonial property" has the same meaning as in section 10(4) and (5);

"relevant date" has the same meaning as in section 10(3);

"salary related occupational pension scheme" has the meaning given by regulation 1A of the Transfer Values Regulations;

"the Transfer Values Regulations" means the Occupational Pension Schemes (Transfer Values) Regulations 1996.

(2) Any reference in these Regulations to —

(*a*)   a numbered section is to a section bearing that number in the Act;

(*b*)   a numbered regulation is to a regulation bearing that number in these Regulations.

Valuation

3.—(1) The value of any benefits under a pension arrangement shall be calculated and verified for the purposes of the Act, in accordance with this regulation and regulation 4.

(2) The value, as at the relevant date, of the rights or interests which a party has or may have in any benefit under a pension arrangement as at that date shall be calculated as follows and in accordance with —

(*a*)   paragraph (3), if the party with pension rights is a deferred member of an occupational pension scheme;

(*b*)   paragraph (4), if the party with pension rights is an active member of an occupational pension scheme;

(*c*)   paragraphs (5) and (6), if —
  (i)   the party with pension rights is a member of a personal pension scheme; or
  (ii) those rights are contained in a retirement annuity contract; or

(*d*)   paragraphs (7) and (8), if —
  (i)   the pension of the party with pension rights is in payment;
  (ii) the party with the pension rights holds an annuity other than a retirement annuity contract; or

(iii) the rights of the party with pension rights are contained in a deferred annuity contract other than a retirement annuity contract; or

(iv) the pension of the person with pension rights is not in payment and the person has attained normal pension age.

(3) Where the party with pension rights is a deferred member of an occupational pension scheme, the value of the benefits which he has under that scheme shall be taken to be —

(*a*) in the case of an occupational pension scheme other than a salary related scheme, the cash equivalent to which he acquired a right under section 94(1)(a) of the 1993 Act (right to cash equivalent) on the termination of his pensionable service, calculated on the assumption that he has made an application under section 95 of that Act (ways of taking right to cash equivalent) on the date on which the request for the valuation was received; or

(*b*) in the case of a salary related occupational pension scheme, the guaranteed cash equivalent to which he would have acquired a right under section 94(1)(aa) of the 1993 Act if he had made an application under section 95(1) of that Act, calculated on the assumption that he has made an application under section 95 of that Act on the date on which the request for the valuation was received.

(4) Where the party with pension rights is an active member of an occupational pension scheme, the valuation of the benefits which he has accrued under that scheme shall be calculated and verified —

(*a*) on the assumption that the member has made a request for an estimate of the cash equivalent that would be available to him were his pensionable service to terminate on the date on which the request for valuation was received; and

(b) in accordance with regulation 11 (disclosure) of, and Schedule 1 to, the Transfer Values Regulations.

(5) Where the party with pension rights is a member of a personal pension scheme, or those rights are contained in a retirement annuity contract, the value of the benefits which he has under that scheme or contract shall be taken to be the cash equivalent to which he would have acquired a right under section 94(1)(b) of the 1993 Act, if he had made an application under section 95(1) of that Act on the date on which the request for the valuation was received.

(6) In relation to a personal pension scheme which is comprised in a retirement annuity contract made before 4th January 1988, paragraph (5) shall apply as if such were not excluded from the scope of Chapter IV of Part IV of the 1993 Act by section 93(1)(b) of that Act (scope of Chapter IV).

(7) Cash equivalents are to be calculated and verified in accordance with regulations 7 to 7C and 7E(1) to (3) of the Transfer Values Regulations as appropriate.

(8) But when calculating and verifying a cash equivalent in accordance with those regulations—

(*a*) references to "trustees" must be read as references to "person responsible for the pension arrangement";

(*b*) where the person with pension rights is a pensioner member on the date on which the request for the valuation is received, the value of his pension must be calculated and verified in accordance with regulations 7 to 7E of the Transfer Values Regulations as appropriate;

(*c*) where the person is over normal pension age but not in receipt of a pension—
   (i) the value of his pension must be calculated and verified in accordance with regulations 7 to 7E of the Transfer Values Regulations as appropriate; and
   (ii) the person responsible for the pension arrangement must assume that the pension came into payment on the date on which the request for the valuation was received; and

(*d*) the date by reference to which the cash equivalent is to be calculated and verified is to be the date on which the request for the valuation was received.

(10) For the purposes of paragraph (3), (4) or (7), section 93(1)(a)(i) of the 1993 Act (scope of Chapter IV) shall be construed as if the words "at least one year" had been omitted from that provision.

(11) For the purposes of paragraphs (3), (4) and (5), where the date on which the request for valuation was received is more than 12 months after the relevant date then the date for the purpose of valuing the benefits shall be the relevant date.

Valuation of relevant state scheme rights

3A. — (1) The value of any benefits in relevant state scheme rights shall be calculated and verified for the purposes of the Act in accordance with this regulation and regulation 4.

(2) The value, as at the relevant date, of the rights or interests which a party has or may have in any benefits in relevant state scheme rights

shall be calculated and verified in such manner as may be approved by the Government Actuary.

Apportionment

4. The value of the proportion of any rights or interests which a party has or may have in any benefits under a pension arrangement or in relevant state scheme rights as at the relevant date and which forms part of the matrimonial property by virtue of section 10(5) shall be calculated in accordance with the following formula —

$$\frac{A \ \text{x} \ B}{C}$$

where —

A   is the value of these rights or interests in any benefits under the pension arrangement which is calculated, as at the relevant date, in accordance with paragraph (2) of regulation 3 above or, as the case may be, is the value of relevant state scheme rights which are calculated, as at the relevant date, in accordance with paragraph (2) of regulation 3A above; and

B   is the period of C which falls within the period of the marriage of the parties before the relevant date and, if there is no such period, the amount shall be zero; and

C   is the period of the membership of that party in the pension arrangement before the relevant date or, as the case may be, the period during which that party has held relevant state scheme rights before the relevant date.

Revocation and saving

5.—(1) Subject to paragraph (2), there are hereby revoked:

(*a*)   regulation 3, and regulations 1 and 2 thereof insofar as they relate to regulation 3, of the Divorce etc. (Pensions) (Scotland) Regulations 1996;

(*b*)   regulation 4, and regulations 1, 2 and 3 thereof insofar as they relate to regulation 4, of the Divorce etc. (Pensions) (Scotland) Amendment Regulations 1997.

(2) Notwithstanding paragraph (1), the Regulations specified in paragraph (1) shall continue to apply to any action for divorce

commenced before 1st December 2000 or any action for declarator of nullity of marriage commenced before that date.

C. The Divorce etc. (Notification and Treatment of Pensions) (Scotland) Regulations 2000[3] (S.I. 2000 No. 1050)

The Secretary of State for Social Security, in exercise of the powers conferred upon him by section 23(1)(a)(ii) of the Welfare Reform and Pensions Act 1999 and sections 10(8) and (10) and 12A(8) of the Family Law (Scotland) Act 1985, and of all other powers enabling him in that behalf hereby makes the following Regulations:

Citation, commencement and interpretation

1.—(1) These Regulations may be cited as the Divorce etc. (Notification and Treatment of Pensions) (Scotland) Regulations 2000 and shall come into force on 1st December 2000.

(2) These Regulations shall not affect any action for divorce commenced before 1st December 2000 or any action for declarator of nullity of marriage commenced before that date.

(3) In these Regulations —

"the 1985 Act" means the Family Law (Scotland) Act 1985;
"the 1999 Act" means the Welfare Reform and Pensions Act 1999;
"the other person" means the other person to a marriage or civil partnership;
"pension arrangement" has the meaning given by section 46(1) of the 1999 Act,

and any expression used in these Regulations to which a meaning is assigned in section 12A of the 1985 Act shall have the same meaning in these Regulations as in that section.

Notices under section 12A of the 1985 Act

2.—(1) This regulation applies in the circumstances set out in section 12A (6)(a) of the 1985 Act.

(2) Where this regulation applies, the person responsible for the first pension arrangement shall, within 21 days after the date of the transfer, give notice in accordance with the following paragraphs of this regulation to: —

---

[3] As amended by S.I. 2007 No. 814.

(*a*) the person responsible for the new pension arrangement; and

(*b*) the other person.

(3) The notice to the person responsible for the new pension arrangement shall consist of a copy of the following documents: —

(*a*) every order made under section 12A(2) or (3) of the 1985 Act imposing any requirement upon the person responsible for the first pension arrangement;

(*b*) any order under section 12A(7) of the 1985 Act varying such an order;

(*c*) any notice given by any other person to the person responsible for the first pension arrangement under regulation 5 of these Regulations; and

(*d*) where the rights of the liable person under the first pension arrangement were derived in whole or in part from a transfer from a previous pension arrangement, any notice under paragraph (2)(a) of this regulation given on the occasion of that transfer.

(4) The notice to the other person shall contain the following particulars —

(*a*) the fact that all the accrued rights of the liable person under the first pension arrangement have been transferred to the new pension arrangement;

(*b*) the date on which the transfer takes effect;

(*c*) the name and address of the person responsible for the new pension arrangement; and

(*d*) the fact that the order made under section 12A(2) or (3) of the 1985 Act is to have effect as if it had been made instead of respect of the person responsible for the new pension arrangement.

3.—(1) This regulation applies where —

(*a*) section 12A(6) of the 1985 Act has already applied; and

(*b*) the liable person has transferred all his accrued rights for the second or any subsequent time to another new pension arrangement.

(2) Where this regulation applies, the person responsible for the pension arrangement from which the transfer is made to the other new pension arrangement shall, within 21 days after the date of the transfer, give notice to the other person of —

(*a*)   the fact that all accrued rights of the liable person have been transferred to the other new pension arrangement;

(*b*)   the date on which the transfer takes effect;

(*c*)   the name and address of the person responsible for the other new pension arrangement; and

(*d*)   the fact that the court may, on an application by any person having interest, vary any order under section 12A(2) or (3) of the 1985 Act.

4.—(1) This regulation applies where —

(*a*)   an order under section 12A(2) or (3) of the 1985 Act has been made imposing any requirement on the person responsible for the pension arrangement; and

(*b*)   some but not all of the accrued rights of the liable person have been transferred from the pension arrangement.

(2) Where this regulation applies, the person responsible for the pension arrangement from which the transfer is made shall, within 21 days after the date of the transfer, give notice to the other person of —

(*a*)   the likely extent of the reduction in the benefits payable under the arrangement as a result of the transfer;

(*b*)   the name and address of the person responsible for the pension arrangement under which the liable person has acquired transfer of credits as a result of the transfer;

(*c*)   the date on which the transfer takes effect; and

(*d*)   the fact that the court may, on an application by any person having an interest, vary an order under section 12A(2) or (3) of the 1985 Act.

5.—(1) This regulation applies where —

(*a*)   an order under section 12A(2) or (3) of the 1985 Act has been made imposing any requirements on the person responsible for the pension arrangement; and

(*b*)   there has been a change in the name or address of the other person.

(2) Where this regulation applies, the other person shall, within 21 days of the occurrence of the change mentioned in paragraph (1)(b) of this regulation, give notice of that change to the person responsible for the pension arrangement.

6.—(1) This regulation applies where —

(*a*) a transfer of accrued rights has taken place in the circumstances set out in section 12A(6)(a) of the 1985 Act;

(*b*) notice has been given in accordance with regulation 2(2)(a) and (b) of these Regulations; and

(*c*) there has been a change in the name or address of the other person but the other person has not, before receiving notice under regulation (2)(2)(b), given notice of that change to the person responsible for the first pension arrangement under regulation 5(2) of these Regulations.

(2) Where this regulation applies, the reference in regulation 5(2) to the person responsible for the pension arrangement shall be construed as a reference to the person responsible for the new pension arrangement and not the person responsible for the first pension arrangement.

(3) Subject to paragraph (4), where this regulation applies and the other person, within one year from the transfer, gives to the person responsible for the first pension arrangement notice of that change in purported compliance with regulation 5(2), the person responsible for the first pension arrangement shall —

(*a*) send that notice to the person responsible for the new pension arrangement; and

(*b*) give the other person a second notice under regulation 2(2) (b),

and the other person shall thereupon be deemed to have given notice under regulation 5(2) to the person responsible for the new pension arrangement.

(4) Upon complying with paragraph (3) above, the person responsible for the first pension arrangement shall be discharged from any further obligation under that paragraph, whether in relation to the change in question or any further change in the name or address of the other person which may be notified to them by the other person.

7. A notice under these Regulations may be sent by ordinary first class post to the last known address of the intended recipient and shall be deemed to have been received on the seventh day following the date of posting.

Revocations

8.—(1) Subject to paragraph (2), there are hereby revoked: —

(*a*) regulations 4 to 10 of the Divorce etc. (Pensions) (Scotland) Regulations 1996, and regulations 1 and 2 thereof insofar as they relate to regulations 4 to 10; and

(*b*) regulations 5 to 8 of the Divorce etc. (Pensions) (Scotland) Amendment Regulations 1997, and regulations 1, 2 and 3 thereof insofar as they relate to regulations 5 to 8.

(2) Notwithstanding paragraph (1), the regulations specified in paragraph (1) shall continue to apply to any action for divorce commenced before 1st December 2000 and any action for declarator of marriage commenced before that date.

D. The Pensions on Divorce etc. (Provision of Information) Regulations 2000[4] (S.I. 2000 No. 1048)

The Secretary of Sate for Social Security, in exercise of the powers conferred upon him by sections 168(1) and (4), 181(1) and 182(2) and (3) of the Pension Schemes Act 1993 and sections 23(1)(a), (b)(i), (c) (i) and (2), 34(1)(b)(ii), 45(1) and 83(4) and (6) of the Welfare Reform and Pensions Act 1999 and of all other powers enabling him in that behalf, after consulting such persons as he considered appropriate, hereby makes the following Regulations:

Citation, commencement and interpretation

1.—(1) These Regulations may be cited as the Pensions on Divorce etc. (Provision of Information) Regulations 2000 and shall come into force on 1st December 2000.

(2) In these Regulations —

"the 1993 Act" means the Pension Schemes Act 1993;
"the 1995 Act" means the Pensions Act 1995;
"the 1999 Act" means the Welfare Reform and Pensions Act 1999;
"the Charging Regulations" means the Pensions on Divorce etc. (Charging) Regulations 2000;
"the Implementation and Discharge of Liability Regulations" means the Pension Sharing (Implementation and Discharge of Liability) Regulations 2000;
"the Valuation Regulations" means the Pension Sharing (Valuation) Regulations 2000;

---

[4] As amended by S.I. 2000 No. 2691, S.I. 2003 No. 1727, S.I. 2005 No. 2877, S.I. 2006 No. 744, S.I. 2008 No. 1050 and S.I. 2009 No. 615.

"active member" has the meaning given by section 124(1) of the 1995 Act;

"day" means any day other than —
(*a*) Christmas Day or Good Friday; or
(*b*) a bank holiday, that is to say, a day which is, or is to be observed as, a bank holiday or a holiday under Schedule 1 to the Banking and Financial Dealings Act 1971;

"deferred member" has the meaning given by section 124(1) of the 1995 Act;

"implementation period" has the meaning given by section 34(1) of the 1999 Act;

"member" means a person who has rights to future benefits, or has rights to benefits payable, under a pension arrangement;

"money purchase benefits" has the meaning given by section 181(1) of the 1993 Act;

"normal benefit age" has the meaning given by section 101B of the 1993 Act;

"notice of discharge of liability" means a notice issued to the member and his former spouse by the person responsible for a pension arrangement when that person has discharged his liability in respect of a pension credit in accordance with Schedule 5 to the 1999 Act;

"normal pension age" has the meaning given in section 180 of the 1993 Act (normal pension age);

"notice of implementation" means a notice issued by the person responsible for a pension arrangement to the member and his former spouse at the beginning of the implementation period notifying them of the day on which the implementation period for the pension credit begins;

"occupational pension scheme" has the meaning given by section 1 of the 1993 Act;

"the party with pension rights" and "the other party" have the meanings given by section 25D(3) of the Matrimonial Causes Act 1997;

"pension arrangement" has the meaning given in section 46(1) of the 1999 Act;

"pension credit" means a credit under section 29(1)(b) of the 1999 Act;

"pension credit benefit" means the benefits payable under a pension arrangement or a qualifying arrangement to or in respect of a person by virtue of rights under the arrangement in question which are attributable (directly or indirectly) to a pension credit;

"pension credit rights" means rights to future benefits under a pension arrangement or a qualifying arrangement which are attributable (directly or indirectly) to a pension credit;

"pension sharing order or provision" means an order or provision which is mentioned in section 28(1) of the 1999 Act;

"pensionable service" has the meaning given by section 124(1) of the 1995 Act;

"person responsible for a pension arrangement" has the meaning given by section 46(2) of the 1999 Act;

"personal pension scheme" has the meaning given by section 1 of the 1993 Act;

"qualifying arrangement" has the meaning given by paragraph 6 of Schedule 5 to the 1999 Act;

"retirement annuity contract" means a contract or scheme which is to be treated as becoming a registered pension scheme under section 153(9) of the Finance Act 2004 in accordance with paragraph 1(1)(f) of Schedule 36 to that Act;

"salary related occupational pension scheme" has the meaning given by regulation 1A of the Transfer Values Regulations;

"the Regulatory Authority" means the Occupational Pensions Regulatory Authority;

"transfer day" has the meaning given by section 29(8) of the 1999 Act;

"the Transfer Values Regulations" means the Occupational Pension Schemes (Transfer Values) Regulations 1996;

"transferee" has the meaning given by section 29(8) of the 1999 Act;

"transferor" has the meaning given by section 29(8) of the 1999 Act;

"trustees or managers" has the meaning given by section 46(1) of the 1999 Act.

Basic information about pensions and divorce

2.—(1) The requirements imposed on a person responsible for a pension arrangement for the purposes of section 23(1)(a) of the 1999 Act (supply of pension information in connection with divorce etc.) are that he shall furnish —

(*a*) on request from a member, the information referred to in paragraphs (2) and (3)(b) to (f);

(*b*) on request from the spouse of a member, the information referred to in paragraph (3); or

(*c*) pursuant to an order of the court, the information referred to in paragraph (2), (3) or (4),

to the member, the spouse of the member, or, as the case may be, to the court.

(2) The information in this paragraph is a valuation of pension rights or benefits accrued under that member's pension arrangement.

(3) The information in this paragraph is —

(*a*) a statement that on request from the member, or pursuant to an order of the court, a valuation of pension rights or benefits accrued under that member's pension arrangement, will be provided to the member, or, as the case may be, to the court;

(*b*) a statement summarising the way in which the valuation referred to in paragraph (2) and sub-paragraph (a) is calculated;

(*c*) the pension benefits which are included in a valuation referred to in paragraph (2) and sub-paragraph (a);

(*d*) whether the person responsible for the pension arrangement offers membership to a person entitled to a pension credit, and if so, the types of benefits available to pension credit members under that arrangement;

(*e*) whether the person responsible for the pension arrangements intends to discharge his liability for a pension credit other than by offering membership to a person entitled to a pension credit; and

(*f*) the schedule of charges which the person responsible for the pension arrangement will levy in accordance with regulation 2(2) of the Charging Regulations (general requirements as to charges).

(4) The information in this paragraph is any other information relevant to any power with respect to the matters specified in section 23(1)(a) of the 1999 Act and which is not specified in Schedule 1 or 2 to the Occupational Pension Schemes (Disclosure of Information) Regulations 1996 (basic information about the scheme and information to be made available to individuals), or in Schedule 1 or 2 to the Personal Pension Schemes (Disclosure of Information) Regulations 1987 (basic information about the scheme and information to be made available to individuals), in a case where either of those Regulations applies.

(5) Where the member's request for, or the court order for the provision of, information includes a request for, or an order for the provision of, a valuation under paragraph (2), the person responsible for the pension arrangement shall furnish all the information requested, or ordered, to the member —

(*a*) within 3 months beginning with the date the person responsible for the pension arrangement receives that request or order for the provision of the information;

(*b*) within 6 weeks beginning with the date the person responsible for the pension arrangement receives that request, or order, for the provision of the information, if the member has notified that person on the date of the request or order that the information is needed in connection with proceedings commenced under any of the provisions referred to in section 23(1)(a) of the 1999 Act; or

(*c*) within such shorter period specified by the court in an order requiring the person responsible for the pension arrangement to provide a valuation in accordance with paragraph (2).

(6) Where —

(*a*) the member's request for, or the court order for the provision of, information does not include a request or an order for a valuation under paragraph (2); or

(*b*) the member's spouse requests the information specified in paragraph (3),

the person responsible for the pension arrangement shall furnish that information to the member, his spouse, or the court as the case may be, within one month beginning with the date that person responsible for the pension arrangement receives the request for, or the court order for the provision of, the information.

(7) At the same time as furnishing the information referred to in paragraph (1), the person responsible for a pension arrangement may furnish the information specified in regulation 4(2) (provision of information in response to a notification that a pension sharing order or provision may be made).

Information about pensions and divorce: valuation of pension benefits

3.—(1) Where an application for financial relief under any of the provisions referred to in section 23(1)(a)(i) or (iii) of the 1999 Act (supply of pension information in connection with domestic and overseas divorce etc. in England and Wales and corresponding Northern Ireland powers) has been made or is in contemplation, the valuation of benefits under a pension arrangement shall be calculated and verified for the purposes of regulation 2 of these Regulations in accordance with —

(*a*) paragraph (3), if the person with pension rights is a deferred member of an occupational pension scheme;

(*b*) paragraph (4), if the person with pension rights is an active member of an occupational pension scheme;

(*c*) paragraphs (5) and (6), if —

(i) the person with pension rights is a member of a personal pension scheme; or

(ii) those pension rights are contained in a retirement annuity contract; or

(*d*) paragraphs (7) and (8), if —
- (i) the pension of the person with pension rights is in payment;
- (ii) the rights of the person with pension rights are contained in an annuity contract other than a retirement annuity contract; or
- (iii) the rights of the person with pension rights are contained in a deferred annuity contract other than a retirement annuity contract; or
- (iv) the pension of the person with pension rights is not in payment and the person has attained normal pension age.

(2) Where an application for financial provision under any of the provisions referred to in section 23(1)(a)(ii) of the 1999 Act (corresponding Scottish powers) has been made, or is in contemplation, the valuation of benefits under a pension arrangement shall be calculated and verified for the purposes of regulation 2 of these Regulations in accordance with regulation 3 of the Divorce etc. (Pensions) (Scotland) Regulations 2000 (valuation).

(3) Where the person with pension rights is a deferred member of an occupational pension scheme, the value of the benefits which he has under that scheme shall be taken to be —

(*a*) in the case of an occupational pension scheme other than a salary related scheme, the cash equivalent to which he acquired a right under section 94(1)(a) of the 1993 Act (right to cash equivalent) on the termination of his pensionable service, calculated on the assumption that he has made an application under section 95 of that Act (ways of taking right to cash equivalent) on the date on which the request for the valuation was received; or

(*b*) in the case of a salary related occupational pension scheme, the guaranteed cash equivalent to which he would have acquired a right under section 94(1)(aa) of the 1993 Act if he had made an application under section 95(1) of that Act, calculated on the assumption that he has made such an application on the date on which the request for the valuation was received.

(4) Where the person with pension rights is an active member of an occupational pension scheme, the valuation of the benefits which he has accrued under that scheme shall be calculated and verified —

(*a*) on the assumption that the member had made a request for an estimate of the cash equivalent that would be available to him were his pensionable service to terminate on the date on which the request for the valuation was received; and

(*b*)   in accordance with regulation 11 of and Schedule 1 to the Transfer Values Regulations (disclosure).

(5) Where the person with pension rights is a member of a personal pension scheme, or those rights are contained in a retirement annuity contract, the value of the benefits which he has under that scheme or contract shall be taken to be the cash equivalent to which he would have acquired a right under section 94(1)(b) of the 1993 Act, if he had made an application under section 95(1) of that Act on the date on which the request for the valuation was received.

(6) In relation to a personal pension scheme which is comprised in a retirement annuity contract made before 4th January 1988, paragraph (5) shall apply as if such a scheme were not excluded from the scope of Chapter IV of Part IV of the 1993 Act by section 93(1)(b) of that Act (scope of Chapter IV).

(7) Cash equivalents are to be calculated and verified in accordance with regulations 7 to 7C and 7E(1) to (3) of the Transfer Values Regulations as appropriate.

(8) But when calculating and verifying a cash equivalent in accordance with those regulations —

(*a*)   references to "trustees" must be read as references to "person responsible for the pension arrangement";

(*b*)   where the person with pension rights is a pensioner member on the date on which the request for the valuation is received, the value of his pension must be calculated and verified in accordance with regulations 7 to 7E of the Transfer Values Regulations as appropriate;

(*c*)   where the person is over normal pension age but not in receipt of a pension —

(i)   the value of his pension must be calculated and verified in accordance with regulations 7 to 7E of the Transfer Values Regulations as appropriate; and

(ii)   the person responsible for the pension arrangement must assume that the pension came into payment on the date on which the request for the date by reference to which the cash equivalent is to be calculated and verified is to be the date on which the request for the valuation was received.

(10) Where paragraph (3), (4) or (7) has effect by reference to provisions of Chapter IV of Part IV of the 1993 Act, section 93(1)(a) (i) of that Act (scope of Chapter IV) shall apply to those provisions as

if the words "at least one year" had been omitted from section 93(1)
(a)(i).

Provision of information in response to a notification that a pension sharing order or provision may be made

4.—(1) A person responsible for a pension arrangement shall furnish
the information specified in paragraph (2) to the member or to the
court, as the case may be —

- (*a*) within 21 days beginning with the date that the person
  responsible for the pension arrangement received the
  notification that a pension sharing order or provision may be
  made; or
- (*b*) if the court has specified a date which is outside the 21 days
  referred to in sub-paragraph (a), by that date.

(2) The information referred to in paragraph (1) is —

- (*a*) the full name of the pension arrangement and address to which
  any order or provision referred to in section 28(1) of the 1999
  Act (activation of pension sharing) should be sent;
- (*b*) in the case of an occupational pension scheme, whether the
  scheme is winding up, and, if so, —
  - (i) the date on which the winding up commenced; and
  - (ii) the name and address of the trustees who are dealing
    with the winding up;
- (*c*) in the case of an occupational pension scheme, whether a cash
  equivalent of the member's pension rights, if calculated on
  the date the notification referred to in paragraph (1)(a) was
  received by the trustees or managers of that scheme, would
  be reduced in accordance with the provisions of paragraphs 2,
  3 and 12 of Schedule 1A to the Transfer Values Regulations
  (reductions in initial cash equivalents);
- (*d*) whether the person responsible for the pension arrangement is
  aware that the member's rights under the pension arrangement
  are subject to any, and if so, to specify which, of the following —
  - (i) any order or provision specified in section 28(1) of the
    1999 Act;
  - (ii) an order under section 23 of the Matrimonial Causes
    Act 1973 (financial provision orders in connection
    with divorce etc.), so far as it includes provision made
    by virtue of section 25B or 25C of that Act (powers to
    include provisions about pensions);
  - (iii) an order under section 12A(2) or (3) of the Family Law

(Scotland) Act 1985 (powers in relation to pensions lump sums when making a capital sum order) which relates to benefits or future benefits to which the member is entitled under the pension arrangement;

(iv) an order under Article 25 of the Matrimonial Causes (Northern Ireland) Order 1978, so far as it includes provision made by virtue of Article 27B or 27C of that Order (Northern Ireland powers corresponding to those mentioned in paragraph (2)(d)(ii));

(v) a forfeiture order;

(vi) a bankruptcy order;

(vii) an award of sequestration on a member's estate or the making of the appointment on his estate of a judicial factor under section 41 of the Solicitors (Scotland) Act 1980 (appointment of judicial factor);

(*e*) whether the member's rights under the pension arrangement include rights specified in regulation 2 of the Valuation Regulations (rights under a pension arrangement which are not shareable);

(*f*) if the person responsible for the pension arrangement has not at an earlier stage provided the following information, whether that person requires the charges specified in regulation 3 (charges recoverable in respect of the provision of basic information), 5 (charges in respect of pension sharing activity), or 6 (additional amounts recoverable in respect of pension sharing activity) of the Charging Regulations to be paid before the commencement of the implementation period, and if so, —

(i) whether that person requires those charges to be paid in full; or

(ii) the proportion of those charges which he requires to be paid;

(*g*) whether the person responsible for the pension arrangement may levy additional charges specified in regulation 6 of the Charging Regulations, and if so, the scale of the additional charges which are likely to be made;

(*h*) whether the member is a trustee of the pension arrangement;

(*i*) whether the person responsible for the pension arrangement may request information about the member's state of health from the member if a pension sharing order or provision were to be made;

(*j*) (repealed); and

(*k*) whether the person responsible for the pension arrangement requires information additional to that specified in regulation 5 (information required by the person responsible for the pension arrangement before the implementation period may begin) in order to implement the pension sharing order or provision.

Information required by the person responsible for the pension arrangement before the implementation period may begin

5. The information prescribed for the purposes of section 34(1) (b) of the 1999 Act (information relating to the transferor and the transferee which the person responsible for the pension arrangement must receive) is —

(*a*) in relation to the transferor —
- (i) all names by which the transferor has been known;
- (ii) date of birth;
- (iii) address;
- (iv) National Insurance number;
- (v) the name of the pension arrangement to which the pension sharing order or provision relates; and
- (vi) the transferor's membership or policy number in that pension arrangement;

(*b*) in relation to the transferee —
- (i) all names by which the transferee has been known;
- (ii) date of birth;
- (iii) address;
- (iv) National Insurance number; and
- (v) if the transferee is a member of the pension arrangement from which the pension credit is derived, his membership or policy number in that pension arrangement;

(*c*) where the transferee has given his consent in accordance with paragraph 1(3)(c), 3(3)(c) or 4(2)(c) of Schedule 5 to the 1999 Act (mode of discharge of liability for a pension credit) to the payment of the pension credit to the person responsible for a qualifying arrangement —
- (i) the full name of that qualifying arrangement;
- (ii) its address;
- (iii) if known, the transferee's membership number or policy number in that arrangement; and
- (iv) the name or title, business address, business telephone number, and, where available, the business facsimile number and electronic mail address of a person who may be contacted in respect of the discharge of liability for the pension credit;

(*d*) where the rights from which the pension credit is derived are held in an occupational pension scheme which is being wound up, whether the transferee has given an indication whether he wishes to transfer his pension credit rights which may have been reduced in accordance with the provisions of regulation 16(1) of the Implementation and Discharge of Liability Regulations (adjustments to the amount of the pension credit — occupational pension schemes which are underfunded on the valuation day) to a qualifying arrangement; and

(*e*) any information requested by the person responsible for the pension arrangement in accordance with regulation 4(2)(i) or (k).

Provision of information after the death of the person entitled to the pension credit before liability in respect of the pension credit has been discharged

6.—(1) Where the person entitled to the pension credit dies before the person responsible for the pension arrangement has discharged his liability in respect of the pension credit, the person responsible for the pension arrangement shall, within 21 days of the date of receipt of the notification of the death of the person entitled to the pension credit, notify in writing any person whom the person responsible for the pension arrangement considers should be notified of the matters specified in paragraph (2).

(2) The matters specified in this paragraph are —

(*a*) how the person responsible for the pension arrangement intends to discharge his liability in respect of the pension credit;

(*b*) whether the person responsible for the pension arrangement intends to recover charges from the person nominated to receive pension credit benefits, in accordance with regulations 2 to 9 of the Charging Regulations, and if so, a copy of the schedule of charges issued to the parties to pension sharing in accordance with regulation 2(2)(b) of the Charging Regulations (general requirements as to charges); and

(*c*) a list of any further information which the person responsible for the pension arrangement requires in order to discharge his liability in respect of the pension credit.

Provision of information after receiving a pension sharing order or provision

7.—(1) A person responsible for a pension arrangement who is in receipt of a pension sharing order or provision relating to that arrangement shall provide in writing to the transferor and transferee, or, where regulation 6(1) applies, to the person other than the person entitled to the pension credit referred to in regulation 6 of the

Implementation and Discharge of Liability Regulations (discharge of liability in respect of a pension credit following the death of the person entitled to the pension credit), as the case may be, —

(*a*) a notice in accordance with the provisions of regulation 7(1) of the Charging Regulations (charges in respect of pension sharing activity — postponement of implementation period);

(*b*) a list of information relating to the transferor or the transferee, or, where regulation 6(1) applies, the person other than the person entitled to the pension credit referred to in regulation 6 of the Implementation and Discharge of Liability Regulations, as the case may be, which —

    (i) has been requested in accordance with regulation 4(2)(i) and (k), or, where appropriate, 6(2)(c), or should have been provided in accordance with regulation 5;

    (ii) the person responsible for the pension arrangement considers he needs in order to begin to implement the pension sharing order or provision; and

    (iii) remains outstanding;

(*c*) a notice of implementation; or

(*d*) a statement by the person responsible for the pension arrangement explaining why he is unable to implement the pension sharing order or agreement.

(2) The information specified in paragraph (1) shall be furnished in accordance with that paragraph within 21 days beginning with —

(*a*) in the case of sub-paragraph (a), (b) or (d) of that paragraph, the day on which the person responsible for the pension arrangement receives the pension sharing order or provision; or

(*b*) in the case of sub-paragraph (c) of that paragraph, the later of the days specified in section 34(1)(a) and (b) of the 1999 Act (implementation period).

Provision of information after the implementation of a pension sharing order or provision

8.—(1) The person responsible for the pension arrangement shall issue a notice of discharge of liability to the transferor and the transferee, or, as the case may be, the person entitled to the pension credit by virtue of regulation 6 of the Implementation and Discharge of Liability Regulations no later than the end of the period of 21 days beginning with the day on which the discharge of liability in respect of the pension credit is completed.

(2) In the case of a transferor whose pension is not in payment, the notice of discharge of liability shall include the following details —

(*a*)　the value of the transferor's accrued rights as determined by reference to the cash equivalent value of those rights calculated and verified in accordance with regulation 3 of the Valuation Regulations (calculation and verification of cash equivalents for the purposes of the creation of pension debits and credits);

(*b*)　the value of the pension debit;

(*c*)　any amount deducted from the value of the pension rights in accordance with regulation 9(2)(c) of the Charging Regulations (charges in respect of pension sharing activity — method of recovery);

(*d*)　the value of the transferor's rights after the amounts referred to in sub-paragraphs (b) and (c) have been deducted; and

(*e*)　the transfer day.

(3) In the case of a transferor whose pension is in payment, the notice of discharge of liability shall include the following details —

(*a*)　the value of the transferor's benefits under the pension arrangement as determined by reference to the cash equivalent value of those rights calculated and verified in accordance with regulation 3 of the Valuation Regulations;

(*b*)　the value of the pension debit;

(*c*)　the amount of the pension which was in payment before liability in respect of the pension credit was discharged;

(*d*)　the amount of pension which is payable following the deduction of the pension debit from the transferor's pension benefits;

(*e*)　the transfer day;

(*f*)　if the person responsible for the pension arrangement intends to recover charges, the amount of any unpaid charges —

　　(i)　not prohibited by regulation 2 of the Charging Regulations (general requirements as to charges); and

　　(ii)　specified in regulations 3 and 6 of those Regulations;

(*g*)　how the person responsible for the pension arrangement will recover the charges referred to in sub-paragraph (f), including —

　　(i)　whether the method of recovery specified in regulation 9(2)(d) of the Charging Regulations will be used;

　　(ii)　the date when payment of those charges in whole or in part is required; and

　　(iii)　the sum which will be payable by the transferor, or which will be deducted from his pension benefits, on that date.

(4) In the case of a transferee —

(*a*) whose pension is not in payment; and
(*b*) who will become a member of the pension arrangement from which the pension credit rights were derived,

the notice of discharge of liability to the transferee shall include the following details —

(i)   the value of the pension credit;
(ii) any amount deducted from the value of the pension credit in accordance with regulation 9(2)(b) of the Charging Regulations;
(iii) the value of the pension credit after the amount referred to in sub-paragraph (b)(ii) has been deducted;
(iv) the transfer day;
(v)   any periodical charges the person responsible for the pension arrangement intends to make, including how and when those charges will be recovered from the transferee; and
(vi) information concerning membership of the pension arrangement which is relevant to the transferee as a pension credit member.

(5) In the case of a transferee who is transferring his pension credit rights out of the pension arrangement from which those rights were derived, the notice of discharge of liability to the transferee shall include the following details —

(*a*) the value of the pension credit;
(*b*) any amount deducted from the value of the pension credit in accordance with regulation 9(2)(b) of the Charging Regulations;
(*c*) the value of the pension credit after the amount referred to in sub-paragraph (b) has been deducted;
(*d*) the transfer day; and
(*e*) details of the pension arrangement, including its name, address, reference number, telephone number, and, where available, the business facsimile number and electronic mail address, to which the pension credit has been transferred.

(6) In the case of a transferee, who has reached normal benefit age on the transfer day, and in respect of whose pension credit liability has been discharged in accordance with paragraph 1(2), 2(2), 3(2) or 4(4) of Schedule 5 to the 1999 Act (pension credits: mode of discharge —

funded pension schemes, unfunded public service pension schemes, other unfunded pension schemes, or other pension arrangements), the notice of discharge of liability to the transferee shall include the following details —

   (*a*) the amount of pension credit benefit which is to be paid to the transferee;

   (*b*) the date when the pension credit benefit is to be paid to the transferee;

   (*c*) the transfer day;

   (*d*) if the person responsible for the pension arrangement intends to recover charges, the amount of any unpaid charges —

      (i) not prohibited by regulation 2 of the Charging Regulations; and

      (ii) specified in regulations 3 and 6 of those Regulations; and

   (*e*) how the person responsible for the pension arrangement will recover the charges referred to in sub-paragraph (d), including —

      (i) whether the method of recovery specified in regulation 9(2)(e) of the Charging Regulations will be used;

      (ii) the date when payment of those charges in whole or in part is required; and

      (iii) the sum which will be payable by the transferee, or which will be deducted from his pension credit benefits, on that date.

(7) In the case of a person entitled to the pension credit by virtue of regulation 6 of the Implementation and Discharge of Liability Regulations, the notice of discharge of liability shall include the following details —

   (*a*) the value of the pension credit rights as determined in accordance with regulation 10 of the Implementation and Discharge of Liability Regulations (calculation of the value of appropriate rights);

   (*b*) any amount deducted from the value of the pension credit in accordance with regulation 9(2)(b) of the Charging Regulations;

   (*c*) the value of the pension credit;

   (*d*) the transfer day; and

   (*e*) any periodical charges the person responsible for the pension arrangement intends to make, including how and when those charges will be recovered from the payments made to the person entitled to the pension credit by virtue of regulation 6 of the Implementation and Discharge of Liability Regulations.

Penalties

9. Where any trustee or manager of an occupational pension scheme fails, without reasonable excuse, to comply with any requirement imposed under regulation 6, 7 or 8, the Regulatory Authority may by notice in writing require that trustee or manager to pay within 28 days from the date of its imposition, a penalty which shall not exceed —

(*a*) £200 in the case of an individual, and
(*b*) £1,000 in any other case.

Provision of information after receipt of an earmarking order

10. — (1) The person responsible for the pension arrangement shall, within 21 days beginning with the day that he receives —

(*a*) an order under section 23 of the Matrimonial Causes Act 1973, so far as it includes provision made by virtue of section 25B or 25C of that Act (powers to include provision about pensions);
(*b*) an order under section 12A(2) or (3) of the Family Law (Scotland) Act 1985; or
(*c*) an order under Article 25 of the Matrimonial Causes (Northern Ireland) Order 1978, so far as it includes provision made by virtue of Article 27B or 27C of that Order (Northern Ireland powers corresponding to those mentioned in sub-paragraph (a)),

issue to the party with pension rights and the other party a notice which includes the information specified in paragraphs (2) and (5), or (3), (4) and (5), as the case may be.

(2) Where an order referred to in paragraph (1)(a), (b) or (c) is made in respect of the pension rights or benefits of a party with pension rights whose pension is not in payment, the notice issued by the person responsible for a pension arrangement to the party with pension rights and the other party shall include a list of the circumstances in respect of any changes of which the party with pension rights or the other party must notify the person responsible for the pension arrangement.

(3) Where an order referred to in paragraph (1)(a) or (c) is made in respect of the pension rights or benefits of a party with pension rights whose pension is in payment, the notice issued by the person responsible for a pension arrangement to the party with pension rights and the other party shall include —

(*a*) the value of the pension rights or benefits of the party with pension rights;

(*b*) the amount of the pension of the party with pension rights after the order has been implemented;

(*c*) the first date when a payment pursuant to the order is to be made; and

(*d*) a list of the circumstances, in respect of any changes of which the party with pension rights or the other party must notify the person responsible for the pension arrangement.

(4) Where an order referred to in paragraph (1)(a) or (c) is made in respect of the pension rights of a party with pension rights whose pension is in payment, the notice issued by the person responsible for a pension arrangement to the party with pension rights shall, in addition to the items specified in paragraph (3), include —

(*a*) the amount of the pension of the party with pension rights which is currently in payment; and

(*b*) the amount of pension which will be payable to the party with pension rights after the order has been implemented.

(5) Where an order referred to in paragraph (1)(a), (b) or (c) is made the notice issued by the person responsible for a pension arrangement to the party with pension rights and the other party shall include —

(*a*) the amount of any charges which remain unpaid by —
    (i) the party with pension rights; or
    (ii) the other party,

in respect of the provision by the person responsible for the pension arrangement of information about pensions and divorce pursuant to regulation 3 of the Charging Regulations, and in respect of complying with an order referred to in paragraph (1)(a), (b) or (c); and

(*b*) information as to the manner in which the person responsible for the pension arrangement will recover the charges referred to in sub-paragraph (a), including
    (i) the date when payment of those charges in whole or in part is required;
    (ii) the sum which will be payable by the party with pension rights or the other party, as the case may be; and
    (iii) whether the sum will be deducted from payments of pension to the party with pension rights, or, as the case may be, from payments to be made to the other party pursuant to an order referred to in paragraph (1)(a), (b) or (c).

E. The Pensions on Divorce etc. (Charging) Regulations 2000[5] (S.I. 2000 No. 1049)

The Secretary of State for Social Security, in exercise of the powers conferred upon him by sections 23(1)(d) and (3), 24, 41(1) and (2) and 83(4) and (6) of the Welfare Reform and Pensions Act 1999 and of all other powers enabling him in that behalf, after consulting such persons as he considered appropriate hereby makes the following Regulations:

Citation, commencement and interpretation

1.—(1) These Regulations may be cited as the Pensions on Divorce etc. (Charging) Regulations 2000 and shall come into force on 1st December 2000.

(2) In these Regulations, unless the context otherwise requires —

"the 1999 Act" means the Welfare Reform and Pensions Act 1999;
"the Provision of Information Regulations" means the Pensions on Divorce etc. (Provision of Information) Regulations 2000;
"day" means any day other than —
    (*a*) Christmas Day or Good Friday; or
    (*b*) a bank holiday, that is to say, a day which is, or is to be observed as, a bank holiday or a holiday under Schedule 1 to the Banking and Financial Dealings Act 1971;
"implementation period" has the meaning given by section 34(1) of the 1999 Act;
"normal pension age" has the meaning given by section 180 of the Pension Schemes Act 1993;
"notice of implementation" has the meaning given by regulation 1(2) of the Provision of Information Regulations;
"pension arrangement" has the meaning given to that expression in section 46(1) of the 1999 Act;
"pension credit" means a credit under section 29(1)(b) of the 1999 Act;
"pension credit benefit" has the meaning given by section 101B of the Pensions Schemes Act 1993;
"pension credit rights" has the meaning given by section 101B of the Pension Schemes Act 1993;
"pension sharing activity" has the meaning given by section 41(5) of the 1999 Act;
"pension sharing order or provision" means an order or provision which is mentioned in section 28(1) of the 1999 Act;

---

[5] As amended by S.I. 2000 No. 2691, S.I. 2005 No. 2877, S.I. 2008 No. 1050 and S.I. 2009 No. 615.

"person responsible for a pension arrangement" has the meaning given to that expression in section 46(2) of the 1999 Act;

"the relevant date" has the meaning given by section 10(3) of the Family Law (Scotland) Act 1985;

"trustees or managers" has the meaning given by section 46(1) of the 1999 Act.

General requirements as to charges

2.—(1) Subject to paragraph (8), a person responsible for a pension arrangement shall not recover any charges incurred in connection with —

(*a*) the provision of information under —
   (i) regulation 2 of the Provision of Information Regulations (basic information about pensions and divorce or dissolution of a civil partnership);
   (ii) regulation 4 of those Regulations (provision of information in response to a notification that a pension sharing order or provision may be made); or
   (iii) regulation 10 of those Regulations (provision of information after receipt of an earmarking order);
(*b*) complying with any order specified in section 24 of the 1999 Act (charges by pension arrangements in relation to earmarking orders); or
(*c*) any descriptions of pension sharing activity specified in regulation 5 of these Regulations,

unless he has complied with the requirements of paragraphs (2) to (5).

(2) The requirements mentioned in paragraph (1) are that the person responsible for a pension arrangement shall, before a pension sharing order or provision is made —

(*a*) inform the member or the member's spouse or civil partner, as the case may be, in writing of his intention to recover costs incurred in connection with any of the matters specified in sub-paragraph (a), (b) or (c) of paragraph (1); and
(*b*) provide the member or the member's spouse or civil partner, as the case may be, with a written schedule of charges in accordance with paragraphs (3) and (4) in respect of those matters specified in sub-paragraph (a) or (c) of paragraph (1) for which a charge may be recoverable.

(3) No charge shall be recoverable in respect of any of the items mentioned in paragraph (4) unless the person responsible for a pension arrangement has specified in the written schedule of charges mentioned

in paragraph (2)(b) that a charge may be recoverable in respect of that item.

(4) The items referred to in paragraph (3) are —

(*a*) the provision of a cash equivalent other than one which is provided in accordance with the provisions of —
  (i) section 93A or 94 of the 1993 Act (salary related schemes: right to statement of entitlement, and right to cash equivalent);
  (ii) regulation 11(1) of the Occupational Pension Schemes (Transfer Values) Regulations 1996 (disclosure); or
  (iii) regulation 5 (information to be made available to individuals) of, and paragraph 2(b) of Schedule 2 (provision of cash equivalent) to the Personal Pension Schemes (Disclosure of Information) Regulations 1987;
(*b*) subject to regulation 3(2)(b) or (c), as the case may be, the provision of a valuation in accordance with regulation 2(2) of the Provision of Information Regulations;
(*c*) whether a person responsible for a pension arrangement intends to recover the cost of providing membership of the pension arrangement to the person entitled to a pension credit, before or after the pension sharing order is implemented;
(*d*) whether the person responsible for a pension arrangement intends to recover additional charges in the circumstances prescribed in regulation 6 of these Regulations in respect of pension sharing activity described in regulation 5 of these Regulations;
(*e*) whether the charges are inclusive or exclusive of value added tax, where the person responsible for a pension arrangement is required to charge value added tax in accordance with the provisions of the Value Added Tax Act 1994;
(*f*) periodical charges in respect of pension sharing activity which the person responsible for a pension arrangement may make when a person entitled to a pension credit becomes a member of the pension arrangement from which the pension credit is derived;
(*g*) whether the person responsible for a pension arrangement intends to recover charges specified in regulation 10 of these Regulations.

(5) In the case of the cost referred to in paragraph (4)(c) or the charges to be imposed in respect of pension sharing activity described in regulation 5 of these Regulations, the person responsible for a pension arrangement shall provide —

(*a*) a single estimate of the overall cost of the pension sharing activity;

(*b*) a range of estimates of the overall cost of the pension sharing activity which is dependent upon the complexity of an individual case; or

(*c*) a breakdown of the cost of each element of pension sharing activity for which a charge shall be made.

(6) Subject to regulation 9(3) and (4), a person responsible for a pension arrangement shall recover only those sums which represent the reasonable administrative expenses which he has incurred or is likely to incur in connection with any of the activities mentioned in paragraph (1), or in relation to a pension sharing order having been made the subject of an application for leave to appeal out of time.

(7) The requirements of paragraph (2) do not apply in connection with the recovery by a person responsible for a pension arrangement of costs incurred in relation to a pension sharing order having been made the subject of an application for leave to appeal out of time.

(8) The information specified in regulation 2(2) and (3) of the Provision of Information Regulations shall be provided to the member or the member's spouse or civil partner without charge unless —

(*a*) the person responsible for the pension arrangement has furnished the information to the member, the member's spouse, civil partner or the court within a period of 12 months immediately prior to the date of the request or the court order for the provision of that information;

(*b*) the member has reached normal pension age on or before the date of the request or the court order for the provision of the information;

(*c*) the request or the court order for the provision of the information is made within 12 months prior to the member reaching normal pension age; or

(*d*) the circumstances referred to in regulation 3(2)(b)(i) apply.

Charges recoverable in respect of the provision of basic information

3.—(1) Subject to paragraph (2), the charges prescribed for the purposes of section 23(1)(d) of the 1999 Act (charges which a person responsible for a pension arrangement may recover in respect of supplying pension information in connection with divorce etc.) are any charges incurred by the person responsible for the pension arrangement in connection with the provision of any of the information set out in —

(*a*) regulation 2 of the Provision of Information Regulations which may be recovered in accordance with regulation 2(8) of these Regulations;

(*b*) regulation 4 of those Regulations; or

(*c*) regulation 10 of those Regulations.

(2) The charges mentioned in paragraph (1) shall not include any costs incurred by a person responsible for a pension arrangement in respect of the matters specified in sub-paragraphs (a) to (f) —

(*a*) any costs incurred by the person responsible for a pension arrangement which are directly related to the fulfilment of his obligations under regulation 2(3) of the Provision of Information Regulations, other than charges which may be recovered in the circumstances described in regulation 2(8) of these Regulations;

(*b*) any costs incurred by the person responsible for the pension arrangement as a result of complying with a request for, or an order of the court requiring, a valuation under regulation 2(2) of the Provision of Information Regulations, unless —

    (i) he is required by a member or a court to provide that valuation in less than 3 months beginning with the date the person responsible for the pension arrangement receives that request or order for the valuation;

    (ii) the valuation is requested by a member who is not entitled to a cash equivalent under any of the provisions referred to in regulation 2(4)(a);

    (iii) a member has requested a cash equivalent in accordance with any of those provisions within 12 months immediately prior to the date of the request for a valuation under regulation 2(2) of the Provision of Information Regulations;

(*c*) any costs incurred by the person responsible for the pension arrangement as a result of providing a valuation of benefits calculated and verified in accordance with regulation 3 of the Divorce etc. (Pensions) (Scotland) Regulations 2000 (valuation), unless —

    (i) he is required by the court to provide that valuation in less than 3 months beginning with the date the person responsible for the pension arrangement receives that order;

    (ii) the valuation is requested by a member who is not entitled to a cash equivalent under any of the provisions referred to in regulation 2(4)(a);

    (iii) a member has requested a cash equivalent in accordance with any of those provisions within 12 months immediately prior to the date of the request for a valuation under regulation 2(2) of the Provision of Information Regulations; or

(iv) the relevant date is more than 12 months immediately prior to the date the person responsible for the pension arrangement receives the request for the valuation;

(*d*) any costs incurred by the trustees or managers of —

(i)   an occupational pension scheme in connection with the provision of information under regulation 4 of the Occupational Pension Schemes (Disclosure of Information) Regulations 1996 (basic information about the scheme); or

(ii) a personal pension scheme in connection with the provision of information under regulation 4 of the Personal Pension Schemes (Disclosure of Information) Regulations 1987 (basic information about the scheme),

which the trustees or managers shall provide to the member free of charge under those Regulations;

(*e*) any costs incurred by the trustees or managers of an occupational pension scheme, or a personal pension scheme, as the case may be, in connection with the provision of a transfer value in accordance with the provisions of —

(i)   section 93A or 94 of the 1993 Act;

(ii) regulation 11(1) of the Occupational Pension Schemes (Transfer Values) Regulations 1996; or

(iii) regulation 5 of, and paragraph 2(b) of Schedule 2 to, the Personal Pension Schemes (Disclosure of Information) Regulations 1987; or

(*f*) any costs not specified by the person responsible for a pension arrangement in the information on charges provided to the member pursuant to regulation 2 of the Provision of Information Regulations with the exception of any additional amounts under regulation 6(1)(a) of these Regulations.

Charges in respect of the provision of information — method of recovery

4.—(1) A person responsible for a pension arrangement may recover the charges specified in regulation 3(1) by using either of the methods described in sub-paragraph (a) or (b) —

(*a*) requiring payment of charges at any specific time between the request for basic information and the completion of the implementation of a pension sharing order or provision, or the

compliance with an order specified in section 24 of the 1999 Act, as the case may be; or
(b) subject to paragraph (2), requiring as a condition of providing information in accordance with —
  (i) regulation 2 of the Provision of Information Regulations; or
  (ii) regulation 10 of those Regulations,

that payment of the charges to which regulation 3(1) refers shall be made in full by the member before the person responsible for the pension arrangement becomes obliged to provide the information.
(2) Paragraph (1)(b) shall not apply —

(a) where a court has ordered a member to obtain the information specified in regulation 2 of the Provision of Information Regulations;
(b) where, in accordance with regulation 2(8) of these Regulations, the person responsible for the pension arrangement shall provide that information without charge, or
(c) where the person responsible for the pension arrangement is required to supply that information by virtue of regulation 4 of the Provision of Information Regulations.

Charges in respect of pension sharing activity

5.—(1) The charges prescribed in respect of prescribed descriptions of pension sharing activity for the purposes of section 41(1) of the 1999 Act (charges in respect of pension sharing costs) are any costs reasonably incurred by the person responsible for the pension arrangement in connection with pension sharing activity other than those costs specified in paragraph (3).

(2) The descriptions of pension sharing activity prescribed for the purposes of section 41(1) of the 1999 Act are any type of activity which fulfills the requirements of section 41(5) of the 1999 Act.

(3) The costs specified in this paragraph are any costs which are not directly related to the costs which arise in relation to an individual case.

Additional amounts recoverable in respect of pension sharing activity

6.—(1) The circumstances in which a person responsible for a pension arrangement may recover additional amounts are —

(a) where a period of more than 12 months has elapsed between the person responsible for the pension arrangement supplying information in accordance with regulation 2 of the Provision of Information Regulations and the taking effect of an order or provision specified in subsection (1) of section 28 of the 1999 Act (activation of pension sharing); or

(b) in the case of an occupational pension scheme, where the trustees or managers of that scheme undertake activity from time to time associated with pension credit rights or pension credit benefit in that scheme which belong to a member.

(2) For the purposes of section 41(2)(d) of the 1999 Act, the additional amounts are —

(a) in the circumstances described in paragraph (1)(a), interest calculated at a rate not exceeding increases in the retail prices index on the amounts of any charges not yet due, or of any charges requested but yet to be recovered, which are specified in the schedule of charges issued to the member in accordance with regulation 2(2)(b) of these Regulations; and

(b) in the circumstances described in paragraph (1)(b), an amount not exceeding an increase calculated by reference to increases in the retail prices index on the amounts which relate to the costs referred to in regulation 2(4)(d) and which are specified in the schedule of charges provided to the member and the member's spouse or civil partner in accordance with regulation 2(2)(b).

(3) Where a person responsible for a pension arrangement intends to recover an additional amount specified in paragraph (2)(a) in the circumstances described in paragraph (1)(a), he shall set out this intention, the rate of interest to be used, and the total costs recoverable in the notice of implementation and final costs issued in accordance with regulation 7 of the Provision of Information Regulations (provision of information after receiving a pension sharing order or provision).

(4) Where the trustees or managers of an occupational pension scheme intend to recover an additional amount specified in paragraph (2)(b) in the circumstances described in paragraph (1)(b), they shall inform the parties involved in pension sharing in writing of this intention in the schedule of charges issued in accordance with regulation 2(2)(b) of these Regulations.

Charges in respect of pension sharing activity — postponement of implementation period

7.—(1) The circumstances when the start of the implementation period may be postponed are when a person responsible for a pension arrangement —

(*a*) issues a notice to the member and the person entitled to the pension credit no later than 21 days after the day on which the person responsible for the pension arrangement receives the pension sharing order or provision; and

(*b*) in that notice, requires the charges specified in regulation 3, 5 or 6 to be paid before the implementation of the pension sharing order or provision is commenced.

(2) Paragraph (1) shall apply only if the person responsible for the pension arrangement has specified at a stage no later than in his response to the notification that a pension sharing order or provision may be made, issued in accordance with regulation 4 of the Provision of Information Regulations —

(*a*) that he requires the charges mentioned in paragraph (1) to be paid before the implementation period is commenced; and either

(*b*) whether he requires those charges to be paid in full; or

(*c*) the proportion of those charges which he requires to be paid as full settlement of those charges.

(3) Once payment of the charges mentioned in paragraph (1) has been made in accordance with the requirements of the person responsible for the pension arrangement —

(*a*) that person shall —
  (i) issue the notice of implementation in accordance with regulation 7(1)(c) of the Provision of Information Regulations, and
  (ii) begin the implementation period for the pension credit,

within 21 days from the date the charges are paid, provided that the person responsible for the pension arrangement would otherwise be able to begin to implement the pension sharing order or provision, and

(*b*) subject to paragraph (4), that person shall not be entitled to recover any further charges in respect of the pension sharing order or provision in question.

(4) Paragraph (3)(b) shall not apply —

(*a*) in relation to the recovery of charges referred to in regulations 2(4)(d) and 6(2)(b); or

(*b*) where the pension credit depends on a pension sharing order and the order is the subject of an application for leave to appeal out of time.

Charges in respect of pension sharing activity — reimbursement as between the parties to pension sharing

8.—A payment in respect of charges recoverable under regulation 3, 5 or 6 made by one party to pension sharing on behalf of the other party to pension sharing, shall be recoverable by the party who made the payment from that other party as a debt.

Charges in respect of pension sharing activity — method of recovery

9.—(1) Subject to paragraphs (7) and (8), a person responsible for a pension arrangement may recover the charges specified in regulations 3, 5 and 6 by using any of the methods described in paragraph (2).

(2) The methods of recovery described in this paragraph are —

(*a*) subject to regulation 7 requiring the charges referred to in paragraph (1) to be paid before the implementation period for the pension sharing order or provision is commenced;

(*b*) deduction from a pension credit;

(*c*) deduction from the accrued rights of the member;

(*d*) where a pension sharing order or provision is made in respect of a pension which is in payment, deduction from the member's pension benefits;

(*e*) where liability in respect of a pension credit is discharged by the person responsible for the pension arrangement in accordance with paragraph 1(2), 2(2), or 3(2) of Schedule 5 to the 1999 Act (mode of discharge of liability for pension credits), deduction from payments of pension credit benefit; or

(*f*) deduction from the amount of a transfer value which is calculated in accordance with —

  (i) regulations 7 to 7E of the Occupational Pension Schemes (Transfer Values) Regulations 1996 (manner of calculation and verification of cash equivalents); or

  (ii) regulation 3 of the Personal Pension Schemes (Transfer Values) Regulations 1987 (manner of calculation and verification of cash equivalents).

(3) A person responsible for a pension arrangement shall not recover charges referred to in paragraph (1) by using any of the methods described in paragraph (2)(b), (c), (d), (e) or (f) unless —

(*a*) a pension sharing order or provision corresponding to any order or provision specified in subsection (1) of section 28 of the 1999 Act has been made;

(*b*) the implementation period has commenced;

(*c*) where a pension sharing order has been made, the person responsible for a pension arrangement is not aware of an appeal against the order having begun on or after the day on which the order takes effect;

(*d*) there are charges which are unpaid and for which the party, to whom paragraph (2)(b), (c), (d), (e) or (f) applies, is liable;

(*e*) the person responsible for the pension arrangement has issued a notice of implementation in accordance with regulation 7 of the Provision of Information Regulations;

(*f*) the person responsible for a pension arrangement specifies in the notice of implementation that recovery of the charges may be made by using any of those methods; and

(*g*) 21 days have elapsed since the notice of implementation was issued to the parties to pension sharing in accordance with the requirements of regulation 7 of the Provision of Information Regulations.

(4) If a pension sharing order or provision includes provision about the apportionment between the parties to pension sharing of any charge under section 41 of the 1999 Act or under corresponding Northern Ireland legislation, by virtue of section 24D of the Matrimonial Causes Act 1973 (pension sharing orders: apportionment of charges) or section 8A of the Family Law (Scotland) Act 1985 (pension sharing orders: apportionment of charges), the recovery of charges using any of the methods described in paragraph (2) by the person responsible for the pension arrangement shall comply with the terms of the order or provision.

(5) A person responsible for a pension arrangement shall not recover charges referred to in paragraph (1) by using any of the methods described in paragraph (2), from a party to pension sharing, if that party has paid in full the proportion of the charges for which he is liable.

(6) A person responsible for a pension arrangement may recover charges by using any of the methods described in paragraph (2)(b), (c) or (d) —

(*a*) at any time within the implementation period prescribed by section 34 of the 1999 Act ("implementation period");

(*b*) following an application by the trustees or managers of an occupational pension scheme, such longer period as the Pensions Regulator may allow in accordance with section 33(4) of the 1999 Act (extension of time for discharge of liability); or

(*c*) within 21 days after the end of the period referred to in sub-paragraph (a) or (b).

(7) Where the commencement of the implementation period is

postponed, or its operation ceases in accordance with regulation 4 of the Pension Sharing (Implementation and Discharge of Liability) Regulations 2000 (postponement or cessation of implementation period where an application is made for leave to appeal out of time) a person responsible for a pension arrangement may require any outstanding charges referred to in paragraph (1) to be paid immediately, in respect of —

(*a*) all costs which have been incurred prior to the date of postponement or cessation; or

(*b*) any reasonable costs related to —
   (i)   the application for leave to appeal out of time; or
   (ii) the appeal out of time itself.

(8) Paragraph (7) applies even if, prior to receiving the notification of the application for leave to appeal out of time, a person responsible for a pension arrangement has indicated to the parties to pension sharing that he will not be using the method of recovery specified in paragraph (2)(a).

Charges in relation to earmarking orders

10.—The prescribed charges which a person responsible for a pension arrangement may recover in respect of complying with an order specified in section 24 of the 1999 Act are those charges which represent the reasonable administrative expenses which he has incurred or is likely to incur by reason of the order.

F. The Pensions on Divorce etc. (Pension Sharing) (Scotland) Regulations 2000[6] (S.I. 2000 No. 1051)

The Secretary of State for Social Security, in exercise of the powers conferred upon him by sections 28(1)(f)(ii) and (3)(a) and 48(1)(f) (ii) and (3)(a) of the Welfare Reform and Pensions Act 1999 and of all other powers enabling him in that behalf, after consulting such persons as he considered appropriate, hereby makes the following Regulations:

---

[6] As amended by S.I. 2007 No. 814.

Citation, commencement and interpretation

1.—(1) These Regulations may be cited as the Pensions on Divorce etc. (Pension Sharing) (Scotland) Regulations 2000 and shall come into force on 1st December 2000.

(2) In these Regulations —

"the 1985 Act" means the Family Law (Scotland) Act 1985;

"the 1999 Act" means the Welfare Reform and Pensions Act 1999;

"pension arrangement" has the meaning given by section 46(1) of the 1999 Act;

"qualifying arrangement" has the meaning given by paragraph 6 of Schedule 5 to the 1999 Act;

"transferee" and "transferor" have, in regulations 2 and 3, the meaning given by section 29(8), and, in regulations 4 and 5, the meaning given by section 49(6), of the 1999 Act.

Sharing of Rights under Pension Arrangements

Prescribed form of provision corresponding to provision in a pension sharing order under the 1985 Act

2. For the purposes of section 28(1)(f)(ii) of the 1999 Act, the provision which corresponds to the provision which may be made by a pension sharing order under the 1985 Act shall be in a form which contains in an annex to, and which is separable from, the qualifying agreement referred to in section 28(1)(f)(i) of the 1999 Act, the following information —

(*a*) in relation to the party who is the transferor —
    (i)   all names by which the transferor has been known;
    (ii) date of birth;
    (iii) address;
    (iv) national insurance number;
    (v) the name and address of the pension arrangement to which the pension sharing provision relates, and
    (vi) the transferor's membership number or policy number in that pension arrangement;

(*b*) in relation to the party who is the transferee —
    (i)   all names by which the transferee has been known;
    (ii) date of birth;
    (iii) address;
    (iv) national insurance number, and

(v)   if the transferee is a member of the pension arrangement from which a pension credit is derived, his membership number in that pension arrangement;

(c)   details of —
  (i)   the amount to be transferred to the transferee, or
  (ii) the specified percentage of the cash equivalent of the relevant benefits on the valuation day to be transferred to the transferee;

(d)   where the transferee has given his consent, in accordance with paragraph 1(3)(c), 3(3)(c), or 4(2)(c) of Schedule 5 to the 1999 Act (mode of discharge of liability for a pension credit), to the payment of a pension credit to the person responsible for a qualifying arrangement —
  (i)   the full name of that qualifying arrangement;
  (ii)   its address;
  (iii) if known, the transferee's membership number or policy number in that arrangement, and
  (iv)   the name or title, business address, business telephone number and, where available, the business facsimile number and electronic mail address of a person who may be contacted in respect of the discharge of liability for the pension credit;

(e)   details of the provision about the apportionment (if any) made by the transferor and the transferee of liability for any charges levied by the person responsible for the pension arrangement in relation to pension sharing under Chapter I of Part IV of the 1999 Act, and

(f)   confirmation by the transferor that he has intimated to the pension arrangement his intention with respect to pension sharing and that the pension arrangement has acknowledged receipt of the intimation.

Circumstances in which an agreement is to be entered into, in order to be considered a "qualifying agreement" under section 28(1)(f) of the 1999 Act

3. A qualifying agreement is, for the purposes of section 28(1)(f) of the 1999 Act, one which the transferor and transferee have entered into in order to determine the financial settlement on divorce or dissolution of a civil partnership and in respect of which the transferor has intimated to the person responsible for a pension arrangement prior to the making of the agreement the intention to have the transferor's pension rights under the pension arrangement shared with the transferee.

Sharing of State Scheme Rights

Prescribed form of provision corresponding to provision in a pension sharing order under the 1985 Act

4. For the purposes of section 48(1)(f)(ii) of the 1999 Act, the provision which corresponds to the provision which may be made by a pension sharing order under the 1985 Act shall be in a form which contains in an annex to, and which is separable from, the qualifying agreement referred to in section 48(1)(f)(i) of the 1999 Act, the following information —

(*a*) in relation to the party who is the transferor —
    (i) full name;
    (ii) date of birth;
    (iii) address;
    (iv) national insurance number, and
    (v) details of the specified amount or, as appropriate, the specified percentage of the cash equivalent on the transfer day of the transferor's relevant state scheme rights immediately before that day;

(*b*) in relation to the party who is the transferee —
    (i) full name by which the transferee is or will be known;
    (ii) date of birth;
    (iii) address, and
    (iv) national insurance number, and

(*c*) a statement by the transferor and the transferee that they have received confirmation from the Secretary of State that shareable state scheme rights are held in the name of the transferor and that on the —
    (i) grant of decree of divorce;
    (ii) declarator of nullity of marriage;
    (iii) dissolution of civil partnership; and
    (iv) declarator of nullity of civil partnership,
    a pension sharing agreement will be implemented.

Circumstances in which an agreement is to be entered into, in order to be considered a "qualifying agreement" under section 48(1)(f) of the 1999 Act

5. A qualifying agreement is, for the purposes of section 48(1)(f) of the 1999 Act, one which the transferor and transferee have entered into in order to determine the financial settlement on divorce or dissolution of a civil partnership and in respect of which they have received confirmation from the Secretary of State that shareable state scheme rights are held in the name of the transferor.

G. The Pension Sharing (Valuation) Regulations 2000[7]
(S.I. 2000 No. 1052)

The Secretary of State for Social Security, in exercise of the powers conferred upon him by sections 27(2), 30(1) and (2) and 83(4) and (6) of the Welfare Reform and Pensions Act 1999, and of all other powers enabling him in that behalf, after consulting such persons as he considered appropriate, hereby makes the following Regulations:

Citation, commencement and interpretation

1.—(1) These Regulations may be cited as the Pension Sharing (Valuation) Regulations 2000 and shall come into force on 1st December 2000.

(2) In these Regulations —

"the 1993 Act" means the Pension Schemes Act 1993;
"the 1995 Act" means the Pensions Act 1995;
"the 1999 Act" means the Welfare Reform and Pensions Act 1999;
"the 2004 Act" means the Pensions Act 2004;
"employer" has the meaning given by section 181(1) of the 1993 Act;
"initial cash equivalent" means the amount calculated in accordance with regulation 7(1)(a) of the Transfer Values Regulations;
"occupational pension scheme" has the meaning given by section 1 of the 1993 Act;
"pension arrangement" has the meaning given by section 46(1) of the 1999 Act;
"relevant arrangement" has the meaning given by section 29(8) of the 1999 Act;
"scheme" means an occupational pension scheme;
"transfer credits" has the meaning given by section 181(1) of the 1993 Act;
"transfer day" has the meaning given by section 29(8) of the 1999 Act;
"the Transfer Values Regulations" means the Occupational Pension Schemes (Transfer Values) Regulations 1996;
"transferor" has the meaning given by section 29(8) of the 1999 Act;

---

[7] As amended by S.I. 2000 No.2691, S.I. 2005 No. 2877, S.I. 2005 No. 3377, S.I. 2006 No. 744 and S.I. 2008 No. 1050.

"trustees or managers" has the meaning given by section 46(1) of the 1999 Act;

"valuation day" has the meaning given by section 29(7) of the 1999 Act.

Rights under a pension arrangement which are not shareable

2.—(1) Rights under a pension arrangement which are not shareable are —

(*a*) subject to paragraph (2), any rights accrued between 1961 and 1975 which relate to contracted-out equivalent pension benefit within the meaning of section 57 of the National Insurance Act 1965 (equivalent pension benefits, etc.);

(*b*) any rights in respect of which a person is in receipt of —
  (i) a pension;
  (ii) an annuity;
  (iii) payments under an interim arrangement within the meaning of section 28(1A) of the 1993 Act (ways of giving effect to protected rights); or
  (iv) dependants' income withdrawal within the meaning of paragraph 21 of Schedule 28 to the Finance Act 2004 (dependants' income withdrawal).

by virtue of being the widow, widower, surviving civil partner or other dependant of a deceased person with pension rights under a pension arrangement; and

(*c*) any rights which will result in the payment of a benefit which is to be provided solely by reason of the—
  (i) disablement, or
  (ii) death,

due to an accident suffered by a person occurring during his pensionable service.

(2) Paragraph (1)(a) applies only when those rights are the only rights held by a person under a pension arrangement.

Calculation and verification of cash equivalents for the purposes of the creation of pension debits and credits

3. For the purposes of section 29 of the 1999 Act (creation of pension debits and credits), cash equivalents may be calculated and verified —

(*a*) where the relevant arrangement is an occupational pension scheme in accordance with regulations 4 and 5; or

(*b*) in any other case, in accordance with regulations 6 and 7.

Manner of calculation and verification of cash equivalents: occupational pension schemes

4.—(1) Subject to this regulation, cash equivalents for members of occupational pension schemes are to be calculated and verified in accordance with regulations 7 to 7E of the Transfer Values regulations.

(2) Reductions to initial cash equivalents can only be made in accordance with regulation 7D of, and paragraphs 1 to 6 and 12 to 14 of Schedule 1A to, those Regulations.

(3) The reduction referred to in paragraph 2 of Schedule 1A to the Transfer Values Regulations must not be applied to a case where liability in respect of a pension credit is to be discharged in accordance with—

    (*a*) paragraph 1(2) of Schedule 5 to the 1999 Act (pension credits: mode of discharge—funded pension schemes); or

    (*b*) paragraph 1(3) of that Schedule, in a case where regulation 7(2) of the Pension Sharing (Implementation and Discharge of Liability) Regulations 2000 (funded pension schemes) applies.

(4) When calculating and verifying the cash equivalent, the Transfer Values Regulations are to be read as if—

    (*a*) in regulation 1(2) (interpretation), there were inserted at the appropriate alphabetical places—

      "'normal pension age' has the meaning given by section 180 of the 1993 Act (normal pension age);"

      "'occupational pension scheme' has the meaning given by section 1 of the 1993 Act (categories of pension scheme);"

      "'transfer day' has the meaning given by section 29(8) of the Welfare Reform and Pensions Act 1999 (creation of pension debits and credits);"

      "'valuation day' has the meaning given by section 29(7) of the Welfare Reform and Pensions Act 1999;"

    (*b*) in regulation 7(1) (manner of calculation and verification of cash equivalents—general provisions), for "paragraphs (4) and (7)" there were substituted "paragraphs (4), (7) and (8) to (11)"; and

    (*c*) after regulation 7(7), there were inserted—

      "(8) Where the person with pension rights is a deferred member of an occupational pension scheme on the transfer day, the value of the benefits which he has accrued under that scheme must be taken to be—

        (a) in the case of an occupational pension scheme other

than a salary related scheme, the cash equivalent to which he acquired a right under section 94(1) (a) of the 1993 Act (right to cash equivalent) on the termination of his pensionable service, calculated and verified on the assumption that he has made an application under section 95(1) of that Act (ways of taking right to cash equivalent); or

(b) in the case of a salary related occupational pension scheme, the guaranteed cash equivalent to which he would have acquired a right under section 94(1) (aa) of the 1993 Act if he had made an application under section 95(1) of that Act.

(9) Where the person with pension rights is an active member of an occupational pension scheme on the transfer day, the value of the benefits which he has accrued under that scheme must be calculated and verified on the assumption that the member had made a request for an estimate of the cash equivalent that would be available to him were his pensionable service to terminate on the transfer day.

(10) Where the person with pension rights is a pensioner member of an occupational pension scheme on the transfer day, the value of his pension must be calculated and verified in accordance with this regulation and regulations 7A to 7C and 7E(1) to (3) as appropriate.

(11) Where the person with pension rights attains, or is over, normal pension age and is not in receipt of a pension—

(a) the pension must be calculated and verified in accordance with this regulation and regulations 7A to 7C and 7E(1) to (3) as appropriate; and

(b) the trustees must assume that the member's pension comes into payment on the transfer day."

Manner of calculation and verification of cash equivalents: other relevant arrangements

5.—(1) Subject to this regulation, cash equivalents for members of a relevant arrangement other than an occupational pension scheme are to be calculated and verified in accordance with regulations 7 to 7E of the Transfer Values Regulations.

(2) When calculating and verifying the cash equivalent, the Transfer Values Regulations are to be read as if—

(a) in regulation 1(2)—
   (i) for the definition of "trustees" there were substituted—
      "'trustees' means the person responsible for the relevant arrangement;" and

(ii) there were inserted at the appropriate alphabetical places—

"'personal pension scheme' has the meaning given by section 1 of the 1993 Act (categories of pension scheme)";

"'transfer day' has the meaning given by section 29(8) of the Welfare Reform and Pensions Act 1999 (creation of pension debits and credits);"

(*b*) in regulation 7(1) (manner of calculation and verification of cash equivalents—general provisions), for "paragraphs (4) and (7)" there were substituted "paragraphs (4), (7) and (8)"; and

(*c*) after regulation 7(7), there were inserted—

"(8) Where the person with pension rights is a member of a personal pension scheme, or those rights are contained in a retirement annuity contract, the value of the benefits which he has accrued under that scheme or contract on the transfer day must be taken to be the cash equivalent to which he would have acquired a right under section 94(1)(b) of the 1993 Act (right to cash equivalent), if he had made an application under section 95(1) of that Act (ways of taking right to cash equivalent) on the date on which the request for the valuation was received."

(3) In relation to a personal pension scheme which is comprised in a retirement annuity contract made before 4th January 1988, this regulation applies as if such a scheme were not excluded from the scope of Chapter IV of Part IV of the 1993 Act by section 93(1)(b) of that Act (scope of Chapter IV).

Other relevant arrangements: reduction of cash equivalents

7.—(1) Where all or any of the benefits to which a cash equivalent relates have been surrendered, commuted or fortified before the date on which the person responsible for the relevant arrangement discharges his liability for the pension credit in accordance with the provisions of Schedule 5 to the 1999 Act, the cash equivalent of the benefits so surrendered, commuted or fortified shall be reduced in proportion to the reduction in the total value of the benefits.

(2) This regulation does not apply to occupational pension schemes.

H. The Pension Sharing (Implementation and Discharge of Liability) Regulations 2000[8] (S.I. 2000 No. 1053)

ARRANGEMENT OF REGULATIONS

PART I

---

[8]As amended by S.I. 2000 No. 2691, S.I. 2005 No. 2877, S.I. 2005 No. 3377, S.I. 2006 No. 744, S.I. 2008 No. 1050 and S.I. 2009 No. 615.

14. Disqualification as a destination for pension credit — occupational pension schemes
15. Disqualification as a destination for pension credit — annuity contracts and insurance policies
16. Adjustments to the amount of the pension credit — occupational pension schemes which are underfunded on the valuation day
17. Adjustments to the amount of the pension credit — payment made without knowledge of the pension debit
18. Adjustments to the amount of the pension credit — increasing the amount of the pension credit

The Secretary of State for Social Security, in exercise of the powers conferred upon him by sections 10(2)(b), 124(1) and 174(2) and (3) of the Pensions Act 1995, sections 33(2)(a) and (4), 34(4)(c), 35(2)(b) and 83(4) and (6) of, and paragraphs 1(2)(b), (3)(c), 3(3)(c), 4(2)(c), (4), 5(b), 6(2)(b), 7(1)(b), (2)(a), (2)(b), (3), (4), (6), 8(1), (2), 9, 10, and 13 of Schedule 5 to, the Welfare Reform and Pensions Act 1999, and of all other powers enabling him in that behalf, after consulting such persons as he considered appropriate, hereby makes the following Regulations:

PART I

GENERAL

Citation, commencement and interpretation

1.—(1) These Regulations may be cited as the Pension Sharing (Implementation and Discharge of Liability) Regulations 2000 and shall come into force on 1 December 2000.

(2) In these Regulations —

"the 1993 Act" means the Pension Schemes Act 1993;
"the 1995 Act" means the Pensions Act 1995;
"the 1999 Act" means the Welfare Reform and Pensions Act 1999;
"the 2004 Act" means the Pensions Act 2004;
"base rate" means the base rate for the time being quoted by the reference banks or, where there is for the time being more than one such base rate, the base rate which, when the base rate quoted by each bank is ranked in a descending sequence of seven, is fourth in the sequence;
"the implementation period" has the meaning given by section 34 of the 1999 Act;
"the Inland Revenue" means the Commissioners of Inland Revenue;
"normal benefit age" has the meaning given by section 101B of the 1993 Act;

"occupational pension scheme" has the meaning given by section 1 of the 1993 Act;

"pension arrangement" has the meaning given by section 46(1) of the 1999 Act;

"pension credit" means a credit under section 29(1)(b) of the 1999 Act;

"pension sharing order" means an order which is mentioned in section 28(1) of the 1999 Act;

"pension sharing order or provision" means an order or provision which is mentioned in section 28(1) of the 1999 Act;

"personal pension scheme" has the meaning given by section 1 of the 1993 Act;

"person responsible for a pension arrangement" has the meaning given to that expression in section 46(2) of the 1999 Act;

"the reference banks" means the seven largest institutions for the time being which —

(a)　are authorised by the Financial Services Authority under the Banking Act 1987;

(b)　are incorporated in and carrying on within the United Kingdom a deposit-taking business (as defined in section 6, but subject to any order under section 7 of that Act); and

(c)　quote a base rate in sterling;

and for the purpose of this definition the size of an institution at any time is to be determined by reference to the gross assets denominated in sterling of that institution, together with any subsidiary (as defined in section 736 of the Companies Act 1985), as shown in the audited end of year accounts last published before that time;

"the Regulatory Authority" means the Pensions Regulator;

"safeguarded rights" has the meaning given in section 68A(1) of the 1993 Act;

"section 9(2B) rights" has the meaning given in regulation 1(2) of the Occupational Pension Schemes (Contracting-out) Regulations 1996;

"the Transfer Values Regulations" means the Occupational Pension Schemes (Transfer Values) Regulations 1996;

"transferee" has the meaning given by section 34(5) of the 1999 Act;

"transferor" has the meaning given by section 34(5) of the 1999 Act;

"trustees or managers", in relation to an occupational pension scheme or a personal pension scheme means —

(a)　in the case of a scheme established under a trust, the trustees of the scheme, and

(b)　in any other case, the managers of the scheme;

"the valuation day" has the meaning given in section 29(7) of the 1999 Act.

PART II

EXTENSION, POSTPONEMENT OR CESSATION OF IMPLEMENTATION PERIOD

Time period for notification to the Regulatory Authority of failure by the trustees or managers of an occupational pension scheme to discharge their liability in respect of a pension credit

2. The period prescribed for the purposes of section 33(2)(a) of the 1999 Act (period within which notice must be given of non-discharge of pension credit liability) is the period of 21 days beginning with the day immediately following the end of the implementation period.

Circumstances in which an application for an extension of the implementation period may be made

3. The circumstances in which an application may be made for the purposes of section 33(4) of the 1999 Act (application for extension of period within which pension credit liability is to be discharged) are that the application is made to the Regulatory Authority before the end of the implementation period; and —

(*a*) the Regulatory Authority is satisfied that —
  (i)   the scheme is being wound up or is about to be wound up;
  (ii) the scheme is ceasing to be a contracted-out scheme;
  (iii) the financial interests of the members of the scheme generally will be prejudiced if the trustees or managers do what is needed to discharge their liability for the pension credit within that period;
  (iv) the transferor or the transferee has not taken such steps as the trustees or managers can reasonably expect in order to satisfy them of any matter which falls to be established before they can properly discharge their liability for the pension credit;
  (v)   the trustees or managers have not been provided with such information as they reasonably require properly to discharge their liability for the pension credit within the implementation period;
  (vi) the transferor or the transferee has disputed the amount of the cash equivalent calculated and verified for the purposes of section 29 of the 1999 Act (creation of pension debits and credits);
(*b*) the provisions of section 53 of the 1993 Act (supervision: former contracted-out schemes) apply; or

(*c*) the application has been made on one or more of the grounds specified in paragraph (a) or (b), and the Regulatory Authority's consideration of the application cannot be completed before the end of the implementation period.

Postponement or cessation of implementation period when an application is made for leave to appeal out of time

4.—(1) The modifications to the operation of section 34 of the 1999 Act ("implementation period") where the pension credit depends on a pension sharing order and the order is the subject of an application for leave to appeal out of time are —

(*a*) where the implementation period has not commenced, its commencement shall be postponed; or

(*b*) where the implementation period has commenced, its operation shall cease and it shall not commence afresh until the person responsible for the pension arrangement has received the documents referred to in paragraph (2).

(2) The postponement or cessation referred to in paragraph (1) (a) or (b) shall continue until the person responsible for the pension arrangement is in receipt of —

(*a*) confirmation from the court that the order which was the subject of the application for leave to appeal out of time has not been varied or discharged; or

(*b*) a copy of the varied pension sharing order.

(3) Where the person responsible for the pension arrangement has discharged his liability in respect of the pension credit which depends on a pension sharing order and that person subsequently receives notification of an application for leave to appeal out of time in respect of that order, he shall inform the court within 21 days from the date on which he received the notification that liability in respect of that pension credit has been discharged.

Civil penalties

5. For the purpose of section 33(2)(b) or (3) of the 1999 Act, the maximum amount of the penalty which may be imposed by the Regulatory Authority under section 10(2)(b) of the 1995 Act is —

(*a*) £1,000 in the case of an individual, and

(*b*) £10,000 in any other case.

PART III

DEATH OF PERSON ENTITLED TO A PENSION CREDIT BEFORE LIABILITY IN RESPECT OF THE PENSION CREDIT IS DISCHARGED

Discharge of liability in respect of a pension credit following the death of the person entitled to the pension credit

6.—(1) The person responsible for the pension arrangement shall following the death of the person entitled to the pension credit discharge his liability in respect of a pension credit in accordance with this regulation.

(2) Where the rules or provisions of a pension arrangement so provide and provided that any requirements of the Inland Revenue under Part 4 of the Finance Act 2004 (pension schemes etc) are satisfied, the person responsible for the pension arrangement shall discharge his liability in respect of a pension credit by undertaking to —

(*a*)   make —
   (i) a payment of a lump sum; or
   (ii) payments of a pension; or
   (iii) payments of both a lump sum and a pension,

to one or more persons; or

(*b*)   enter into an annuity contract or take out a policy of insurance with an insurance company for the benefit of one or more persons; or

(*c*)   make a payment or, as the case may be, payments under sub-paragraph (a) and enter into an annuity contract or take out an insurance policy under sub-paragraph (b).

(3) Where paragraph (2)(b) or (c) applies, the annuity contract entered into or insurance policy taken out must satisfy the requirements of paragraph 6(2) of Schedule 5 to the 1999 Act (qualifying arrangements) and regulation 11 of these Regulations.

(4) Where the provisions of paragraph (2) do not apply, liability in respect of a pension credit shall be discharged by retaining the value of the pension credit in the pension arrangement from which that pension credit was derived.

(5) Where —

(*a*)   liability in respect of a pension credit has been discharged in accordance with paragraph (2); and (*b*) the value of the payment or payments made, the annuity contract entered into or the insurance policy taken out, as the case may be, is less than the value of the pension credit,

the value of an amount equal to the difference between the value of the pension credit and the value of that payment or those payments, that contract or policy, as the case may be, shall be retained in the pension arrangement from which that pension credit was derived.

PART IV

DISCHARGE OF LIABILITY IN RESPECT OF A PENSION CREDIT

Funded pension schemes

7.—(1) The circumstances in which the trustees or managers of a scheme, to which paragraph 1 of Schedule 5 to the 1999 Act applies, may discharge their liability in respect of a pension credit in accordance with sub-paragraph (2)(b) of that paragraph are where —

(*a*) the person entitled to the credit has failed to provide his consent in accordance with paragraph 1(2)(a) and (4) of that Schedule; and
(*b*) the circumstances set out in paragraph 1(3) of that Schedule do not apply.

(2) The circumstances in which the trustees or managers of a scheme, to which paragraph 1 of Schedule 5 to the 1999 Act applies, may discharge their liability in respect of a pension credit in accordance with sub-paragraph (3)(c) of that paragraph are where —

(*a*) the person entitled to the credit has failed to provide his consent in accordance with paragraph 1(3)(c) of that Schedule; and
(*b*) either —
　(i) the person entitled to the pension credit has failed to provide his consent in accordance with paragraph 1(2) (a) and (4) of that Schedule; or
　(ii) the trustees or managers of the scheme have not discharged their liability in accordance with paragraph (1) above.

Unfunded occupational pension schemes other than public service pension schemes

8.—(1) The circumstances in which the trustees or managers of a scheme, to which paragraph 3 of Schedule 5 to the 1999 Act applies, may discharge their liability in respect of a pension credit in accordance with sub-paragraph (3)(c) of that paragraph are those specified in —

(*a*) sub-paragraphs (a) and (b) of paragraph (2), in the case of a registered scheme; and

(*b*) sub-paragraphs (a), (b) and (c) of paragraph (2), in the case of an unregistered scheme.

(2) The circumstances specified in this paragraph are —

(*a*) the liability of the trustees or managers has not been discharged in accordance with the provisions of paragraph 3(2) of that Schedule;

(*b*) the person entitled to the pension credit has not consented to the discharge of liability in accordance with paragraph 3(3) of that Schedule; and

(*c*) the employer who is associated with the scheme from which the pension credit derives —

(i) consents to the trustees or managers discharging their liability for the credit in accordance with paragraph 3(3) of that Schedule; and

(ii) agrees to compensate the person entitled to the credit fully for any tax liability which he may incur as a result of the trustees or managers of the scheme discharging their liability for the credit in accordance with paragraph 3(3) of that Schedule.

(3) In this Regulation—

(*a*) "registered scheme" means an occupational pension scheme which is registered under section 153 of the Finance Act 2004; and

(*b*) "unregistered scheme" means an occupational pension scheme which is not a registered scheme under section 153 of the Finance Act 2004.

Other pension arrangements

9.—(1) The circumstances in which the person responsible for a pension arrangement, to which paragraph 4 of Schedule 5 to the 1999 Act applies, may discharge his liability in respect of a pension credit in accordance with sub-paragraph (2)(c) of that paragraph are where his liability has not been discharged in accordance with the provisions of paragraph 4(3) or (4) of that Schedule.

(2) The circumstances in which the person responsible for the pension arrangement may discharge his liability in respect of the pension credit under paragraph 4(4) of Schedule 5 to the 1999 Act are where the person responsible for the pension arrangement has not discharged his liability in accordance with the provisions of —

(*a*) paragraph (1) above;
(*b*) paragraph 4(2) of that Schedule; or
(*c*) paragraph 4(3) of that Schedule.

Calculation of the value of appropriate rights

10. The value of rights conferred on a person entitled to a pension credit are to be calculated in a manner which is consistent with the methods adopted and assumptions made when transfers of other pension rights are received by the person responsible for the pension arrangement.

Qualifying arrangements

11.—(1) The requirements referred to in paragraph 6(2)(b) of Schedule 5 to the 1999 Act (requirements applying to annuity contracts or policies of insurance for the purpose of sub-paragraph (1) of that paragraph) are that the annuity contract is entered into or the insurance policy is taken out with an insurance company which is —

(*a*) authorised under section 3 or 4 of the Insurance Companies Act 1982 (authorisation of insurance business) to carry on long term business (within the meaning of section 1 of that Act (classification));
(*b*) in the case of a friendly society authorised under section 32 of the Friendly Societies Act 1992 (grant of authorisation by Commission: general) to carry out long term business under any of the Classes specified in Head A of Schedule 2 to that Act (the activities of a friendly society: long term business); or
(*c*) an EC company as defined in section 2 of the Insurance Companies Act 1982 (restriction on carrying on insurance business), and which falls within paragraph (2).

(2) An EC company falls within this paragraph if it —

(*a*) carries on ordinary long term insurance business (within the meaning of section 96(1) of the Insurance Companies Act 1982) in the United Kingdom through a branch in respect of which such of the requirements of Part I of Schedule 2F to that Act (recognition in the United Kingdom of EC and EFTA companies: EC companies carrying on business etc. in the United Kingdom) as are applicable have been complied with; or

(*b*) provides ordinary long term insurance in the United Kingdom and such of the requirements of Part I of Schedule 2F to that Act as are applicable have been complied with in respect of insurance.

Disqualification as a destination for pension credit — general

12. The requirements referred to in paragraph 7(1)(b) of Schedule 5 to the 1999 Act (requirements to be satisfied to qualify pension arrangements as destinations for pension credits) are that the pension arrangement —

(*a*) is an arrangement which carries on pension business as defined by section 431B of the Income and Corporation Taxes Act 1988 (meaning of "pension business");

(*b*) is an overseas arrangement within the meaning given by regulation 1(2) of the Contracting-out (Transfer and Transfer Payment) Regulations 1996 (citation, commencement and interpretation); or

(*c*) is an overseas scheme within the meaning given by regulation 1(2) of the Contracting-out (Transfer and Transfer Payment) Regulations 1996.

Disqualification as a destination for pension credit — contracted-out or safeguarded rights

13.—(1) The descriptions of pension arrangements referred to in paragraph 7(2)(a) of Schedule 5 to the 1999 Act (pension arrangements which qualify as destinations for pension credits, where the rights by reference to which the amount of the credits are determined are or include contracted-out rights or safeguarded rights) are —

(*a*) a contracted-out salary related occupational pension scheme which satisfies the requirements of section 9(2) of the 1993 Act (requirements for certification of occupational salary related schemes);

(*b*) a contracted-out money purchase occupational pension scheme which satisfies the requirements of section 9(3) of the 1993 Act (requirements for certification of occupational money purchase schemes);

(*bb*) a contracted-out occupational pension scheme to which section 149 of the 1995 Act (hybrid occupational pension schemes) applies;

(*c*) an appropriate personal pension scheme within the meaning of section 7(4) of the 1993 Act (issue of appropriate scheme certificates);

(*d*) an annuity contract or an insurance policy which satisfies the requirements of paragraph 6 of Schedule 5 to the 1999 Act (qualifying arrangements);

(*e*) an overseas arrangement within the meaning given by regulation 1(2) of the Contracting-out (Transfer and Transfer Payment) Regulations 1996; or

(*f*) an overseas scheme within the meaning given by regulation 1(2) of the Contracting-out (Transfer and Transfer Payment) Regulations 1996.

(2) The requirements referred to in paragraph 7(2)(b) of Schedule 5 to the 1999 Act (requirements to be satisfied by a pension arrangement which qualifies as a destination for a pension credit, where the rights by reference to which the amount of the credit are determined are or include contracted-out rights or safeguarded rights) are —

(*a*) in relation to the descriptions of pension arrangement referred to in paragraph (1)(a) to (d), the requirements specified in the Pension Sharing (Safeguarded Rights) Regulations 2000 to be met by an occupational pension scheme or a personal pension scheme;

(*b*) in relation to the descriptions of pension arrangement referred to in paragraph (1)(e), the requirements specified in regulation 15 (disqualification as a destination for pension credit — annuity contracts and insurance policies) and regulation 7(3) and (4) of the Pension Sharing (Safeguarded Rights) Regulations 2000 (the pension and annuity requirements — money purchase schemes);

(*c*) in relation to the descriptions of pension arrangement referred to in paragraph (1)(f) and (g), the requirements specified in regulation 11 of the Contracting-out (Transfer and Transfer Payment) Regulations 1996 (transfer payments to overseas schemes or arrangements in respect of section 9(2B) rights), as if the references in that regulation to —

    (i) "earner" were to "the person entitled to a pension credit"; and

    (ii) "accrued section 9(2B) rights" were to "safeguarded rights".

(3) The rights for the purposes of paragraph 7(6) of Schedule 5 to the 1999 Act (meaning of "contracted-out" rights under or derived from an occupational pension scheme or a personal pension scheme)

are those which fall within the categories specified in regulation 2 of the Pension Sharing (Safeguarded Rights) Regulations 2000 (definition of contracted-out rights).

Disqualification as a destination for pension credit — occupational pension schemes

14. The calculation of the value of the rights of the person entitled to the pension credit for the purposes of paragraph 7(3) of Schedule 5 to the 1999 Act shall be made in accordance with the methods adopted and assumptions made by the scheme which are consistent with the methods adopted and assumptions made by that scheme when transfers of other pension rights are received by the scheme.

Disqualification as a destination for pension credit — annuity contracts and insurance policies

15.—(1) The circumstances referred to in paragraph 7(4) of Schedule 5 to the 1999 Act (circumstances in which an annuity contract or insurance policy is disqualified as a destination for pension credit) are where the requirements specified in paragraphs (2) to (7) are not satisfied.

(2) The annuity contract or insurance policy must provide that that contract or policy, as the case may be, may not be assigned or surrendered unless —

(*a*)   the person entitled to the pension credit; or

(*b*)   if the person entitled to the pension credit has died, his widow, widower or surviving civil partner.

has consented to the assignment or surrender.

(3) The benefits previously secured by the annuity contract or insurance policy become secured, or are replaced by benefits which are secured by another qualifying arrangement.

(4) The annuity contract or insurance policy, as the case may be, must provide that the benefits secured by that contract or policy may be commuted if either —

(*a*)   the conditions set out in paragraph (5) are satisfied; or

(*b*)   the conditions set out in paragraph (6) are satisfied.

(5) The conditions referred to in paragraph (4)(a) are —

(*a*)   the benefits secured by the annuity contract or insurance policy have become payable;

(*b*) any lump sum payment—
    (i)   is permitted by the lump sum rule in section 166 of the Finance Act 2004; and
    (ii) qualifies as a trivial commutation lump sum for the purposes of paragraph 7 of Part I of Schedule 29 to that Act;
(*c*) all of the interest of the person entitled to the pension credit under the annuity contract or insurance policy is discharged upon payment of a lump sum.

(6) The conditions referred to in paragraph (4)(b) are —

(*a*) the benefits secured by the annuity contract or insurance policy have become payable and the person entitled to the pension credit requests or consents to the commutation;
(*b*) the person entitled to the pension credit is suffering from serious ill health prior to normal benefit age; and
(*c*) the insurance company with which the annuity contract is entered into, or with which the insurance policy is taken out, assumes an obligation to pay the benefits secured by the annuity contract or insurance policy to —
    (i)   the person entitled to the pension credit;
    (ii) the trustees of a trust for the benefit of the person entitled to the pension credit; or
    (iii) the trustees of a trust for the benefit of the dependants of the person entitled to the pension credit.

(7) The annuity contract or insurance policy must contain, or be endorsed with, terms so as to provide for any increase in accordance with regulation 32 of the Pension Sharing (Pension Credit Benefit) Regulations 2000 (increase of relevant pension) which would have been applied to the benefits which have become secured or been replaced by the annuity contract or insurance policy had the discharge of liability not taken place.

(8) In this regulation —

> "serious ill health" means ill health which is such as to give rise to a life expectancy of less than one year from the date on which commutation of the benefits secured by the annuity contract or insurance policy is applied for.

Adjustments to the amount of the pension credit — occupational pension schemes which are underfunded on the valuation day

16.—(1) The circumstances referred to in paragraph 8(1)(d) of

Schedule 5 to the 1999 Act (adjustments to amount of pension credit) are —

- (*a*) the discharge of liability in respect of the pension credit in accordance with paragraph 1(3) of Schedule 5 to the 1999 Act is at the request, or with the consent, of the person entitled to the pension credit;
- (*b*) the person entitled to the pension credit has refused an offer by the trustees or managers of the occupational pension scheme from which the pension credit is derived to discharge their liability in respect of the pension credit, without any reduction in the amount of the credit, in accordance with the provisions of paragraph 1(2) of Schedule 5 to the 1999 Act (conferring appropriate rights in that scheme on the person entitled to the pension credit); and
- (*c*) prior to making his request or giving his consent in accordance with sub-paragraph (a) the person entitled to the pension credit has received from the trustees or managers of the occupational pension scheme from which the pension credit is derived, a written statement which provides the following information —
  - (i) the reasons why the amount of the pension credit has been reduced;
  - (ii) the amount by which the pension credit has been reduced; and
  - (iii) where possible, an estimate of the date by which it will be possible to pay the full, unadjusted amount of the pension credit.

(2) Reductions may be made to a pension credit in accordance with paragraphs 2 to 6 of Schedule 1A to the Transfer Values Regulations modified as if—

- (*a*) in paragraph 2, the reference to "initial cash equivalent" were a reference to "pension credit";
- (*b*) in paragraph 3(b), the words "in respect of which the member's cash equivalent is being calculated and verified" were "to which the pension credit relates";
- (*c*) in paragraph 4, the words "member's initial cash equivalent that is payable in respect of" were "pension credit that relates to"; and
- (*d*) in paragraph 5, the words "a member's initial cash equivalent" were "the pension credit"

Adjustments to the amount of the pension credit — payments made without knowledge of the pension debit

17. For the purposes of paragraph 9 of Schedule 5 to the 1999 Act (adjustments to amount of pension credit), where the cash equivalent of the member's shareable rights after deduction of the payment referred to in sub-paragraph (b) of that paragraph, is less than the amount of the pension debit, the pension credit shall be reduced to that lesser amount.

Adjustments to the amount of the pension credit — increasing the amount of the pension credit

18.—(1) For the purposes of paragraph 10 of Schedule 5 to the 1999 Act (adjustments to amount of pension credit) the trustees or managers of an occupational pension scheme to which paragraph 1(3) or 3(3) of Schedule 5 to the 1999 Act applies shall increase the amount of the pension credit by —

(*a*) the amount, if any, by which the amount of that pension credit falls short of what it would have been if the valuation day had been the day on which the trustees or managers make the payment; or

(*b*) if it is greater, interest on the amount of that pension credit calculated on a daily basis over the period from the valuation day to the day on which the trustees or managers make the payment, at an annual rate of one per cent above the base rate.

(2) For the purposes of paragraph 10 of Schedule 5 to the 1999 Act the trustees or managers of a personal pension scheme to which paragraph 1(3) of Schedule 5 to the 1999 Act applies, or a person responsible for a pension arrangement to which paragraph 4(2) of Schedule 5 to the 1999 Act applies, shall increase the amount of the pension credit by —

(*a*) the interest on the amount of that pension credit, calculated on a daily basis over the period from the valuation day to the day on which the trustees or managers or the person responsible for the pension arrangement make the payment, at the same rate as that payable for the time being on judgment debts by virtue of section 17 of the Judgments Act 1838; or

(*b*) if it is greater, the amount, if any, by which the amount of that pension credit falls short of what it would have been if the valuation day had been the day on which the trustees or managers or the person responsible for the pension arrangement make the payment.

I. The Sharing of State Scheme Rights (Provision of Information and Valuation) (No. 2) Regulations 2000[9] (S.I. 2000 No. 2914)

The Secretary of State for Social Security, in exercise of the powers conferred upon him by sections 45B(7), 55A(6), 55B(7), 122(1) and 175(3) and (4) of the Social Security Contributions and Benefits Act 1992 and sections 23(1)(a), (b)(ii) and (c)(i) and (2), 49(4) and 83(4) and (6) of the Welfare Reform and Pensions Act 1999 and of all other powers enabling him in that behalf, after agreement by the Social Security Advisory Committee that proposals to make regulation 4 of these Regulations should not be referred to it and after consulting such person as he considered appropriate, hereby makes the following Regulations:

Citation, commencement and interpretation

1.—(1) These Regulations may be cited as the Sharing of State Scheme Rights (Provision of Information and Valuation) (No. 2) Regulations 2000 and shall come into force on 1st December 2000.

(2) In these Regulations —

"the 1992 Act" means the Social Security Contributions and Benefits Act 1992;
"the 1999 Act" means the Welfare Reform and Pensions Act 1999;
"shareable state scheme rights" has the meaning given by section 47(2) of the 1999 Act.

Basic information about the sharing of state scheme rights and divorce or the dissolution of a civil partnership

2.—(1) The requirements imposed on the Secretary of State for the purposes of section 23(1)(a) of the 1999 Act (supply of pension information in connection with divorce etc.) are that he shall furnish —

(*a*) the information specified in paragraphs (2) and (3) —
    (i) to a person who has shareable state scheme rights on request from that person; or
    (ii) to the court, pursuant to an order of the court; or
(*b*) the information specified in paragraph (3) to the spouse or civil partner of a person who has shareable state scheme rights, on request from that spouse or civil partner.

---

[9] As amended by S.I. 2005 No. 2877.

(2) The information specified in this paragraph is a valuation of the person's shareable state scheme rights.

(3) The information in this paragraph is an explanation of —

(*a*) the state scheme rights which are shareable;

(*b*) how a pension sharing order or provision will affect a person's shareable state scheme rights; and

(*c*) how a pension sharing order or provision in respect of a person's shareable state scheme rights will result in the spouse or civil partner of the person who has shareable state scheme rights becoming entitled to a shared additional pension.

(4) The Secretary of State shall furnish the information specified in paragraphs (2) and (3) to the court, or as the case may be, to the person who has shareable state scheme rights within —

(*a*) 3 months beginning with the date the Secretary of State receives the request or, as the case may be, the order for the provision of that information;

(*b*) 6 weeks beginning with the date the Secretary of State receives the request or, as the case may be, the order for the provision of the information, if the person who has shareable state scheme rights has notified the Secretary of State on the date of the request or order that the information is needed in connection with proceedings commenced under any of the provisions referred to in section 23(1)(a) of the 1999 Act; or

(*c*) such shorter period specified by the court in an order requiring the Secretary of State to provide a valuation in accordance with paragraph (2).

(5) Where —

(*a*) the request made by the person with shareable state scheme rights for, or the court order requiring, the provision of information does not include a request or, as the case may be, an order for a valuation under paragraph (2); or

(*b*) the spouse or civil partner of the person with shareable state scheme rights requests the information specified in paragraph (3),

the Secretary of State shall furnish that information to the person who has shareable state scheme rights, his spouse, civil partner, or the court, as the case may be, within one month beginning with the date the Secretary of State receives the request or the court order for the provision of that information.

Information about the sharing of state scheme rights and divorce or dissolution of a civil partnership: valuation of shareable state scheme rights

3. Where an application for financial relief or financial provision under any of the provisions referred to in section 23(1)(a) of the 1999 Act has been made or is in contemplation, the valuation of shareable state scheme rights shall be calculated and verified for the purposes of regulation 2(2) of these Regulations in such manner as may be approved by or on behalf of the Government Actuary.

Calculation and verification of cash equivalents for the purposes of the creation of state scheme pension debits and credits

4. For the purposes of —

    (*a*) section 49 of the 1999 Act (creation of state scheme pension debits and credits);

    (*b*) section 45B of the 1992 Act (reduction of additional pension in Category A retirement pension: pension sharing);

    (*c*) section 55A of the 1992 Act (shared additional pension); and

    (*d*) section 55B of the 1992 Act (reduction of shared additional pension: pension sharing),

cash equivalents shall be calculated and verified in such manner as may be approved by or on behalf of the Government Actuary.

Revocation

5. The Sharing of State Scheme Rights (Provision of Information and Valuation) Regulations 2000 are revoked.

J. The Divorce and Dissolution etc. (Pension Protection Fund) (Scotland) Regulations 2006 (S.S.I. 2006 No. 254)

The Scottish Ministers, in exercise of the powers conferred by section 10(8B) of the Family Law (Scotland) Act 1985 and of all other powers enabling them in that behalf, hereby make the following Regulations:

Citation and commencement

1. These Regulations may be cited as the Divorce and Dissolution etc. (Pension Protection Fund)(Scotland) Regulations 2006 and shall come into force on 3rd June 2006.

Apportionment

2.—(1) The value of the proportion of any rights or interests which a party to a marriage or civil partnership has or may have to any pension protection fund compensation payable under Chapter 3 of Part 2 of the Pensions Act 2004 as at the relevant date and which forms part of the matrimonial property or partnership property by virtue of section 10(5A) shall be calculated in accordance with the following formula—

$$\frac{A \ \text{x} \ B}{C}$$

where—

A is the value of these rights or interests to any pension protection fund compensation which is calculated as at the relevant date, in accordance with the provisions referred to in section 162 of the Pensions Act 2004;

B is the period of C which falls within the period of the marriage or civil partnership of the parties before the relevant date and, if there is no such period, the amount shall be zero; and

C is the period before the relevant date during which pension protection fund compensation is payable to that party.

(2) In this regulation—

"matrimonial property" has the same meaning as in section 10(4), (5) and (5A);
"partnership property" has the same meaning as in section 10(4A), (5) and (5A);
and
"relevant date" has the same meaning as in section 10(3).

(3) Any reference in this regulation to a numbered section is to a section bearing that number in the Family Law (Scotland) Act 1985.

K. The Pension Protection Fund (Pensions on Divorce etc.: Charges) Regulations 2011 (S.I. 2011 No. 726)

The Secretary of State for Work and Pensions, in exercise of the powers conferred by sections 168A, 203(1)(a), 315(2), (4) and (5) and 318(1) of the Pensions Act 2004, makes the following Regulations . . .

Citation, commencement and interpretation

1.—(1) These Regulations may be cited as the Pension Protection Fund (Pensions on Divorce etc: Charges) Regulations 2011 and shall come into force on 6th April 2011.

(2) In these Regulations—

"implementation period" has the same meaning as in section 34(1) of the Welfare Reform and Pensions Act 1999;

"party" means a party to a pension sharing order or provision, or to a pension attachment order or provision;

"pension attachment order or provision" means an order or provision which is made under or by virtue of any of the provisions specified in regulation 1(1)(b) to (f), or (in Scotland) a provision contained in a qualifying agreement corresponding to provision which may be made by an order under section 8(1)(ba) of the Family Law (Scotland) Act 1985 (orders for financial provision);

"pension sharing order or provision" means an order or (in Scotland) a provision contained in a qualifying agreement, which provides that one party's shareable rights under a specified occupational pension scheme be subject to pension sharing for the benefit of the other party, and specifies the percentage value or (in Scotland) the amount to be transferred.

"PPF compensation" means compensation payable under the pension compensation provisions specified in section 162(2) of the Pensions Act 2004 or Article 146(2) of the Pensions (Northern Ireland) Order 2005.

Information to be provided where the Board is under a duty to comply with a pension sharing or attachment order or provision

2.—(1) This regulation applies where the Board has assumed responsibility for a scheme in accordance with Chapter 3 of Part 2 of the Pensions Act 2004 (pension protection), and is required to—

(*a*)   implement a pension sharing order or provision by virtue of the modifications made by the Pension Protection Fund (Pension Sharing) Regulations 2006;

(*b*)   make payments in accordance with an order made under section 23 of the Matrimonial Causes Act 1973 (financial provision orders in connection with divorce proceedings, etc.), which—

(i)   includes provision made by virtue of section 25B (pensions) or 25C (pensions: lump sums) of that Act; and

    (ii) applies in relation to the Board by virtue of section 25E (the Pension Protection Fund) of that Act;

(*c*) make payments in accordance with an order made under Part I of Schedule 5 to the Civil Partnership Act 2004 (financial provision in connection with dissolution, nullity or separation), which—

    (i) includes provision made by virtue of Part 6 of that Schedule (making of Part I orders having regard to pension benefits); and

    (ii) applies in relation to the Board by virtue of Part 7 of that Schedule (Pension Protection Fund compensation etc.) of that Act;

(*d*) make payments in accordance with an order under Article 25 of the Matrimonial Causes (Northern Ireland) Order 1978 (financial provision orders in connection with divorce proceedings, etc.), which—

    (i) includes provision made by virtue of Article 27B (pensions) or 27C (pensions: lump sums) of that Order; and

    (ii) applies in relation to the Board by virtue of Article 27E the Pension Protection Fund) of that Order;

(*e*) make payments in accordance with an order made under Part I of Schedule 15 to the Civil Partnership Act 2004 (financial provision in connection with dissolution, nullity or separation), which—

    (i) includes provision made by virtue of Part 5 (making of Part I orders having regard to pension benefits) of that Schedule; and

    (ii) applies in relation to the Board by virtue of Part 6 (Pension Protection Fund compensation etc.) of that Schedule;

(*f*) make payments in accordance with an order made under section 8(1)(ba) of the Family Law (Scotland) Act 1985 which applies in relation to the Board; or

(*g*) make payments under any provision corresponding to provision which may be made by a pension sharing order or an order under section 8(1)(ba) of that Act and—

    (i) which is contained in a qualifying agreement (to which section 28(3) of the Welfare Reform and Pensions Act 1999 relates; and

    (ii) applies in relation to the Board.

(2) The Board must inform the parties of—

(*a*) the date on which the Board assumed responsibility for the scheme; and (*b*) the fact that the Board will implement the order or provision or, as the case may be, will comply with the pension attachment order or provision.

(3) The Board must provide the information specified in paragraph (2) within the period of 14 days beginning with the date on which the Board assumed responsibility for the scheme.

(4) Where the Board has previously provided the information specified in paragraph (2)(a), nothing in this regulation requires that information to be provided again to the same party.

General requirements as to charges

3.—(1) The Board may not recover any of the charges specified in regulation 4 unless—

(*a*) before the pension sharing order or provision or pension attachment order or provision was made, the trustees or managers of the scheme had—

(i) informed the member or the member's spouse or civil partner, as the case may be, in writing, of their intention to recover costs incurred in connection with implementation of a pension sharing order or provision, or compliance with a pension attachment order or provision; and

(ii) provided the member or the member's spouse or civil partner, as the case may be, with a written schedule of the charges which they intended to impose; and

(*b*) the Board has provided the party from whom the Board intends to recover the charges with a written schedule of charges owed by that party and the date by which payment in whole or in part is required.

(2) If a pension sharing order or provision includes provision about the apportionment of charges between the parties to pension sharing, any recovery of charges by the Board must comply with the terms of the order or provision.

Charges in respect of pension sharing and pension attachment

4.—(1) For the purposes of section 168A(1)(charges in respect of pension sharing etc.) of the Pensions Act 2004, the prescribed charges which the Board may recover from the parties are costs which are reasonably incurred by the Board in respect of—

(*a*) implementation of a pension sharing order or provision which applies in relation to the Board;

(*b*) provision of information associated with that implementation; and

(*c*) charges which represent the reasonable administrative expenses which the Board has incurred by reason of complying with a pension attachment order or provision.

Charges in respect of pension sharing and pension attachment—methods of recovery

5.—(1) In the circumstances prescribed in paragraph (3), and subject to paragraph (4), the Board may recover the charges specified in regulation 4 by using either of the methods specified in paragraph (2).

(2) The methods of recovery specified in this paragraph are—

(*a*) requiring payment from a party liable for payment of the charges; and

(*b*) deducting the charges from PPF compensation which would otherwise be payable to a party liable for payment of the charges.

(3) The circumstances prescribed in this paragraph are—

(*a*) in the case of a pension sharing order or provision, that—
    (i) the implementation period for the pension sharing order or provision has commenced;
    (ii) the Board is not aware of any appeal against the order having begun on or after the day on which the order takes effect; and
    (iii) the Board has informed the party from whom the Board intends to recover the charges of the date on or after which the charges may be recovered, together with details of the methods which may be used to recover the charges; or

(*b*) in the case of a pension attachment order or provision, that the circumstances prescribed in paragraph (3)(a)(ii) and (iii) apply.

(4) The Board may not recover any of the charges specified in regulation 4 from a party by using either of the methods prescribed in paragraph (2) if that party has paid in full all the charges for which they are liable.

L. The Pension Protection Fund (Pension Compensation Sharing and Attachment on Divorce etc) Regulations 2011 (S.I. 2011 No. 731)

The Secretary of State for Work and Pensions makes the following Regulations in exercise of the powers conferred by sections 168A(1) and (3), 206(4)(a), 207, 315(2) to (5) and 318(1) of the Pensions Act 2004 and sections 107(2), 108, 109(g)(ii), 110(1)(a), 112, 114(3), 115(1)(b)(ii) and (4), 116(6) and (8)(b), 117(1), (2)(b) and (c), 118, 119 and 144(2) and (4) of, and paragraphs 5(4), 7(5), 8(4)(a), 9(1), (2) and (6), 10(1), 17(6), 18 and 19 of Schedule 5 to the Pensions Act 2008. . .

PART I

GENERAL

Citation, commencement and interpretation

1.—(1) These Regulations may be cited as the Pension Protection Fund (Pension Compensation Sharing and Attachment on Divorce etc) Regulations 2011 and shall come into force on 6th April 2011.

(2) In these Regulations—

"the Act" means the Pensions Act 2008;

"the 2004 Act" means the Pensions Act 2004;

"admissible rules" has the same meaning as in paragraph 35 (scheme rules, admissible rules etc) of Schedule 7 to the 2004 Act;

"child of the family" means—

(*a*) a child of the transferee; or

(*b*) any other child who has been treated by the transferee as a child of the family, other than a child placed with the transferee as a foster parent by a local authority or voluntary organisation;

"compensation cap" has the same meaning as in paragraph 26(7) of Schedule 7 to the 2004 Act (compensation cap);

"member" means the party who is entitled to present or future payment of PPF compensation under the pension compensation provisions and includes a pension compensation credit member;

"pension compensation attachment order" means an order made under any of the provisions specified in regulation 17(1)(a) to (e);

"pension compensation credit member" means a person who has

rights to PPF compensation which are attributable to a pension compensation credit;

"pension compensation debit" means a debit of the appropriate amount, to be applied to the transferor's shareable rights to PPF compensation, on the taking effect of a pension compensation sharing order or provision (see section 111 of the Act (creation of pension compensation debits and credits));

"qualifying course" means a full time educational or vocational course at a recognised educational establishment where, in pursuit of that course, the time spent receiving instruction or tuition, undertaking supervised study, examination or practical work or taking part in any exercise, experiment or project for which provision is made in the curriculum of the course, exceeds 12 hours per week in normal term time, and includes any gaps between the ending of one course and the commencement of another, where the person is enrolled on and commences the latter course;

"PPF" means the Pension Protection Fund;

"relevant compensation" means the payments to which the member is entitled (or will become entitled on attaining normal pension age) under the pension compensation provisions by virtue of the member's shareable rights to PPF compensation that derive from rights under a specified scheme;

"relevant partner" means a person of either sex who was not married to, or in a civil partnership with, the transferee and who was living with the transferee—

(*a*) as if that person and the transferee were husband and wife; or

(*b*) in the case of two adults of the same sex, as if they were civil partners;

"surviving dependant" means—

(*a*) a child of the family who was financially dependent on the transferee at the time of the transferee's death and who is aged less than 18;

(*b*) a child of the family who was financially dependent on the transferee at the time of the transferee's death, who is aged less than 23 and who is—

(i) attending a qualifying course; or

(ii) incapable of engaging in full time paid employment due to a condition that falls within the definition of a disability under section 6 (disability) of the Equality Act 2010; or

(*c*) a child of the transferee who is born after the transferee's death;

"surviving partner" means the surviving widow, widower or civil
partner of a deceased transferee;
"valid nomination" means a signed written notice.

(3) "Day", in regulations 3, 5, 9, 11, 12, 17 and 18, means any day
other than—

(*a*)   Christmas Day or Good Friday; or
(*b*)   a day which is, or is to be observed as, a bank holiday under
        Schedule 1 (bank holidays) to the Banking and Financial
        Dealings Act 1971;

and where the Board receives a request or order to provide information,
an order or provision, a notification or other documents on a day which
falls on one of the days specified in sub-paragraph (a) or (b), any period
of time specified in regulation 3, 5, 9, 11, 12, 17 or 18 is to run from
the next day after the day of receipt which is not a day specified in
sub-paragraph (a) or (b).

PART 2

SHAREABLE RIGHTS

Rights to PPF compensation which are not shareable

2. Any right of a person to PPF compensation is not shareable
if—

(*a*)   the compensation is in payment; and
(*b*)   the compensation is derived directly or indirectly from the
        rights of a deceased person by virtue of being the surviving
        partner or surviving dependant of that person.

PART 3

SUPPLY OF INFORMATION ABOUT PENSION
COMPENSATION IN RELATION TO DIVORCE ETC

**Basic information about pension compensation and divorce or
dissolution of a civil partnership**

3.—(1) The requirements imposed on the Board for the purposes
of section 118(1)(a) of the Act (supply of information about pension

compensation in relation to divorce etc.) are that the Board must supply—

(*a*) on request from a member, the information specified in paragraphs (2) and (3)(b) and (c);

(*b*) on request from the spouse or civil partner of the member, the information specified in paragraph (3); and

(*c*) pursuant to an order of the court, the information specified in paragraph (2), (3), or (4), to the member, the spouse or civil partner of the member, or, as the case may be, to the court.

(2) The information specified in this paragraph is a valuation of the member's rights to PPF compensation and (if not the same as the member's rights to PPF compensation) a valuation of the member's rights to relevant compensation.

(3) The information specified in this paragraph is—

(*a*) a statement that on request from the member, or pursuant to an order of the court, a valuation of the member's rights to PPF compensation and to relevant compensation (if not the same as the member's rights to PPF compensation), will be supplied to the member, or, as the case may be, to the court;

(*b*) a statement summarising the way in which the valuations referred to in paragraph (2) and sub-paragraph (a) are calculated;

(*c*) a schedule of the charges that the Board will impose in accordance with regulation 18 (charges in respect of pension compensation sharing costs etc recoverable by the Board), and the method by which those charges may be recovered;

(*d*) a statement that a person entitled to a pension compensation credit against the Board will be entitled to periodic compensation calculated in accordance with Schedule 5 (pension compensation payable on discharge of pension compensation credit) to the Act.

(4) The information specified in this paragraph is any other information about the calculation and payment of PPF compensation relevant to any power exercisable under the provisions specified in section 118(1)(a) of the Act.

(5) Where the member's request or the court order for the provision of information includes a request or an order for provision of a valuation under paragraph (2), the Board must supply all the information in that request or order within—

(*a*)   3 months, beginning with the day that the Board receives the request or order for the provision of information;

(*b*)   6 weeks, beginning with the day that the Board receives the request or order for the provision of information, where the member or the court has notified the Board on the date of the request or order that the information is needed in connection with proceedings commenced under any of the provisions specified in section 118(1)(a) of the Act; or

(*c*)   any shorter period, where the court specifies such a period in an order requiring the Board to supply a valuation in accordance with paragraph (2).

(6) Where—

(*a*)   the member's request or the court order for supply of information does not include a request or an order for provision of a valuation under paragraph (2); or

(*b*)   the member's spouse or civil partner requests the information specified in paragraph (3),

the Board must supply that information within one month beginning with the day that the Board receives the request or the court order for the provision of the information.

Valuation of relevant compensation for the purposes of an application for financial relief or financial provision

4.—(1) Where the Board is notified that—

(*a*)   an application for financial relief or financial provision under any of the provisions specified in section 118(1)(a) of the Act has been made or is in contemplation; or

(*b*)   a qualifying agreement containing provision corresponding to provision which may be made by an order under section 8 (orders for financial provision) of the Family Law (Scotland) Act 1985 is to be made or is in contemplation,

the value of the PPF compensation or relevant compensation to which the member is entitled or will become entitled must be calculated and verified for the purposes of section 118(1)(b) of the Act, or of regulation 3(2), in accordance with paragraphs (2) and (3).

(2) The value of the PPF compensation or relevant compensation is the cash equivalent of the amount that would be required to make provision for the member's entitlement to PPF compensation or relevant compensation under the pension compensation provisions.

(3) The cash equivalent of the PPF compensation or relevant compensation must be calculated and verified—

(*a*) in accordance with actuarial assumptions approved by the Board; and

(*b*) on the assumption that the date on which the valuation is carried out is the date that the Board received the request for the valuation.

Provision of information in response to a notification that a pension compensation sharing order etc may be made

5.—(1) On a direction from the court or a request from the member, the Board must supply the information specified in paragraph (2) to the member or to the court, as the case may be—

(*a*) within 21 days beginning with the day that the Board received the notification that a pension compensation sharing order, a pension compensation attachment order, or a qualifying agreement containing provision equivalent to such orders, may be made; or

(*b*) if the court has specified a date which is before or after the 21 day period specified in sub-paragraph (a), by that date.

(2) The information referred to in paragraph (1) is—

(*a*) the full name and address of the person to whom any order or provision specified in section 109 of the Act (activation of pension compensation sharing) should be sent;

(b) whether the Board is aware that the member's rights to PPF compensation are subject to any, and if so, which, of the following—

    (i) any order or provision specified in section 109 of the Act;

    (ii) any order or provision specified in section 28(1) (activation of pension sharing) of the Welfare Reform and Pensions Act 1999;

    (iii) an order under section 23 (financial provision orders in connection with divorce proceedings etc.) of the Matrimonial Causes Act 1973, which includes provision made by virtue of section 25B (pensions) or 25C (pensions: lump sums) of that Act;

    (iv) an order under Part 1 of Schedule 5 (financial provision orders in connection with dissolution of civil partnerships etc: England and Wales) to the Civil Partnership Act

2004, which includes provision made by virtue of Part 6 of that Schedule (powers to include provision about pensions);

(v) an order under section 23 of the Matrimonial Causes Act 1973, which includes provision made by virtue of section 25F (attachment of pension compensation) of that Act;

(vi) an order under Part 1 of Schedule 5 to the Civil Partnership Act 2004, which includes provision made by virtue of paragraph 34A (attachment of PPF compensation) of Part 7 of that Schedule;

(vii) an order under Article 25 (financial provision orders in connection with divorce proceedings, etc.) of the Matrimonial Causes (Northern Ireland) Order 1978, which includes provision made by virtue of Article 27B (pensions) or 27C (pensions: lump sums) of that Order;

(viii) an order under Part 1 (financial provision in connection with divorce, nullity or separation) of Schedule 15 to the Civil Partnership Act 2004, which includes provision made by virtue of Part 5 (making of Part 1 orders having regard to pension benefits) of that Schedule;

(ix) an order under Article 25 of the Matrimonial Causes (Northern Ireland) Order 1978, which includes provision made by virtue of Article 27F (attachment of pension compensation) of that Order;

(x) an order under Part 1 of Schedule 15 to the Civil Partnership Act 2004, which includes provision made by virtue of paragraph 29A (attachment of PPF compensation) of Part 6 of that Schedule;

(xi) an order under section 8 (orders for financial provision) of the Family Law (Scotland) Act 1985, which includes provision made by virtue of section 12A(2) (orders for payment of capital sum: pensions lump sums) or (3) or 12B (order for payment of capital sum: pension compensation) of that Act;

(xii) any provision corresponding to provision which may be made by such an order, and which is contained in a qualifying agreement between the parties to a marriage or the partners to a civil partnership;

(xiii) a forfeiture order;

(xiv) a bankruptcy order;

(xv) an award of sequestration on a member's estate or the making of the appointment on the member's estate of a judicial factor under section 41 (appointment of judicial factor) of the Solicitors (Scotland) Act 1980;

(*c*) whether the member's rights to PPF compensation include rights which are not shareable or cannot be subject to a pension compensation attachment order;

(*d*) if such information has not already been supplied, details of any charges that the Board will impose in accordance with regulation 18 (charges in respect of pension compensation sharing costs etc recoverable by the Board) and the method by which they may be recovered; and

(*e*) whether the Board requires any information additional to that specified in regulation 9 (information to be supplied in order for the implementation period to begin) in order to implement the pension sharing order or provision.

Information to be provided by the Board to pension compensation credit members

6. The information to be provided by the Board to pension compensation credit members and to beneficiaries of pension compensation credit members is to be determined in accordance with the provisions of the Schedule.

PART 4

PENSION COMPENSATION SHARING AND QUALIFYING AGREEMENTS (SCOTLAND)

Prescribed form of provision corresponding to provision which may be made by a pension compensation sharing order

7. For the purposes of section 109(g)(ii) of the Act, the form of a provision corresponding to provision which may be made by a pension compensation sharing order, and which is contained in a qualifying agreement between the parties to a marriage or the partners in a civil partnership, is that the provision must include —

(*a*) in relation to the transferor, the information specified in regulation 9(1)(a);

(*b*) in relation to the transferee, the information specified in regulation 9(1)(b);

(*c*) details of —
  (i) the amount to be transferred to the transferee, or
  (ii) the percentage of the cash equivalent of the relevant compensation which is to be transferred to the transferee;

(*d*) details of provision about the apportionment between the transferor and transferee (if any) of charges imposed by the Board in accordance with regulation 18(1);

(*e*) confirmation by the transferor that the Board has been sent notification that a qualifying agreement is to be made, and that the Board has acknowledged receipt of that notification.

Circumstances in which an agreement is to be entered into, in order to be considered a "qualifying agreement" for the purposes of section 110(1)(a) of the Act

8. The circumstances prescribed for the purposes of section 110(1)(a) of the Act are that —

(*a*) the transferor has notified the Board that a qualifying agreement which makes provision corresponding to—
  (i) a pension compensation sharing order under section 8 of the Family Law (Scotland) Act 1985; or
  (ii) a capital sum order made under section 8 containing provision by virtue of section 12B of that Act, is to be made; and

(*b*) the transferor and transferee have entered into the agreement in order to determine the financial settlement on divorce or dissolution of a civil partnership.

PART 5

IMPLEMENTATION AND DISCHARGE OF LIABILITY

Information to be supplied in order for the implementation period to begin

9.—(1) Subject to paragraph (2), the information prescribed for the purposes of section 115(1)(b)(ii) of the Act ("implementation period") is—

(*a*) in relation to the transferor—
  (i) all names by which the transferor is or has been known;
  (ii) date of birth;
  (iii) address;
  (iv) National Insurance number; and
  (v) the name of the pension scheme for which the Board has assumed responsibility and to which the pension compensation sharing order or provision relates, or such other information as the Board may require to identify the pension scheme concerned;

(*b*) in relation to the transferee —
> (i) the name of the transferee and, if the transferee is or will be entitled to PPF compensation other than by reason of the pension compensation credit, all other names by which the transferee is or has been known;
> (ii) date of birth;
> (iii) address;
> (iv) National Insurance number; and
> (v) if the transferee is or will be entitled to PPF compensation other than by reason of the pension compensation credit, the name of the pension scheme or such other information as the Board may require to identify the pension scheme concerned.

(2) Where —

(*a*) the Board has not received all the information specified in paragraph (1)(a); but
(*b*) considers that it has sufficient information relating to the transferor to enable it to begin implementation of the pension compensation credit,

the prescribed information for the purposes of section 115(1)(b)(ii) of the Act is such information relating to the transferor as the Board considers sufficient.

(3) Where the Board is subject to a liability in respect of a pension compensation credit and the transferee dies before the implementation period has begun, the start of the implementation period is to be postponed until the Board has received notification of —

(*a*) the date of the transferee's death; and
(*b*) the name and address of the executor or personal representative of the deceased transferee.

Extension of implementation period

10. The circumstances in which the implementation period for a pension compensation credit is extended for the purposes of section 114 of the Act (time for discharge of liability) are that —

(*a*) the transferor or the transferee has not taken such steps as the Board can reasonably expect in order to satisfy it of any matter which falls to be established before it can discharge its liability for the pension compensation credit within the implementation period;

(*b*) the Board has not been supplied with such information as it reasonably requires to discharge its liability for the pension compensation credit within the implementation period; or

(*c*) the transferor or the transferee has disputed the amount of the cash equivalent calculated and verified for the purposes of section 111 of the Act (creation of pension compensation debits and credits).

Postponement or cessation of implementation period when an application for leave to appeal out of time is made

11.—(1) Where a pension compensation credit depends on a pension compensation sharing order which is the subject of an application for leave to appeal out of time, the modifications to the effect of section 115 of the Act are—

(*a*) where the implementation period has not commenced, its commencement is postponed; or

(*b*) where the implementation period has commenced, its operation ceases.

(2) The postponement or cessation referred to in paragraph (1)(a) or (b) is to continue until the Board receives—

(*a*) confirmation from the court that the order which was the subject of the application for leave to appeal out of time has not been varied, discharged or recalled; or

(*b*) a copy of the varied pension compensation sharing order.

(3) If the Board—

(*a*) has already discharged its liability in respect of the pension compensation credit which depends on a pension compensation sharing order; and

(*b*) subsequently receives notification of an application for leave to appeal out of time in respect of that order,

it must inform the court, within 21 days from the date on which the notification was received, that the Board's liability in respect of that pension compensation credit has been discharged.

Notification about the implementation period by the Board

12.—(1) Within a period of 21 days beginning on the day on which the implementation period begins in accordance with section 115(1) of the Act ("implementation period"), the Board must notify the transferor and transferee of the date that the implementation period began.

(2) Where the implementation period cannot begin because the Board has not received all of the documents or information specified in section 115(1)(b)(i) and regulation 9(1) or (3) (information to be supplied in order for the implementation period to begin), the Board must, as soon as practicable after becoming aware that it has not received all such documents and information—

(*a*) notify the transferor and the transferee, or (in cases where the transferee has died before the implementation period has begun) the executor or personal representative of the transferee, that the start of the implementation period is delayed because the Board has not been supplied with relevant information; and

(*b*) specify the information required and (if applicable) the date on which it was requested.

(3) Where the implementation period—

(*a*) is extended in accordance with regulation 10; or

(*b*) is postponed or ceases to operate in accordance with regulation 11,

the Board must, within 21 days of the date of the extension, postpone-ment or cessation of the implementation period, notify the transferor and transferee of the reasons for that extension, postponement or cessation, including details of any information which the Board requires in order to complete implementation.

(4) If any charges imposed by the Board in accordance with regulation 18 (charges in respect of pension compensation sharing costs etc recoverable by the Board) are due or will become due to be paid, the Board must notify the transferor and transferee of—

(*a*) the amount of the charges;

(*b*) the party who, in accordance with section 117(3) of the Act (charges in respect of pension compensation sharing costs), is responsible for paying the charges;

(*c*) the date on which the charges were due or will become due to be paid;

(*d*) the method, in accordance with regulation 18(4), by which the charges may be recovered if not paid by the date specified in sub-paragraph (c); and

(*e*) the date, calculated in accordance with regulation 18(6)(e), on or after which the Board may recover the charges if not paid by the date specified in sub-paragraph (c).

Calculation and verification of cash equivalent

13.—(1) For the purposes of calculating the appropriate amount in accordance with section 111 of the Act, the cash equivalent of the relevant compensation is the amount that immediately before the transfer day would be required to make provision for the member's entitlement to relevant compensation under the pension compensation provisions.

(2) The cash equivalent must be calculated and verified in accordance with actuarial assumptions approved by the Board.

Determination of cash equivalent value of pension compensation credit

14. The Board must calculate the cash equivalent value of the compensation to which the transferee becomes entitled on the sending of a notice under section 116(3) (discharge of liability) using actuarial assumptions which are consistent with the actuarial assumptions used to calculate and verify the cash equivalent of the member's entitlement to relevant compensation under the pension compensation provisions.

Discharge of liability where the transferee dies before the Board has discharged liability for a pension compensation credit

15.—(1) This regulation applies where—

(*a*) the Board is subject to a liability in respect of a pension compensation credit; and

(*b*) the transferee dies before liability in respect of that pension compensation credit has been discharged.

(2) The Board must discharge the liability by sending a notice to the personal representative or executor of the deceased.

(3) On the sending of the notice—

(*a*) either—
   (i) where regulation 20 does not apply, a surviving partner is entitled to compensation calculated in accordance with regulation 21; or
   (ii) a relevant partner is entitled to compensation in the circumstances prescribed in regulation 22(2); and

(*b*) a surviving dependant is entitled to compensation in the circumstances prescribed in regulation 22(5).

Notification of discharge of liability

16. — (1) Where the Board discharges liability in respect of a pension compensation credit in accordance with section 116 of the Act, it must also supply —

(*a*) to the transferor —
   (i)   in a case where the transferor has not attained pension compensation age before or on the transfer day, the information specified in paragraphs (2) and (3); or
   (ii) in a case where the transferor has attained pension compensation age before or on the transfer day, the information specified in paragraphs (2) and (4);

(*b*) to the transferee —
   (i)   in a case where the transferee has not attained pension compensation age before or on the transfer day, the information specified in paragraphs (5) and (6); or
   (ii) in a case where the transferee has attained pension compensation age before or on the transfer day, the information specified in paragraphs (5) and (7); or

(*c*) in a case where the transferee has died prior to discharge of liability by the Board, to the personal representative or executor of the transferee, the information specified in paragraphs (5) (with the exception of the information specified in paragraph (5)(e)) and (8).

(2) The information specified in this paragraph is —

(*a*) the cash equivalent value as at the valuation day of the transferor's entitlement to relevant compensation;
(*b*) the cash equivalent value of the pension compensation debit;
(*c*) the transfer day;
(*d*) any charges which may be deducted in accordance with regulation 18 from the transferor's remaining rights to relevant compensation (if any); and
(*e*) the cash equivalent value of the transferor's rights to relevant compensation (if any) immediately after the relevant compensation is reduced in accordance with section 113 of the Act (reduction of compensation) and after any deduction in respect of charges owed.

(3) The information specified in this paragraph is the annual rate of PPF compensation which would be payable if the transferor had reached pension compensation age immediately after the relevant compensation is reduced in accordance with section 113 of the Act and after the deduction of any charges owed.

(4) The information specified in this paragraph is the annual rate of the PPF compensation which is payable to the transferor—

(*a*) immediately before; and
(*b*) immediately after, the relevant compensation is reduced in accordance with section 113 and any charges owed are deducted.

(5) The information specified in this paragraph is—

(*a*) the cash equivalent value of the pension compensation credit;
(*b*) the transfer day;
(*c*) any charges which may be deducted in accordance with regulation 18 from the transferee's entitlement to compensation;
(*d*) the cash equivalent value of the pension compensation credit following the deduction of any charges owed; and
(*e*) the date at which payment of PPF compensation will commence.

(6) The information specified in this paragraph is an estimate of the annual rate of PPF compensation which is likely to be payable to the transferee on reaching pension compensation age.
(7) The information specified in this paragraph is the annual rate of compensation which is payable to the transferee from the transfer day.
(8) The information specified in this paragraph is the fact that compensation may be payable to a surviving partner, relevant partner or surviving dependant in accordance with Part 7.

Provision of information after receipt of a pension compensation attachment order or provision

17.—(1) The Board must, within 21 days beginning with the day it receives—

(*a*) an order under section 23 of the Matrimonial Causes Act 1973, which includes provision made by virtue of section 25F (attachment of pension compensation) of that Act;
(*b*) an order under Part 1 of Schedule 5 to the Civil Partnership Act 2004, which includes provision made by virtue of paragraph 34A (attachment of PPF compensation) of Part 7 of that Schedule;
(*c*) an order under Article 25 of the Matrimonial Causes (Northern Ireland) Order 1978, which includes provision made by virtue of Article 27F (attachment of pension compensation) of that Order;

(*d*) an order under Part 1 of Schedule 15 to the Civil Partnership Act 2004, which includes provision made by virtue of paragraph 29A (attachment of PPF compensation) of Part 6 of that Schedule;

(*e*) an order under section 8 (orders for financial provision) of the Family Law (Scotland) Act 1985 containing provision made by virtue of section 12B(2) of that Act; or

(*f*) a qualifying agreement containing provision equivalent to such an order,

issue to the member and to the person entitled to payments by virtue of the pension compensation attachment order or provision ("the other party") a notice which includes the information specified in paragraphs (2) and (4), or (2), (3) and (4), as the case may be.

(2) Where an order or provision specified in paragraph (1) is made in relation to relevant compensation that is not in payment, the notice issued by the Board to the member and to the other party must include—

(*a*) the cash equivalent value of the relevant compensation;

(*b*) the first date when a payment pursuant to the order or provision is to be made; and

(*c*) a list of any changes in circumstances which, under the terms of the order or provision, the member or the other party must notify to the Board.

(3) Where an order or provision specified in paragraph (1) is made in relation to relevant compensation that is in payment, the notice issued by the Board to the member must, in addition to the items specified in paragraph (2), include—

(*a*) the annual rate of the relevant compensation payable to the member immediately before implementation of the order or provision; and

(*b*) the annual rate of the relevant compensation which will be payable to the member and to the other party immediately after implementation of the order or provision.

(4) Where an order or provision specified in paragraph (1) is made (whether or not in relation to relevant compensation that is in payment), the notice issued by the Board to the member and to the other party must include—

(*a*) the amount of any charges made in accordance with regulation 18(2)(d) which remain unpaid;

(*b*)   the date by which payment in whole or in part is required;
(*c*)   the amount of the charges which are attributable to the member and to the other party; and
(*d*)   whether the charges may be set off, in accordance with regulation 18(4)(c), against payments made to the member or the other party.

PART 6

CHARGES IN RESPECT OF PENSION COMPENSATION SHARING COSTS ETC

Charges in respect of pension compensation sharing costs etc recoverable by the Board

18.—(1) Subject to paragraph (3), the Board may recover from a party to proceedings under any of the provisions specified in section 118(1)(a)(i) to (iv), or to a qualifying agreement specified in section 118(1)(a)(v) of the Act ("a party"), charges of the description specified in paragraph (2).

(2) The charges that the Board may recover are those in respect of —

(*a*)   provision of information or a valuation in accordance with regulation 3, 4 or 5;
(*b*)   the reasonable costs of implementing and discharging liability for a pension compensation credit;
(*c*)   any other reasonable costs associated with pension compensation sharing activity in relation to the parties; and
(*d*)   those charges which represent the reasonable administrative expenses which the Board incurs by reason of a pension compensation attachment order or provision.

(3) The Board must not recover charges in relation to the costs specified in paragraph (2) if it is required to supply the same information to a member by regulations made under section 203 of the 2004 Act (provision of information to members of schemes etc) or to a pension compensation credit member by regulation 6 (information to be provided by the Board to pension compensation credit members).

(4) Subject to paragraph (3), the Board may recover charges in relation to the costs specified in paragraph (2)(a) to (c) by —

(*a*)   requiring payment of charges to be made by any specified date on or after the date that the costs giving rise to the charges were incurred;

(*b*) where compensation is not in payment, making a deduction from a member's future entitlement to relevant compensation, or from a transferee's future entitlement to compensation (calculated in accordance with paragraph 6 of Schedule 5 to the Act (compensation payable to transferee)); or

(*c*) where—
    (i) relevant compensation is in payment to a member; or
    (ii) compensation is in payment to a transferee in accordance with paragraph 4 (compensation payable to transferee) of Schedule 5 to the Act,
setting off the charges owed against such payments.

(5) Subject to paragraph (3), the Board may recover charges in relation to the costs specified in paragraph (2)(d) by either of the methods specified in paragraph (4)(a) and (c).

(6) The Board must not recover charges in relation to the costs specified in paragraph (2) by either of the methods specified in paragraph (4)(b) and (c) unless—

(*a*) there are charges which are unpaid;

(*b*) the party from whose entitlement the Board intends to make the deduction is liable to pay those charges;

(*c*) the Board has notified the parties of the charges which the Board will impose in accordance with regulation 3(3)(c), 5(2) (d), 12(4) or 17(4), as the case may be;

(*d*) the Board has notified the party liable to pay the charges of the method by and the date on which the charges may be recovered; and

(*e*) a period of 21 days from the date that the charges were due to be paid has elapsed.

Reimbursement between parties to pension compensation sharing

19. A payment in respect of charges in accordance with regulation 18 made by one of the parties to pension compensation sharing on behalf of the other party is recoverable as a debt by the party who made the payment from that other party.

PART 7

COMPENSATION FOR SURVIVORS

Circumstances where a surviving partner is not entitled to periodic compensation

20. A surviving partner is not entitled to periodic compensation under paragraph 5 or 7 of Schedule 5 to the Act (compensation payable to widow, widower or surviving civil partner) or under regulation 15(3)(a)(i) where there is—

- (*a*) a valid nomination in favour of a relevant partner made by the transferee in accordance with either—
  - (i) the admissible rules of the scheme; or
  - (ii) regulation 22(3)(a); or
- (*b*) no provision to pay a survivor's pension under the admissible rules of the scheme.

Compensation payable on discharge of liability under regulation 15 in the case of surviving partners

21. Where a surviving partner is entitled to compensation under regulation 15(3)(a)(i), the annual rate and duration of the periodic compensation payable to the surviving partner is to be calculated—

- (*a*) where the transferee, had they not died, would have become entitled to periodic compensation under paragraph 4 of Schedule 5 to the Act commencing on the transfer day, in accordance with paragraph 5(2) and (3) of Schedule 5 to the Act (compensation payable to widow, widower or surviving civil partner);
- (*b*) where the transferee, had they not died, would have become entitled to periodic compensation under paragraph 6 of Schedule 5 to the Act commencing at pension compensation age, in accordance with paragraph 7(2) and (3) of Schedule 5 to the Act (compensation payable to widow, widower or surviving civil partner).

Compensation payable in the case of relevant partners and surviving dependants

22.—(1) This regulation applies where the transferee—

- (*a*) was before death entitled to present or future payment of periodic compensation calculated in accordance with paragraph 4 or 6 of Schedule 5 to the Act; or
- (*b*) would have become so entitled had they not died before the Board discharged liability for a pension compensation credit.

(2) Subject to paragraph (4), a relevant partner is entitled to periodic compensation in the circumstances prescribed in paragraph (3).

(3) The circumstances are where there is provision to pay a survivor's pension to a relevant partner under the admissible rules of the scheme (whether discretionary or otherwise); and —

    (*a*) the transferee —
        (i) has supplied the Board with a valid nomination in favour of the relevant partner; and
        (ii) the relevant partner has demonstrated to the satisfaction of the Board that they were living with the transferee at the date of the transferee's death; or
    (*b*) where the transferee has not supplied the Board with a valid nomination in accordance with sub-paragraph (a)(i), the relevant partner supplies evidence to the satisfaction of the Board that, at the date of the transferee's death, they were —
        (i) financially dependent, or interdependent, on the transferee; and
        (ii) living with the transferee.

(4) No compensation may be paid under paragraph (2) where the transferee had a civil partner or a spouse at the date of the transferee's death and there is no valid nomination in favour of the relevant partner.

(5) A surviving dependant is entitled to periodic compensation in the circumstances prescribed in paragraph (6).

(6) In the case of a surviving dependant, the circumstances are where there is supplied to the Board —

    (*a*) in the case of a natural child of the transferee, a birth certificate or other evidence demonstrating to the satisfaction of the Board that they are the natural child of the transferee;
    (*b*) in the case of an adopted child of the transferee, the adoption certificate demonstrating that they are the adopted child of the transferee; or
    (*c*) in the case of any other surviving dependant, evidence demonstrating to the satisfaction of the Board that they are a dependant of the transferee.

Amount and duration of periodic compensation that can be paid in the case of a relevant partner

23. — (1) Where a relevant partner is entitled to payment of periodic compensation under regulation 22, compensation is to commence on the day following the transferee's death and is payable for life.

(2) The amount of periodic compensation payable is to be calculated —

(a) where the transferee was entitled to payment of periodic compensation commencing on the transfer day, or would have become so entitled had they not died, in accordance with paragraph 5(3) of Schedule 5 to the Act; or

(b) where the transferee was entitled to payment of periodic compensation commencing at pension compensation age, or would have become so entitled had they not died, in accordance with paragraph 7(3) of Schedule 5 to the Act.

Amount of periodic compensation that can be paid in the case of a surviving dependant

24.—(1) Subject to paragraphs (2) and (3) and regulation 26, where a surviving dependant is entitled to periodic compensation under regulation 22(5) the amount is to be calculated—

(a) where the transferee was entitled to payment of periodic compensation commencing on the transfer day, or would have become so entitled had they not died, in accordance with paragraph 4 of Schedule 5 to the Act (including any increases under paragraph 17 of Schedule 5 to the Act (annual increase in periodic compensation) to which the transferee would have been entitled); or

(b) where the transferee was entitled to payment of periodic compensation commencing at pension compensation age, or would have become so entitled had they not died, in accordance with paragraph 6 of Schedule 5 to the Act (including any revaluation amount under paragraph 8 (revaluation) and any increases under paragraph 17 of Schedule 5 to the Act to which the transferee would have been entitled).

(2) Where periodic compensation is also payable to a surviving partner or relevant partner and—

(a) there is only one surviving dependant, the amount of periodic compensation is 25% of the amount calculated under paragraph (1); or

(b) there are two or more surviving dependants, the amount of periodic compensation is half of the amount calculated under paragraph (1), divided equally between the surviving dependants.

(3) Where periodic compensation is not payable to a surviving partner or relevant partner and—

(*a*) there is only one surviving dependant, the amount of periodic compensation is half of the amount calculated under paragraph (1); or

(*b*) there are two or more surviving dependants, the amount of periodic compensation is the amount calculated under paragraph (1), divided equally between the surviving dependants.

Period of payment

25.—(1) Except in the circumstances prescribed in paragraph (2), where periodic compensation is payable to a surviving dependant under regulation 22(5), it is payable from the day following the transferee's death.

(2) Where a surviving dependant—

(*a*) is a child born after the transferee's death, periodic compensation is payable from the date of the child's birth;

(*b*) has left a qualifying course, as a consequence of which payment of periodic compensation has ceased in accordance with paragraph (4)(a), but within one year begins another qualifying course before attaining the age of 23, periodic compensation is payable from the date that the later qualifying course begins; or

(*c*) becomes disabled and is incapable of engaging in full time paid employment due to a condition that falls within the definition of a disability under section 6 of the Equality Act 2010, after attaining the age of 18 but before attaining the age of 23, periodic compensation is payable from the date that the surviving dependant became disabled.

(3) Except where paragraph (4) or (5) applies, periodic compensation is payable until the surviving dependant attains the age of 18.

(4) Where the surviving dependant is attending a qualifying course, periodic compensation is payable either—

(*a*) until they leave the course; or

(*b*) until they attain the age of 23,

whichever is the earlier.

(5) Where the surviving dependant is incapable of engaging in full time paid employment due to a condition that falls within the definition of a disability under section 6 of the Equality Act 2010, periodic compensation is payable until the surviving dependant attains the age of 23.

Change of circumstances and backdating

26.—(1) The amount of periodic compensation payable to a surviving dependant under these Regulations may be varied where—

(*a*) there is a change in the circumstances of a person to whom periodic compensation is payable; and
(*b*) that change would have resulted in—
　　(i) a different rate of periodic compensation being payable (including where a rate of nil may apply); or
　　(ii) periodic compensation being payable from a different date, and such a variation must take effect from the date that the change in circumstances occurred.

(2) The amount of periodic compensation calculated under paragraph (1) must include any increases under paragraphs 17 (annual increase in periodic compensation) and 20 (Board's power to alter rates of revaluation and indexation) of Schedule 5 to the Act.

(3) Where a person makes a claim for periodic compensation, the claim must be backdated to the date that the person became eligible to claim periodic compensation, or where that date is more than five years before the date of the claim, to a date five years before the date of the claim.

PART 8

REVALUATION

Manner in which percentage increase in general level of prices is to be determined

27.—(1) For the purposes of paragraph 8(4)(a) of Schedule 5 to the Act (revaluation), the manner in which the percentage increase in the general level of prices in Great Britain is to be determined is—

$$100 \times \left(\tfrac{A}{B}\right) - 100$$

where—

(*a*) A is the general level of prices in Great Britain determined in such manner as the Secretary of State may from time to time decide for the month which falls two complete months before the first day of the month in which the transferee—
　　(i) attains pension compensation age; or

(ii) becomes entitled to early payment of periodic compensation or lump sum compensation under paragraph 6 or paragraph 9 (commutation of periodic compensation) of Schedule 5 to the Act, calculated in accordance with paragraph 10 of Schedule 5 to the Act (early payment of compensation); and

(*b*) B is the general level of prices in Great Britain determined in such manner as the Secretary of State may from time to time decide for the month which falls two complete months before the first day of the month during which the transfer day falls.

(2) In this regulation, where the Secretary of State makes a decision about the manner in which the general level of prices in Great Britain is to be determined, the Secretary of State must publish that decision.

PART 9

COMMUTATION OF PERIODIC COMPENSATION

Circumstances in which periodic compensation may be commuted

28.—(1) The circumstances prescribed for the purposes of paragraph 9(1) (commutation) of Schedule 5 to the Act are specified in paragraph (2).

(2) The circumstances are that—

(*a*) the transferor must not have previously exercised an option to commute for a lump sum either—
 (i) a portion of the pension from which the pension compensation credit was derived; or
 (ii) a portion of the relevant pension compensation from which the pension compensation credit was derived;

(*b*) the transferee must not have previously exercised an option to commute for a lump sum a portion of the pension compensation credit in respect of which they are entitled to periodic compensation; and

(*c*) the transferee exercises the option to commute within the period of six months beginning with the day on which payment of periodic compensation commences.

Circumstances in which the portion of compensation to be commuted may exceed 25%

29.—(1) The prescribed circumstances for the purposes of paragraph 9(2) of Schedule 5 to the Act are that—

(*a*) the transferee must have attained the age of 60 but not have attained the age of 75 on the date specified in paragraph (4) (the nominated date); and

(*b*) the portion to be commuted is a PPF trivial commutation lump sum.

(2) A payment is a PPF trivial commutation lump sum if—

(*a*) either—
    (i) no trivial commutation lump sum or PPF trivial commutation lump sum has previously been paid to the transferee by either a registered pension scheme; or the Board; or
    (ii) if such a lump sum has previously been paid, the PPF trivial commutation lump sum is paid before the end of the commutation period;

(*b*) on the nominated date the value of the transferee's pension rights and entitlement to PPF compensation does not exceed the commutation limit;

(*c*) it is paid when all or part of the transferee's standard lifetime allowance is available; and

(*d*) it extinguishes the transferee's entitlement to PPF compensation.

(3) "The commutation period" is the period beginning with the day on which a trivial commutation lump sum or PPF trivial commutation lump sum was first paid to the transferee and ending 12 months after that day.

(4) The nominated date is—

(*a*) a date nominated by the transferee which is within the period of three months ending with the day on which the transferee proposes to exercise the option to commute; or

(*b*) if no date is nominated by the transferee, a date within that period nominated by the Board.

(5) The commutation limit is 1% of the standard lifetime allowance on the nominated date.

(6) For the purposes of paragraph (2)(b)—

(*a*) the value of the transferee's pension rights is the aggregate of—
  (i) the value of the transferee's relevant crystallised pension rights (calculated in accordance with paragraph 8 (trivial commutation lump sum) of Schedule 29 to the Finance Act 2004 ("the Finance Act")); and
  (ii) the value of the transferee's uncrystallised rights (calculated in accordance with paragraph 9 (trivial commutation lump sum) of Schedule 29 to the Finance Act); and
(*b*) the value of the transferee's entitlement to PPF compensation is the aggregate of—
  (i) any entitlement to lump sum compensation under the pension compensation provisions; and
  (ii) any entitlement to periodic compensation under the pension compensation provisions.

(7) For the purposes of paragraph (6)(b)—

(*a*) the value of any entitlement to lump sum compensation is the full amount of lump sum compensation to which the transferee is entitled on the nominated date; and
(*b*) the value of periodic compensation is to be calculated by multiplying the annual periodic compensation to which the transferee is entitled on the nominated date by 20.

(8) In this regulation—

(*a*) "registered pension scheme" has the same meaning as in section 150(2) of the Finance Act (meaning of "pension scheme");
(*b*) "standard lifetime allowance" means the amount specified in the relevant order for that tax year, made under section 218(3) of the Finance Act (individual's lifetime allowance and standard lifetime allowance);
(*c*) "tax year" has the same meaning as section 4(2), (3) and (4) of the Income Tax Act 2007 (income tax an annual tax); and
(*d*) "trivial commutation lump sum" has the same meaning as in paragraph 7 of Schedule 29 to the Finance Act (trivial commutation lump sum).

Manner in which an option to commute may be exercised

30.—(1) The manner in which an option to commute periodic compensation under paragraph 9 of Schedule 5 to the Act may be exercised is specified in paragraphs (2) to (4).

(2) A transferee may only exercise an option to commute a portion of the periodic compensation to which they are entitled by giving notice to the Board in writing.

(3) A notice given under paragraph (2) must include—

(*a*) the name, address, date of birth and national insurance number of the transferee; and

(*b*) the percentage of the periodic compensation which the transferee opts to commute.

(4) The Board may require a transferee exercising an option to commute to produce any document or provide any other information relevant to the Board's functions in relation to the transferee's request for commutation.

PART 10

EARLY PAYMENT OF PERIODIC COMPENSATION

Circumstances where a transferee is entitled to early payment of periodic compensation

31.—(1) The conditions under which, by virtue of paragraph 10 of Schedule 5 to the Act (early payment of compensation), a transferee may become entitled to early payment of lump sum compensation (by virtue of paragraph 9 of Schedule 5 to the Act (commutation of periodic compensation) and regulation 28 or 29) and periodic compensation under paragraph 6 of Schedule 5 to the Act (compensation payable to transferee) are specified in paragraph (2).

(2) Those conditions are that —

(*a*) the transferee has given notice to the Board, in accordance with paragraph (3), that they wish to receive periodic compensation or lump sum compensation before attaining pension compensation age; and

(*b*) the transferee has attained the age of 55 on the date on which they would like the periodic compensation or lump sum compensation to be paid.

(3) The notice referred to in paragraph (2)(a) must include—

(*a*) the transferee's name, address, date of birth and national insurance number; and

(*b*) the date on which the transferee would like the periodic compensation or lump sum compensation to become payable.

PART 11

ANNUAL INCREASE IN PERIODIC COMPENSATION

Determination of indexed proportion

32. In any case where it is unclear whether the pension compensation credit or any part of it is derived from rights of the transferor relating to pensionable service (whether actual or notional) occurring—

(*a*) before 6th April 1997; or
(*b*) on or after 6th April 1997,

the Board may determine as best as it is able, having regard to the admissible rules of the scheme and all the circumstances of the case, how much of the service or notional service of the transferor should be treated for the purposes of paragraph 17 of Schedule 5 to the Act as having occurred before 6th April 1997 and how much should be treated as having occurred on or after that date.

PART 12

COMPENSATION CAP

Restriction of amount of compensation payable

33.—(1) This regulation applies where, in respect of a pension compensation credit—

(*a*) the transferee becomes entitled to payment of compensation under paragraph 4 or 6 of Schedule 5 to the Act; and
(*b*) on the transfer day the transferor was not entitled to present payment of relevant compensation.

(2) Except where regulation 34 applies, where the annual value of the periodic compensation payable to the transferee under paragraph 4 or 6 of Schedule 5 to the Act in respect of that pension compensation credit exceeds the compensation cap, the amount of compensation payable to the transferee is restricted in accordance with paragraph (3).

(3) Where compensation payable to the transferee is required to be restricted in accordance with this paragraph, the compensation payable is the cap fraction of the amount which would otherwise be payable to the transferee, in respect of that pension compensation credit, under paragraph 4 or 6 of Schedule 5 to the Act.

(4) The annual value of the periodic compensation payable to the transferee under paragraph 4 or 6 of Schedule 5 to the Act in respect of a pension compensation credit is to be determined in accordance with this paragraph—

(*a*)   where no portion of the compensation to which the transferee is entitled under the pension compensation credit has been commuted, the annual value of the periodic compensation is the annual value of the compensation to which the transferee is entitled in respect of that credit; or

(*b*)   where a portion of the compensation to which the transferee is entitled under the pension compensation credit has been commuted, the annual value of the periodic compensation is the amount which would have been the annual value of the periodic compensation in respect of that credit, had a portion not been commuted.

(5) In this regulation—

"the cap fraction" means—
$$C/V$$
where C is the compensation cap, and V is the annual value of the periodic compensation payable under the pension compensation credit.

Application of compensation cap where compensation becomes payable on different dates

34.—(1) This regulation applies where—

(*a*)   the transferee becomes entitled to payment of compensation in accordance with paragraph 4 or 6 of Schedule 5 to the Act; and

(*b*)   the transferee has previously become entitled to payment of compensation, in accordance with either of those paragraphs, which is derived from the rights of the same transferor under the same or a connected scheme.

(2) For the purposes of paragraph (1), a scheme is a connected scheme if the same person is or was the employer in relation to both schemes.

(3) Where this regulation applies, the amount of compensation payable to the transferee in accordance with paragraph 4 or 6 of Schedule 5 of the Act is to be restricted in accordance with paragraph (4) or (5).

(4) If the previous cap percentage is or exceeds 100, the compensation payable in respect of a subsequent tranche of compensation is nil.

(5) If the previous cap percentage is less than 100, the amount of compensation payable in respect of the previous and subsequent tranches of compensation is restricted in accordance with paragraph (8).

(6) "The previous cap percentage" is the cap percentage for the previous tranche of compensation.

(7) "The cap percentage" means (AAV x 100)/ACC, where AAV is the appropriate annual value of the previous or, as the case may be, a subsequent tranche of compensation at the time when each tranche first becomes payable and ACC is the appropriate compensation cap at that time.

(8) Where paragraph (5) applies—

(*a*) the amount of a subsequent tranche of compensation is restricted in accordance with regulation 33(3), but taking the reference to the cap fraction in that paragraph as a reference to the revised cap fraction; and

(*b*) the amount of the previous tranche of compensation is restricted to the revised cap fraction of the amount that would be payable apart from this sub-paragraph.

(9) "The revised cap fraction" means 100 / the aggregate cap percentage.

(10) "The aggregate cap percentage" means the aggregate of the cap percentages for the previous and subsequent tranches of compensation.

. . .

SCHEDULE Regulation 6

Information to be provided by the Board

1. In this Schedule—

"beneficiary" means any person who is entitled to compensation as a surviving partner, relevant partner or other surviving dependant of a pension compensation credit member;

"interested person" has the same meaning as in section 207(2) of the 2004 Act (review and reconsideration of reviewable matters);

"reviewable matter" has the same meaning as in section 206(1) of the 2004 Act (meaning of "reviewable matters").

2. Information to be provided by the Board to pension compensation credit members and beneficiaries shall be determined in accordance with the provisions of the table of information to be provided by the Board set out below—

Table of information to be provided by the Board

Description of person to whom information is to be provided	Description of information to be provided	Period during which the Board must provide information
Any pension compensation credit member who makes a request in writing to the Board for it to provide a forecast of the pension compensation credit member's entitlement to compensation.	A forecast, determined in accordance with the provisions of Schedule 5 to the Act, of the compensation to be paid to the pension compensation credit member	The period of 28 days beginning on the day on which the Board receives the request.
Any pension compensation credit member who will attain pension compensation age on their next birthday.	1. A forecast, determined in accordance with the provisions of Schedule 5 to the Act, of the compensation to be paid to the pension compensation credit member. 2. Details of any options to commute which may be exercised by the pension compensation credit member in accordance with paragraph 9 of Schedule 5 to the Act (commutation of periodic compensation) and regulations 28 and 29; and forecasts of— (a) the lump sum to be paid under any such option; and (b) the reduced level of annual compensation payment which the pension compensation credit member would receive if they exercised any such option.	The period of 6 months beginning 12 months before the day on which the pension compensation credit member will attain pension compensation age.

Any pension compensation credit member who makes a request in writing to the Board for it to provide— (i) information about any options to commute which may be exercised by the pension compensation credit member in accordance with paragraph 9 of Schedule 5 to the Act and regulations 28 and 29; or (ii) a forecast of the lump sum payable to the pension compensation credit member on the exercise of any such option.	Details of any options to commute available to the pension compensation credit member, and forecasts of— (a) the lump sum to be paid to the pension compensation credit member under any such option; and (b) the reduced level of annual compensation payments which the pension compensation credit member would receive if they exercised such an option.	The period of 28 days beginning on the day on which the Board receives the request.
Any pension compensation credit member who makes a request in writing to the Board for it to provide information about any entitlement the pension compensation credit member may have to early payment of compensation under paragraph 10 of Schedule 5 to the Act (early payment of compensation) and regulation 31.	Details of any entitlement the pension compensation credit member may have to early payment of compensation and a forecast of the periodic compensation and of any lump sum payment payable to the pension compensation credit member.	The period of 28 days beginning on the day on which the Board receives the request.
All pension compensation credit members, surviving or relevant partners or dependants of such members.	Details of any variation in the amount of compensation payable where the variation will result from the operation of paragraph 27 (increasing the compensation cap in line with earnings) of Schedule 7 to the 2004 Act, paragraph 17 (annual increase in periodic compensation) or 20 (Board's power to alter rate of revaluation and indexation) of Schedule 5 to the Act, and the date when the variation will become effective ('the operative date').	Not less than 28 days before the operative date.

Any pension compensation credit member who is an interested person in relation to a particular reviewable matter.	A statement describing how an application may be made to the Board for the review of the reviewable matter, how the application will be considered, and the Board's powers on making a review decision.	The period of 28 days beginning on the day on which the Board knew or ought to have known that the reviewable matter had occurred.
Any pension compensation credit member who is either a party to matrimonial or civil partnership proceedings, or may be a party to such proceedings, who makes a request in writing to the Board for information about their compensation entitlement.	A statement, determined in accordance with Schedule 5 to the Act, of the compensation to be paid to the pension compensation credit member.	The period of three months beginning on the day on which the Board receives the request, or by the date that the Board must comply with a court order to provide such information, whichever is the sooner.

INDEX

409